CHINA'S INTEGRATION INTO THE WORLD ECONOMY

CHINA'S INTEGRATION INTO THE WORLD ECONOMY

edited by

John Whalley

The University of Western Ontario, Canada

World Scientific

NEW JERSEY • LONDON • SINGAPORE • BEIJING • SHANGHAI • HONG KONG • TAIPEI • CHENNAI

Published by

World Scientific Publishing Co. Pte. Ltd.
5 Toh Tuck Link, Singapore 596224
USA office: 27 Warren Street, Suite 401-402, Hackensack, NJ 07601
UK office: 57 Shelton Street, Covent Garden, London WC2H 9HE

British Library Cataloguing-in-Publication Data
A catalogue record for this book is available from the British Library.

CHINA'S INTEGRATION INTO THE WORLD ECONOMY

ISBN-13 978-981-4304-78-8
ISBN-10 981-4304-78-6

Typeset by Stallion Press
Email: enquiries@stallionpress.com

Printed in Singapore by B & Jo Enterprise Pte Ltd

ACKNOWLEDGEMENTS

During the period of writing or co-writing these papers, I have been fortunate to have received financial and intellectual support from a number of sources. On the financial front, I have been greatly aided by the China Programme of the Centre for International Governance Innovation (CIGI), Waterloo, Ontario, as well as research grants from the Social Sciences and Humanities Research Council (SSHRC), and the Ontario Research Fund during the later stages of work on the volume. Discussion, comment and academic collegial input has come from many sources, including Shuming Zhang, Xin Xian, Li Shi, Yuezhou Cai, Tongsan Wang, Yu Yongding, Wang Li, Yiming Wang, Yao Li, Yan Dong, Huifang Tian. Logistical and organizational support has been provided by Kun Peng. To all, I am grateful.

INTRODUCTION

This volume contains twelve papers that I have either authored or co-authored over the last six years dealing with China's integration into the world economy. This integration has been one of the most dramatic economic events since the period of the Second World War. Since the mid-1970s, China has increased its real income per capita by approximately eight times. China has grown from having trade substantially smaller than that of Hong Kong back in the 1970s to a position today where China is the second largest trading country among all global traders. China accounts for nearly 50% of all inward foreign investment coming from the OECD. China has made tremendous progress in terms of poverty alleviation, with sharp reductions in the numbers of individuals and households below the poverty line, although this has been accompanied by a sharp increase in relative inequality particularly between urban and rural areas.

How all this has been accomplished is still a subject of substantial debate and difference of position in literature. There are those, such as Paul Krugman, who characterize Chinese growth as a triumph of perspiration over inspiration, emphasizing the role that physical capital accumulation has played in this process. However, more recent policy announcements in China attach great significance to the educational process in China, where there has been an enormous four-fold increase in the number of graduate and undergraduate students since the late 1990s and the generation of ideas, and the sharp growth which has taken place in China's trade in information technology products. These products now account for nearly 40% of China's exports, whereas back in the mid-1990s, they were perhaps no more than 2%, with textiles and apparel being a much more prominent and important component of China's exports.

These controversies are central to this integration process. Insofar as the widely held belief in China has been that the major driver of China's growth has been its integration into the global economy, which accelerated greatly after 1992 with changes in policy structure and large inflows of foreign direct investment. Following this there was significant growth of exports, then with further elevation following China's successful accession to the WTO in 2001. In recent years, China's export growth had been running at nearly 30% per year, pre-financial crisis, but in the crisis fell sharply. There is also a belief in Chinese policy circles that accumulation of human capital and infrastructure development in China (roads, ports, telecomm, airports, etc.) have been as instrumental in the growth process as physical capital accumulation. As noted above, the contrast in view is notable with Western literature, which tends to emphasize physical capital accumulation.

The chapters in the volume which follow deal with various dimensions and aspects of this overall set of issues, arising with any assessment of the contribution into the global economy for its development. In the first part China's growth strategy, in light of the growing participation of the global economy, is discussed. The first paper deals with China's inward foreign direct investment and uses a decomposition of the Chinese economy into the Chinese FDI and non-FDI sectors and to assess how FDI flows relate to the sustainability of future Chinese growth. Using an extension of conventional single sector growth accounting, due to Solow, Dennison and others, this paper takes a two-sector approach and uses data classified on a FDI, non-FDI sectoral basis. Results suggest that the majority of China's growth is accounted for by FDI in the period from the early 1990s on, and that, in turn, a significant portion of China's technical progress is concentrated in the FDI portion of the economy. This suggests that if in the future, there is a plateauing or even a fall in FDI, this could significantly affect Chinese growth prospects. Foreign direct investment into China was already beginning to plateau in the period before the financial crisis and the crisis has taken its toll both on Chinese exports and on inward FDI, although China, seemingly, has been able to maintain a relatively high growth rate of 6–8% through the financial crisis.

The second paper deals with technology upgrading as part of China's growth strategy out to 2020. It discusses and evaluates the eleventh 5-year plan, published in 2005 in China which emphasizes the need for China to move from export growth based on lower quality products such as textiles and apparel and into higher quality items such as electronics, machine tools, autos and engineering products. This 5 year plan sets out the whole strategy as to how this is to be accomplished: major increases in educational spending, R&D tax credits, geographical zones which will promote these policies, large spending on mega-projects, and intellectual property arrangements which are designed both to protect new innovations that the Chinese produce, but also reduce dependency on expensive foreign intellectual property. All this is set out in the Chapter and an evaluation of this strategy proceeds, emphasizing many of the fundamental divisions which exist between Western and Chinese literature in terms of the determinants of Chinese growth processes.

The third paper in this section, presents both data on and forward projections of China's rapidly growing trade and investment flows with Southern countries. The South is defined to exclude Hong Kong (China), Korea and Singapore, large bilateral trade links for China. The data indicate that from a low base in the 1990's when Southern trade was growing more slowly than China's overall trade it subsequently grows rapidly. After 2001 (WTO accession) there is a significant acceleration, which pre crisis was in turn further accelerating. In 1995 Southern trade was 13% of China's total trade; but by 2007 it was 28% of China's total trade and growing at 42% per year on the export side in contrast to 26% for all exports. By country, India (with a 33-fold increase between 1995–2007) is the most rapidly growing bilateral partner, followed by Brazil (18 fold increase between 1995–2007). By region, Latin America and Africa are the largest regional sources of trade growth, with more dispersion across countries in Asia. Also, in contrast to its total trade, China runs a significant trade deficit in its Southern trade due to imports of resource products. We report projections that by 2015 Southern trade (assuming unchanged growth rates) would be over 50% of China's trade, and by 2025 India will account for over 50% of China's trade.

It also presents data on Southern and bilateral FDI flows involving China and developing countries. From a very small base in the 1990s, these are now growing at even more rapid rates than China's trade. Bilateral flows between India and China, for instance, grew 90-fold between 1995 and 2007.

Part two of the volume then goes on to discuss China's aid and trade policies. In Chapter 4 on China's new regional trade agreements, the emphasis is on the range, scope and form of these regional agreements, and how they emerged so quickly in the period following China's accession to the WTO in 2001. Unlike other large entities earlier acceding to the WTO, who remained strongly committed to multilateralism for several decades prior to entry into significant regional agreements, China's approach seems to be more pragmatic, with a combined multilateral and regional approach, beginning by way of initial agreements with Hong Kong and then spreading to agreements with Australia, New Zealand, ASEAN and Singapore, and elsewhere. Interestingly, these agreements are also very different in form one from another. They appear to dovetail with the interests of the bilateral negotiating participant, rather than following a common template structure as is common with the US and the EU. Increasingly in the years ahead, the expectation is that regional agreements of this form will grow in significance and scope for China, as China's trade policies take ever more centre stage in her developmental strategy.

Chapter 5 discusses liberalization in China's key service sectors following WTO accession, exploring some scenarios as to how this liberalization will play out and raising some issues of measurement. The key sectors involved are banking, insurance and telecoms. Interestingly, at the point of WTO accession by China in 2001, a major demand from OECD countries, particularly the US and EU, was for the unilateral liberalization by China in these key service sectors. The decision made by China to join the WTO with these commitments was the more broad ranging one of prioritizing engagement with the international community over insulation from global interactions rather than the precise details of what were to be involved.

China thus largely accepted the terms of accession in services as they were presented to them by the OECD countries through the WTO accession process. In the banking area, the commitments are breathtaking in scope. They involve China effectively moving to open international banking over the period out to 2008. This is to allow entry of foreign banks into branch banking in China, entry into banking using both domestic and foreign currencies, and with almost no restrictions on banking activities within China. The paper in the volume suggests that, if fully implemented as committed, China's banking system would be on par with banking activity in the Cayman Islands in terms of openness. The reality of banking liberalization however, has been far more limited in practice. There have been major changes in banking structure in China, but not change to the extent which these commitments would suggest. Changes in insurance arrangements are less dramatic, as they were relatively liberal towards foreign insurers before the accession negotiations. The issue had been much more the degree of uptake by foreign insurance companies, with opportunities in the Chinese market with few formal barriers to constrain them. In telecoms, the agreement focuses on the degree of foreign participation in and ownership of Chinese telecom operators and also access of those operators to the Chinese market.

This section concludes with Chapter 6 discussing China's post-WTO accession trade stance. Prior to the completion of the lengthy negotiations on Chinese WTO accession, there was extensive debate inside China on the merits of this step from a Chinese perspective. This debate has continued despite the initiation of implementation of the terms of accession now due to be completed by 2007. The talk in China today is of post-WTO China; and every new policy initiative is discussed not only in terms of its WTO compatibility, but also in terms of its ability to contribute to the implementation of the accession process and the eventual harnessing of China's resulting WTO benefits. The completion of accession negotiations was been hailed internally as a milestone in China's economic development, with claims of significant additions to growth potential, and a new policy environment underpinned by the single most important policy departure since Deng Xiao Ping's introduction of the responsibility system in 1976. At the same time, WTO accession has been criticized by detractors as establishing too quickly a western-style market-oriented environment in China, which will likely lead to greater inequality and over-centralization, and has resulted in China giving away too many WTO bargaining chips which could have been more effectively used in later global negotiations.

There has been much discussion at the policy level of Chinese exchange rate policy in recent years of these issues, with repeated pressures from the US in particular for China to change its exchange rate policy, which is believed to be a source of both major accumulation of reserves and a source of artificial stimulus to Chinese export performance by maintaining export volumes at higher levels than would otherwise be the case.

This issue has always been difficult for economists to analyze using conventional models because traditional models of international trade are pure barter economies in which money is neutral and with a simple monetized extension, exchange rates have no effects. In such models trade is either balanced, or there is a fixed exogenous trade imbalance. This chapter therefore departs from previous literature by modeling the exchange rate regime in terms of a fixed exchange rate at which the Chinese central bank stands ready to accumulate foreign reserves at the fixed exchange rate, and as such, the trade imbalance is endogenously determined. Using this structure and calibrating to Chinese data from 2005, the model is able to be used to analyze numerically the impacts of the renminbi appreciation on the trade imbalance and welfare. In the simple static framework used, policies which reduce reserve accumulation and increase imports are welfare improving.

Part three of the volume continues with a chapter discussing how China's tax policies are best designed under global integration. China's tax policy has been a surprisingly important component of Chinese policy in recent years. China is relatively highly taxed, with more than 30% of GDP flowing through the tax system. The value-added tax in particular has grown since its initial introduction in 1994 into a tax which accounts for nearly 40% of tax revenues. The enterprise tax has also undergone major change from effectively an accumulation of surpluses of state-owned enterprises to a formal enterprise tax with a clearly defined base and statutory rate and moving close to the corporate tax structure in use in the OECD, but with major tax incentives towards R&D and investment.

The first of the chapters in this section deals with the Unified Enterprise Tax and the behavior of state-owned enterprises of China. In 1992, a key element in the changes in policy structure towards foreign investment, in this was to introduce a special tax regime for FDI, under which FDI and the income accruing to it were effectively taxed at around half the rate compared to income accruing to domestic enterprises. This is widely believed by some at the time to be one of the significant sources of stimulus for inward foreign investment, although by no means necessarily the only or dominant source. However, these elements of tax structure were seen in 1992 as only a temporary arrangement, pending a move to a unified tax. The movement to the unified tax took place in 2006, with legislation which removed these tax preferences over a four year period out to 2010.

This chapter uses modeling techniques to analyze the impact of these tax changes. It suggests that if conventional competitive models are used to analyze such tax changes, then they will be viewed as desirable on the grounds that they remove a distortion. But, once the differential structure of state owned relative to private enterprises is taken into account, things change. Different prototype models of SOE are used where, representative of the earlier Iron Rice bowl period, enterprise managers are treated as politically appointed and receiving credits from the state banking system in ways such that any losses are automatically recapitalized. In such a world, if managers try to maximize their personal network or *guanxi*, then they would maximize the size of the enterprise, effectively hiring labor up to the point where the wage paid to labour is equal to the average product of labor rather than the marginal product. In such a world, the numerical modeling reported on in this chapter shows that the move to a unified enterprise tax is no longer so clearly welfare-improving, and under some circumstances may even be welfare-worsening.

A second chapter in this section evaluates the Chinese Value Added Tax (VAT) in its current impure form relative to a pure form using a monetary trade model similar in structure to that used in the chapter on China's renminbi appreciation. The impurities in the Chinese VAT stem from two separate sources. The first relates to the export rebates which are common in all VATs throughout the world but are different in China. China's experience with export rebates was one of rapid growth of both exports and revenue losses. In 1994, when the tax was introduced, the value of rebates which were claimed far exceeded the budgetary revenues available to finance such rebates. So rebates were initially frozen for a few years and were then reintroduced at rates which were significantly lower that the statutory rate when the VAT was introduced. As such, a completely separate system of rebates on exports came to coexist with the rest of the VAT regime. This is atypical compared to VAT regimes from around the world. In addition, the VAT in China has, since 1994, operated on an income basis rather than a consumption basis, (again unusual) in which the expensing of capital goods is not allowed. This chapter evaluates these features and emphasizes how, in a model such as the renminbi appreciation model where there is an endogenous trade surplus. Features of tax structure which tend to retard exports can be welfare-improving because they reduce the size of the trade surplus, which in turn, reflects the exchange of goods on the one hand and paper, which is non-contributive to utility in static models, on the other. Thus this impure form of VAT, which in the conventional model used in most public finance analysis would be welfare inferior compared to the pure form, turns out to be welfare-improving.

The volume then continues with a fourth part on China and global architecture. The first Chapter in this part discusses Chinese activity in Africa. China's large and growing presence in Africa, which has become especially prominent in the last two to three years, is now the subject of substantial curiosity and even puzzlement outside of China. The focus of this curiosity is primarily Sub-Saharan Africa, where the majority of this activity is concentrated. While for now still small relative to China's reserves and overall trade, it is nonetheless sizable relative to current resource flows into Africa. As a source of development finance to Africa, if this involvement continues to grow, China will in a few years be poised to outrank combined financial flows from multilateral agencies (the World Bank, the IMF) and private in-flows from OECD countries. Trade between China and Africa is growing at rates in the order of 30% per year, from an admittedly low base. FDI inflows to Africa from China are growing at similar rates.

The African Development Bank now has its annual meetings not in Africa, but in Shanghai. The elevation of mean growth rates in Sub-Saharan Africa from around 4.5% to 6–6.5% in the last two years can in part be linked to the growing Chinese presence in Africa. Chinese enterprises are centrally involved in Africa in resources, textiles and apparel, construction, finance, and many other fields. Seemingly, everywhere one looks in Africa, one finds present or recent Chinese activity. This charter documents this phenomenon and explore the factors which underlie it.

Chapter 10 discusses post-MFA performance of developing Asia, and China in particular, noting that with the termination of the Multi-Fibre Arrangement (MFA) in 2005 under the WTO agreement on textiles in the Uruguay Round in 1994, major changes took place in the structure of global production and trade which significantly influenced China. It had been anticipated that there would be a large surge in China's exports of textiles and apparel following MFA removal. This discusses the size, and dimensions, and geographical composition of this surge and the policy reponse outside of China. The surges which occurred reflected many years of pent-up supply and generated new China containment trade measures, which came into place driven by protectionist pressures in the EU and the US and spread elsewhere including into the developing world (Brazil and Peni for example). How and why this occurred is set out in Chapter 10.

Chapter 11 is in the final part of the volume dealing with China and inequality which has grown substantially over the period of China's global engagement. China has made major progress dealing with absolute poverty and numbers below poverty lines have fallen. But relative inequality has widened. Here, emphasis is on the contributing factors to inequality in China in recent years and the sources of growth of relative inequality. One of the important factors has been the *hukou* system of labor mobility restrictions between urban and rural areas, under which significant portions of the population in rural areas have been constrained in terms of their ability to move into other areas. It has rather been through temporary migrant workers that migration has taken place, and many typically return to their villages within 3–4 years after their migration. This policy structure has generates a segmentation of labor markets within China, and in this chapter using calibrated models and data from 2005, numerical simulation methods are used to evaluate the impact on inequality of these mobility restrictions. This is done in a variety of models of increasing complexity, including models of form in which the dampening effect of increased house prices generated by migration surges into rural areas also come into play.

The conclusion is that *hukou* restrictions have been a significant factor in restraining migration which in turn would lessen relative inequality.

The volume concludes with a chapter which focuses on volatility of incomes in rural areas and its contribution to inequality in China. It is often argued that because of rural income volatility that inequality is in some sense a less serious problem in China than is perceived because over a period of time, people will move above and below the poverty line threshold and so the numbers of people who are permanently below the line is smaller than might appear in annual poverty related data.

This paper argues an opposite position which suggests that in the presence of inequality, one has to account for the presence of volatility and account for it in terms of its impact on expected income. Thus an increase in volatility in rural incomes reduces the certainty equivalence of income, and therefore increases overall inequality. This analysis uses data from the Chinese Household Income Panel, collected by Li Shi and others at the Chinese Academy of Social Sciences to analyze this issue.

All these papers contribute in one way or another to debate on China's participation in the global economy. How important has it been for China's strong growth performance? How should that engagement proceed given the special elements of China's economic structure? How sustainable is this strategy for growth in the medium to long run? These issues will remain central to China's future developmental strategy for decades to come and especially after the current financial crisis.

CONTENTS

Part I

FDI and Technology

CHINA AND FDI*

John Whalley
University of Western Ontario, CIGI and NBER

Xian Xin
China Agricultural University

That China's economy is now deeply integrated into the wider global economy and that inward FDI flows and trade growth have been mechanisms for this integration over the last 15 years is hardly news. The growth of exports, imports, and GDP increasingly reflect FDI inflows. China's deep integration into the global economy must therefore be judged not only by trade growth, but also by capital flows. In the paper we discuss three issues related to FDI, and primarily FDI inflows. The first is their contribution to growth, which we suggest is substantial and if any plateauing of FDI growth occurs then GDP growth may be significantly reduced. We also discuss the links between regional inequality and geographic concentration of FDI. Macro data suggests limited linkage, while micro studies claim to find it. Finally, we discuss recent proposals to remove tax preferences to FDI and RMB revaluation suggesting potential negative effects on FDI inflows. FDI has become so central to Chinese economic performance that what happens on the FDI front in the short term will likely determine the speed of China's development.

1. Introduction

That China's economy is now deeply integrated into the wider global economy and that inward FDI flows and trade growth have been mechanisms for this integration over the last 15 years is hardly news. But the dimensions and speed of change continue at a torrid pace. Here we discuss the size and geographical concentration of the FDI, and raise several key issues linking FDI and wider economic performance. One is whether FDI-lead growth can continue to be the prime developmental path for China, or do constraints on global aggregate flows, rising wage rates,

* This paper has been prepared for a conference to be held at Brookings, Washington, DC. May 10–11 2007. We are grateful to Li Wang for help with data, and also comments on an earlier draft.

on the absorptive capacity abroad for Chinese exports at some point serve to limit growth. If this is the case, there is an issue of when this may occur and what an alternative growth path may be. Another is whether regionally concentrated location-specific FDI has been a prime contributor to the growing inequality which threatens to politically constrain growth. Yet another is whether proposed or likely policy change, such as the removal of substantial tax preferences towards FDI under the proposed unified tax, and/or significant Renminbi revaluation could also serve to limit FDI inflows.

In what follows, we first document the dimensions of FDI inflows into China in recent years, emphasizing its links to China's large processing trade. FDI inflows to China, which now account for nearly half of all OECD outflows, are split between horizontal (serving the Chinese market) and vertical (export oriented), and are highly regionally concentrated. We then go on to discuss the contribution of FDI inflows to China's growth, drawing on an earlier growth accounting chapter of ours (Whalley and Xin, 2006) which argues that a plateauing of FDI inflows to China could reduce growth rates by 3–4 percentage points. We then use this as a bridge to discuss potential constraints on China's future growth linked to FDI and trade. We note that for more than 20 years western economists have been predicting the demise of Chinese high growth, which has not happened. Sections follow on regional concentration of FDI and inequality in China, and the potential impacts of tax preference removal and Renminbi revaluation on FDI inflows.

2. Inward and Outward FDI in China

2.1. *Inward FDI*

Before 1979 FDI was prohibited in China, a restriction which was lifted as part of China's open door policy of 1979, when a new foreign investment law was adopted. In its early stages, FDI was restricted to China's Four Special Economic Zones and limited to equity joint ventures. Most of the FDI went into hotel construction and energy. In 1984, a new foreign investment law accelerated FDI growth and a number of preferential policies were also used by both central and local governments to attract FDI.

A sharp increase in FDI only occurred after 1992 when China reaffirmed the policies of openness and market-oriented reforms introduced earlier. Significant tax preferences towards FDI introduced in 1991 and 1994 were also instrumental in the post-1992 surge. The resulting growth in China's inward FDI has been spectacular. In 1985, annual FDI inflows were less than US$ 2 billion; while in 2006, they were around US$ 70 billion (MOFCOM, 2007), 35 times those of 20 years earlier. Between 1985 and 1991, the annual growth rate of FDI inflows into China was 14%. Annual FDI inflows during this period were less than US$ 4.5 billion, but increased sharply to US$ 11 billion in 1992 and again to US$ 28 billion in 1993, with growth rates of over 150% in both years.

The sharpest increases in inflows occurred in the early 1990s, and the late 1990s saw a small decrease in FDI inflows. But by 1997, China had FDI inflows of US$ 49 billion. China's FDI inflows increased again after China joined into the WTO in 2001. During the three years 2001, 2002 and 2003, world FDI inflows declined sharply by 41%, 26% and 10% respectively each year, but China saw FDI inflows grow at 15%, 13% and 1.4% (UNCTAD, 2006). China again saw inward FDI grow at 13% in 2004 and 19.4% in 2005,[1] but a small decrease of 4% in 2006 as the result of inward FDI in financial services falling by 47%. China is now the world's largest developing country FDI recipient and was the world's 2nd largest FDI recipient overall after the US in 2004, 3rd in 2005 and 4th in 2006. By contrast, FDI inflows into India were only US$ 5.5 billion in 2004 and US$ 6.6 billion in 2005 (UNCTAD, 2006).

A feature of China's inward FDI is the large and increasing share involved with manufacturing. Before China's accession to the WTO, less than 60% of inward FDI went to the manufacturing sector. But after China joined the WTO, more inward FDI went to the manufacturing sector and this reached over 70% in 2005 as the share of FDI going to the real estate sector decreased. Because labour productivity in China's FIEs is sharply higher than elsewhere in the economy, (maybe by a factor of four compared to the rest of the industrial sector), one can argue that the primary attraction of FDI is access to a high quality low wage labour pool which they can use effectively with foreign technology in processing trade of various forms. In 2005 FIEs accounted for only 3% (25 million out of a 778.8 million labour force) of China's workforce (including agriculture), but over 20% of GDP and over 58% of exports.

[1]China's official inward FDI data did not include FDI to financial services (including banking, securities, and insurance) before 2005 since FDI inflows to these service sectors are relatively small. FDI inflows to financial services soared to US$12.1 billion in 2005 and declined to US$ 6.45 billion in 2006 (MOFCOM, 2007).

The size distribution of the Foreign Invested Enterprises (FIEs) funded by FDI is a further feature. By 2005 553 thousand FIEs using FDI had been established, with around 47% (260 thousand out of 553 thousand) of them still in operation. Among the 260 thousand functioning FIEs 186 thousand are industrial enterprises, though the large majority are small. Only 56 thousand FIEs with annual sales income of over 5 million Yuan (US$ 0.61 million equivalent) are tracked by statistical agencies in China for data purposes.

A key link between FDI and overall world economic performance is that a large portion of China's trade is conducted via foreign invested enterprises (FIEs). MOFCOM (Ministry of Commerce of China) estimates that 46% of the output of FIEs in the manufacturing sector is for export from China, while for non-FIEs it is only 17% (MOFCOM, 2004). The export growth rate of FIEs in most years since the early 1990s has been over 30% and over 40% in some years; a much higher growth rate than that for non-FIEs. Whalley and Xin (2006) note the sharp change in share of China's exports of FIEs from less than 2% in 1990 to nearly 60% in 2005. The share of exports from FIEs has thus increased steadily since 1990, reaching 30% in 1995, more than 40% in 1996, 50% by 2001, and 58% by 2005. Since 1990 FIEs have also accounted for most of China's export growth. Without growth in FIE exports, China's export growth rate would have been only about 10% in most years after 1990, and negative in some years.

Along with rapid export growth, FIEs have also accounted for progressively more of China's imports. FIEs are heavily involved in component import, assembly and re-export as processing trade. In 2005, the ratio of imports by China's FIEs to total imports was about 60%, although compared to exports, the ratio of imports by FIEs to China's total imports is more volatile. This ratio was 55% in 1998, declined to 37% by 2001, and rebounded by almost 20 percentage points in 2002.

Lenovie (2000) reports that most of the vertical and export-oriented FDI inflows to China originate from elsewhere in Asia (primarily from Hong Kong, Korea, and Taiwan). But while Hong Kong, Macao and Taiwan accounted for 66% of FDI inflows between 1979 and 1992, and later this share declined, it was still around 40% in 2004. Many of these businesses are owner-managed from initial investments, with the core business growth occurring inside rather than outside of China. Fung (2004) also reports that, in contrast to the 1990s, the majority of foreign investment inflows to China now take the form of wholly foreign-owned entities rather than joint ventures. He reports that in 2002, 64% of FDI was of this form. Also, FDI in China from North America and Europe is claimed to be more heavily horizontal and aimed more at the Chinese domestic market rather than exports. Fung (2004) reports an estimate that US-origin FIEs sold more than 80% of their products locally in 2002, while Japanese-origin FIEs sold only 45% of their production locally.

A large amount of China's FDI-related trade is conducted through middlemen and distribution arrangements centered on Hong Kong, Korea and Taiwan. Fung (2004) notes that 28.3% of China's exports in 2002 were re-exported via Hong Kong and 21.9% of Chinese imports were imported via Hong Kong. Trade through middlemen is a reflection of trade in textiles and apparel and the impact of bilateral multilateral fibre agreement (MFA) quota restraints on China in the US and EU markets. As Whalley (2006) notes, the termination of the MFA in January, 2005, has seen large increases in China's exports of clothing to the US and EU, accompanied by sharp falls in exports to Hong Kong as these quotas are removed. But at the same time this Hong Kong trade also involves considerably more products than apparel, and especially electronics.

A considerable amount of China's trade is also related to processing and assembly, with sourcing via retailers in OECD and other markets abroad the common organizational form. Processed exports typically largely embody labour as the domestic value-added, and have smaller value-added content than non-processed exports. Processed exports are typically products for final rather than intermediate sale, as again typified by consumer electronics and clothing. Fung (2004) reports official estimates that 55.2% of China's exports in 2003 were processed exports, while 39.5% of China's imports were inputs for processing. Feenstra and Hanson (2005) report similar estimates that 55.6% of China's exports between 1997 and 2002 were processed. The most recent official data indicates that in 2005, 78% of China's FIE exports are processed exports and 60% of FIE imports are inputs to processing. FIE processed exports and imports accounted for 83% and 84% of China's total processed exports and imports respectively in 2005 (MOFCOM, 2006) indicating the importance of FDI to processing trade.

As Fung (2004) notes, there has been substantial growth in China's technology trade within this component. He notes that 2003 data from China's Custom Statistics report 25.9% of China's exports as high technology products, along with 28.9% of imports as high technology products. Two-way trade in high technology products would thus seem to be substantial. MOFCOM (2006) estimates that 88% of China's exports of high technology products are conducted by FIEs and, in 2005, 43%

of China's FIE exports are high technology products (of which 94% are processed exports).

While Tomiura (2005) finds that relatively few Japanese firms outsource directly to China, Xing (2004) found that Japanese-affiliated manufacturers in China, operating as subsidiaries, sold about 1/3 of their products back to Japan. In industrial machinery, more than half of the products were exported to the Japanese market either as final goods or intermediate inputs. In the textile and transportation equipment sectors, ratios of re-export increased between 1997 and 2002. In 1997, only 31% of textile products were produced for the Japanese market while the share rose to 47% in 2002. In transportation equipment, Japanese-affiliated manufacturers also exported 47% of their products to Japan in 2002, much higher than the 27% re-export ratio in 1997. Re-exports increased by 23% in 2000, and continued to grow in 2001 and 2002 with 36% and 16% growth respectively. This suggests growing Japanese-affiliate production in China for the Japanese market via FDI.

Finally, the geographical concentration within China of both China's trade and FDI inflows is pronounced. The majority of FDI inflows still go to the Eastern and South Eastern coastal areas, although the picture is changing. As Table 1 indicates in 2000 nearly 44% of FDI is located in two provinces (Guangdong and Jiangsu); by 2003 the share in Guangdong has fallen sharply, but five provinces still account for 56% of FDI in 2003 and 59% in 2005 (NBSC, 2006). Fung (2004) also notes that Guangdong accounted for 31.7% of China's imports in 2003, and 34.9% of China's exports in the same year. These two figures are relatively stable and are 30% and 32% in 2005 for imports and exports respectively. Among both of these exports and imports over 60% are conducted via FIEs in 2005 (NBSC, 2006).

All these studies and data thus suggest that China has indeed become a significant production base both for final products consumed abroad (and largely in OECD markets) and intermediate inputs purchased by foreign firms using FDI. Both Roach (2003) and Rauch (2001) characterize China as now being part of a global supply chain network in certain key industries and engaged in both importing and exporting various components and parts and FDI is at the heart of this. This suggests increasing vertical integration between OECD and Chinese industrial activity, and the creation of linkage between firms through FDI. A significant portion of this is affiliate activity and a further portion involves owner-operated firms from Taiwan and Hong Kong.

Table 1. The Shares of FDI by Province/City in Total FDI (%), 2000, 2003, and 2005.

	2000	2003	2005
Eastern China	**86.50**	**85.73**	**88.78**
Guangdong	27.97	14.78	20.50
Jiangsu	15.93	19.95	15.75
Shandong	7.37	11.36	14.73
Shanghai	7.84	10.33	11.12
Zhejiang	4.00	9.41	8.64
Beijing	4.17	4.14	5.85
Tianjin	2.89	2.90	4.03
Liaoning	5.07	5.33	3.82
Fujian	8.51	4.91	3.42
Hebei	1.68	1.82	0.85
Hainan	1.07	0.80	0.07
Central China	**7.65**	**11.02**	**8.00**
Hunan	1.68	1.92	1.90
Jiangxi	0.56	3.04	1.71
Hubei	2.34	2.96	1.25
Anhui	0.79	0.69	0.89
Henan	1.40	1.02	0.86
Heilongjiang	0.26	0.61	0.67
Jilin	0.36	0.36	0.55
Shanxi	0.26	0.40	0.16
Western China	**4.59**	**3.25**	**3.22**
Sichuan	1.08	0.78	1.01
Guangxi	1.30	0.79	0.62
Inner Mongolia	0.26	0.17	0.44
Chongqing	0.61	0.49	0.37
Shaanxi	0.72	0.63	0.32
Yunnan	0.32	0.16	0.29
Ningxia	0.04	0.03	0.07
Guizhou	0.06	0.09	0.06
Gansu	0.15	0.04	0.03
Xinjiang	0.05	0.03	0.01
Qinghai	0.00	0.05	0.01
Tibet	0.00	0.00	0.00

Source: NBSC (2001, 2004) and MOFCOM (2006).

2.1.1. *Outward FDI*

In contrast to inward FDI, Chinese outward foreign direct investment (FDI) has been relatively small until recently (US$ 5.5 billion in 2004, 12.3 billion in 2005 and 16.1 billion in 2006, NBSC, 2006) and also heavily concentrated on both greenfield and joint venture activity abroad, much of it focused on Hong Kong. But, in the last year or two, direct acquisition of foreign firms by Chinese entities involving potentially large transactions have become prominent, in some instances in the US$ 15–20 billion range, and with a focus well beyond Hong Kong. Examples include: the Lenovo buyout of IBM's PC business, CNOOC's bid for Unocal, a prospective bid by MinMetals for Noranda, the Haier Group bid for Maytag, and others (Antkiewicz and Whalley, 2006). In part, the motivation is for the Chinese acquirer to combine the acquired foreign distribution system with growing lower wage Chinese manufacturing output which slowly displaces higher wage supplies abroad. Access to foreign brands in the distribution process is an element behind this.

Chinese outward FDI has previously been concentrated outside of the OECD (Table 2). Data in geographical locations for Chinese FDI are made hard to interpret by the sizeable amount flowing through intermediary tax haven locations such as the Cayman Islands. By the end of 2003, 84.3% of China's accumulated outward FDI was in Asia, 8.2% in Latin America (and mainly in the Cayman Islands), around 2% each in Europe, Africa, and North America, and 0.8% in Oceania. The top five destinations of China's cumulative outward FDI by 2003 were Hong Kong, Cayman Islands, Macao, the US, and Virgin Islands (77.2%, 6.3%, 1.4%, 1.2%, and 0.9% in that order). China's outward FDI share in different regions has changed rapidly in recent years. The largest changes have happened in Latin America where the share rose to 52.7% from 32.1% during the same period, of which 42.1% was to the Cayman Islands. The share in Europe changed from 3.1% to 4.1%, North America from 2.3% to 2.6%, Africa 5.8% to 3.2%, and Oceania 2.2% to 1.7%.

China's outward FDI has been heavily concentrated in five sectors: leasing and business services (28.9% of China's accumulated outward FDI by 2005), distribution, wholesale and retail (20.0%), mining (15.1%), transport, storage and post (12.4%), and manufacturing (10.1%). In 2006, Chinese outward investment was only US$ 16.1 billion, only one-fifth of FDI flowing into China, despite the growth rate of outward FDI shares outpacing that of inward FDI for several prior years (in 2006, 32% and −4% respectively, year on year; in 2005, 123% and 20% respectively).

A recent joint study undertaken by the Chinese Academy of International Trade and Economic Cooperation (CAITEC) and the Welsh Development Agency (WDA) used a questionnaire to investigate key factors involved in Chinese outward FDI. These included market expansion, implementation of long-term development strategies for firms, more access to technology, accessing advanced management methods, avoiding trade

Table 2. China's Outward FDI (US$).

	Accumulated outward FDI at the end of 2003		Outward FDI in 2004		Outward FDI in 2005		Accumulated outward FDI at the end of 2005	
	Amount (million)	Share (%)	Amount (million)	Share (%)	Amount (million)	Share (%)	Amount (million)	Share (%)
Total	**39446.5**	**100.0**	**5498.0**	**100.0**	**12261.2**	**100.0**	**57205.6**	**100.0**
Asia	**33254.1**	**84.3**	**3000.3**	**54.6**	**4374.6**	**35.7**	**40629.0**	**71.0**
Hong Kong	30459.0	77.2	2628.4	47.8	3419.7	27.9	36507.1	63.8
Indonesia	67.1	0.2	62.0	1.1	11.8	0.1	140.9	0.2
Japan	118.2	0.3	15.3	0.3	17.2	0.1	150.7	0.3
Macao	563.8	1.4	26.6	0.5	8.3	0.1	598.7	1.0
Singapore	257.2	0.7	48.0	0.9	20.3	0.2	325.5	0.6
Republic of Korea	253.2	0.6	40.2	0.7	588.8	4.8	882.2	1.5
Thailand	191.0	0.5	23.4	0.4	4.8	0.0	219.2	0.4
Vietnam	191.6	0.5	16.9	0.3	20.8	0.2	229.2	0.4
Africa	**886.2**	**2.2**	**317.4**	**5.8**	**391.7**	**3.2**	**1595.3**	**2.8**
Algeria	75.1	0.2	11.2	0.2	84.9	0.7	171.2	0.3
Sudan	113.7	0.3	146.7	2.7	91.1	0.7	351.5	0.6
Guinea	13.4	0.0	14.4	0.3	16.3	0.1	44.2	0.1
Madagascar	36.2	0.1	13.6	0.2	0.1	0.0	49.9	0.1
Nigeria	−4.7	0.0	45.5	0.8	53.3	0.4	94.1	0.2
South Africa	47.0	0.1	17.8	0.3	47.5	0.4	112.3	0.2
Europe	**922.3**	**2.3**	**170.9**	**3.1**	**505.0**	**4.1**	**1598.2**	**2.8**
United Kingdom	53.8	0.1	29.4	0.5	24.8	0.2	108.0	0.2
Germany	112.1	0.3	27.5	0.5	128.7	1.0	268.4	0.5
France	17.4	0.0	10.3	0.2	6.1	0.0	33.8	0.1
Russia	184.9	0.5	77.3	1.4	203.3	1.7	465.6	0.8
Latin America	**3240.7**	**8.2**	**1762.7**	**32.1**	**6466.2**	**52.7**	**11469.6**	**20.0**
Bahamas	−51.8	−0.1	43.6	0.8	23.0	0.2	14.7	0.0
Cayman Islands	2486.7	6.3	1286.1	23.4	5162.8	42.1	8935.6	15.6
Mexico	111.2	0.3	27.1	0.5	3.6	0.0	141.9	0.2
Virgin Is. (E)	372.0	0.9	385.5	7.0	1226.1	10.0	1983.6	3.5
North America	**815.9**	**2.1**	**126.5**	**2.3**	**320.8**	**2.6**	**1263.2**	**2.2**
Canada	65.7	0.2	5.1	0.1	32.4	0.3	103.3	0.2
United States	470.9	1.2	119.9	2.2	231.8	1.9	822.7	1.4
Oceania	**327.3**	**0.8**	**120.2**	**2.2**	**202.8**	**1.7**	**650.3**	**1.1**
Australia	269.4	0.7	125.0	2.3	193.1	1.6	587.5	1.0
New Zealand	36.6	0.1	−4.9	−0.1	3.5	0.0	35.2	0.1

Source: NBSC (2006, Table 18–20).

barriers, taking advantage of foreign preferential investment policies, achieving cost reductions, acquisition of material inputs (resources), and transferring excess production capacity abroad. The use of overseas investment as a way around official Chinese restrictions on access to foreign exchange and foreign capital markets was also cited as a factor (CAITEC, 2005).

Other studies have pointed to non-economic reasons for Chinese enterprises investing abroad, such as the possibility of gaining residency rights and other benefits in the host country for managerial staff (such as health services, social security, access to education). But the decision by a Chinese company to buy a foreign company is also often linked to an intent to move manufacturing activity to China to benefit from lower labour costs while keeping existing distribution networks of the acquired business in the host country; similar considerations to that involving foreign firms in their outsourcing activities in China.

Recent widely publicized Chinese bids for large firms in the OECD are also portrayed in Chinese media as involving a prestige factor; going abroad to either buy a recognizable foreign brand (Lenovo's takeover of IBM) or to build their own brand's identity by establishing manufacturing plants in the target country (such as Haier's factory in South Carolina).

However, recent Chinese outward FDI also reflects official Chinese government policy to encourage domestic enterprises to invest abroad. Government regulatory approval processes for overseas investment projects have been significantly simplified in the recent years, increasing outward FDI flows. Chinese companies are also supported by low interest loans if their overseas activity involves, among other things, resource exploration and acquisition of advanced foreign technology. This use of low interest loans made available to Chinese SOEs reflects China's large and growing foreign reserves. These reserves today stand at close to US$ 1 trillion reflecting both large Chinese trade surpluses in recent years and inward foreign investment. With concerns in China over security of supply of resource inputs, and the prospect of possible further falls in the US dollar and the impact on the large holdings of US treasuries in the reserve portfolio, deploying Chinese reserves in this way is seen in China as a reasonable policy.

Chinese government policy promotes the use outward-oriented investment largely by large state-owned enterprises (SOEs) to secure access to resources and raw materials (especially iron ore, coal, oil and natural gas), acquire new technology for transfer back to China, expand Chinese export markets, and strengthen international relationships with and gain more influence in other countries. In 2003, SOEs accounted for only 43% of total Chinese investments abroad with limited liability, shareholding and private companies taken together, accounting for another 43%. With the recent large scale acquisition activity abroad these proportions seems poised to change.

Political resistance to these transactions has emerged in the OECD with questions of subsidization, lack of transparency, and national security being raised. National security issues regarding foreign acquisitions are not new and, in the US, go back to the Exxon-Florio provisions of the American Defense Production Act of 1998 following concerns in the US in the late 1980s over Japanese buyouts. However, issues of subsidization of foreign acquisitions through low interest loans from central banks and the transparency of organizational form of acquiring entities (state-owned enterprises) are new.

For now, outward FDI from China (insourcing to China) is still relatively small but growing much more rapidly that inward FDI, and the size of China's foreign reserves suggests this could change significantly in future years. Here the linkage to distribution and marketing networks seems even more marked than in the inward FDI area.

3. Inward FDI and Growth Performance in China

How much of China's strong growth performance can be attributed to inward FDI is an issue discussed in a recent joint chapter of ours (Whalley and Xin, 2006). In it, we use an extension of the growth accounting approach long associated with Solow (1957) and Dennison (1967), extending the original Solow framework by using a two-stage production growth accounting approach.

Solow's original purpose was to investigate the contribution of technical progress relative to factor accumulation in US long term growth, which he puts at 87.5% of growth. Dennison (1967) later used Solow's framework to explore the factors explaining why growth rates differed across OECD counties, and Jorgenson and Griliches (1967) investigated the role of embodied technical progress on growth, concluding it was substantial. Young (1995) later used this growth accounting approach to analyze growth experiences more broadly in Asia, finding that the higher growth in the newly industrializing countries of east Asia was not due to rapid technological progress and other factors affecting the Solow residual, but rather capital accumulation. The Solow framework has recently been extended to open economies by Kohli (2003a and 2003b) to capture terms of trade effects in growth performance of open economies.

Following the trade literature, at the first stage we use a GDP function in which the outputs of the FIE and non-FIE portions of the Chinese economy aggregate to yield GDP,

$$O(t) = g(FIE(t), NFIE(t)) \tag{1}$$

where $O(t)$ refers to aggregate output, and FIE(t) and NFIE(t) are outputs of the FIE and non-FIE portions of the economy.

In the second stage we use separate production functions for each sector, i.e.

$$FIE(t) = A^F(t)f(FDI(t), L^F(t)) \tag{2}$$
$$NFIE(t) = A^N(t)h(K(t), L^N(t)) \tag{3}$$

where $A^F(t)$ and $A^N(t)$ are the Hicksian neutral technical change terms, $L^F(t)$ and $L^N(t)$ are the labor inputs used in the FIE and non-FIE parts of the economy, FDI(t) and K(t) are the stocks of accumulated FDI and capital used in the FIE and non-FIE parts of the economy. The strong assumption is made that foreign supplied capital (FDI) is the only non-labor input in the FIE portion of the economy.

Taking time derivatives through (2) and (3) yields,

$$\frac{\dot{FIE}}{FIE} = \frac{\dot{A^F}}{A^F} + S^F_{FDI}\frac{\dot{FDI}}{FDI} + S^F_L\frac{\dot{L^F}}{L^F} \tag{4}$$

and,

$$\frac{\dot{NFIE}}{NFIE} = \frac{\dot{A^N}}{A^N} + S^N_K\frac{\dot{K}}{K} + S^N_L\frac{\dot{L^N}}{L^N} \tag{5}$$

where S^F_L and S^F_{FDI} are the shares of labor and FDI in FIE production and S^N_L and S^N_K are the shares of labor and capital in non-FIE production.

The economy wide growth accounting equation for this two-stage production structure can thus be expressed as,

$$\frac{\dot{O}}{O} = g^F\left(\frac{\dot{A^F}}{A^F} + S^F_{FDI}\frac{\dot{FDI}}{FDI} + S^F_L\frac{\dot{L^F}}{L^F}\right) + g^N\left(\frac{\dot{A^N}}{A^N} + S^N_K\frac{\dot{K}}{K} + S^N_L\frac{\dot{L^N}}{L^N}\right) \tag{6}$$

where g^F and g^N are shares of FIE and non-FIE output in the GDP function. If (1), (2), and (3) are Cobb-Douglas, then the associated share parameters are constant. If (1), (2), and (3) are CES then the share parameters in (6) change over time.

If g^F is the share of FIE output in national income, g^N can then be obtained by residual since the sum of g^F and g^N is one. The labor share parameters, S_L^F and S_L^N in FIE and non-FIE production functions are calculated using the labor force wage bill divided by value-added for the two parts of the economy, and S_{FDI}^F and S_K^N are obtained by residual. The wage bill of FIEs is estimated by multiplying wage rate (NBSC, 2005, p. 174) and labor force data (NBSC, p. 506, p. 121). The wage bill of non-FIEs is China's total labor remuneration (NBSC, 2005, p. 62; and other various years) minus the FIE wage bill. Data on China's labor force is from NBSC (2005, p. 118) and the labor force in non-FIEs is taken to be the total labor force minus that in FIEs.

To determine the capital stock and growth variables, we first estimate the Chinese total capital stock along with the FIE capital stock as accumulated FDI net of depreciation. We use the total capital stock minus the FDI stock as our estimate of the non-FIE capital stock.

The Chinese capital stock is obtained by firstly deflating annual capital formation data using a fixed investment price index NBSC (2005, p. 301). A depreciation rate of 0.04, similar to that used by Chow (1993 and 2003), is assumed for the depreciation of the annual capital stock after 1985. Before 1985, a depreciation factor of 0.10 is used instead to account for outmoded fixed equipment. Annual capital formation is from the World Bank database (World Bank, 2005) in US$.

The resulting growth rates of variables from 1995 to 2004, along with the estimated share parameters are reported in Table 3. These data indicate that while FIEs produce one fifth of China's total GDP, the FIE subpart of the Chinese economy grew three times faster than the non-FIE portion between 1995 and 2004, and considerably faster than China's economy as a whole. In the two years 2003 and 2004, over 40% of China's growth comes from FIEs and in the last decade (from 1995 to 2004), over 30% of China's economic growth.

A further striking feature of these data is the high capital share in the non-FIE portion of the economy (declining from 70% to only 50% in 2004), and the even higher share of FDI in FIE output (over 80% in most years after 1995). The high (and volatile) $\dot{L}^F/L^F$ variable reflects rapid labor

Table 3. Growth Rates of Output and Accumulated FDI, Capital Stock and Labor Force in FIEs and the Non-FIEs Portion of the Chinese Economy and Share Parameters.

	$\frac{\dot{FIE}}{FIE}$	$\frac{\dot{NFIE}}{NFIE}$	g^F	g^N	S_L^F	S_{FDI}^F	S_L^N	S_K^N	$\frac{\dot{L}^F}{L^F}$	$\frac{\dot{FDI}}{FDI}$	$\frac{\dot{L}^N}{L^N}$	$\frac{\dot{K}}{K}$
1995	–	–	10.3	89.7	19.6	80.4	29.9	70.1	41.0	41.8	0.5	14.0
1996	18.9	8.5	11.2	88.8	20.8	79.2	30.2	69.8	26.4	32.6	1.0	14.2
1997	24.8	6.8	12.8	87.2	19.8	80.2	30.3	69.7	5.3	26.6	1.2	13.3
1998	23.5	5.5	14.7	85.3	21.1	78.9	32.8	67.2	7.6	20.7	1.1	12.3
1999	15.9	5.6	15.9	84.1	20.1	79.9	34.9	65.1	2.2	14.2	1.1	11.4
2000	17.4	6.2	17.2	82.8	18.4	81.6	36.9	63.1	7.7	11.9	0.8	10.5
2001	12.5	6.5	18.0	82.0	18.7	81.3	40.4	59.6	10.1	12.4	1.1	11.2
2002	12.3	7.4	18.7	81.3	19.5	80.5	42.7	57.3	12.3	12.5	0.7	11.5
2003	20.4	6.7	20.6	79.4	18.5	81.5	45.2	54.8	19.4	10.6	0.5	13.0
2004	18.8	7.1	22.4	77.6	15.9	84.1	48.8	51.2	14.8	10.4	0.6	13.3

Source: Whalley and Xin (2006).

growth forces in FIEs from a low base, and the high $\dot{K}/K$ variable reflects high rates of domestic saving in China.

Following Solow's original procedure of specifying no functional form for the production functions (4) and (5), and allowing shares to vary each year, we use data from Table 4 and (6) to decompose the growth performance of the FIE and non-FIE parts of China's economy and assess their respective contributions to the total GDP growth. If we instead assume (2) and (3) to be Cobb-Douglas, and time invariant, shares are constant over time. If we assume CES, then shares vary over time in ways which reflect the elasticity of substitution, output, and factor input data and need not be the same as observed shares.

Table 4 reports growth accounting results using the conventional Solow methodology. These suggest that over 90% of growth in the non-FIE sub-economy in China between 1995 and 2004 has been from growth in the capital stock. In contrast, 20–40% of FIE growth came from technological progress and a further 15% from growth in the FIE labor force. These decomposition results also suggest that without FDI inflows, in 2004 growth in China would be lowered by the 1.8% attributed to the $\dot{FDI}/FDI$ term. If TFP growth in the FIE portion of the economy of 1.6% is attributed to technical progress embodied in FDI, this component of growth would also be lost. This yields an estimate of forgone growth were FDI growth to have been interrupted in 2004 of 3.4%. The 3% labor force growth rate in the FIE portion would remain as a growth contribution through redeployment of labor elsewhere.

Table 4. **A Two Stage Solow Decomposition of FIE and Non-FIE Growth Rates in China by Year and Component (%).**

	GDP growth rate	Growth rate (A)								Contribution to GDP growth (B)							
		FIE				Non-FIE				FIE				Non-FIE			
		Total	TFP	L	FDI	Total	TFP	L	K	Total	TFP	L	FDI	Total	TFP	L	K
1996	9.6	18.9	−12.4	5.5	25.8	8.5	−1.7	0.3	9.9	1.9	−1.3	0.6	2.7	7.7	−1.5	0.3	8.9
1997	8.8	24.8	2.4	1.0	21.3	6.8	−2.8	0.4	9.3	2.8	0.3	0.1	2.4	6.0	−2.5	0.3	8.2
1998	7.8	23.5	5.5	1.6	16.4	5.5	−3.1	0.3	8.2	3.0	0.7	0.2	2.1	4.8	−2.7	0.3	7.2
1999	7.1	15.9	4.2	0.4	11.3	5.6	−2.2	0.4	7.4	2.3	0.6	0.1	1.7	4.8	−1.8	0.3	6.3
2000	8.0	17.4	6.3	1.4	9.7	6.2	−0.7	0.3	6.6	2.8	1.0	0.2	1.5	5.2	−0.6	0.3	5.6
2001	7.5	12.5	0.5	1.9	10.1	6.5	−0.7	0.5	6.7	2.2	0.1	0.3	1.7	5.3	−0.6	0.4	5.5
2002	8.3	12.3	−0.2	2.4	10.0	7.4	0.5	0.3	6.6	2.2	0.0	0.4	1.8	6.1	0.4	0.3	5.4
2003	9.3	20.4	8.2	3.6	8.6	6.7	−0.6	0.2	7.2	3.8	1.5	0.7	1.6	5.5	−0.5	0.2	5.8
2004	9.5	18.8	7.7	2.4	8.8	7.1	−0.1	0.3	6.8	3.9	1.6	0.5	1.8	5.6	0.0	0.2	5.4

(*Continued*)

Table 4. *(Continued)*

	Contribution share to total GDP growth (C)									Factor contribution share inside (D)					
		FIE				Non-FIE				FIE			Non-FIE		
	GDP	Total	TFP	L	FDI	Total	TFP	L	K	TFP	L	FDI	TFP	L	K
1996	100	20.2	−13.3	5.9	27.6	79.8	−15.7	2.7	92.7	−65.8	29.1	136.7	−19.7	3.4	116.2
1997	100	31.4	3.0	1.3	27.0	68.6	−28.5	3.7	93.4	9.7	4.2	86.1	−41.5	5.3	136.2
1998	100	38.5	9.0	2.6	26.8	61.5	−34.2	3.9	91.9	23.5	6.8	69.7	−55.7	6.3	149.3
1999	100	32.7	8.5	0.9	23.3	67.3	−25.8	4.4	88.7	26.1	2.7	71.2	−38.3	6.5	131.8
2000	100	34.5	12.5	2.8	19.2	65.5	−7.6	3.3	69.8	36.3	8.2	55.5	−11.6	5.0	106.6
2001	100	28.8	1.2	4.3	23.2	71.2	−7.8	5.0	74.0	4.2	15.1	80.7	−11.0	7.1	103.9
2002	100	26.7	−0.4	5.2	21.8	73.3	5.0	3.1	65.2	−1.4	19.6	81.8	6.8	4.2	89.0
2003	100	41.1	16.5	7.2	17.3	58.9	−5.6	2.0	62.5	40.3	17.5	42.2	−9.5	3.3	106.1
2004	100	40.8	16.6	5.1	19.1	59.2	−0.5	2.6	57.1	40.8	12.5	46.7	−0.8	4.4	96.4

Source: Whalley and Xin (2006).

While the FIE sub-economy in China is still only 20% of the whole economy, it nonetheless accounts for over 40% of China's recent economic growth. This part of the Chinese economy thus has substantial implications for the sustainability of China's future economic growth, and whether rapid growth will continue into the future, in turn, depends on both continued growth in inward FDI along with access to international export markets abroad.

While China's FDI inflow growth rate has averaged over 10% since 2002 and China's accession to the WTO, in the years ahead it seems likely to plateau or slightly decline. An important feature of China's FDI performance has been the falling share of OECD FDI going to other non-OECD countries (in Brazil it fell to US$ 10 billion in 2003 and 18 billion in 2004 from US$ 33 billion in 2000). As overall OECD FDI has increased little, the prospects seem to be for plateauing or even falling FDI flows to China as some further FDI moves to other low wage countries such as Vietnam and Indonesia.

China's WTO commitments imply both capital market liberalization (in banking) and further progress on commitments on rule-based WTO issues, including TRIPs and TRIMs, and these changes may help attract more FDI. China is also continuing to see changes in the legal forms that FIEs take, and this may also help with continued FDI inflows. The share of inward FDI occurring through wholly foreign-owned enterprises at the end of 2000 was 46.9% of accumulated FDI, and in recent years, wholly foreign-owned enterprises provide the dominant legal form (over 66% of inward FDI in 2004) (NBSC, 2005 and various issues). This increasing share of wholly-owned FIEs may accelerate technology transfer and product upgrading, and access to foreign equipment and technology and intermediate goods will improve with trade liberalization and lower tariffs will apply to imports.

China's rapid export growth, which FDI inflows have generated, also raises concerns over the continued absorptive capacities of the OECD. China's share of world exports is now around 8% and with a 35% growth rate in exports is doubling every three years. Continued FDI flows thus may also encounter problems here if they are export-oriented. China's large trade surplus with the EU and the US also fuels protectionist pressure in these countries.

This leaves the issue of whether the non-FIE part of the economy can generate higher growth in the future to compensate for slowing growth in the FIE sub-economy. The reform process for SOEs and labor market and competition related reforms provide the major hope, but results from these reforms thus far are not conclusive.

Overall then, plateauing or falling FDI, limits to FDI diversification from other non-OECD countries, and continued growth of exports all raise cautions for continued high growth in China in the future based on FDI inflows. These negatives are counterbalanced by an ever improving policy environment for FDI in China, but they seem unlikely to support yet more FDI growth into China. Whether growth in the non-FIE sub-economy can compensate is the issue.

4. FDI and Regional Inequality

A central policy concern in China is growing inequality and whether FDI plays a central role is a topic now much debated. While absolute poverty in China measured by headcount ratios (fraction of the population below various poverty lines) has been falling sharply, relative inequality has grown quickly. A widely used measure is the ratio of urban to rural incomes, which has increased from around 1.8 in the mid-1980s to around 3.2 today (calculation based on Table 10-1 (NBSC, 2006)). The national Gini coefficient has increased from under 0.28 in the 1981 to 0.41 today (World Bank, 2007).

The geographically concentrated nature of China's development which has occurred primarily in a relatively small number of Western and Coastal provinces is widely thought to be a key determinant in this outcome. In turn, as these same provinces are the largest recipients of inward FDI, the link between FDI inflows and relative inequality surfaces as an issue.

In Table 5 we report real GDP/capita by province for the years between 1978 and 2004. Provinces are stratified by Coastal and Interior with interior provinces showing GDP/capita well below the national average and coastal provinces well above the national average. The gap between highest and lowest provinces in 2004 is approximately ten times, narrowing from approximately 15 times in 1978. The trend indicates a narrowing over time in the dispersion of provincial GDP/capita both within the two groups of coastal and interior provinces and across the two groups. As national inequality has been increasing in China, this seems to indicate increasing inequality within provinces over time, and especially across the urban rural divide within provinces.

In Table 6 we report FDI inflows by province for individual years from 1978 onwards, cumulating them forward after allowing for 4% depreciation.

Table 5. Real Provincial Per Capital GDP in China, Various Years.

	Per capita GDP (in 1978 RMB)				As per cent of national average			
	1978	1990	2000	2004	1978	1990	2000	2004
National Average	374.57	888.98	2099.9	2858.14	100	100	100	100
Coastal								
Beijing	1248.2	2558.6	4811.4	6666.8	333.24	287.81	229.13	233.26
Tianjin	1141.6	1951.6	4393.2	6653.4	304.78	219.53	209.21	232.79
Liaoning	675.3	1350.6	2955.4	3787.2	180.29	151.93	140.74	132.51
Changhai	2484.6	3090.2	7293.1	9938.5	663.32	347.61	347.31	347.73
Jiangsu	427.2	1078.8	3095.4	4849.7	114.05	121.35	147.41	169.68
Zhejiang	329.8	1114.0	3462.2	5535.3	88.05	125.31	164.87	193.67
Fujian	270.6	839.4	2039.6	3954.0	72.24	94.42	144.27	138.34
Shangdong	314.9	871.0	2524.0	3921.3	84.07	97.98	120.20	137.20
Guangdong	364.8	1286.8	2999.2	4488.5	97.39	144.75	142.83	157.04
Hainan	310.6	795.1	1767.3	2185.6	82.92	89.44	84.16	76.47
Interior								
Hebei	362.0	753.2	2024.2	3015.9	96.64	84.73	96.40	105.52
Shanxi	363.0	765.3	1337.4	2187.1	96.91	86.09	63.69	76.52
Inner Mongolia	318.4	735.5	1581.8	2643.6	85.00	82.74	75.33	92.49
Jilin	381.5	880.3	1790.8	2720.0	101.85	99.02	85.28	95.17
Helongiang	558.4	1031.9	2365.5	2985.8	149.08	116.08	112.65	104.47
Anhui	241.8	593.0	1361.5	1731.7	64.55	66.71	64.84	60.59
Jiangxi	273.3	610.9	1297.9	1900.9	72.96	68.72	81.81	66.51
Henan	230.5	574.6	1489.0	2108.1	61.54	64.64	70.91	73.76
Hubei	330.1	807.0	1903.0	2447.1	88.13	90.78	90.62	85.62
Hunan	284.5	636.2	1537.8	1947.1	75.95	71.57	73.23	68.12
Guangxi	223.0	511.1	1225.1	1578.1	59.53	57.54	58.34	55.21
Chongqin			1379.8	2043.4			65.71	71.49
Sichuan	252.2	587.9	1291.6	1746.1	67.33	66.13	61.51	61.09
Guizhou	173.6	432.7	756.1	947.6	46.35	48.67	36.01	33.15
Yunnan	223.3	588.9	1223.1	1557.7	59.62	66.24	58.25	54.50
Xizhang	371.5	611.1	1202.7	1794.1	99.18	68.74	57.27	62.77
Shaanxi	291.6	625.8	1235.9	1808.6	77.85	70.40	58.86	63.28
Gamsu	346.1	575.6	1029.6	1383.2	92.40	64.75	49.03	48.40
Qinghai	425.8	821.6	1365.0	2007.9	113.68	92.42	65.00	70.25
Ningxia	365.2	721.3	1267.6	1819.3	97.50	81.14	60.36	63.65
Xinjiang	316.9	914.0	1901.3	2604.5	84.60	102.81	90.54	91.13

Sources: NBSC (various years).

These are in real terms after adjustments by the GDP deflator for the year. These data show substantial growth through the 1990s in FDI by province, as well as extreme concentration with Guangdong, Fujian, Jiangsu, Shangdong, and Shanghai, accounting for nearly 70% of the FDI stock in 2003.

Table 6. Cumulative FDI Capital Stock by Province by Year (1990 Prices, and Assuming A 4% Depreciation Rate), US$, Million.

Province	1988	1989	1990	1991	1992	1993	1994	1995
Beijing	668.40	983.003	1220.633	1401.953	1654.9	2078.136	2825.8665	3285.968
Tianjin	42.34	70.67025	102.7734	222.9011	309.1879	747.1675	1332.1312	2085.983
Hebei	22.24	50.14094	87.4853	125.6964	220.5618	502.739	799.68934	1057.818
Shanxi	8.67	17.77465	20.46367	23.21735	29.84592	130.4785	144.46224	172.5575
Inner Mongolia	4.48	4.558158	15.01583	15.44927	19.42449	81.23989	102.23989	128.8293
Liaoning	153.21	274.1738	506.9369	814.6281	1238.2	2127.358	2914.6571	3554.092
Jilin	8.24	11.50332	28.64318	44.41857	109.1902	306.8286	441.10332	639.99
Helongjiang	53.30	75.18416	96.6668	101.6649	161.3466	325.38	522.92438	776.2981
Shanghai	309.98	750.0233	894.0324	994.7586	1390.978	3654.478	5006.4224	6341.235
Jiangsu	136.97	231.793	346.6813	532.408	1962.597	3970.941	6091.7064	8602.737
Zhejiang	39.31	93.27012	137.9693	218.579	421.6352	1161.916	1812.2325	2407.379
Anhui	15.30	19.81286	28.63034	36.45332	83.27676	269.014	482.38829	719.1809
Fujian	173.05	518.5472	787.8254	1194.654	2404.379	4417.603	6490.2311	8376.666
Jiangxi	6.89	12.90258	18.59648	36.17442	122.8108	270.6633	418.35463	554.9252
Shangdong	57.28	195.7465	338.7566	493.9474	1360.518	2681.421	4120.3436	5382.536

(*Continued*)

Table 6. *(Continued)*

Province	1988	1989	1990	1991	1992	1993	1994	1995
Henan	85.32	127.6334	183.018	211.3351	249.8383	463.602	679.23729	906.1143
Hubei	29.66	53.07147	79.94861	120.3977	295.008	679.874	1017.2676	1308.83
Hunan	10.25	16.73169	27.22242	47.52933	162.3749	476.9085	658.42683	901.5353
Guangdong	1273.39	2461.97	3823.491	5384.152	8438.003	13645.25	18832.104	23523.72
Guangxi	27.45	75.60513	101.2409	120.9936	276.9246	914.9793	1385.0036	1686.559
Hainan	151.83	247.5512	340.6692	492.6437	872.6786	1356.675	1858.5588	2347.843
Chongqin	0.00	0.00	0.00	0.00	0.00	0.00	0.00	0.00
Sichuan	31.39	38.71735	53.20866	74.00842	170.1021	582.6255	1117.6828	1360.39
Guizhou	5.85	13.62205	17.75717	23.94694	40.46971	70.36231	106.09295	132.1143
Yunnan	4.12	11.88792	14.0224	16.24409	40.9894	110.5477	145.50079	191.5235
Xizhang	0.04	0.038287	0.036756	0.035285	0.033874	0.032519	0.0312183	0.02997
Shanxi	148.54	278.805	278.805	297.3493	325.6723	484.5858	609.86019	757.4454
Gansu	2.66	4.442522	4.442522	5.139079	5.242673	13.80244	66.4127	97.67769
Qinghai	3.59	3.308006	3.308006	3.175685	3.649307	5.880999	7.105664	7.691754
Ningxia	0.40	0.617556	0.617556	0.762065	3.840824	12.41997	16.327117	17.74371
Xinjiang	6.70	12.45043	12.45043	12.15923	11.67286	50.09983	77.35452	103.395

(Continued)

Table 6. *(Continued)*

Province	1996	1997	1998	1999	2000	2001	2002	2003
Beijing	3925.989	4544.906	5428.39	6189.589	6756.058	7317.344	7825.075	8298.674
Tianjin	3071.991	4172.507	5044.161	5716.093	6051.211	6812.481	7274.183	7674.219
Hebei	1427.947	1908.191	2533.867	2948.621	3159.081	3347.75	3577.104	3868.078
Shanxi	234.2515	355.8898	461.7979	637.1306	720.2966	801.4958	867.6605	929.1307
Inner Mongolia	159.3752	188.6837	225.7621	248.708	289.8555	328.5947	397.6033	421.5638
Liaoning	4275.254	5257.004	6123.034	6403.984	7316.313	8034.125	9296.16	10195.85
Jilin	838.7143	1001.13	1162.137	1264.835	1377.184	1480.89	1535.213	1559.616
Helongjiang	1026.879	1343.784	1548.682	1644.378	1724.068	1815.534	1907.723	1976.303
Shanghai	8045.392	9781.946	11160.32	12118.89	13162.05	14653.79	16050.46	17870.59
Jiangsu	10846.93	13060.75	15796.95	18175.27	20554.96	22984.62	26794.34	30478.79
Zhejiang	3066.448	3676.19	4176.772	4620.214	5215.12	6046.581	7232.372	9185.539
Anhui	942.0907	1116.038	1207.372	1288.503	1390.942	1493.44	1612.012	1712.861
Fujian	10070.75	11712.52	13313.71	14774.25	15842.59	17051.44	18150.81	18594.98
Jiangxi	682.3901	889.4267	1082.315	1197.913	1259.866	1395.582	1841.914	2494.04
Shangdong	6475.547	7568.629	8348.234	9133.071	10204.31	11451.93	13190.98	15372.08

(Continued)

Table 6. *(Continued)*

Province	1996	1997	1998	1999	2000	2001	2002	2003
Henan	1129.967	1421.894	1667.964	1859.468	2057.796	2190.536	2290.708	2441.774
Hubei	1594.194	1943.848	2344.163	2703.534	3051.658	3488.559	4011.141	4557.065
Hunan	1235.729	1633.023	1969.717	2214.724	2454.105	2736.914	3045.24	3381.936
Guangdong	28422.04	33440.23	38008.8	42262.37	46026.15	49796.42	53064.81	54464.45
Guangxi	1948.531	2302.099	2645.429	2854.184	2993.688	3054.601	3126.072	3189.483
Hainan	2645.934	2883.798	3120.828	3235.961	3314.813	3401.796	3503.331	3552.863
Chongqin	0	203.637	407.3044	509.3534	607.1264	703.4617	766.1778	852.9678
Sichuan	1525.008	1585.044	1704.666	1805.38	1944.424	2140.29	2312.645	2405.779
Guizhou	142.4189	160.9674	176.8121	189.9973	194.4896	200.0141	209.7472	221.7219
Yunnan	216.3375	288.3847	348.4314	410.6956	456.2133	468.3303	501.4337	519.1248
Xizhang	0.028771	0.02762	0.026515	0.025455	0.024436	0.023459	0.022521	0.02162
Shanxi	889.1447	1159.585	1260.66	1330.081	1416.328	1525.088	1631.188	1715.377
Gansu	138.4913	153.139	165.9998	179.6868	202.6453	229.5231	248.7505	249.3452
Qinghai	7.88088	8.768897	8.418141	10.35483	9.940634	26.70328	47.56907	57.02146
Ningxia	19.79113	22.26824	30.49725	54.70589	60.93532	66.3985	73.95301	78.84265
Xinjiang	131.0039	137.806	142.9417	149.1309	152.4053	155.8791	158.8791	159.0259

Sources: NBSC (various years) and authors' calculations.

These two tables suggest however that while FDI is concentrated by province on both a stock and a flow basis, changes in regional inequality run opposite to FDI trends. Among coastal provinces there is more relative income growth in those provinces receiving relatively smaller amounts of FDI. In addition, there is generally a narrowing of income disparities between coastal and non-coastal provinces. This leaves the issue of whether the concentration of FDI inflows into urban areas within provinces is a more critical determinant of growing relative inequality that is not revealed in this data.

For these FDI flows the resulting foreign-invested enterprises also employ a relatively small amount of labour, even though they account for a majority of China's exports and imports. Whalley and Xin (2006) report this figure at 3% of the workforce (including agriculture). If the channel for FDI to impact on inequality is through wage rate effects in localized labour markets effectively segmented by an absence of labour mobility, the aggregate impact on inequality of 3% of the workforce being hired by FIEs would at first sight appear to be small.

At the micro level, a recent paper by Ma (2006) analyzes in some detail the geographical location of trade flows involving FIEs in an effort to capture regional inequality change resulting from both FDI and transportation costs. Ma notes the dramatic changes in Guangdong with wage rates growing from only 97% of the national average in 1978 to 172% of the national average by 1997. Reflecting its proximity to Hong Kong, by 1997 Guangdong accounts for 43% of China's total exports, and 88% of exports from coastal provinces. Guangdong in 1999 accounted for 58% and 55% of exports and imports used in processing trade in which domestic value-added is applied to imported components which are reshipped. These dramatic changes in the Guangdong case seem to suggest a link between FDI and wage inequality despite the small size of the FIE labour force in aggregate.

Ma uses an economic geography model based on Redding and Venables (2004) to test the two hypotheses that provinces where, due to transport cost differentials, there is lower cost market access abroad, will have FIEs who pay higher wages reflecting competitive pressures on wage rates, and in turn FIEs with lower cost supplier access will also have FIEs who pay higher wages. Ma uses the same structure as Redding and Venables to generate a wage equation which implies that the maximum wage a representative FIE in any province would pay is a function of two distance weighted market capability measures on the import and export side. Higher market and supplier access reduce production costs and with immobile labour wage rates in FIEs will rise. Market and supplier access variables are estimated from a gravity model since they are not directly observable and applied to a dataset of trade between 29 Chinese provinces and 120 export receiving and import supplying countries for the 10 years 1990–2000. Results suggest that the interaction between transport costs and FDI through FIE behaviour explains around 1/3 to 1/4 of the provincial wage differentials. Ma also finds similar transport-related access impacts involved in processing trade for local firms (State-Owned Enterprises, Communally-Owned Enterprises) and attributes these to competitive effects from FIE wage behaviour even though their involvement in processing trade is small.

Overall then, the links between FDI and relative inequality in China seem hard to support from broad macro data and the orders of magnitude for the workforce involved, but in more detailed micro studies these effects do seem to emerge. Despite this, it is hard to envisage a policy of limiting FDI flows into China being consciously used by the National Government as a way of reducing inequality given the developmental strategy now so central to China's growth. But the issue does highlight the potentially central role that labour market segmentation (due either to policy or other factors) plays in Chinese performance and hence the importance of how this interacts with FDI inflows.

5. Future Policy Change and Impacts on FDI Inflows

A key issue for the future is whether policy change in China might retard further growth in FDI inflows. Here we discuss two key elements in this: tax policy change and Renminbi revaluation.

5.1. *Tax policy change*

While a central element in China's recent strong growth performance has been large inflows of foreign direct investment, a key factor in attracting foreign investment has been substantial tax preferences. Currently there is a proposal for a unified and single equal yield tax rate to apply to all enterprises and for tax preferences towards FIEs to be removed. This suggests possible negative impacts on future FDI inflows.

The tax preferences currently given to FIEs are both substantial and complex. If they are in special economic zones, national hi-tech industrial zones and national grade economic and technical development zones, they pay a reduced enterprise tax rate of 15% compared to the general rate of 30%. FIEs in coastal regions and all provincial capitals pay 24%. FIEs also receive extensive tax holidays with a full exemption for two years, a 50% exemption for the next three years and (if in particular geographical zones) a tax reduction of 15–30% for a further 3–5 years. In addition, local governments frequently exempt them from local surcharges applied to other enterprises of 3% of taxable income, and taxable income can again be reduced if income is reinvested. There is also differential tax treatment of wages paid to employees between FIEs and other enterprises. There are no formal estimates for effective tax rates on Chinese enterprises comparable to those for OECD economies, but instead indications widely circulate that FIEs on average may face tax rates in the 10–15% range, while non-FIEs face tax rates of between 22% and 28%.

Converting these tax preferences into effective tax rates by enterprise type is treacherous, as the effective tax rate varies with the time profile of returns to investment (most FIEs make no profit in their first two years, for instance), their location, their financing, and labor costs. There are no estimates of effective tax rates for Chinese enterprises comparable to those of OECD economies (such as in King and Fullerton, 1984 and the studies which have followed), but various Chinese sources put the capital tax rates faced by FIEs in the range of 10–14%, while for the non-FIEs a range of 22–28% is widely used. In 2004, 23% of total enterprise taxes were paid by FIEs, and 77% were paid by the other types of enterprises, even though FIEs accounted for a significantly larger part of the total return to capital.

With more than two decades of reform completed and accession to the WTO accomplished the, government position now is that FDI inflows are mainly attracted by non-tax factors. These include China's economic environment, a growing domestic market, low wage rates, well trained and hard working labor, a market system and a stronger judicial system. With tax preferences seen as less important, the government proposal is thus to unify enterprise tax rates and to remove what are seen as distortions associated with the various incentive schemes for FIEs.

The most recent proposal on unified tax reform has been discussed by members of the Standing Committee of the National People's Congress in the end of December, 2006, and they produced a draft of a new corporate income tax law which includes following. (1) The draft bill suggests a unified tax rate of 25% for both domestic and foreign-funded businesses. (2) For small business enterprises, according to the draft law, the income tax for small businesses will be 20%. Depending on what region and what industry they are active in, small businesses now pay either 18% or 27%. (3) The bill allows domestic companies to deduct employees' full salaries from taxable income as foreign companies now do. (4) There will be transitional measures for FIEs under which the current two-year full tax exemption and three-year partial tax exemption for foreign manufacturers will be removed and export-oriented foreign-funded businesses will no longer enjoy an additional 50% tax reduction. But existing FIEs will continue to receive tax preferences for five years after the new law is implemented and will only gradually face increased income taxes. (5) The bill also extends some existing tax preferences. For instance, all hi-tech companies will enjoy a 15% tax rate to stimulate innovation, while at present only those in state hi-tech zones enjoy this privilege. Investments in equipment for environmental protection and water conservancy purposes and for production safety will be able to be used to offset taxes payable. (6) The new enterprise tax structure is expected to take effect in 2008 if the bill is adopted by the NPC plenary session in March, 2007.

How large the impact of these tax changes will be on FDI flows into China is conjectural and has not been the source of study but the indications are that it could be substantial. A relevant consideration would seem to be that China's FDI growth has partly come from reduced FDI flowing elsewhere (such as Brazil), and so if the aggregate FDI outflows from the OECD remain largely unchanged tax induced intercountry reallocation effects could be key. There are already indications that FDI inflows into India are beginning to grow, and in the textile and apparel area, inflows to Cambodia, Vietnam, Indonesia and economies with wage rates lower than those in China are increasing.

The largest yearly increases in FDI in China occurred in 1992 and 1993 immediately after the introduction of tax preferences towards FIEs in 1991. While the more general policy reform package and market orientation of those reforms is usually taken to be the main trigger for these FDI surges, the issue remains as to how important the tax component was. If it was significant, unwinding it now could also have large effects in the other direction, although the attraction of FDI is to a high skilled and reliable low wage labour force, good infrastructure, and an ever deepening judicial structure remains as well as tax preferences.

5.1.1. *Renminbi revaluation and FDI*

A second key policy area which could impact FDI inflows is Renminbi (RMB) revaluation. A commonly held view is that China's RMB is under-valued and a number of studies further indicate that the undervaluation is on the order of 10–30% (Chang and Shao, 2004; Goldstein, 2004; Funke and Rahn, 2005). In response to both international and internal pressures, The People's Bank of China allowed an effective nominal 2.1% appreciation of the RMB against the US dollar in July, 2005, and the RMB had appreciated by 5.6% by the end of 2006. China's rapid export growth and associated trade surplus have brought with it pressure to revalue the RMB to reduce the trade surplus, especially since 2003 and especially from the US.

Existing literature in general suggests that RMB revaluation may reduce China's inward FDI flows. Both theoretical and empirical studies from other countries (e.g. Cushman, 1985; Froot and Stein, 1991; Klein and Rosengren, 1994; Blonigen, 1997; Goldberg and Klein, 1997; Bayoumi and Lipworth, 1998; Xing, 2006a and 2006b; Xing and Wan, 2006) imply that the revaluation of host county's currency can substantially decrease its FDI inflows. The revaluation of a FDI host country's currency increases production costs (measured in foreign currency) and limits inward FDI flows through a relative production cost effect. For the Chinese case, Xing (2006a) sets up a theoretical model and then empirically tests the model projections of the effects of devaluation of RMB on FDI inflows from Japan. His results imply that RMB revaluation will significantly reduce China's inward FDI flows from Japan.

The size of such effects will also depend on how heavily China's inward FDI has been involved with China's processing trade since imports used in processing are denominated in foreign currency and the relative production cost effect will be reduced. Both exports from and imports by FIEs in China are heavily involved in processing trade. MOFCOM (2006) estimates that 78% of China's FIE exports are processed exports and 60% of FIE imports are processed imports in 2005. FIE processed exports and imports accounted for 83% and 84% of China's total processed exports and imports respectively in 2005. Moreover, FIEs account for more than 50% of China's trade surplus in 2005. These data suggest that China's total trade is composed of distinct parts; processing trade which involves imports receiving upgrading via added value, and other trade, and the impacts of RMB revaluation on these two types of trade differ. This suggests differentiated studies of the impacts of RMB revaluation on FDI since the trade-FDI link reflects the nature of the trade. There is for now little literature on the trade impacts of RMB revaluation other than econometric models which specify no structural form for trade patters. These are discussed in Marquez and Schindler (2006). Willenbockel (2006) uses a CGE framework to assess the structural effects on trade and production of a real exchange rate revaluation in China but does not differentiate processing trade and general trade and does not directly evaluate FDI impacts. Quantitative estimates of the effects are thus for now missing. But if FDI is heavily trade-driven, then the null hypothesis Renminbi revaluation of the size speculated in the literature can have significant effects which will compound tax-related effects.

6. Concluding Remarks

We discuss recent literature and policy debate on FDI and China. FDI inflows have grown rapidly in recent years and China now accounts for nearly 50% of OECD outflows. In turn, growth of exports, imports, and GDP increasingly reflect FDI inflows. China's deep integration into the global economy must therefore be judged not only by its trade growth, but also by the size of capital flows. These are also now starting to grow on the outward FDI side.

In the chapter we discuss three issues related to FDI, and primarily FDI inflows. The first is their contribution to growth, which we suggest is substantial and if any plateauing of FDI growth occurs then GDP growth may be significantly reduced. We also discuss the links between regional inequality and geographic concentration of FDI. Macro data suggests limited linkage, while micro studies claim to find it. Finally, we discuss recent proposals to remove tax preferences to FDI and RMB revaluation suggesting potential negative effects on FDI inflows.

FDI has become so central to Chinese economic performance that what happens on the FDI front in the short term will likely determine the speed of China's development. Many factors influence these flows including global factors not discussed here. How these all interact and play out remains to be seen.

References

Antkiewicz, A. and J. Whalley (2006). Recent Chinese Buyout Activity and the Implications for Global Architecture. NBER Working Paper No. 12072.

Bayoumi, T. and G. Lipworth (1998). Japanese Foreign Direct Investment and Regional Trade, *Journal of Asian Economics*, 9(4): 581–607.

Blonigen, B. (1997). Firm-specific assets and the link between exchange rates and foreign direct investment, *American Economic Review*, 87: 447–465.

Brean, D. (1998). Fiscal Reform in Modern China: An Overview. in *Taxation in Modern China*, edited by D. Brean. London, UK: Routledge.

CAITEC (Chinese Academy of International Trade and Economic Cooperation and Welsh Development Agency) (2005). Chinese Enterprises' Expansion into European and North American Markets.

Campa, J. (1993). Entry by foreign firms in the United States under exchange rate uncertainty, *Review of Economics and Statistics*, 75: 614–622.

Chang, G. H. and Q. Shao (2004). How Much is the Chinese Currency Undervalued? A Quantitative Estimation. *China Economic Review*, 15: 366–371.

Chow, G. C. (1993). Capital Formation and Economic Growth in China, *Quarterly Journal of Economics*, 108(3): 809–842.

Chow, G. C. and A. Lin (2003). Accounting for Economic Growth in Taiwan and Mainland China: A Comparative Analysis, EWP-GE/0306003.

Cushman, D. O. (1985). Real Exchange Rate Risk, Expectation, and the Level of Direct Investment. *Review of Economics and Statistics*, 67(2): 297–308.

Dennison, E. F. (1967). Why Growth Rates Differ. Washington, DC: The Brookings Institution.

Feenstra, R. C. and G. H. Hanson (2005). Ownership and Control in Outsourcing to China: Estimating the Property-Rights Theory of the Firm, *Quarterly Journal of Economics*, 120(2): 729–761.

Froot, K. and J. Stein (1991). Exchange rates and foreign direct investment: An imperfect capital markets approach, *Quarterly Journal of Economics* 106: 1191–1217.

Fung, K. C. (2004). Trade and Investment: China, the United States, and the Asia–Pacific Economies, U.S.–China Economic and Security Review Commission Hearing on China as an Emerging Regional and Technological Power: Implications for U.S. Economic and Security Interests, February, 12–13, 2004.

Funke, M. and J. Rahn (2005). Just How Undervalued is the Chinese Renminbi? *World Economy*, 28(4): 465–489.

Goldberg, L. and M. W. Klein (1997). Foreign Direct Investment, Trade and Real Exchange Rate Linkages in Southeast Asia and Latin America, *NBER working paper*, 6344.

Goldberg, L. S. and C. D. Kolstad (1995). Foreign direct investment, Exchange rate variability and demand uncertainty, *International Economic Review*, 36(4). No. 4.

Goldstein, M. (2004). Adjusting China's Exchange Rate Policies, Institute for International Economics Working Paper No.04-1, IIE: Washington, D.C.

Gong, M. and W. Li (2006). Does China function as a Bridge to Increase Regional Trade?; An Empirical Analysis of the Trade Relations between Chine and its Main Trade Partners, China: Xiamen University. (mimeo)

Jorgensen, D. W. and Zvi Griliches (1967). The Explanation of Productivity Change, *Review of Economic Studies*, 34(3): 349–383.

King, M. and D. Fullerton (1984). *The Taxation of Income from Capital*, Chicago: The University of Chicago Press.

Klein, M. and E. Rosengren (1994). The real exchange rate and foreign direct investment in the United States: Relative wealth vs. relative wage effects, *Journal of International Economics*, 36: 373–389.

Kohli, U. (2003a). Growth Accounting in the Open Economy: International Comparisons, *International Review of Economics and Finance*, 12: 417–435.

Kohli, U. (2003b). GDP Growth Accounting: A National Income Function Approach, *Review of Income and Wealth*, 49(1): 23–34.

Lenovie, F. (2000). FDI and the Opening up of China's Economy, CEPII Working Paper No. 2000-11.

Ma, A. S. (2006). Geographical Location of Foreign Direct Investment and Wage Inequality in China, *The World Economy*, 29(8): 1031–1055.

Marquez, J. and J. W. Schindler (2006). Exchange-Rate Effects on China's Trade: An Interim Report, Federal Reserve Bank of San Francisco Working Paper 2006-41.

MOFCOM. (2004). Foreign Direct Investment Report.

MOFCOM. (2006). Foreign Direct Investment Report.

MOFCOM. (2007). Statistics about Utilization of Foreign Investment in China from Jan to Dec 2006, Available at http://www.fdi.gov.cn/pub/FDI_EN/Statistics/FDI%20Statistics/Statistics%20of%20Foreign%20Investment/t20070119_73060.htm

OECD. (2000). Main Determinants and Impacts of Foreign Direct Investment on China's Economy, OECD Working Papers on International Investment No. 2000/4, Paris.

OECD. (2006). The Internationalization of Production, International Outsourcing, and OECD Labour Markets, Economics Dept., OECD, March 2006. (mimeo)

Rauch, J. E. (2001). Business and Social Networks in International Trade, *Journal of Economic Literature*, 34: 1177–1203.

Redding, S. and A. J. Venables (2004). Economic Geography and International Inequality, *Journal of International Economics*, 62(1): 53–82.

Roach, S. (2003). Getting China, *Morgan Stanley Special Economic Study*, September.

Solow, R. M. (1957). Technical Change and the Aggregate Production Function, *Review of Economics and Statistics*, 39(3): 312–320.

Tomiura, E. (2005). Foreign Outsourcing and Firm-level Characteristics: Evidence from Japanese Manufacturers, *Journal of the Japanese and International Economies*, 19: 255–271.

UNCTAD. (2006). World Investment Report.

Whalley, J. and X. Xin (2006). China's FDI and Non-FDI Economies and the Sustainability of Future High Chinese Growth, NBER working paper W12249, National Bureau of Economic Research.

Whalley, J. (2006). The Post-MFA Performance of Developing Asia, NBER Working Papers 12178, National Bureau of Economic Research.

World Bank. (2005). WDI database, Available at http://devdata.worldbank.org/data-query/.

World Bank. (2007). China Quick Facts, Available at http://web.worldbank.org/WBSITE/EXTERNAL/COUNTRIES/EASTASIAPACIFICEXT/CHINAEXTN/0,,contentMDK:20680895~pagePK:1497618~piPK:217854~theSitePK:318950,00.html

Xing, Y. and G. Wan (2006). Exchange Rates and Competition for FDI in Asia, *World Economy*, 29(4): 419–34.

Xing, Y. (2004). Japanese FDI in China: Trend, Structure, and the Role of Exchange Rates, in K. H. Zhang (ed.), *China as a World Workshop*. Armonk, NY: M. E. Sharp.

Xing, Y. (2006a). Exchange Rate Policy and the Relative Distribution of FDI among Host Countries, BOFIT Discussion Papers 15/2006.

Xing, Y. (2006b). Why is China so Attractive for FDI? The Role of Exchange Rate, *China Economic Review*, 17(2): 198–209.

Young, A. (1995). The Tyranny of Numbers: Confronting the Statistical Reality of the East Asian Growth Experience, *Quarterly Journal of Economics*, 110: 641–680.

TECHNOLOGY UPGRADING AND CHINA'S GROWTH STRATEGY TO 2020*

John Whalley
University of Western Ontario, NBER and CIGI

Weimin Zhou
University of Waterloo,
Shanghai Jiaotong University, and CIGI

It is widely believed in China that in order to meet the target of tripling GDP per capita between 2005 and 2020 set out in China's 11th 5-year plan in 2005, a change in China's growth strategy from FDI promotion and export-led growth towards technology upgrading and higher productivity growth in manufacturing needs to occur. Recent government documents set out measures to be taken to achieve these ends and include increased educational spending, tax incentives, large R&D projects, and changes to the regulatory environment. This chapter seeks to evaluate their potential effectiveness.

1. Introduction

China's growth, if one accepts the data, has been characterized by remarkably high rates of between 8 and 12% for over 20 years. This growth has significantly raised income per capita and sharply reduced absolute poverty as measured by numbers of people below the poverty line. The latest targets adopted in the 11th 5-year plan in 2005 are to maintain growth at rates of at least 7.5% until 2020 with the aim of raising GDP per capita from current levels of a little over $1,000 at the end of 2004 to around $3,000.

Like other growth processes elsewhere and earlier in Asia (most notably in Japan and South Korea), China's growth has been characterized by

*An earlier version of this paper was prepared for the annual conference of the Centre for International Governance Innovation (CIGI), Waterloo, September 14–15, 2006. We are grateful to Xin Xian, Agata Antkiewicz and O. G. Dayaratna Banda for remarks and discussion.

changing and shifting elements as alternative factors and forces have come into play. Both Japanese and Korean growth were achieved, in part, by shifting priorities for credit rationing and government support among key sectors and only increasing openness to trade as both production and exports grew rapidly. There were first of labor intensive manufactures (clothing and textiles), and then heavy industrial products (steel, chemicals), assembled electronics, and subsequently autos and higher technology products. Growth was not a simple application of capital accumulation and input growth as economists often model the process analytically.

China thus far has partly followed, but also departed, from the Korean and Japanese experiences in having had two distinct phases of growth which have taken different forms. The first was agriculture-led growth from the mid-1970s until the late 1980s driven by the adoption of an incentive-based responsibility system in place of existing collective arrangements. This was accompanied by sharp increases in yields and productivity in agriculture (see MacMillan, Whalley and Zhu, 1989). The second has been manufacturing-led growth since the 1990s until today and characterized by large FDI inflows and with it, large increases in manufacturing production and exports (see Xin and Whalley (2006) for a discussion of the contribution of FDI inflow to this process). Outward orientation, China's integration into the world economy, and WTO accession in 2002 have been central to this strategy. The emphasis has been placed on increasing manufacturing output, and exports and FDI have been the key drivers. Manufacturing today accounts for a little over 50% of GDP in contrast to numbers of around 20% in OECD economies,[1] and nearly a half of manufacturing output is exported.

For some time, however, it has been accepted in China that this strategy alone would not be sufficient to maintain Chinese growth at the target rates set out in the 11th 5-year plan out to 2020 and beyond for a number of reasons. One is that further growth driven by simply increasing the share of manufacturing to GDP is unrealistic given its current size. If anything, this share would likely fall with growth in services and increases in public services such as education and health care. Another is that FDI inflows had grown rapidly by the mid-2000s to around $60 billion per year and accounted for over 40% of total OECD outflows to non-OECD economies.

[1] At the peak in the early 1980s, similar numbers characterized Korea.

With manufacturing costs beginning to increase in China, the prospect seen was for a plateau or even fall in FDI in the future as some of it moved to lower cost locations elsewhere in Asia (such as Indonesia, Vietnam, Cambodia, and others). Yet another was that 40% export growth achieved in 2004 and 2005 was unsustainable as it implied an approximate doubling of China's share of world trade every 2 years. If these export growth rates were to continue, by 2010 China would account for around 50% of world trade.

This sense that changes are needed to facilitate continued high growth in China provides the background for this paper. In both the latest and earlier 5-year plans, targets for accelerating technological upgrading have been set out, typically in terms of raising the portion of growth coming from total factor productivity growth rather than input growth and raising the ratio of R&D expenditures to GDP. The instruments for achieving these targets have been seen as (i) large R&D projects in a wide range of targeted areas to be co-financed by national governments, provincial governments and enterprises; (ii) tax incentives for R&D; (iii) new approaches to standards settings and the regulatory environment to foster innovation and (iv) increased expenditures on education and research both in general and in top rank educational institutions. The range of programs and institutions is wide and large. Our focus is the potential contribution to sustaining Chinese growth from any new technology-based productivity growth that results.

Our discussion comprises of three elements. One is conventional growth accounting, asking how large the technology upgrading is likely to be that is needed to sustain high growth. Another is whether each of the instruments is likely to deliver their required contributions more narrowly, such as tax incentives for R&D. Finally, we discuss Japanese and Korean historical experience, seeking pointers regarding both likely pitfalls and sources of success.

Our view is that Chinese growth, as it is currently evolving, is clearly unsustainable in its present form, but change has been true of growth profiles first in Europe following the industrial revolution, in North America since the 1850s, and in Asia since 1945 (earlier in Japan). If Chinese growth is to complete a historic transformation in Polanyi's (1944) sense, and even build further on it, something has to change and new elements need to emerge. Whether technology upgrading will provide sustainability is the issue.

2. The Broad Strategy and Targets for Technology Upgrading for Continued Chinese Economic Growth

Not only has China's recent growth primarily reflected high levels of capital accumulation more so than productivity growth, but the majority of productivity growth has reflected imported technologies. Whalley and Xin (2006) in a recent study, focusing on the contrasts between the foreign direct investment (FDI) part of the Chinese economy and the remainder, report differences in labour productivity of 6:1 excluding agriculture, and 8:1 including agriculture. They report growth rates of 18.8% and 20.4% for the FDI part of the economy in 2003 and 2004 in contrast to growth rates of 6.7% and 7.1% for the remainder, and show that nearly all total factor productivity growth occurred in the FDI portion. The latter suggests that Chinese growth has relied heavily on importing technological improvements, rather than generating these at home.

While relying more on imported technology to achieve high growth and also the technology gap may be the more efficient route, since the late 1990s, the Chinese government has repeatedly argued the need to refocus economic growth from investment-driven to efficiency improving growth by highlighting the need to also generate technical change at home. In the 10th 5-year plan for 2001–2005, a series of planned changes to the current science and technology system were set out. The latest 11th 5-year plan (2006–2010) sets out a strategy which relies on the development of China's own innovative capacity to achieve whatever technology upgrading may be needed for its future economic growth as the main element in sustaining high growth. *The Guidelines on National Medium- and Long-term Program for Science and Technology Development 2006–2020* (hereafter referred to as *S&T Guidelines 2006–2020*) were issued on January 26th, 2006, by the State Council[2] together with complimentary policies on February 7th, 2006, and specify a series of targets and instruments for science and technology development to achieve the objective of continued high economic growth. The stated aim is to become what the government calls an "innovative country" by 2020, a term used to justify a series of qualitative and quantitative targets as well as institutional reforms, with indigenous technological development to become the integral part of China's economic growth strategy.

[2]China: Something New — Getting serious about innovation, *The Economist*, published on August 5th, 2006.

Table 1. A Schematic Representation of China's Technology Upgrading Growth Strategy.

Objectives of the economic growth strategy out to 2020	Targets for technology upgrading to meet objectives	Major instruments for achieving targets
• GDP growth rate to exceed 7.5% annually until 2010, then 7.0% up to 2020 • Energy consumption per GDP to be reduced by 20% by 2010 • Pollution emissions to be reduced by 10% by 2010 • Water consumption per unit of industrial value-added to fall by 30%	Qualitative Targets: • Improvement of domestic innovation capacities • Transformation of the national innovation system from state-based to enterprise-based • Development and upgrade of a wide series of strategic technologies, frontline technologies and basic research Quantitative Targets: • TFP growth to reach 60% of GDP growth by 2020 • GERD/GDP is to reach 2.5% by 2020 • Foreign technology reliance to reduce to 30% by 2020 • The number of invention-type patent grants gained by Chinese inventors to rank in the top five in the world by 2020 • The number of internationally cited scientific papers by Chinese authors to rank in the top five in the world[3] by 2020	• Increase in Science and Technology expenditures from various sources • Tax incentives • Government procurement • Foreign technology import regulation • Strengthened IPR protection • Talent force and education

Source: The Guidelines on National Medium- and Long-term Program for Science and Technology Development 2006–2020.

Table 1 sets out the broad elements of this strategy. The objectives set for this strategy are achieving an overall growth rate of 7% until 2020, while

[3]Institute of Scientific and Technical Information of China (ISTIC) uses three established index — SCI, EI and ISTP — as ranking tools.

reducing the energy consumption to GDP ratio, pollution emission and water consumption. A series of more concrete qualitative and quantitative targets are then set for achieving these objectives, and, in turn, instruments set for achieving the targets.

Qualitative targets include: improvements in domestic innovation capacity; a change in the national innovation system from state-based to enterprise-based; and the development of a series of new strategic technologies, frontline technologies and basic research which cover sophisticated manufacturing facilities and product areas such as large-scale integrated equipment, aeroplanes and automobiles, IT, agriculture, energy (energy exploitation, energy saving and clean energy development), recycling technology, medicine and medical equipment and national defensive technologies.

Among the quantitative targets, the most significant is that TFP (Total Factor Productivity) is set to increase. TFP measures that portion of growth not directly attributable to input growth, and may be neutral (equal for all inputs) or biased in favour of one input or the other. It is generally believed in China that the current TFP contribution to GDP growth is below 40%. Weiguo Song, a researcher at the National Research Centre for Science and Technology for Development under the Ministry of Science and Technology, along with Jun Li have summarized[4] TFP studies by various government agencies and scholars, and claim this shows that TFP growth over GDP growth was below 40% during the 9th 5-year development plan period (1996–2000). The proposed 60% target reflects a recognition that future increases in both labor and capital inputs will be insufficient to continue to fuel high GDP growth. China's one-child policy since the 1970s implies that while the labor force growth will grow at an average rate of 1.1% during 2004–2010, it will decline to 0.3% during 2010–2020 and labor's contribution to GDP growth will be close to zero by 2020.[5] With regard to capital's contribution, it is assumed that both FDI and, more broadly, capital's contribution to GDP growth will likely decrease as capital deepening occurs. In order to keep high GDP growth, the argument is that

[4]Guanhua Xu, Minister of Science and Technology in China, at a press conference of the 4th Session of the 10th National People's Congress, argued that in order to achieve the aim of quadrupling GDP by 2020, China has to increase TFP growth over GDP growth ratio from the current 39% to 60%.

[5]Li *et al.*, 2005, China's Economic Growth Potential and Prospect Analysis, *Management World*, Vol. 9, in Chinese.

TFP has to make more of a contribution, although as already noted how a residual contributes is unclear.

TFP changes can reflect a variety of factors such as improved resource reallocation, institutional reforms, factor productivity improvements, and the use of new technologies. Many earlier papers have discussed sources of China's economic growth, some questioning the reliability of China's statistics (Young, 2003), some arguing that China's growth would face a limit sooner or later as growth depended heavily on large increases in inputs with only small improvements in productivity (Krugman, 1994). Borensztein and Ostry (1996) also argued that China's TFP growth would slow as the potential for factors other than pure technical progress weakened.

Recent work by Li *et al.* (2005) summarized in Table 2 claims that China's TFP growth reached its high point at the beginning of China's reforms in the early 1990s when outward-oriented reforms took hold, then fell by the end of the 1990s. This seems to point to the need for dramatic change over the next decade or so if overall growth rates are to be preserved, and that without heightened technical progress China's current high economic growth is unsustainable.

In order to achieve a higher rate of technical progress, the target has been set in the growth strategy for the GERD (Gross Expenditures on Research and Development) over GDP ratio to reach 2.5% by 2020. Currently, this ratio is only around 1.3% (see Table 3). By comparison, OECD countries on average invested around 2.5% of GDP in Research and Development in 2004.[6] This GERD/GDP ratio has increased sharply in recent years and is targeted for further rises.

Table 2. Sources of China's Economic Growth since 1978 from Li et al. (2005) (%).

	GDP growth	Capital growth	Labor growth	TFP growth
1978–1985	9.8	8.5	3.1	3.5 (35.3)
1985–1989	8.9	9.8	2.6	2 (22.2)
1990–1997	11.2	11.2	1.1	4 (36.1)
1997–2000	7.7	10.7	1.1	0.8 (10.9)
2000–2003	8.4	10.5	1.1	1.6 (19.8)

Note: The parentheses are the factor contribution share to total GDP growth.
Sources: Li *et al.* (2005).

[6]OECD, Main Science and Technology Indicators, June 2006.

Table 3. China R&D Expenditures 1991–2005 (RMB 100 million).

	1991	1992	1993	1994	1995	1996	1997	1998	1999	2000	2001	2002	2003	2004	2005
GERD	150.8	209.8	256.2	309.8	349.1	404.8	481.9	551.1	678.9	895.7	1043	1288	1540	1966	2450
Annual growth (%)	—	29.0	6.6	0.6	–0.2	9.5	17.6	10.9	20.3	16.9	15.0	23.8	17.2	27.7	20.4
GERD/GDP(%)	0.7	0.8	0.7	0.7	0.6	0.6	0.6	0.70	0.76*	0.90*	0.95*	1.07*	1.13*	1.23*	1.34*

*based on revised GDP

Source: China Science and Technology Statistics Data Book 1998–2006.

Table 4. Foreign Technology Purchases by China in 2005.

	Foreign technology purchases by China (million US$)	Share (%)
Total	19050.57	100
Patents	1278.38	6.7
Know-how	5095.33	26.7
Technical consulting and other services	4735.99	24.9
Software	432.50	2.3
Trademark licensing	271.81	1.4
Joint Ventures	1722.93	9.0
Key equipment and production lines	5333.11	28.0
Others	180.49	0.9

Source: Science and Technology Agency, Ministry of Commerce. http://kjs.mofcom.gov.cn/aarticle/ztxx/dwmyxs/u/200601/20060101418975.html.

Table 5. China Foreign Technology Reliance in 2004 and 2005 (billion US$).

	2004	2005
GDP (1)	1930	2230
GERD/GDP	1.23%	1.34%
GERD (2)	23.7	29.9
Foreign Technology Purchases (3)	13.9	19.1
Foreign Technology Reliance = (3)/((2)+(3))	36.9%	38.9%

Sources: (1) from World Development Indicator; (2) from Science and Technology Agency, Ministry of Commerce. http://kjs.mofcom.gov.cn/aarticle/ztxx/dwmyxs/u/200601/20060101418975.html.

A third target set as part of the technology upgrading strategy is to reduce foreign technology reliance to 30% by 2020. The Chinese government computes a ratio of foreign technology reliance calculated as foreign technology purchases (see Table 4) over these plus GERD. Currently, this ratio is around 40% (see Tables 4 and 5) and China's aim is to improve domestic innovation capacity. The claim is that purchases of foreign technology have not resulted in enhanced domestic innovative capability because too little effort has been put in absorption and assimilation. Chinese manufacturers are claimed to be stuck in a cycle of purchasing foreign technology, then purchasing again the upgraded technology when the previous version is outdated. This argument is supported by several Western economists. Howard Pack (2000), for example, argues that technology inflows that are not complemented by domestic absorptive capability will have little, if any, impact on a country's productivity. The claim goes specifically to the purchase of key equipment and production lines which account for over a quarter of total purchases. Table 4 indicates that patents and trademark licensing, which are often regarded as among the major forms of technology imports, account for only about 8% of the total.

The last two targets set for the growth strategy aim to enhance China's intellectual property inventory. One emphasizes invention-type patents which are thought to have more value than appliance or design patents (the latter two are also referred to as mini-patents). The target is set for China to rank in the top five countries in numbers of invention-type patents by 2020. The existing government incentives such as patent application fee subsidies have resulted in China already ranking number ten globally in terms of the number of patent applications.[7] However, China's effective capacity in this area is a lot weaker than this ranking suggests. As shown in Table 6, the total number of patents granted to domestic applicants is four times that for foreign applicants, but the number of invention-type patents granted to domestic applicants is only about two thirds that for foreign applicants.

The final target in this area focuses on international rankings of China's published scientific research papers. China ranks number four in the world in terms of the total number of papers,[8] but high quality papers as measured

Table 6. Number of Patents Awarded in China by the State Intellectual Property Office (2004).

	Total	To domestic applicants	To foreign applicants
Invention	49360	18241	31119
Applied Patents	70623	70019	604
Industrial Design	70255	63068	7187
Total	190238	151328	38910

Source: Ministry of Science and Technology (2006), http://www.most.gov.cn/eng/statistics/2005.

[7]WIPO, 2006.

[8]National Science and Technology Plan Annual Report (2006) stated that "in 2003, the number of published scientific papers registered in SCI, EI and ISTP is 93,000, ranking number 5 in the world." In 2005, the ranking went up to number 4 according to the statistics provided on the official website of Ministry of Science and Technology (http://www.sts.org.cn/nwdt/gndt/document/0611091.htm).

by citation frequency are only a small portion. The target of a top of 5 ranking is now to apply to citations as well as the number of papers.

3. Instruments to be Used to Meet Targets

To implement this indigenous technology upgrading growth strategy, a series of instruments are to be used to meet the targets set. Some increase R&D funding by augmenting existing sources, others create new financing sources; others aim to trigger enterprise innovation using government procurement practices, foreign technology import regulation and intellectual property law reform; yet others aim to strengthen long-term innovative capacity through educational improvements.

3.1. *Government expenditures on science and technology (S&T)*

Since the mid-1990s, both China's central and local budgetary revenues have grown sharply, but the share of expenditures on science and technology in state budgetary expenditures has not reflected this growth, even though they have grown absolutely. This can be seen from Table 7. To improve on this, the growth in state budgetary expenditures on science and research are to be set at a higher rate than the government financial revenue growth rate in general. The share of budgetary expenditures on science and technology in total budget revenue is to be at least 4%, and its growth to be higher than the state revenue growth. For 2006, planned budgetary expenditures from central government increased 19.2% compared to 2005.

Table 7. State Budgetary Expenditures on Science and Research.

	1999	2000	2001	2002	2003	2004	2005
State budgetary expenditures on science and research (100 million RMB)	543.9	575.62	703.26	816.22	975.54	1095.3	1334.9
Share of state budgetary expenditures (excluding debt) (%)	4.12	3.62	3.72	3.7	3.96	3.8	3.9

Sources: Ministry of Finance official website, http://www.mof.gov.cn/1162.htm and Ministry of Science and Technology official website, http://www.sts.org.cn/nwdt/gndt/document/060925.htm.

State budgetary expenditures on science and technology are in three categories: basic research, public research and research on frontline technologies. The *S&T Guidelines 2006–2020* list a wide series of projects covering strategic technologies, frontline technologies and basic research which are now expected to be substantially funded by the government. The earlier 10th 5-year development plan (2001–2005) already organized China's Science and Technology system as what is known as a "3 + 2" system. "3" refers to a National High-Tech R&D Program labeled "863", and a National Key Technologies R&D Program and a National Program of Key Basic Research Projects labeled "973". "2" refers to R&D Infrastructure and Facility Development and Environment Building for S&T Industries. In this structure, a series of Mega-Projects became the top priority.[9] These projects emphasized the development of a chain of integrated products or technologies instead of piecemeal invention with the aim of enhancing product and industrial capabilities. Among the "3" programs, the 863 and 973 programs were fully financed by state sources.

Since many projects in the existing National Key Technologies R&D program and Mega-Projects are thought to be able to be commercialized quickly, enterprises are now encouraged to participate and become the dominating funding source. Hao and Gong (2006) document several big projects often dubbed China's billion-dollar babies. Some are basic research programs such as protein science, quantum research, nanotechnology, development and reproductive biology. Others are engineering programs in Mega-Projects such as next-generation broadband, large-scale oil and gas exploitation, transgenic plant breeding, drug development and even manned moon exploitation.

Hao and Gong (2006) also provide details of the Chinese government's planning for GERD and budget expenditures on R&D for 2010 and 2020 (see Table 8). GERD is to grow to 2.5% of GDP by 2020. In 2004, China's

Table 8. China GERD and Budget Planning for 2010 and 2020.

	GERD ($ billion)	Percent of GDP	Government contribution ($ billions)
2004	$24.60 (actual)	1.23%	$8.7
2010	$45.00 (planned)	2.00%	$18.00
2020	$113.00 (planned)	2.50%	NA

Source: Hao and Gong, 2006, Research Funding: China Bets Big on Big Science, *Science*, Vol. 311. no. 5767, pp. 1548–1549.

[9]In the 10th 5-year plan, 12 Mega-Projects were carried out.

GERD already ranked number seven in the world, even though its absolute value was substantially below that of OECD countries; e.g., US$ 313 billion for the United States and US$ 118 billion for Japan. The government-funded part in the United States was also substantial, around US$ 90 billion.[10] By 2020, China is set to move up in these rankings.

3.2. *Tax incentives aiming to improve domestic innovation*

A further set of instruments set out in the *S&T Guidelines 2006–2020* to help meet targets for GERD are new tax measures designed to encourage innovation. In the 1990s, a series of tax incentives were introduced to encourage high technology development. The *S&T Guidelines 2006–2020* take these measures further. Table 9 compares these new planned incentives with prior ones.

Existing S&T tax incentives have not been effective in stimulating enterprises to invest in R&D because few enterprises benefited. Only profitable enterprises with an annual 10% increase in R&D inputs could use tax deductions, and deductions could not be carried forward or backward. When companies made considerable R&D investments, they were typically not profitable immediately, and even if they made future profits, the deduction would go unused in full since it could not be carried forward.

Depreciation rules were similar in effect. The allowable enterprise capital investment depreciation rate was only 4%, much lower than in OECD countries. The government later raised this to 7%. But as the central government set the aim of improving the financial position of loss-making SOEs in 1997, many SOEs resorted to depreciation rate reductions as a way of removing accounting losses, and increases in depreciation rates for tax purposes went unclaimed for many SOEs.

Another tax issue is the different tax treatment of domestic enterprises and Foreign Invested Enterprises (FIEs). Because of efforts to attract foreign direct investment, China's tax system evolved in the early 1990s to be biased in favor of FIEs. The corporate income tax rate for FIEs is 10–24% while that for Chinese domestic enterprises is usually 33%. 40% of FIEs' reinvestment is tax-deductible while Chinese domestic companies

[10] See OECD Main Science and Technology Indicator 2005/1. The other four countries before China are Germany (US$ 59 billion), France (US$ 39 billion), United Kingdom (US$ 33 billion), South Korea (US$ 28 billion).

Table 9. Improvement on Tax Incentives under the New Technology Upgrading Strategy.

Item	Prior tax rules	New tax rules
Deduction for R&D and training	150% of R&D expenses could be deducted from annual taxable income on the condition that the enterprise had made a profit and its R&D expenses were 10% higher than that of the previous year. The redundant part was not allowed to be carried forward or backward.	150% of R&D expenses can now be deducted from annual taxable income; and can be carried forward for five years, but not carried backward. Employees' education training expenses up to 2.5% of total taxable income can now be deducted from corporate income taxable.
R&D equipment and instrument depreciation	Equipment or instruments below RMB 100,000 could be deducted.	Equipment or instruments below RMB 300,000 can now be expensed. Those over RMB 300,000 have shortened asset lives.
High-tech enterprises	Only high-tech exports got VAT totally refunded, software and integrated circuit manufacturing companies enjoyed a favorable VAT rate of 3–6% instead of 17% Approved high-tech foreign-funded enterprises in high-tech parks enjoyed a favorable tax rate of 15%. New enterprises could have two years of tax holiday.	VAT (Value-added Tax) for high-tech enterprises are to move from production-type to consumption-type allowing for deduction of capital expenditures. Approved high-tech enterprises in high-tech parks are to get two years tax holiday after earning profit, then enjoy a favorable tax rate of 15% (regular rate is 33%).
Import tariff and import-related VAT exemption	An exemption usually applied to software and integrated-circuit manufacturing companies together with those listed in National High-tech Products List.	Custom duties and import-related VAT are to be removed for imports of R&D-related products by approved enterprises, technology centres, national engineering centres, Mega-projects, National Key Technologies R&D Program and other major projects.
Tech transfer service institutions	Tax exemptions involved mainly the corporate income tax.	For technology enterprises, incubators and national university science and technology parks, business tax, corporate income tax, real estate tax, urban and township land use tax are exempt during an initial period.

(*Continued*)

Table 9. (Continued)

Item	Prior tax rules	New tax rules
Transformed science and research institutions	Favorable policies applied in terms of corporate income tax, land, urban and township land use tax, real estate tax are adopted.	Upon expiration of current favorable policies, extensions are expected to apply.
Donation		Donations to S&T SME Innovation Funds and other similar funds are deductible for corporate income taxes.
Venture Capital		Favorable taxation terms for venture capital which invest mainly in small and medium-sized high-tech enterprises.

Sources: *The Guidelines on National Medium- and Long-term Program for Science and Technology Development 2006–2020*, and various official documents from Ministry of Finance.

have no tax deduction for capital investment. Chinese domestic companies are only allowed to deduct a portion of employee compensation from corporate taxable income while FIEs can take a full deduction. As a large part of enterprise R&D expenditures (around 50% in OECD countries) goes to employee compensation, China's tax system does not encourage domestic companies to invest in R&D through the tax treatment of wage costs.

3.3. *Financial services to support science and technology (S&T) enterprises*

Besides tax incentives, the Chinese government also plans to improve financial services to encourage enterprise investment in research and development. State policy banks (i.e. the National Development Bank, the China Import and Export Bank and the China Agriculture Development Bank)[11] are instructed to provide loans to S&T enterprises, finance S&T imports and exports, and support agricultural technology application and industrialization. Commercial banks and other financial institutions are encouraged to provide loans to S&T enterprises based on government

[11] These three banks were separated from the four major commercial banks in 1994 when bank reform was adopted. They are responsible for supporting state policies.

guarantees, provide discounted interest rates, and create funds for innovative collateral property, including intellectual property. Venture Capital (VC) is also a new source that the government aims to use to develop financing for S&T SMEs. In addition, a series of measures will be adopted to facilitate S&T enterprises' public listings. Corporate bond issuance is also to be allowed for qualified S&T enterprises.

3.4. *Government procurement of innovative products, regulation of foreign technology imports and IPR protection*

A further group of instruments to be used to support domestic enterprise innovation include procurement practices, regulation of technology imports and IPR protection. These are all areas that involve commitments made as part of China's WTO accession terms, and so how they can be used in these ways are constrained. Government procurement practices will be used to create or ensure demand for domestic innovation products. Key engineering projects undertaken by central or local governments are to be used to support domestic equipment procurement. The government aims to purchase trial or new products which are seen as having potential in the future. Foreign technology import regulation is to be used to reduce foreign technology reliance. Technology import regulation focuses on limiting repeated purchases of foreign technology or obsolete foreign technology and equipment imports. If foreign capital equipment has to be introduced, then after-purchase absorption and innovative capability generated is to be assessed before licenses are issued.

Along with China's commitment to reduce foreign technology reliance and strengthen domestic innovation, IPR protection is to become more rigorous to allow for swifter and more extensive new technology adoption. The idea is to use IPR laws to provide support for enterprises to create new products and technology. Measures include strengthening of intellectual property protection through legislative regulation, improvement of the appraisal efficiency of invention-type patents, and subsidies to domestic applicants for foreign intellectual property. While IPR protection has been a highly controversial issue in China, its strengthening is now seen as a workable incentive to encourage technology upgrading strategy in that it will not only increase the potential profits of inventors but also reduce profits from direct capital good usage, and encourage indigenous R&D.

3.5. *Talent force and the education system*

The education system is another instrument to be used to heighten innovative capacity and technical progress in the longer term. Currently China's higher education system is seen as having two main problems regarding innovation. First, there is a shortage of leading scientists in various disciplines. Second, there is perceived to be poor communication between science and technology development organizations (such as universities and research institutions) and enterprises.

Responding to the first, the Chinese government has launched a series of initiatives as part of the *S&T Guidelines 2006–2020*, including the cultivation of a younger generation of talent to take the lead in academic research; the cultivation of innovative talent while implementing key national projects; the attraction of overseas talent; and the establishment of a group of world-class universities domestically.

The second thrust in this area is linked to China's institutional reform of its science and technology system. To improve linkage between the science and technology system and enterprises, the Chinese government will shift the system from state-based to enterprise-based by transferring a portion of research institutes (those not responsible for basic research or public research) to enterprises. It will also encourage enterprises to establish new incentives such as stock options to motivate researchers to develop more market-friendly inventions and establish interaction between enterprises and universities and research institutes by allowing senior engineers in enterprises to act as part-time professors or researchers in universities as well as encouraging researchers in universities or research institutes to take part-time jobs in enterprises. These measures also aim to facilitate the diffusion of technology and improve the speed of technology adoption.

4. Evaluation of China's Technology Upgrading Strategy

While it is the recognition of limits to the current growth process that has caused the Chinese government to set out the objectives, targets and instruments we describe above, the question which follows is whether these will be effective? Can the objectives be met by the instruments and are the targets sufficient to meet the instruments and assure continued high economic growth?

4.1. *Meeting growth targets through TFP targets*

The central quantitative target set for maintaining GDP growth is to raise the TFP growth rate by 2020 to 60% of overall growth. The most commonly explored analyses linking between economic growth and TFP utilize a growth accounting framework. Following Solow (1957) and Denison (1967), we can write a simple aggregate production function as

$$Y(t) = A(t)F(K(t), L(t)) \tag{1}$$

where $Y(t)$ is output in period t, $A(t)$ is a measure of overall factor productivity, $K(t)$ and $L(t)$ are measures of capital and labor inputs. A time derivative of (1) yields the growth accounting equation

$$\frac{\dot{Y}}{Y} = \frac{\dot{A}}{A} + s_k \frac{\dot{K}}{K} + s_L \frac{\dot{L}}{L} \tag{2}$$

where s_K and s_L represent the shares of capital and labour in national income, and $\frac{\dot{A}}{A}$ measures TFP growth. Solow first applied his approach to US growth from the 1870s to the 1950s concluding that the majority of growth (around 87%) was attributable to technical progress rather than input growth. Jorgensen and Griliches (1967) later showed however that a substantial fraction of the residual could be explained by changes in the quality of inputs, such as average years of schooling and better health.

The studies mentioned earlier use a similar approach in analyzing Chinese TFP growth and come to the conclusion that only 40% of Chinese growth since the 1990s is due to technical innovation. This sharply lower proportion also occurred in other Asian economies at earlier stages of industrialization such as Japan and South Korea. This phenomenon is often attributed to the high savings rates in these economies, and large capital accumulation relative to a small initial capital stock as industrialization occurs.

Using the study by Li *et al.* (2005) summarized in Table 2, one can make computations of the required change in $\frac{\dot{A}}{A}$ as a ratio of $\frac{\dot{Y}}{Y}$ for given reductions in factor input growth rates. These are summarized in Table 10 and suggest that a TFP growth target set as 60% of GDP growth may be realistic to sustain the overall GDP growth objective if the value of $\frac{\dot{A}}{A}$ declines to 7.5% from 10.5% and $\frac{\dot{L}}{L}$ falls from 1.1% to 0%. In the worst case

Table 10. Required Changes in $\frac{\dot{A}}{A}$ based on Li *et al.* (2005) to Maintain Chinese Growth under Falling Factor Input Growth Rates.

	GDP growth rate	Capital growth rate	Labour growth rate	$\frac{\dot{A}}{A}$
Li (2005) results for 2000–2003	8.4	10.5	1.1	1.6 (19.8%)
Under reduction in $\frac{\dot{K}}{K}$ to 7.5	8.4	7.5	1.1	3.5 (41.2%)
Under reduction in $\frac{\dot{L}}{L}$ to 0	8.4	10.5	0	2.1 (25.0%)
Under reduction both in $\frac{\dot{K}}{K}$ to 7.5 and $\frac{\dot{L}}{L}$ to 0	8.4	7.5	0	3.9 (46.4%)

Note: The parentheses are the percentage of TFP contribution to total GDP growth.

scenario that both capital and labour inputs fall in these ways, the highest required $\frac{\dot{A}}{A}$ component of GDP growth is still less than 50%.

In more recent work, Whalley and Xin (2006) apply a two-stage growth accounting approach to China in which they consider the Chinese economy to be segmented into two distinct subparts. One uses foreign direct investment (FDI) and labour as inputs; the other domestic capital and labour. The outputs from these two sub sectors then aggregate into a single output, as shown in the Solow approach.

Based on their Equation (8) (reproduced here as (3)) and relevant data in Table 2 and Table 5 for 2004 we can make some further speculative calculations. Their growth accounting equation is

$$\frac{\dot{Y}}{Y} = g^F\left(\frac{\dot{A}^F}{A^F} + s^F_{FDI}\frac{F\dot{D}I}{FDI} + s^F_L\frac{\dot{L}^F}{L^F}\right) + g^N\left(\frac{\dot{A}^N}{A^N} + s^N_K\frac{\dot{K}}{K} + s^N_L\frac{\dot{L}^N}{L^N}\right) \tag{3}$$

where the superscripts F and N relate to the FDI and non-FDI sectors, and g^F and g^N are the shares of output in the FDI and non-FDI sectors. In their calculations for 2004, $\frac{\dot{Y}}{Y} = 9.5$, $g^F = 0.224$, $g^N = 0.776$, $s^F_{FDI} = 0.841$, $s^F_L = 0.159$, $s^N_L = 0.488$, $\frac{F\dot{D}I}{FDI} = 10.4$, $\frac{\dot{L}^F}{L^F} = 14.8$, $\frac{\dot{L}^N}{L^N} = 0.6$, $\frac{\dot{A}^F}{A^F} = 7.7$, $\frac{\dot{A}^N}{A^N} = -0.1$. Their calculations thus show that all technological progress occurs in the FDI part of the economy, which is also not the indigenous TFP growth that the new Chinese growth strategy focuses on.

If input growth in the FDI sector were to fall due to stagnating FDI, the lost contribution to GDP growth would be about 2.8%. If labor growth by 2020 were zero as predicted by Li *et al.* (2005), Chinese GDP growth would lose another 0.75%, and GDP growth would be a little less than 6%. The TFP component of GDP growth as calculated by Whalley and Xin (2005) is 17.3% for 2004, but this comprises an FDI part which accounts for nearly all TFP growth. If both parts of TFP growth were to increase to 60%, that would yield an increase of $\frac{\dot{A}}{A}$ by about 4%, which is enough to cover the lost growth due to plateauing FDI and labor growth. But if only the non-FDI part of TFP growth is affected by a strategy focused on indigenous technological progress, there is little impact on overall growth which will now fall short of its target. However, if as expected by Chinese officials, both the TFP components of GDP growth were to increase only by 20% (from 40% to 60%), then $\frac{\dot{A}}{A}$ increases by about 2%, inadequate to cover the loss, but still maintaining a 7.5% economic growth rate. If only the non-FDI component increases by 20%, then once again there is no impact on the growth rate and the strategy's objective is not met.

These calculations build on the premise that $\frac{\dot{A}}{A}$ constitutes a meaningful target for policy. However, as a residual there are no direct instruments available in the growth accounting framework to achieve a particular $\frac{\dot{A}}{A}$ value. As such, it also makes speculation on the feasibility of achieving this objective hard to translate into firm policy recommendation.

4.2. *GERD targets, objectives and TFP growth*

The next issue is whether achieving the individual targets set for instruments can assure meeting the overall TFP growth objective. The first target is set for R&D expenditures. The relationship between R&D investment and technological change has been the subject of substantial academic debate with several models developed. Romer (1990), Grossman and Helpman (1991) and Barro and Sala-i-Martin (1995) apply a product-variety approach to technological change under which an increase in product varieties are treated as representative of R&D. In contrast, Griliches (1973) uses a regression approach to assess the effect of R&D on the TFP growth rate. Aghion and Howitt (1992) and Grossman and Helpman (1991) apply a quality-ladders formulation to technological change, presuming that quality upgrading is proportional to R&D outlays. These models calculate TFP growth as the sum of $\frac{\dot{A}}{A}$ and an R&D-specific term. Other models tackle the relationship between R&D and economic growth by treating R&D as a special form of capital (Romer, 2006; Barro and Xavier, 2004).

There is no clear theory relating GERD/GDP ratios to TFP growth rates, and so assessing the impact of meeting GERD/GDP targets on

TFP growth (and hence broader economic growth) is difficult. Some economists (Kim and Nelson, 2000) have argued that R&D investment, the number of researchers and scientists, the number of published papers and IPR awards are four major factors determining a country's innovative capacity.

Meeting the GERD to GDP target seems likely. The goal of a 2.0% and 2.5% share for GERD in GDP for 2010 and 2020 respectively implies an annual growth rate of GERD at 8.6% up to 2010 and 9.6% beyond to 2020. This targeted rate of 8–10% should be possible, since Table 3 shows China's average GERD real annual growth is around 15% since 1996, higher than the required figure.

4.3. *Meeting GERD targets with instruments*

Meeting GERD/GDP targets implies using a series of budgetary and tax measures. Table 11 also shows GERD by source of funds, recipient of funding, and sector of performance in 2004. Government-financed R&D accounts for 26.6% of GERD, industry-financed R&D accounts for 65.7%, and GERD financed from abroad and other sources is 7.7%. The time trend of this funding over the last five years thus shows an increase in industrial funding and a decrease in government funding,[12] while GERD grows at around 20% annually in the last five years, and at around 17% in the last ten years. This implies substantial growth in industry funding,

Table 11. GERD by Source of Funds, Recipient of Funding and Sector of Performance in 2004.

(RMB 100 million)

	Research institutes	Business	Higher education	Others	Total
Government	344.3	62.6	108.8	7.8	523.6
Business	22.4	1189.3	74.5	5.1	1291.3
Abroad	2.6	19.8	2.6	0.1	25.2
Others	62.4	42.3	14.9	6.6	126.2
Total	431.7	1314.0	200.9	19.7	1966.3

Source: China Science and Technology Statistics Data Book (2005).

[12] In 2003, industry-financed R&D accounts for 60.1% of total GERD, increasing 2.5% compared to that in 2000. The percentage of industry-financed R&D investment in GERD surpasses 50% for the first time in 2000. Government-financed R&D accounts for 29.9%, decreasing 3.5% compared to that in 2000. Foreign funds and other national sources account for 1.9% and 8.0% respectively.

in large part reflecting encouragement from the central government. Since 1995 more government budgetary funds have been appropriated to science and technology, together with a series of incentives to encourage industry funding. These incentives are not equally available to all enterprises; usually FIEs enjoy more favorable tax terms and State-Owned Enterprises (SOEs) have more government subsidies. The new strategy seeks to remove this discriminatory treatment, and the major increase in industry financed R&D investment is expected to come from non-FIEs.

A problem area with meeting GERD targets is that the percentage of R&D expenditures over sales for private S&T enterprises has fallen sharply from 11.5% in 1993 to 2.1% in 2002. According to the Economic Census Report by the National Statistics Bureau (2005), among all the medium-to-large enterprises in China, only 10% invest in science and technology activities and R&D expenditures are only 0.56% of sales[13] while in major developed countries R&D expenditures account for 5% of sales. Among the Large and Medium-size Enterprises (LMEs), only 32% have R&D centers and R&D researchers account for less than 35% of total engineers and researchers in LMEs. The situation in central government-affiliated enterprises is better, with R&D accounting for around 1.5% of sales, with most having set up R&D centers.

Several research papers show a positive relationship between financial incentives and R&D investment by enterprises and as China's latest financial incentives are substantial, it may be that a substantial increase in enterprise R&D spending occurs nonetheless. Wang and Tsai (2004) studied the impact of three promotional tools in the Taiwanese electronic component industry: R&D tax credits, exemption from tariffs, and accelerated depreciation. Their results indicate that the scheme generated an increase in industrial R&D investment of about 16%. Russo (2004) also concluded that R&D tax credits produce relatively large increases in research effort in Canada and the United States. Hall and Van Reenan (2000) reviewed the evidence in various studies about the effects of tax systems in OECD countries on the user cost of R&D and concluded that in the current imperfect state of knowledge, a dollar in tax credit for R&D might stimulate a dollar of additional R&D. The conclusions confirm the results of surveys by Edwin Mansfield in the United States in 1986. A target of increasing GERD over GDP from the current ratio

[13]See http://news.xinhuanet.com/fortune/2005-12/14/content_3919214.htm.

of 1.3% to 2.5% in 2020 implies (given GDP growth of 7.5%) that the annual growth rate of industry financed R&D (after inflation) should be about 12% providing the industry-financed share in GERD remains around 60%.[14]

Similarly, if we suppose the government-financed R&D share in GERD remains at the current ratio of around 30%, the real annual growth rate of government-financed R&D may need to be 12%[15] implying a larger share of budgetary revenues will need to be directed into government-financed R&D to achieve the targets set. Over the past 10 years, the share of budgetary expenditures on science and research is around 4% (see Table 12) while total budget revenues grow at over 14%. A trend of budgetary revenue growth higher than GDP growth may be difficult to sustain in the mid-to-long term given that the tax load is already heavy in China.[16] In addition, China's tax incentives for R&D investment and the upcoming Value-Added Tax (VAT) reform aiming to change VAT from production-type to consumption-type[17] narrow the tax base further.

Other sources of funding for R&D include bank loans, the stock market and foreign funds. The fragility of China's financial system (see Yingli Pan, 2006), however, raises doubts about these as sources of R&D finances. The use of venture capital will be a new initiative to support R&D activities, but will have to build from a small base.

4.4. *Other targets and instruments*

The targets of paper citations and rankings in patent awards have not been supported by any new and clear initiatives thus far. Some observers argue that the brain drain and the lack of an innovative culture in the education system are constraints on the achievement of both of these (Economist, August 5th, 2006). There are more young leaders in research programs who are expected to bring more creativity and innovation to

[14]This calculation is the rate r from the equation: $(1 + 7.5\%)^{15} \times 2.5\% \times 60\% = 1.3\% \times 60\% \times (1 + r)^{15}$ where $r \approx 12.3\%$.

[15]Using a similar calculation to that for industry-financed R&D.

[16]Since 1995, China's budgetary revenue over GDP has risen from 10% to 18.5%, an average annual growth rate of 1.4%. Though the figure in the USA is 28.4% in 2002, given that social security is only a small share in the total budgetary revenue in China and low GDP per capita, China's tax load on enterprises may be heavier than that in USA. Relevant data is from Xianghong Wu (2005), Is China's Tax Heavy or Not? http://business.sohu.com/20050609/n225876070.shtml.

[17]Currently VAT accounts for over 30% of total budgetary revenue.

Table 12. Budgetary Expenditures on Science and Research (RMB 100 million).

	1996	1997	1998	1999	2000	2001	2002	2003
Budgetary Expenditures on Science and Research (1)	348.63	408.86	438.60	543.85	575.62	703.26	816.22	975.54
Budgetary Expenditures (growth rate) (2)	7937.55	9233.56	10798.18	13187.67	15886.50	18902.58	22053.15	24649.95
	(16.3%)	(16.3%)	(16.9%)	(22.1%)	(20.5%)	(19.0%)	(16.7%)	(11.8%)
(1)/(2)	4.39	4.43	4.06	4.12	3.62	3.72	3.70	3.96
Government Revenue (growth rate)	7407.99	8651.14	9875.95	11444.08	13395.23	16386.04	18903.64	21715.25
	(18.7%)	(16.8%)	(14.2%)	(15.9%)	(17.0%)	(22.3%)	(15.4%)	(14.9%)

Source: China's Ministry of Finance official website, http://www.mof.gov.cn/1162.htm.

their tasks,[18] and an increasing number of returning overseas Chinese as a result of continued high economic growth and policy encouragement.[19] If the Chinese government can create mechanisms to ensure that talented people can devote their time and energy to research, then China might be able to achieve these two targets, but the link is tenuous at best.

Another target is foreign technology reliance. To meet this target, foreign technology purchases will need to be limited to an 8% annual growth rate on average over the next fifteen years.[20] Between 2000 and 2005, the average annual growth rates of foreign technology purchases exceeded 30%, though with large fluctuations (the lowest around −20% in 2004 and the highest up to nearly 100% in 2002).[21] Hence a substantial change is needed for China to meet this target. The linkage of this target to broader TFP and GDP growth is also an issue, and in all probability implies negative impacts.

The last set of issues involve education. Human capital is typically seen as important for economic growth for two reasons (see Barro, 2001). First, more human capital facilitates the absorption of superior technologies from technology-leading countries. Second, since human capital is slower to adjust than physical capital, a country that starts with a high ratio of human to physical capital can grow rapidly by adjusting upwards the quantity of physical capital. In view of the importance of education in China's economic growth and a shortage of education financing, a series of reforms have been carried out since 1990s, including decentralization of financial responsibilities for education (Mark Bray *et al.*, 2001), participation of enterprises, placing companies and research agencies in the management and administration of institutions, and institutional

---

[18]For example, in the 973 program, those under 45 have accounted for 44.6% of all chief scientists and 62.8% of all project heads. See National Science and Technology Plan Annual Report (2006).

[19]David Zweig in *Is China a Magnet for Global Talent?* says "A similar 'reverse brain drain' is underway in mainland China. The number of returnees hit 30,000 in 2005, up from 7,000 in 1999." However, over 50% of the returnees lack working experience, "they might be as much a burden as a benefit to the Chinese state." *Horizons*, special issue on Canada–China, Vol. 9, No. 2, August 2006.

[20]We calculate y/x from the two equations $\begin{cases} x/[x + (GDP \times 1.57 \times 1.34\%)] = 38.9\% \\ y/[y + (GDP \times 4 \times 2.5\%)] = 30\% \end{cases}$, where GDP is in constant 2000 US dollar, then GDP*1.57*1.34% in the upper equation reflects GERD in 2005, and GDP*4*2.5% in the lower equation reflects expected GERD in 2020. These imply that x/y is about 3.2. The average annual growth rate is derived using a similar calculation to that for industrial R&D.

[21]See http://www.kjzg.com.cn/newver/browarticle.php?articleid=1069.

amalgamation (combination of previous separate institutions) (Rui Yang, 2000).

But these reforms have also been criticized. Rui Yang (2000) argues that China separates the underlying values from the system when it adopts from Western education. For instance, China may promote science and technology, but without respect for academic freedom and institutional autonomy. Gopinathan (1997) argues that global economic competitiveness cannot be assured by a model of schooling with a heavy emphasis on a common curriculum and mastery of content as currently emphasized in the Chinese education system. Another problem is rising education expenditures becoming a heavy burden for Chinese households to the point that educational attainment suffers. A survey[22] conducted by Horizon Key, a private market survey company, indicates that education expenses may now account for about one third of household outlays on average. The National Economic and Social Development Statistics issued by National Bureau of Statistics (2004) show that the growth of education expenses in rural households has been over 20% since 1997, while their net income has increased only 6.8%.

The impacts of qualitative targets in the growth strategy remain. Though achieving quantitative targets may lead to changes in scientific and technical activities, they do not in themselves explain how these activities lead to product or process innovations. Thus Freeman (1995), Kim and Nelson (2000) and others have argued that qualitative factors affecting the national system of innovation need to be taken into account as well as quantitative indicators since they facilitate change. For China's case, the qualitative targets as listed in Table 1 summarizing the *S&T Guidelines 2006–2020* are supported by institutional reform initiatives, but as these changes can only be implemented gradually, their impact will likely be slow and diffuse.

4.5. *Summary*

In summary, a TFP target set as 60% of GDP growth could meet a GDP growth objective of a minimum of 7.5% per year until 2020 both if the initial TFP residual is high enough and policy initiatives are assumed to affect TFP growth of both foreign-invested enterprises and other enterprises equally. If only TFP growth of non-FIEs is affected, the initiative would

[22] Hui Zhang and Yue Yuan, 2006, Chinese Residents' Life Quality Index Research Report in 2005.

seem likely to fall short. Moreover, the links between TFP growth and various instruments to raise it, such as the GERD/GDP ratio, foreign technology reliance, number of patents or published scientific papers, are unclear. It is also unclear whether targets for these instruments can be met. Among the four, GERD/GDP is the most likely to be achieved given the substantial budgetary commitments and tax incentives the Chinese government is providing. Changes in foreign technology reliance seem hard to achieve if there is little change in foreign technology purchases and it is also unclear if these affect TFP growth positively or negatively. The two remaining targets, i.e. number of invention-type patents and number of internationally cited scientific papers rely heavily on domestic intellectual capabilities, and if human capital is slow to adjust, these targets may be ambitious.

5. Comparisons with Japan and South Korea

We finally turn to the issue of whether experience elsewhere in Asia offers any guide as to the likelihood of success in the Chinese technology upgrading strategy. Japan and South Korea are two clear examples representing extraordinary success first at both technological and economic catch-up and subsequently sustained growth — Japan's growth is of long standing, going back to the Meiji restoration of 1868. After the Second World War, Japan rapidly recovered and achieved "Miracle Growth" from 1953 to the late 1970s. However, in the 1990s, growth slowed substantially and turned negative for several years. South Korea achieved rapid growth per capita output of 7% annually from the 1960s, while growth rates were especially high in the 1980s and 1990s, and still has strong growth today.

What were the sources of this high economic growth and are there common features with China accounting for their success? Could China's technology policy improve the chances of maintaining a high growth rate by drawing on these experiences?

From a historical perspective, all three of these countries have followed (or will follow) a similar sequencing in terms of sources of output growth in the process of the industrialization, i.e. physical capital, human capital and finally technical progress. Though the sequencing seems to apply to most developed and developing countries in their industrialization processes,[23] what distinguishes Japan is the relatively long high growth

[23] Lau (1996) argues that much of the economic growth in the late nineteenth and early twentieth centuries can be similarly [now with New Industrialized Economies] explained by the growth in tangible capital and labor inputs. Technical progress was not found to

period. Japan underwent industrialization for nine decades from the 1880s to the 1970s. Thus even before it entered the "Miracle Growth" stage, it has already established the necessary infrastructure, enhanced human capital, accumulated physical capital, imported and adapted of foreign technology, and achieved scale economies (Mosk, 2004). South Korea's industrialization is more recent, beginning in the 1960s. At that time, it was short of both capital and technology, so it had to rely on long-term foreign loans to finance industrial investment and promote technology transfer.

Exploring sources of high output growth, Denison and Chung (1976) estimate that of Japan's average annual real national income growth of 8.77% over 1953–71, input growth accounts for 3.95% (accounting for 45% of total growth) and growth in output per unit of input contributes 4.82% (accounting for 55% of total growth). Maddison (1998) produces similar findings, indicating that productivity growth was important, but not the sole determinant of growth. Hayami (1999) compares the changes in the sources of modern economic growth in Japan and the United States, finding that the Japanese High Growth period (1958–1970) was characterized by both high capital input growth and technical progress while US growth was mainly driven by technical progress in the comparable period (1929–1966) as reflected in the TFP contribution figure of 53% in Japan and 80% in the United States.

This raises the issue of why Japan did not make the same shift to efficiency-based growth as in the United States, especially in the "High Growth" period when Japan was able to catch up the advanced industrial economies in the West. Hayami (1999) concludes that a significant lag in any shift to efficiency-based growth characterizes newly industrializing economies in their process of catching up to advanced economies using borrowed technology. According to Alexander Gerschenkron (1962), the later a country starts industrialization, the more heavily it relies on technology borrowed from its predecessors. Furthermore, the later the start of industrialization the more advanced high capital intensity and labor-saving technology tends to be imported.

Hayami (1999) argues that capital-using and labor-saving biases in borrowed technology for recipient economies can be strengthened by international trade and foreign direct investment. One explanation lies in

---

be a significant source of US economic growth until the studies of Abramobitz (1986) and Solow (1957) for the period starting in the late 1920s. The same was also true of the Japanese experience.

the theory of product cycles of Raymond Vernon (1966) which implies that advanced industrial economies tend to specialize in R&D and new product development activities with intensive use of high human capital, whereas Newly Industrializing Economies (NIEs) tend to specialize in standardized mass production based on automatic machinery and cheap labor. Another explanation lies in the fact that more capital goods embodying new technologies are imported from advanced economies. Thus the physical capital-using bias in NIEs and the human capital-using bias in advanced economies reinforce each other through international trade and foreign direct investment.

Both of these features — sequencing of sources of output growth and catch-up development based on technology borrowing — imply that low wage countries will rely more heavily on capital input growth than technological progress during their early industrialization period. However, such a development pattern is not sustainable. Chang-Soo Lee (1998) studied the South Korean Manufacturing Sector using a disaggregated growth accounting approach and found that the contribution of capital to growth is high for South Korean manufacturing. However, productivity growth was still the largest contributor to output growth in eight of fifteen industries, and productivity growth explained about 38% of output growth for manufacturing overall. He also found that an interaction between productivity growth and capital input growth was present for nine of the fifteen industries, supporting the hypothesis of embodied technology in capital input growth. He drew the conclusion that the argument that disembodied technological change is the only source of sustainable economic growth may hold for a leader country which achieves higher productivity growth mainly by accumulating new knowledge through innovation. However, the growth process for a follower country is different — it will adopt neither a typical accumulation-based nor an efficiency-based growth pattern but a mixture of the two.

There are both common and different elements between all three countries. The high savings rate shared by Japan, South Korea and China is also an important source of high capital input growth. Savings rates were especially high during high growth periods for these countries. The ways in which these three countries have executed transfers of technology are, however, different. Japan was import substitution-oriented while both South Korea and China were export-oriented. Given the channel of technology transfer, China is more reliant on FDI for technology transfer while Japan was more dependent on technology trade.

Sakakibara and Cho (2002) document how Japanese policies restricted imports and direct investment until 1964 when Japan obtained the status of an article eight country in the International Monetary Fund. They also argue that restrictions on imports and direct investment facilitated technology transfer from western countries to Japan in the early post-war years because the only way foreign firms were able to profit from their technology in Japan was to sell it. In Japan, the introduction of foreign technology was mainly through licensing of essential technologies, and the Ministry of International Trade and Industry (MITI) played an important role. Acting as a single buyer of technology, it successfully reduced the royalties Japanese firms had to pay for technology licenses. It also encouraged rapid diffusion of technology by keeping domestic patent periods short (Mosk, 2004). This strategy worked so successfully that even developed countries admitted that the rate of technical change and of economic growth depended more on efficient diffusion than on being first in the world with radical innovations, and as much on social innovation as on technical innovation (Freeman, 1995).

In South Korea, its first five-year economic development plan which started in 1962 began with the promotion of import-substituting industries, but soon shifted to export-oriented industries to repay foreign loans. However, its technology transfer has been more reliant on foreign loans than on FDI. In order to expedite the development of export industries, the government adopted a policy of promoting assembly industries of final goods which prompted importation of foreign capital goods, essentially the "turnkey" system. The government organized large-scale foreign loans and allocated them for investments in selected industries, and industries later reverse-engineered the imported capital goods to acquire the necessary technology. But the pattern was different across sectors. Its light industries relied on OEM production arrangements, chemical industries resorted to turn key-plant importation with technical training, and electric and machinery industries depended relatively more on foreign loans.

China adopted its policy of opening in the early 1980s and its policy of promoting FDI inflows in the early 1990s. Since then, China has become progressively more reliant on foreign trade and FDI. In 2004, FIEs produced 22% of China's GDP and over 55% of China's exports (Whalley and Xin, 2006). Trade surpluses and inward FDI have also contributed to capital supply, and in turn, economic growth. The growth of FDI has brought with it new technologies, termed by the Chinese government the "market for technology".

Even though FDI's positive role in technology transfer (or technology spillover) is emphasized in older studies (e.g. Caves, 1974; Globerman, 1979; Blomstrom, 1989), more recent work casts doubt on this conclusion. Aitken and Harrison (1999) showed that earlier findings in support of positive spillovers are likely to be driven by the endogeneity of FDI which means FDI chooses to go to better performing industries. Once industry specific factors are controlled for, there is no evidence for positive spillovers. Hu and Jefferson (2002) studied China's electronic and textile industries and argued that in the short run, firm level FDI enhances the productivity of FDI receiving firms, but it also depresses that of non-FDI domestic firms. FDI can thus reduce the productivity and market share of domestic firms in the short term, but in the longer term those domestic Chinese firms that are able to survive in the face of competition from FDI firms seem able to capture some of the technology and know-how that is introduced from abroad. Hu *et al.* (2005) also argue based on Chinese LME data that FDI can create channels that reduce the transactions cost of technology transfer within firms, but that the presence of foreign investment and foreign expertise need not enhance arm's length market-mediated foreign technology transfer. Both Hu *et al.* (2004) and Markusen and Venables (1999) thus argue that R&D and technology transfer are highly complementary.

This phenomenon of shift is supported by Kim and Stewart's (1993) empirical study on the relationship between domestic R&D and imports of technology for 10 countries. They found strong complementarity between technology imports and domestic R&D for Japan and South Korea, weak for France, none for Germany and the US. However, Japan revealed a sharp decline in the ratio of technology payments to R&D spending; and Korea followed in its steps. So they argue that complementarity appears to weaken in later stages as technology development strategies shift from dependent to imitative to autonomous or offensive technology development.

Consistent with the hypothesis of sequencing of sources of output growth, Japan and South Korea both moved to indigenous R&D, the route that China is now attempting to follow. In Japan, the shift from technology licensing to domestic R&D occurred in the 1960s when the technology cycle was still relatively long, and Japanese firms were able to digest and sequentially develop activities in the whole value chain. R&D in Japan was mostly undertaken by the private sector, and industrial policy was mainly focused on encouraging companies to conduct R&D. By the early 1970s, large Japanese manufacturing enterprises had by and large become internationally competitive, and later Japan continued to close the gap in income per capita between itself and the United States (Mosk, 2004).

In South Korea, indigenous R&D promotion occurred in the 1980s.[24] At that time, there was an increased demand for complex and sophisticated technologies and an increasing reluctance of foreign countries to transfer technology. Korea now ranks 6th in R&D investment among OECD countries. GERD over GNP has risen from 0.77% in 1980 to 2.96% in 2001. The ratio of government to private funding has fallen from 64:36 in 1980 to 26:74 in 2001.[25] However, it is also widely accepted that Korea has not achieved the same degree of success as Japan in indigenous R&D, and the research component in R&D is small. A summary of this might be that Japan has been successful in both imitation and indigenous R&D while Korean successes lie in creative imitation rather than in indigenous R&D, while China, up to now, has not been especially successful even in creative imitation.

The challenge that China sees for itself is to encourage indigenous R&D. According to the World Development Indicator database, GDP per capita measured in constant 2000 US$ was already above 7,000 in Japan in the 1960s, over 3,000 in South Korea in the 1980s when their technologically led growth accelerated, however China is now only around 1,500 in 2006. If the domestic market is insufficient to absorb high technology products, China has to rely on world market, and will face more competition than South Korea from world markets. Competition also comes from FIEs in domestic markets as well. Both Japanese Keiretsu and Korean Chaebol played an important role in the catching-up process, but comparable firms have yet to emerge so strongly in the manufacturing sector in China.

The later a country starts industrialization, the more capital rather than technology reliant it must be in its early growth phase. In South Korea and China, export-oriented growth increased reliance on growth of capital inputs. In the face of competition in export markets, they resorted to capital good imports to increase productivity. South Korea probably did better than China in acquiring technology embodied in capital goods

---

[24]Sakakibara and Cho (2002) argue that the first R&D promotion policy can be found in the Technology Development Promotion Law of 1972. However, the Korean government did not play a significant role in R&D promotion until the 1980s. The role of the government in R&D promotion was limited to the establishment of national research to support industrial technological learning, and funding university-based R&D.

[25]These numbers are cited from Youngrak Choi's presentation at PICMET'04 Symposium, July 31–August 4, 2004.

through reverse-engineering, perhaps due to their indigenous R&D effort. If China is to use an indigenous R&D strategy, domestic demand and domestic enterprise structure pose two outstanding challenges. China does have some advantages, such as potential but as yet unapplied technology based on a long-standing national science and technology system and defense industry, overseas talent is expected to be attracted by China's high economic growth, financial support reflecting the size of both current GDP and further economic growth. Under this view, China might have a promising future in technology upgrading and in turn continued economic growth through indigenous R&D, but it is far from certain that it will be sufficient alone to sustain current high growth rate.

6. Conclusion

As China's current trade- and FDI-driven growth is perceived to face growing problems in the years ahead, this paper turns to an analysis of China's latest technology upgrading strategy. Relative to previous science and technology strategies for sustaining high growth, developing domestic innovation capacity is emphasized as the dominant focal point.

A series of objectives, targets and instruments are set out in both the 11th 5-year plan and the guidelines for the period 2006–2020. The overall objective set is to meet a minimum annual growth rate of 7.5% until 2010, and 7.0% until 2020 under the constraints of mandatory indicators for environmental protection and energy saving. Shifting growth from input-driven (including capital, energy and environment) to technology upgrading-driven is thus the priority issue on Chinese government's growth agenda. A series of targets have been set for the next 15 years, including: TFP growth is to reach 60% of GDP growth; GERD over GDP ratio to reach 2.5%; foreign technology reliance to fall to 30%; the number of invention-type patent grants gained by Chinese inventors to rank in the top five in the world; and the number of internationally cited scientific papers by Chinese authors to rank in the top five in the world.

Instruments for achieving these targets have also been announced. The first is to increase funding for science and technology from both government and private sectors. The second is to improve the efficiency of the use of funds through monitoring mechanisms, enterprise-based market mechanism, large capital equipment and knowledge sharing platforms and basic scientific information sharing platforms. The third is to promote domestic innovation through government procurement of domestically-innovated products, foreign technology import regulation aiming to force advanced technology import and prevent repeated imports of technology; intellectual property rights protection and integration of innovation indicators into performance appraisal systems for both local government and state-owned enterprises; and finally, talent force accumulation through domestic talent cultivation and overseas talent attraction.

The question is whether these instruments can meet the required targets and whether the technology upgrading strategy can meet overall GDP growth objectives consistent with environmental protection and resource-saving targets. We report calculations based on growth accounting studies, suggesting that a TFP target of 60% of GDP growth may help to meet the GDP growth objective, but also note that TFP as a target is hard to discuss in a growth accounting framework since TFP is a residual. Also, there is a critical issue of whether the majority of TFP growth is currently FDI-related and non-indigenous, and hence largely beyond the reach of current policy. Given the substantial R&D tax and other incentives in the strategy, targets for GERD over GDP may well be achieved. In turn, the targets for foreign technology reliance might be achievable, but whether they relate positively to TFP targets remains unclear. Two remaining targets relate to scientific papers and invention-type patents and these will be subject to a slow adjustment process and might take longer to realize.

Finally, we examine Japanese and South Korean growth experience to see whether there are any indications from international comparison as to whether it is possible for China to sustain its future growth using a technology upgrading strategy. The commonality of experience shared by these three countries is that they have initially achieved extraordinarily high growth based largely on technology borrowing, and large capital input contribution to GDP growth, but this growth eventually becomes unsustainable. Japan and South Korea thus moved to indigenous R&D generation along with improved foreign technology adoption as well as enhanced domestic innovation capacity. To implement China's indigenous R&D strategy, there are new challenges, including more competition in both export market and from FIEs on domestic market, together with limited domestic demand. However, China has advantages that Japan and South Korea did not have, among which are large potential labor transfers from rural to urban areas.

Whether China will be successful with their strategy remains to be seen. The current expectation globally seems to be that China is embarked on a historic transformation involving sustained growth for several decades, and so continued growth is factored into both asset markets and investment decisions in China. But we have seen interruptions of growth elsewhere in the world, and interruptions cannot be ruled out in the Chinese case. The new strategy while vague, however, is concrete and seems realistic and can only help in maintaining growth. Whether the cost in foregone consumption today of implementing the strategy pays is perhaps the harder question to answer.

References

Aghion, P. and P. Howitt (1992). A Model of Growth Through Creative Destruction, *Econometrica*, 60(2): 323–351.

Aitken, B. J. and A. E. Harrison (1999). Do Domestic Firms Benefit from Direct Foreign Investment? Evidence from Venezuela, *American Economic Review*, 89: 605–18.

Barro, R. and X. Sala-i-Martin (1995). *Economic Growth.* New York: McGraw-Hill.

Barro, R. J. (2001). Human Capital and Growth, *American Economic Review*, 91(2): 12–17.

Barro, R. and X. Sala-i-Martin (2004). *Economic Growth.* Cambridge, MA: MIT Press.

Blomstrom, M. (1986). Foreign Investment and Productive Efficiency: The Case of Mexico, *Journal of Industrial Economics*, 35: 97–110.

Borenszstein, E. and J. D. Ostry (1996). Accounting for China's growth performance, *American Economic Review* (*Papers and Proceedings*), 86: 225–228.

Bray, M. and G. Qin (2001). Comparative Education in Greater China: Contexts, Characteristics, Contrasts and Contributions. *Comparative Education*, 37(4): *Special Number* (24): *Comparative Education for the Twenty-First Century: An International Response*, 451–473.

Caves, R. E. (1974). Multinational Firms, Competition and Productivity in Host-Country Markets, *Econometrica*, 41: 176–93.

China's Ministry of Science and Technology (2006). National Science and Technology Plan Annual Report.

Chow, G. (1993). Capital Formation and Economic Growth in China, *Quarterly Journal of Economics*, 108: 809–842.

Denison, E. and W. Chung, (1976). *Economic Growth and its Sources.* In *Asia's Next Giant: How the Japanese Economy Works* (Patrick, H. and H. Rosovsky, Eds.), Washington D.C.: Brookings Institution.

Denison, E. F. (1967). *Why Growth Rates Differ: Postwar Experience in Nine Western Countries.* Washington D.C.: Brookings Institution.

Freeman, C. (1995). The 'National System of Innovation' in Historical Perspective, *Cambridge Journal of Economics*, 19: 5–24.

Gerschenkron, A. (1962). *Economic Backwardness in Historical Perspective: A Book of Essays.* Cambridge, MA: Belknap Press of Harvard University Press.

Globerman, S. (1979). Foreign Direct Investment and "Spillover" Efficiency Benefits in Canadian Manufacturing Industries, *Canadian Journal of Economics*, 12: 42–56.

Gopinathan, S. C. (1997). Educational Development in Singapore: Connecting the National Regional and the Global, *The Australian Educational Researcher*, 24(1): 1–12.

Griliches, Z. (1973). *Research Expenditures and Growth Accounting.* In *Science and Technology in Economic Growth* (Williams, B. R., Ed.). New York: Macmillan.

Grossman, G. M. and E. Helpman (1991). *Innovation and Growth in the Global Economy.* Cambridge, MA: MIT Press.

Hall, B. and J. V. Reenen (2000). How Effective are Fiscal Incentives for R&D? A Review of the Evidence, *Research Policy*, 29: 449–469.

Hao, X. and Y. Gong (2006). Research Funding: China Bets Big on Big Science, *Science*, 311(5767): 1548–1549.

Hayami, Y. (1999). Changes in Sources of Modern Economic Growth: Japan Compared with the United States, *Journal of the Japanese and International Economies*, 13: 1–21.

Hu, A. G. Z. and G. H. Jefferson (2002). FDI Impact and Spillover: Evidence from China's Electronic and Textile Industries, *The World Economy*, 25: 1063–76.

Hu, A. G. Z., G. H. Jefferson and J. Qian (2005). R&D Technology Transfer: Firm-Level Evidence from Chinese Industry, *The Review of Economics and Statistics*, 87(4): 780–86.

Hu, A. (2003, April 7–9). Macroeconomic Policy and Employment Promotion: Economic Growth and Employment Growth, International Labor Organization and Social Welfare Department. China Employment Forum.

Jorgensen, D. W. and Z. Griliches (1967). The Explanation of Productivity Change, *Review of Economic Studies*, 34: 249–83.

Kim, J. B. and C. T. Stewart (1993). The Relation Between Technology Import and Domestic R&D, *The Journal of Technology Transfer*, 18(3–4): 94–103.

Kim, L. and R. Nelson (2000). *Technology, Learning and Innovation: Experiences of Newly Industrializing Economies.* Cambridge, UK: Cambridge University Press.

Krugman, P. (1994). The Myth of Asia's Miracle, *Foreign Affairs*, 73: 62–78.

Lau, L. J. (1996). *The Sources of Long-Term Economic Growth: Observations from the Experience of Developed and Developing Countries.* In *The Mosaic of Economic Growth* (Landau, R., T. Taylor and G. Wright, Eds.). Stanford University Press.

Lee, C. S. (1998). Sustainability of Growth in the Korean Manufacturing Sector, *Pacific Economic Paper*, 279.

Li, S., Y. Hou, Y. Liu and J. He (2005). China's Economic Growth Potential and Prospect Analysis, *Management World*, 9.

MacMillan, J. Whalley and L. Zhu (1989). The Impact of China's Economic Reform on Agricultural Productivity Growth, *Journal of Political Economy*, 97: 781–807.

Maddison, A. (1998). *Chinese Economic Performance in the Long-Run*. Paris: OECD Development Centre.

Markusen, J. R. and A. J. Venables (1999). Foreign Direct Investment as a Catalyst for Industrial Development, *European Economic Review*, 43: 335–356.

Mosk, C. (2004). Japan, Industrialization and Economic Growth. Available at EH.Net Encyclopedia at http://eh.net/encyclopedia/article/mosk.japan.final. (accessed January 19).

National Statistic Bureau (2005). Economic Census Report.

Pack, H. (2000). *Research and Development in the Industrial Development Process*. In *Technology, Learning & Innovation: Experiences of Newly Industrializing Economies* (Kim, L. and R. R. Nelson, Eds.). Cambridge, UK: Cambridge University Press.

Pan, Y. L., X. Wu and Y. Yuan (2006). Liberalization of China's Financial System with Intrinsic Defects, mimeo.

Polanyi, K. (1944). *The Great Transformation*. Boston: Beacon Press.

Romer, D. (2006). *Advanced Macroeconomics*. New York: McGraw-Hill/Irwin Press.

Romer, P. M. (1990). Endogenous Technological Change, *Journal of Political Economy*, 98(2): 71–102.

Russo, B. (2004). A Cost-Benefit Analysis of R&D Tax Incentives, *Canadian Journal of Economics*, 37(2).

Sakakibara, M. and D. Cho (2002). Cooperative R&D in Japan and Korea: A Comparison of Industrial Policy, *Research Policy*, 31: 673–692.

Solow, R. (1957). Technical Change and the Aggregate Production Function, *Review of Economics and Statistics*, 39: 312–320.

Song, W. and J. Li (2000). TFP Growth Contribution as an Indicator in "China's 10th Five-year Plan", *Forum on Science and Technology in China*, 6: 10–14.

Vernon, R. (1966). International Investment and International Trade in the Product Cycle. *Quarterly Journal of Economics*.

Wang, J. C. and K. H. Tsai (1998). The Impact of Research and Development Promotion Schemes in the Taiwanese Electronic Component Industry, *R&D Management*, 28.

Whalley, J. and X. Xin (2005). The Growth Performance of China's FDI and Non-FDI Economics, Working Paper.

Yang, R. (2000). Tensions Between the Global and the Local: A Comparative Illustration of the Reorganization of China's Higher Education in the 1950s and 1990s, *Higher Education*, 39(3).

Young, A. (2003). Gold Into Base Metals: Productivity Growth in the People's Republic of China During the Reform Period, *Journal of Political Economy*, 111(6): 1220–1242.

Zhang, H. and Y. Yuan (2006). Chinese Residents' Life Quality Index Research Report in 2005.

Zweig, D. (2006). Is China A Magnet for Global Talent? *Horizons, special issue on Canada–China*, 9(2).

CHINA'S RAPIDLY CHANGING TRADE AND INVESTMENT INVOLVEMENT WITH THE SOUTH[1]

Jing Wang
Chinese Academy of Social Science (CASS)
University of Western Ontario

John Whalley
University of Western Ontario; CIGI and NBER

We present both data on and forward projections of China's rapidly growing trade and investment flows with Southern countries. In this study, we exclude Hong Kong (China), Korea and Singapore. The data indicate that from a low base in the 1990's when Southern trade was growing more slowly than China's overall trade it subsequently grows rapidly. After 2001, (WTO accession) there has been a significant acceleration, which pre crisis was in turn further accelerating. In 1995, Southern trade was 13% of China's total trade; but by 2007 it was 28% of China's total trade and growing at 42% per year on the export side in contrast to 26% for all exports. India (with a 33-fold increase between 1995–2007) is the most rapidly growing bilateral partner, followed by Brazil (18-fold increase between 1995–2007). In Latin America and Africa are the largest regional sources of trade growth, with more dispersion across countries in Asia. In contrast to its total trade, China runs a significant trade deficit in its Southern trade due to imports of resource products. We report projections that by 2015 Southern trade (assuming unchanged growth rates) would be over 50% of China's trade, and by 2025 India will account for over 50% of China's trade.

We also present data on Southern and bilateral FDI flows involving China and developing countries. From a very small base in the 1990's, these are now growing at even more rapid rates than China's trade. Bilateral flows between India and China, for instance, grew 90-fold between 1995 and 2007.

We finally present data on the initial impact of the financial crisis on China's Southern trade and investment. Southern trade show compression, but this is smaller in percentage keeping in view China's overall total flows. There has been slightly slowed investment of China in the South and the South in China relative to that of total FDI. Despite sharp contraction in some countries

[1]We are grateful to the Ontario Research Fund (ORF) for financial support. We are grateful to Yan Dong for discussions.

(Russia, Singapore), the wider impact elsewhere (Brazil, India) seems to be the dominant effect and Southern relative to North involvement continues to grow for China.

1. Introduction

China's remarkable growth has seen as an eight-fold increase in real GDP/capita since the mid 1970's and has been accompanied by a large increase in trade and (since the early 1990's) inward foreign investment. More recently, it is China's growing engagement with the South (excluding Hong Kong, Taiwan, Korea and Singapore) which has been changing rapidly and growing at higher rates than total trade and investment, albeit from a small base. This is what we focus on in this paper and attempt to synthesize data and make forward projections. To our knowledge there are no other papers which attempt this. We draw heavily on the Chinese source material.

The share of Southern trade in China's total trade shows little change in the 1990's, but then begins to increase at an accelerating rate. Southern trade is now over 25% of China's total trade; 35% of imports by value and in the around 20% for exports. Southern trade on both the import and export side relative to non-Southern (OECD) trade after some relative slippage in the 1990's, began to accelerate following China's entry into WTO and its share increased consistently though the 2000's until 2007. On the import side, imports of oil and materials from Africa exports to Asia showed the highest growth.

Trade between India and China increased by a factor of 33 between 1995 and 2007, or at a little less than four times faster than the growth rate of China's total trade. By 2007, China was India's largest export market and India was China's fourth largest market. Trade with Brazil also showed rapid growth, at a factor of 18 between 1995 and 2007.

Given this pace of change, we also make some forward projections assuming that the average 2005–2007 trade growth rates remain unchanged (which in the current crisis is a strong assumption). These projections indicate even higher acceleration in these trends, as the levels of fast-growing Southern trade rise. Our projections forecast China's Southern trade growing to 50% of China's total trade by 2020 and 60% of total trade by 2027. The compounding effects of the extremely high growth rates of Chinese–Indian and Chinese–Brazilian trade are such that these bilateral trade flows will come to dominate China's trade in a surprisingly short period of time. In turn, China will become the world's largest trading entity even earlier.

We then turn to China's FDI involvement with the South. Data show that China's FDI inflows from the South are small and slow-changing, with a small dip in the early 2000s, and a rise in 2006–2007. Shares are steady in the 10% range of total FDI inflows. On the FDI outflow side, the picture is different, with sharp growth in recent years. This is reflected in the even higher growth rates of FDI from China to India, Brazil, Africa and elsewhere compared to trade. FDI flows to India increased by over 90-fold in the 1995–2007 period.

We also discuss how these rapidly accelerating growth rates for China's involvement with the South have been seemingly affected by the financial crisis. We present data on trade for 2008 and early 2009 that shows compression in China's Southern trade, but at a much lower rate than for China's total trade. The relative share of Southern trade out of the total trade thus continues to increase at an accelerating rate. According to data on FDI flows in 2008, China's FDI inflows and outflows continued to increase in 2008, but with Southern growth rates slightly below the total growth rates. FDI outflows doubled in 2008, and inflows increased by over 20%.

Finally, we situate this discussion within a broader policy, context, noting China's growing ties with India and China's regional trade arrangements, which focus heavily on the South. Combined with the emergence of an assertive South on climate change policy, the prospect seems to be one of change at diplomatic and strategic levels.

2. China's Trade with the South 1995–2007

Care is needed in defining what is meant by the South. In particular, we must be careful with our treatment of Hong Kong (China) and Taiwan (province of China). Hong Kong and Taiwan are two of China's major trading partners, and are not members of the OECD. Both countries have a high per capita GDP. For our purposes, we define the South as Africa, Latin America and Asia, excluding Japan, Hong Kong (China), Taiwan (China), the Republic of Korea and Singapore. Trade with Taiwan and Hong Kong grows at about the same rate as China's total trade, and we emphasize that including China's trade with Taiwan and Hong Kong considerably lowers China–South trade flow growth rates. The South is thus defined as Asia*, Latin America and Africa, where Asia* refers to India, Indonesia, Thailand, Malaysia, and Vietnam. It does not include other developing countries in Europe and Central America, or the Oceanic and Pacific Islands. A small

Table 1. Size of China's Imports and Exports to the South (Billions of USD).

	Exports			Imports		
Region	1995	2001	2007	1995	2001	2007
Asia*	14.3	26.1	172.3	12.0	39.1	250.9
Africa	2.5	6.0	37.3	1.4	4.8	36.4
Latin America	3.1	8.2	51.5	3.0	6.7	51.1
South (total above)	19.9	40.4	261.1	16.4	50.6	338.3
Of Which:		Exports			Imports	
India	0.8	1.9	24.0	0.4	1.7	14.6
Indonesia	1.4	2.8	12.6	2.1	3.9	12.4
Thailand	1.8	2.3	12.0	1.6	4.7	22.7
Malaysia	1.3	3.2	17.7	2.1	6.2	28.7
Vietnam	0.7	1.8	11.9	0.3	1.0	3.2
Brazil	0.8	1.4	11.4	1.2	2.3	18.3
Argentina	0.3	0.6	3.6	0.4	1.3	6.3
Mexico	0.2	1.8	11.7	0.2	0.8	3.3
North Africa	0.6	1.0	7.4	0.7	1.2	6.6
Egypt	0.4	0.8	4.4	0.03	0.08	0.2

Source: China Statistical Yearbook, 1996, 2002, 2008.
Note: Asia* is defined as Asia excluding Japan, Hong Kong, Taiwan, the Republic of Korea and Singapore.

downward bias may therefore exist in our calculations of Southern trade shares for China.

We first begin with the pre-crisis period of 1995–2007. The size of China's trade (imports/exports) with major Southern countries and regions for 1995, 2001, and 2007 are set out in Table 1. The absolute value of exports to Southern regions and major countries all almost doubled (except Mexico with a nine-fold increase) between 1995 and 2001. Exports in 2007 increased by a factor of more than six to every region compared to 2001, with China's exports to India increasing by a factor of 13 between 2001 and 2007. China's imports from the South increased about two times (except India and Mexico with factors over four) between 1995 and 2001, and simultaneously imports increased by factors of more than six between 2001 and 2007 with imports from India and Brazil increasing by factors of more than 8 over the same period. China's 2007 exports to and imports from the South were 21% and 35% of total trade respectively. Over 70% of China's Southern trade is with developing countries in Asia.

Thus, trade has increased steadily over time with dramatic changes taking place between 2001 and 2007. Table 2 reports both China's imports and exports with Southern countries and shares of trade for each year

Table 2. China's Exports and Imports from the South, 1995–2007 (Billions of USD).

	Exports to the South	Imports from the South	Southern exports as % of total Chinese exports	Southern imports as % of total Chinese imports
1995	19.9	16.4	13.4	12.4
1996	19.1	19.2	12.6	13.9
1997	24.3	22.8	13.3	16.0
1998	25.0	20.8	13.6	14.8
1999	26.4	25.6	13.6	15.4
2000	36.3	47.6	14.6	21.2
2001	40.4	50.6	15.2	20.8
2002	51.8	67.6	15.9	22.9
2003	71.0	107.9	16.2	26.2
2004	99.1	159.7	16.7	28.5
2005	132.0	208.7	17.3	31.6
2006	183.1	267.4	18.9	33.8
2007	261.1	338.3	21.4	35.4

Source: Authors' calculations based on data from the China Statistical Yearbook, 1996–2008.

between 1995 and 2007. The growth in both the size of this trade and the trade share with the South are evident, especially from 2002 when China attained both higher overall GDP growth and export growth of 25% per year. The 2002–2007 period also corresponds to proportionally stronger GDP growth in non-OECD than OECD countries.

The average annual growth rates of Southern trade for China are reported in Table 3 for sub-periods from 1995 to 2007. China's trade growth with Southern regions and major countries is remarkably high, with the highest (Indian–Chinese) trade running at 35% per year over the whole period and accelerating to 64% on the export side in 2007. We have also calculated the growth rates on both exports and imports with Northern countries over the same period and sub-periods. The growth rates of China's Southern trade across all time periods are much higher than those of Northern trade. On the export side, China's exports to India are the highest; growth rates of exports to Brazil are also high. On the import side, China's imports from Africa increased most from 1995 to 2007, but these growth rates have slowed in recent years. The same is true of Asia* and the South as a whole. Growth rates of imports from Latin America, Brazil and South Africa are set to continue increasing quickly.

China's entry into WTO also seems to have had significant impacts on China's Southern trade. Kowalski and Shepherd (2006) observe that trade barriers affecting South–South trade are much higher than those

Table 3. Average Annual Growth Rates of China's Trade, 1995–2007 (%).

	Export			Import		
Region/Country	1995–2000	2000–2005	2007	1995–2000	2000–2005	2007
Asia*	25.4	37.0	43.1	30.6	27.1	22.7
Africa	27.4	39.3	39.8	40.3	32.5	26.4
Latin America	27.7	41.7	43.1	30.1	33.4	49.6
South (above)	25.9	38.2	42.6	31.0	28.4	26.5
North (rest of the world)	18.9	24.8	22.0	15.0	15.4	18.2
Of South:						
India	35.4	59.5	64.7	37.4	24.9	42.2
Indonesia	24.3	26.7	33.4	18.1	19.9	29.0
Brazil	34.3	46.1	54.1	28.3	28.8	42.1
North Africa	28.0	36.4	28.8	23.1	32.3	62.0

Source: Authors' calculations based on data from the China Statistical Yearbook, 1996–2008.

Note: "North" refers to the rest of the world, excluding the South as defined above. It includes Europe, North America, Oceanic and Pacific Islands, and developed countries and regions in Asia, such as Japan, Hong Kong of China, Taiwan of China, Republic of Korea, and Singapore.

affecting North–North or North–South trades, according to data from 1985 to 2002. Their econometric analysis suggests that South–South trade is more sensitive to tariff reductions. Their simulation also suggests that China would gain more than twice as much from liberalizing trade with Latin American, MENA and sub-Saharan countries as it would from liberalization with other Asian countries.

China's Southern trade performance after its entry into the WTO supports this position. We have calculated changes in average growth rates for sub-periods before and after 2001. These are reported in Table 4. On the export side, growth rates after 2001 accelerated by at least 40% compared to those before 2001 (Indonesia), and increased three-fold in the most extreme case (India). On the import side, growth rates increased by at least 10% (Africa, before 2001 had a high growth of 39%), with a maximum of 1.8 times (North Africa). For total Southern trade, growth rates of both exports and imports doubled after 2001. These large differences in the growth rates of China's Southern and Northern trade reflect the trend of rapid growth in China's Southern trade after 2001.

Table 5 reports the differences in growth rates of China's Southern and total trade by year. Difference in growth rates fluctuate substantially between 1995 and 2007, but yearly variation decreases after China's entry into WTO, and is consistently positive with acceleration later in the period.

Table 4. Average Annual Growth Rates in China's Trade with the South Before/After 2001 (%).

	Export			Import		
Region/Country	1995–2001	2002–2007	Change	1995–2001	2002–2007	Change
Asia*	15.6	37.0	2.4	25.3	36.8	1.5
Africa	20.0	35.9	1.8	38.8	42.0	1.1
Latin America	20.1	36.5	1.8	20.3	41.6	2.0
South (above)	16.8	36.6	2.2	25.2	37.8	1.5
North (rest of world)	11.7	27.3	2.3	9.6	21.2	2.2
In the South:						
India	19.7	53.7	2.7	30.1	46.0	1.5
Indonesia	20.7	28.5	1.4	15.2	21.5	1.4
Brazil	25.9	44.1	1.7	15.8	42.9	2.7
North Africa	18.5	39.1	2.1	12.7	35.2	2.8

Source: Authors' calculations based on data from the China Statistical Yearbook, 1996–2008.
Note: "Change" = Growth rate after 2001/Growth rate before 2001.

Table 5. Growth Rates of China's South Trade and Total Trade (%).

	Export to			Import from		
	South	World	Difference	South	World	Difference
1995	37.2	23.0	14.2	33.8	14.2	19.5
1996	−4.1	1.5	−5.6	17.5	5.1	12.4
1997	27.4	21.0	6.4	18.5	2.5	16.0
1998	3.0	0.5	2.5	−8.8	−1.5	−7.2
1999	5.4	6.1	−0.6	22.9	18.2	4.7
2000	37.3	27.8	9.5	86.1	35.8	50.3
2001	11.3	6.8	4.5	6.3	8.2	−2.0
2002	28.2	22.3	5.8	33.7	21.2	12.5
2003	37.2	34.6	2.6	59.6	39.8	19.8
2004	39.6	35.4	4.2	48.0	36.0	12.0
2005	33.2	28.4	4.8	30.7	17.6	13.1
2006	38.7	27.2	11.5	28.1	19.9	8.2
2007	42.6	25.7	16.9	26.5	20.8	5.8
Average	25.9	20.0	5.9	31.0	18.3	12.7

Source: Authors' calculations based on data from the China Statistical Yearbook, 1996–2008.

We can also compare the growth rates of China's Southern trade to those of worldwide South–South trade. These data are given in Table 6 and show China's share of South–South trade growing for a little over 3% to 9% on the export side and 12% on the import side by 2006. World South–South

Table 6. Comparing Growth Rates of China's and World's South–South Trade (%).

	Growth rate of Southern trade in exports		China's export share in	Growth rate of Southern trade of imports		China's imports share in
	China	The world	Southern trade	China	The world	Southern trade
1995	37.2	22.7	3.4	33.8	23.0	3.0
1996	−4.1	9.3	3.0	17.5	9.8	3.2
1997	27.4	8.3	3.5	18.5	7.4	3.5
1998	3.0	−12.9	4.2	−8.8	−10.7	3.6
1999	5.4	6.2	4.2	22.9	8.1	4.0
2000	37.3	26.4	4.5	86.1	25.5	6.0
2001	11.3	−4.6	5.3	6.3	−2.3	6.5
2002	28.2	10.7	6.1	33.7	8.6	8.0
2003	37.2	23.4	6.8	59.6	22.0	10.5
2004	39.6	30.6	7.3	48.0	35.2	11.5
2005	33.2	21.7	7.9	30.7	21.8	12.3
2006	38.7	22.3	9.0	28.1	23.4	12.8
2007	42.6	12.9	11.4	26.5		

Source: China's data is from the authors' calculations based on the China Statistical Yearbook, 1996–2008. World data for 1995–2006 is from the authors' calculations based on UNCTAD International Merchandise Trade Database. World South–South export data for 2007 is from the authors' calculations based on Lynn (2009).

trade tends to be dominated by inter-regional trade, and these shares are considerably smaller than Southern trade in China's trade. According to Kowalski and Shepherd (2006), world South–South trade has expanded much more rapidly than either North–North or North–South trade, though it started from a much lower base. We note that the South–South trade growth rate data reported by Kowalski and Shepherd (2006) used the World Bank's definition of low- and middle-income countries as having per capita gross national income not exceeding US$ 9075 in 2003 as the South. Thus the country coverage of world South–South trade is different from our definition for China's trade. But using these two data sources, China's Southern trade growth was more rapid than world South–South trade and this is reflected in China's Southern trade share of world South–South trade which increased continually between 1995 and 2002. For 2007, this ratio is likely higher given the growth in China's trade.

The product composition of China's trade with the South is reported in Table 7. On the export side, the export shares of most products decreased sharply after China's entry into the WTO. The South dominated China's export in (and before) 1999, with over 90% of chemicals and

Table 7. Product Composition of China's Southern Trade Shares in 1999–2007 (%).

Item	Exports to the South			Imports from the South		
Year	1999	2004	2007	1999	2004	2007
Oil	17.3	39.3	34.5	37.0	54.0	78.9
Minerals (excluding oil)	69.7	17.8	24.2	56.3	65.0	63.8
Base metals and related products	61.1	18.9	28.7	8.0	18.3	25.8
Chemicals and related products	92.6	36.1	36.4	9.4	15.2	15.0
Manufactured products	50.2	13.6	17.0	4.8	11.9	28.1

Source: Authors' calculations. Data for 1999 and 2004 are based on the China Customs Statistical Yearbook 1999 and 2004 respectively. Data for 2007 are based on the DRCNET (Development Research Center of the State Council of China) database.
Note: Manufacturing products here include electrical and mechanical products, audio and video equipment and related accessories, vehicles, aircrafts, ships, and other transportation equipments, optical instruments, medical instruments, timepieces, musical instruments, and miscellaneous manufactures.

related products, and over half of minerals, base metals and manufacturing products. While the volume of China's Southern exports keep growing (see the growth rates of Southern market above), the fact that Southern shares decreased steadily suggests a more balanced Chinese export market structure and intensified competition in the world market. On the import side, the South is an important provider of strategic raw materials for China, and one of growing importance. The South accounts for 37% and 79% of China's oil imports and 56% and 64% of mineral imports in 1999 and 2007 respectively. For other product groups, China's Southern imports at least doubled, and imports of base metals and related products trebled between 1999 and 2007. In short, China's economic linkage with the South has also deepened in every industry group.

All this data thus points in one direction. China's trade involvement with the South is growing rapidly and at an accelerating rate. The strongest trends, of this trade seem to be with other large and rapidly expanding Southern economies such as India and Brazil.

3. China's Future Trade with the South

Next we turn to some projections of China's future Southern trade based on the annual country trade growth rates that applied from 2005 to 2007, which we report in Table 8. These projections strongly suggest growing Southern trade for China, but the speed and implications for the trading system are striking. In Table 8 we report what could happen if China's Southern trade

Table 8. Forward Projections of China's Imports and Exports with the South Assuming 2005–2007 Growth Rates (Billion USD).

Region/Country	Item	2010	2015	2020
Asia*	Export	443.1	2139.4	10330.4
	Import	515.2	1709.4	5671.9
Africa	Export	100.8	528.4	2769.8
	Import	84.6	346.1	1414.9
Latin America	Export	146.6	836.7	4776.5
	Import	121.4	512.8	2167.2
Total South	Export	690.4	3504.5	17876.7
	Import	721.2	2568.3	9253.9
Total North	Export	1902.6	6285.5	21869.7
	Import	963.3	2075.2	4645.8
Total China	Export	2593.0	9789.9	39746.5
	Import	1684.5	4643.5	13899.8
India	Export	97.4	1003.9	10351.4
	Import	28.5	86.5	262.7
Indonesia	Export	25.6	83.5	272.2
	Import	21.4	53.1	131.7
Brazil	Export	35.5	236.3	1574.4
	Import	39.2	139.2	493.9
North Africa	Export	18.8	88.9	419.6
	Import	15.3	62.2	252.3

Source: Authors' calculations.

were to keep growing at these rates out to different dates. We also assume China's trade with the world grows at rates applying in 2005–2007. For these projections, the sum of China's Southern and Northern trade in the year yields China's total trade, and we project trade levels with the South in the future.

According to these projections, China's trade with the South will rapidly grow. Though at present China's Southern trade is substantially less than half of China's total trade, its more rapid growth implies China's southern export and import shares will continue to climb. Also, as China's exports grow more rapidly than imports, China's trade surplus keeps growing. If China's trade with India were to keep growing as it did during 2005 to 2007, India will become China's largest market in about 10 years, and China's trade with the South will be about twice of that with the North. Even though China's productivity growth, the absorptive capacities of Indian and Brazilian markets, and countries' economic growth in the mid and long term are uncertain, these projections indicate what could happen if China's Southern trade was to keep growing at 2005–2007 rates.

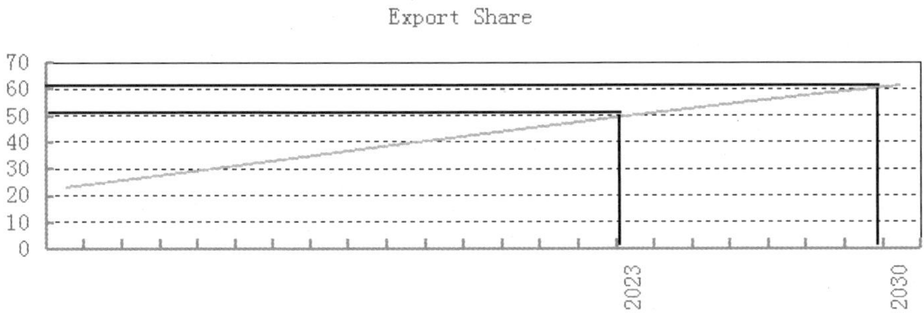

Fig. 1. Projections of China's Southern export share.
Source: Authors' calculations.

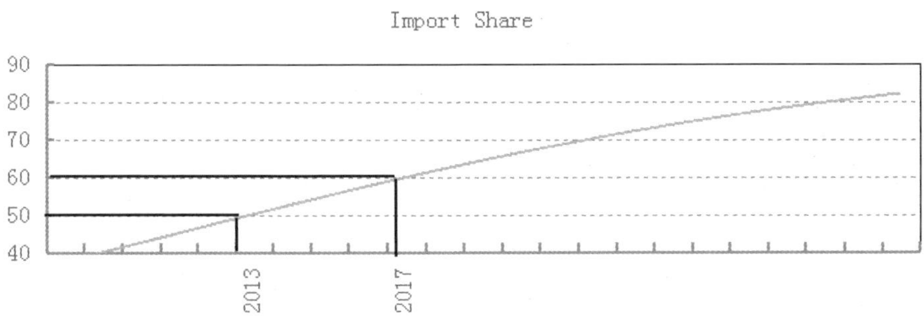

Fig. 2. Projections of China's Southern import share.
Source: Authors' calculations.

Using the same assumptions, we can also project when China's Southern trade will dominant China's foreign trade. These projections are shown in Figs. 1 and 2. China's exports to the South will exceed 50% and 60% of China's total exports by 2023 and 2030 respectively, and imports from the South will exceed 50% and 60% of China's total imports by 2013 and 2017 respectively. South–South trade will exceed 50% of China's total trade by 2020, and will exceed 60% by 2027. The South will surprisingly soon be China's major trade partner if such growth rates are maintained.

4. China's FDI Flows with the South

Besides trade, China has also experienced growing interactions with Southern economies through FDI flows, and especially through outflows from China. Both FDI inflows and outflows began from very small bases in the 1990s, but outflows have experienced very rapid growth in the last few years. As with trade, we can evaluate whether China's Southern investment (both inflows and outflows) grew more quickly than China's total foreign investment flows. In passing, we note that the South here is the South as above, and exclude the Cayman Islands and the British Virgin Islands (which are both large recipients of Chinese outward FDI) as tax-haven based conduits. Both of them rank in the top 5 destinations of Chinese outward FDI.

Before China's entry into the WTO, China's outward investment was very small. Data on China's Southern investment activity is reported in Tables 9 and 10. Table 9 reports the levels involved for various sub-regions and Table 10 gives the breakdown of countries for 2007. Total Chinese outward foreign investment over the whole 1978–2001 period was only US$8.4 billion, in contrast to annual flows today of over US$2 billion. There was also a lack of statistics before 2003, although we can still calculate growth rates for China's foreign investment using the limited information available.

China's FDI inflows increase from an average of $45 billion between 1997–2002 and to $74 billion in 2007 and the Southern share increases from 3.2% to 6.2%. On the outflow side, outflows grow from $2.8 billion in 2003 to $26 billion in 2007, and the Southern share doubles from 8% to 16.5%. Much more rapid growth therefore occurs for the Southern share than for the Northern share and the changes (from a small base) is larger than for trade. Also, by region and country the geographical composition of FDI flows are more balanced than is the case with trade. According to the World Investment Report (2008), global FDI inflows rose in 2007 by 30% to reach $1,833 billion and surpassed the previous all-time high set in

Table 9. Average China's FDI Inflows and Outflows to the South and the World Over Sub-periods between 1997 and 2007 (Millions of USD, %).

	Inflows from			Outflows to		
	South	World	South share	South	World	South share
1997–2002 (Average)	1690.3	45229.0	3.7	NA	NA	NA
2003–2006 (Average)	3064.5	59369.9	5.2	760.9	9561.9	8.0
2007	4669.1	74767.9	6.2	4366.4	26506.1	16.5

Source: Authors' calculations. The inflow data is based on the China Statistical Yearbook 2008. The outflow data is from the 2007 Statistical Bulletin of China's Outward Foreign Direct Investment.

Note: The inflow data is from China's foreign direct investment flows, and is smaller than the data from the UNCTAD database. The outflow data refers to non-financial outward FDI flows.

Table 10. China's FDI Inflows and Outflows to and from the South in Recent Years (Millions of USD).

	Inflows			Outflows		
Region	2003	2007	2007/2003	2003	2007	2007/2003
Asia*	1423.2	2187.5	1.5	198.0	2367.4	12.0
Africa	617.8	1486.8	2.4	74.8	1574.3	21.0
Latin America*	263.6	994.8	3.8	21.9	424.7	19.4
South (Total above)	2304.6	4669.1	2.0	294.6	4366.4	14.8
Of Which:		Inflows			Outflows	
India	15.9	34.0	2.1	0.2	22.0	146.8
Brazil	16.7	31.6	1.9	6.7	51.1	7.7
North Africa	32.5	69.2	2.1	8.9	454.4	51.3
ASEAN*	867.0	1206.7	1.4	122.5	570.4	4.7
ASEAN	2925.4	4391.2	1.5	119.3	968.1	8.1

Source: China Statistical Yearbook 2008, Statistical Bulletin of China's Outward Foreign Direct Investment 2007.
Note: ASEAN* denotes ASEAN except Singapore.

Table 11. Average Annual Growth Rates of China's FDI Flows with the South and North (%).

	China's inflows			China's outflow		
Region/Country	1998–2007	2005–2007	2007	2004–2007	2005–2007	2007
Asia*	6.5	7.1	11.4	115.9	140.3	343.9
Africa	35.8	24.6	22.1	145.8	86.3	202.8
Latin America*	32.4	64.7	21.4	165.5	115.1	333.7
South (Above)	13.2	18.2	16.7	118.0	112.5	279.3
North (rest of the world)	5.5	7.6	19.7	75.9	120.1	157.7
Of South:						
India	356.9	39.9	−35.0	866.2	1110.5	292.5
Brazil	202.4	21.0	−43.1	126.2	169.4	406.7
North Africa	100.4	−13.6	−27.1	368.2	457.3	1015.4
ASEAN*	5.0	4.9	10.6	60.5	73.8	180.1
ASEAN	3.6	13.2	31.0	86.4	94.0	181.1

Source: Authors' calculations based on data from the China Statistical Yearbook 1996–2008 and the Statistical Bulletin of China's Outward Foreign Direct Investment 2007.

2000, for developing countries FDI inflows also reached their highest level, with China the largest recipient among developing countries.

Table 11 reports the annual average growth rates of China's FDI flows by region and country. The contrast between Northern and Southern flows is striking. Inflows from the South grew substantially, but decreased in 2007 with sharp country declines for India, Brazil and North Africa. The growth rates on the outflows side from China were dramatically different with a growth rate in 2007 of several hundred percent. According to the World Investment Report, FDI inflows into developing countries experienced a 21% increase over 2006. This is almost the same as the growth rates of African and Latin American FDI investment in China, but a slower growth rate than that of Asian developing countries FDI into China — China's Southern FDI inflow increased by only 16.7%. In 2007, FDI outflows from South, East and South–East Asia reached a new high with a growth rate of 46%.

Table 12 reports growth rates of China's Southern FDI and total FDI. Here the striking feature on the inflow side is the persistently higher growth rate of Southern origin FDI. On the outflow side, there is sharp volatility in relative North–South outflows both of which grow. However, in 2007 there is a significantly higher outflow to the South that resulted in a higher averaged growth rate over the period 2004–2007.

As with trade, the picture conveyed by FDI data is one of accelerating integration with the South through FDI flows, and especially on the outflow side. As with trade, we can project China's FDI with regions and major countries if we assume that growth rates between 2005 and 2007 remain unchanged in the future. Again, the sum of Southern and Northern projected FDI yields China's total FDI.

According to these calculations (reported in Table 13), China's FDI inflows and outflows will grow very quickly if growth rates between 2005

Table 12. Growth Rates of China's Southern FDI and Total FDI (%).

	Inflow from			Outflow to		
	South	World	Difference	South	World	Difference
1998	13.5	0.5	13.0	NA	NA	NA
1999	−19.3	−11.3	−8.0	NA	NA	NA
2000	15.7	1.0	14.8	NA	NA	NA
2001	15.8	15.1	0.7	NA	NA	NA
2002	28.1	12.5	15.6	NA	NA	NA
2003	−0.1	1.4	−1.6	NA	NA	NA
2004	23.4	13.3	10.0	134.4	92.6	41.8
2005	9.4	−0.5	9.9	31.4	123.0	−91.7
2006	28.6	4.5	24.1	26.9	43.8	−16.9
2007	16.7	18.6	−1.9	279.3	50.3	229.0
Average	13.2	5.5	7.7	118.0	77.4	40.6

Source: Authors' calculations based on data from the China Statistical Yearbook 1996–2008 and the Statistical Bulletin of China's Outward Foreign Direct Investment 2007.

Table 13. Forward Projections of China's FDI Inflows and Outflows by Region (Billions of USD).

Region/Country	Item	2010	2020	2030
Asia*	Inflow	2.7	5.3	10.6
	Outflow	32.9	210981.9	1354922553.4
Africa	Inflow	2.9	26.0	235.0
	Outflow	10.2	5132.9	2587509.0
Latin America*	Inflow	4.4	650.9	95400.3
	Outflow	4.2	8956.4	18982149.4
Total South	Inflow	10.0	682.3	95645.9
	Outflow	47.3	225071.3	1.4E+09
Total North	Inflow	107.5	1058.8	18153.1
	Outflow	197.3	295224704.3	8.6E+15
Total China	Inflow	117.5	1741.1	113799.1
	Outflow	244.6	295449775.6	8.6E+15
Of South:				
India	Inflow	0.1	2.7	76.6
	Outflow	39.1	2.6E+12	1.8E+23
Brazil	Inflow	0.1	0.4	2.5
	Outflow	1.0	20157.9	4.1E+08
ASEAN*	Inflow	1.4	2.2	3.6
	Outflow	3.0	753.4	189552.8

Source: Authors' calculations.

and 2007 remain. More striking growth would occur on the outflows side. China's outward investment boomed in recent years and its growth rates between 2005 to 2007 were very large. China's investments in India, for instance, increased eleven-fold in these years. These projections thus paint a dramatic picture, but China would still be a large FDI source even if these growth rates were halved.

Since the markets of developed countries are the main destination for China's outward investments and have had higher growth rates in recent years than the South, these projections suggest that the Southern share of China's total outward investments will decline in the future. For inflows, the situation is quite the opposite. China's FDI inflows from the South grew more rapidly in recent years than from the North, with the result that China's FDI inflows from the South exceeded 50% and 60% of China's total FDI inflow by 2022 and 2024 respectively. These projections are displayed in Fig. 3.

5. The Financial Crisis and China's Southern Trade and FDI

China's export-oriented economy has been affected severely by the financial crisis. Here, we report preliminary data for 2008 and 2009 on trade, FDI

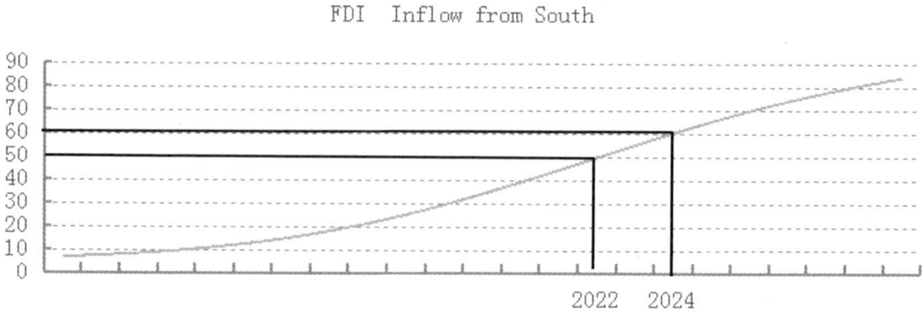

Fig. 3. Projections of Southern FDI inflow share for China.
Source: Authors' calculations.

Table 14. China's Southern Trade, Post-financial Crisis (Billions of USD).

	Exports			Imports		
Region	2008	2009 Q1	2009 Q2	2008	2009 Q1	2009 Q2
Asia*	225.1	39.5	47.7	303.4	46.9	60.4
Africa	51.2	10.1	11.7	56.0	5.7	9.5
Latin America	71.8	10.5	12.6	71.6	9.4	16.5
South (Total above)	348.1	60.1	72.1	431.0	61.9	86.4
Of which:		Exports			Imports	
India	31.6	6.0	7.0	20.3	3.3	3.3
Indonesia	17.2	2.6	3.5	14.3	2.3	3.3
Thailand	15.6	2.6	2.9	25.7	4.4	6.0
Malaysia	21.5	3.6	4.7	32.1	5.6	7.1
Vietnam	15.1	2.8	3.6	4.3	0.9	1.2
Brazil	18.8	2.3	2.7	29.9	3.4	8.0
Argentina	5.1	0.6	0.8	9.4	0.9	1.2
Mexico	13.9	2.3	2.8	3.7	0.8	0.9
North Africa	8.6	1.6	1.6	9.2	1.5	2.2
Egypt	5.9	1.1	1.3	0.4	0.0	0.1

Source: Data for 2009 Q2 was calculated by the authors using available January to June data from the China Customs Statistics.

flows and shares in the South. For trade data, the absolute values of China's Southern trade are considerably higher in 2008 than 2007, but decrease substantially in Spring 2009 and increase again in Summer 2009. Trade levels in 2009 Q2 are still far lower than 2008 levels. Detailed data by country and region is reported in Table 14.

Table 15 reports growth rates of China's Southern trade post-crisis. Here, we see that China's Southern trade played a more important role after the crisis. China's Southern trade grew by more than 30% in 2008; in

Table 15. Growth Rates of China's Trade, Post-financial Crisis (%).

Region	Exports			Imports		
	2008	2009 Q1	2009 Q2	2008	2009 Q1	2009 Q2
Asia*	30.7	−14.9	−16.8	20.9	−34.2	−24.2
Africa	37.4	0.7	−9.4	53.9	−59.2	−41.2
Latin America	39.2	−24.7	−30.4	40.2	−35.8	−15.6
South	33.3	−14.6	−18.5	27.4	−37.9	−25.1
North	13.2	−20.9	−24.6	15.8	−23.1	−15.1
Total China	17.5	−19.7	−23.4	18.5	−30.7	−20.3
Of South:		Exports			Imports	
India	31.5	−12.7	−19.9	38.6	−47.7	−53.2
Indonesia	36.4	−25.9	−20.9	15.6	−38.0	−20.2
Thailand	30.0	−26.8	−30.0	13.2	−29.2	−6.4
Malaysia	21.5	−23.2	−12.2	11.8	−25.0	−16.9
Vietnam	26.9	−30.3	−17.5	34.4	−14.1	21.6
Brazil	65.4	−36.2	−43.1	62.8	−29.4	−1.1
Argentina	41.7	−46.3	−46.3	49.2	−47.2	−30.8
Mexico	18.8	−17.7	−23.2	12.1	−9.3	−7.2
North Africa	16.0	−16.3	−25.5	39.5	−22.6	−15.9
Egypt	34.1	−14.0	−10.2	100.0	−31.9	−57.7

Source: Authors' calculations based on data from the China Customs Statistics.

contrast, China's Northern growth rate was only 13%. China's total trade grew by 18% in 2008. Compared with the same period in 2008, China's trade with almost every market shrank during Spring and Summer 2009 (except exports to Africa, which increased 0.7% in 2009 Q1 and imports from Vietnam, which increased 22% in 2009 Q2). On the export side, China's Southern trade fell less than Northern trade during the first half of 2009, with the Latin American trade falling the most. On the import side, China's Northern trade performed better than Southern trade. Imports from India were only half that of Spring and Summer 2008.

Table 16 suggests that while China's imports from the South in Summer 2009 increased at a slower rate than the previous year, they grew more rapidly compared to Spring 2009. This raised the share of Southern trade, which increased in Summer 2009. China's export to and import from the South in 2009 Q2 were 26% and 36% of the total trade respectively, marking an increase by 1.6 and 3 points respectively over 2009 Q1. The share of exports is higher than that of 2008, but the share of imports is still lower by 2.3 points than that of 2008. This suggest that China's Southern trade has played a more prominent role in China's trade recovery on the export side. The relative fall on the import side reflects lower oil prices and large oil imports from Africa.

Table 16. China's Southern Trade Shares, Post-financial Crisis (%).

	Exports			Imports		
Region	2008	2009 Q1	2009 Q2	2008	2009 Q1	2009 Q2
Asia*	15.7	16.1	17.3	26.8	25.6	25.0
Africa	3.6	4.1	4.2	4.9	3.1	4.0
Latin America	5.0	4.3	4.6	6.3	5.1	6.8
South	24.3	24.5	26.1	38.1	33.8	35.8

Source: Authors' calculations based on the data from the China Customs Statistics.

Compared with global FDI inflows which decreased sharply in 2008, China's foreign direct investment flows point a different picture. As Table 17 indicates, both Southern and Northern FDI to China grew by over 20% in 2008, which gives China FDI an inflow growth rate of 24%. By region, Latin American FDI in China increased the most, at 81%. By country, Indian FDI in China increased by 158%. China's outward investment flows also saw dramatic growth, except to Latin America. Total outflows doubled in 2008 and outflows to Africa and South Africa increased by 249% and 958% respectively. Investments involved with India also grew rapidly with an inflow growth of 159% and an outflow growth of 363%. The rapid growth of outward FDI flows partly reflects the severity of the financial crisis on Chinese domestic enterprises, especially on foreign trade enterprises, as these enterprises looked abroad to seek profits.

6. Institutional Dimensions of China's Growing Southern Linkage

China's growing trade and investment links are matched by growing institutional linkages with the South. These are a result of China and other developing countries recognizing common interests, and so China should emphasize the strengthening of cooperation with other developing countries as the starting point for China's Southern diplomacy. As Wen Jiabao indicated in 2004, China has good political relationships with other developing countries and economic cooperation should bring with it mutual empowerment. China thus seeks to combine trade and investment as well as foreign aid to deepen multilateral and regional cooperation with developing countries, and safeguard the interests of developing countries in international trade organizations and multilateral mechanisms.

China's diplomatic initiatives toward the South are thus reflective of the growing economic interest in the South. After China's entry into

Table 17. China's FDI Flows with the South in 2008 (Millions of USD, %).

	Inflows		Outflows	
	Size	Growth rate	Size	Growth rate
Asia*	2187.1	0.0	3201.0	35.2
Africa	1667.9	12.2	5490.6	248.8
Latin America*	1804.6	81.4	48.9	−88.5
South (All above)	5659.6	21.2	8740.4	100.2
North	85843.9	23.4	47166.7	113.0
World	92395.4	23.6	55907.2	110.9
Of South:	Inflows		Outflows	
India	88.1	158.7	101.9	362.7
Brazil	38.8	22.6	22.4	−56.2
South Africa	25.6	−63.0	4807.9	958.0
ASEAN*	1025.7	−15.0	933.4	63.7
ASEAN	5461.0	24.4	2484.4	156.6

Source: Inflow data obtained from the China Yearbook 2009. Outflow data obtained from China's Statistical Bulletin of Outward Foreign Direct Investment for the same year.

WTO, China's foreign trade policies focused on two major areas. One was to support the WTO system and the others were to try to play a more important role in negotiations. China first tried to strengthen cooperation, especially with developing countries, and emphasize links to least developing countries and small economies. Another was to deepen bilateral and regional trade cooperation, and especially building FTAs. This began with adjacent countries, then extended to a wider area, and especially emerging economies such as Africa and Latin America. At the same time, China sought closer cooperation with energy and strategic material suppliers, especially Arab countries.

China's regional free trade arrangements with developing countries started when China joined the Bangkok Agreement in 2001. The Bangkok Agreement settled the origin of products eligible for preferential concessions among members. China then concluded a Framework Agreement on Comprehensive Economic Cooperation between China and ASEAN in 2002, a starting point at China's FTAs. They then agreed tariff concessions from 2005 and will now build a China and ASEAN Free Trade Area (CAFTA) by 2015.

With FTAs in place with both ASEAN and Pakistan, China already has closer trade relationships with most major developing countries in Asia except India, although here there is the prospect of an agreement. In April

2005, during Wen Jiabao's visit to India, the two governments announced a joint feasibility study on a China–India regional trade arrangement. The study was completed in October 2007 and reached a consensus on trade in goods, trade in services, investment, trade facilitation, and economic cooperation. Formal negotiations for a China–India FTA have not commenced, and the progress of bilateral FTA negotiations between China and India is slower than that between India and Japan and Korea.

China has also reached agreements with Africa. Given the good political relations between China and Africa since 1949, and the simultaneous liberalization of the two countries in the 1970s, economic cooperation between China and Africa has grown rapidly (Zhang Qingmin, 2007). Evidence of this is the Forum on China–Africa Cooperation jointly set up by China and Africa in October 2000. China made major commitments including relief of RMB 10 billion of debts for African countries. China also gave some least-developed African countries tariff-free treatment for 190 tariff headings of goods. This tariff preference was later extended to nearly 500 tariff headings. Negotiations on a China–SACU (Southern Africa Customs Union, including North Africa, Botswana, Namibia, Lesotho, and Swaziland) FTA started in 2004, and South Africa recognized China's market economy status at the same time. Both sides are now pushing forward with negotiations.

China's relationship with Latin America has also developed rapidly following the increased openness of developing countries in Latin America from the end of the 1980s. A China–Chile FTA was signed in 2005 and covers trade issues, such as market access, rules of origin, sanitary and phytosanitary measures, technical trade barriers, trade remedies, dispute settlement mechanisms. A China–Chile investment agreement is now under negotiation. Also, a China–Costa Rica FTA is now under negotiation. A feasible study was completed in 2008 and three negotiations have been carried out until now and some progress has been made on trade in goods and services.

A China–Peru FTA was signed in 2009. On the trade in goods side, over 90% of Chinese and Peruvian goods will be zero tariff in stages. On services, both countries will open further their service markets to each other, based on WTO commitments. On the investment side, both countries will grant investors national treatment and most favoured nation treatment. China and Peru also reached consensus in other fields such as intellectual property rights, trade remedies, rules of origin, customs procedures, technical barriers to trade, and sanitary and phytosanitary measures.

The China–Peru FTA has become a symbol for new bilateral relations between China and other developing countries in Latin America. For instance, Brazil is a founding member of the Rio Group, a member of MERCOSUR (Southern Common Market), a leading member of the Group 77 and the Group 15, an observer of the Non-Aligned Movement, and is rich in minerals and oil. Chinese and Brazilian governments have proposed in-depth consultations on issues of common interest such as an FTA (China–Brazil Joint Communique 2004). Economic cooperation between China and Brazil has become closer in recent years and China has become the largest trading partner of Brazil in 2009. Lula sought to strengthen cooperation between these two countries and to play a greater role in dealing with global financial crisis when he visited China in April 2009. During this visit, Brazil and China signed cooperation protocols involving fields such as agriculture, science and technology, space, energy, ports cooperation, mining, renewable energy and so on. With these, a "loans-for-oil" deal over 10 years involving 10 billion between the China Development Bank and the Brazilian national oil company (Petrobras) was signed. Further, the two governments planned a Joint Action Plan 2010–2014.

FTA negotiations between China and the Gulf Cooperation Council (CCC, including Saudi Arabia, United Arab Emirates, Oman, Kuwait, Qatar, and Bahrain) started in 2004, and have reached a consensus in most merchandise trade areas after four rounds of negotiation. A negotiation on trade in service has since been underway. To promote FDI investment, China has also negotiated double taxation tax treaties with 89 countries, among them India, Brazil, Indonesia, South Africa, Egypt, Nigeria and other 59 developing countries.

The picture is therefore one of rapidly increasing institutional involvement by China, with the South complementing and supporting growing trade and Southern investment linkage. This, like trade and investment, may well be poised to accelerate further in the next decade.

7. Concluding Remarks

This paper assesses China's growing interactions through trade and FDI with the South. Using Chinese source data, the picture that emerges is one of rapidly growing trade and FDI linkage which (pre-crisis) accelerating has been in recent years. At 2005–2007 growth rates, we project that China's Southern trade will be around 50% by 2015, and in the case of India (where trade increases by a factor of 33% between 1997 and 2007) around 50% by

2023. Initial data show this rapid relative growth in Southern engagement has, if anything, been accelerated further by the financial crisis, especially on the export side.

China is rapidly becoming the manufacturing center of the global economy. With more rapid growth in India, Brazil, Indonesia, and other Southern countries than in the OECD, the prospect is for even more significant Southern investment by China. In FDI flows, this seems to be accelerating even more rapidly, if from a lower base. It would seem that the South is poised to become the epicenter of trade in the global economy by 2030, with China at its hub.

References

China Customs Statistics. China Custom Monthly Report, March 2008–June 2009. Available at http://www.haiguan.info.

China Economic Website: Experts say the possibility of Sino-Indian border conflict have been minimal progress in the negotiations. Available at http://www.ce.cn/xwzx/gnsz/gdxw/200801/19/t20080119_14287133.shtml.

China FTA Network: China's Free Trade Agreements. Available at http://fta.mofcom.gov.cn/topic/enperu.shtml.

China Statistics Yearbook (2009). China Statistics Press.

Fenghuang News Website: India's Foreign Trade Policy 2009–2014. Available at http://finance.ifeng.com/roll/20090911/1227546.shtml.

Kowalski, P. and B. Shepherd (2006). South-South TradeIn Goods, *OECD Trade Policy Working Paper, No. 40*, OECD Publishing. doi:10.1787/314103237622.

Lynn, J. (2009). Developing countries turn to South-South trade. Available at http://www.reuters.com/article/idUST-RE5170BC20090208.

Ministry of Commerce of the People's Republic of China. 2007 Statistical Bulletin of China's Outward Foreign Direct Investment. Available at http://hzs.mofcom.gov.cn/accessory/200809/1222502733006.pdf.

Ministry of Commerce of the People's Republic of China (2008). *Statistical Bulletin of China's Outward Foreign Direct Investment.* Available at http://hzs.mofcom.gov.cn/accessory/200909/1253868856016.pdf.

Ministry of Foreign Affairs of Peoples Republic of China. China and Brazil signed Joint Communique, Available at http://www.chineseembassy.org/chn/gxh/zlb/smgg/t118446.htm.

National Bureau of Statistics of China. *China Statistics Yearbook* 1996–2008. Available at http://www.stats.gov.cn/english/statisticaldata/yearlydata/.

Permanent Mission of the People's Republic of China to the UN. Statement by Ambassador Liu Zhenmin at the 33rd Annual Meeting of Foreign Ministers of the Group of 77, 25 September 2009. Available at http://www.china-un.org/eng/lhghyywj/smhwj/2009/t608134.htm.

UNCTAD (2007). World Investment Report 2007: Transnational Corporations, Extractive Industries and Development. Available at http://www.unctad.org/en/docs/wir2007_en.pdf.

UNCTAD (2008). World Investment Report 2008: Transnational Corporations, and the Infrastructure Challenge. Available at http://www.unctad.org/en/docs/wir2008_en.pdf.

UNCTAD International Merchandise Trade Database. Available at http://www.unctad.org/Templates/Page.asp?intItemID=1890&lang=1.

Xinhua News Agency. Insiders said that China and India have great potential for trade development. Available at http://www.hq.xinhuanet.com/focus/2007-04/22/content_9856992.htm.

Zhang, Q. (2007). China's Foreign Relations, *Foreign Affairs Review*, Vol 94, pp. 22–28.

Part II

China's Trade Policies

CHINA'S NEW REGIONAL TRADE AGREEMENTS*

Agata Antkiewicz
Centre for International Governance Innovation (CIGI), Waterloo

John Whalley
University of Western Ontario, CIGI, NBER, and Peking University

This chapter discusses the recent regional trade agreements that China has concluded rapidly following accession to the WTO in 2002. Agreements are in place with Hong Kong, Macao, ASEAN, Australia, and New Zealand, and are either in negotiation or under discussion with South Africa, Chile, India, and the Gulf Cooperation Council. These agreements differ sharply in form and substance, and involve process commitments to ongoing negotiation and cooperation on a wide range of issues. Differences relating to the regional agreements negotiated by the EU and the US are emphasized, as are later potential difficulties these agreements create in moving to an Asian trade bloc centred on them.

1. Introduction

Most of the recent discussion of Chinese trade policy from outside China has been of China's WTO accession, assessing both the commitments themselves and the process of implementation (Bhattasali, Li, and Martin, 2004; Whalley, 2003). Less attention has been given to the network of post WTO accession regional trade agreements that China is now in the process of negotiating. Agreements, or initial frameworks of agreements are now in place with Hong Kong, Macao, ASEAN, Australia, and New Zealand. Discussions on possible FTAs with India, Chile, Singapore, South Africa, and the Gulf Cooperation Council are underway. Possible direct

*This chapter has been prepared as part of the Economic Governance Programme of the Centre for International Governance Innovation, Waterloo, Ontario. We are grateful to Li Wu Shi, Liang Fan, Yi Ming Wang, Shuming Zhang, and Terry Sicular for comments and discussion. We are grateful to a seminar group at University of Western Ontario for comments.

or indirect arrangements involving Korea and Japan are the subject of speculation. Thus, what we may be witnessing with China's new regional trade agreements is the emergence of a third wave of large power regional agreements which will likely set the precedent for other Chinese regional agreements to follow in future years.

China, like other large powers in the trading system (the US and the EU) has clear incentive to commit to multilateral disciplines in the WTO as a way of gaining non-discriminatory access to large markets and head off discrimination against her either in both these or smaller third country markets by fellow large powers. But closer to home (and as with the US and the EU) China has equally clear incentive to negotiate supplemental regional arrangements which deal with interests in local markets in ways which go beyond WTO disciplines. The US with NAFTA, and the EU with accession and other agreements, have encountered similar incentives with similar results.

But there are several striking features of China's emerging network of agreements which differentiate it both from the one-off negotiation of NAFTA by the US in 1991 and the process of ever deeper EU integration initiated by the 1957 Treaty of Rome. The first is the diversity of these agreements, both in form and coverage. For example, the agreement with Hong Kong is concrete and focused on both goods trade and cross border investment and financial activities, while the agreements with Australia and New Zealand are largely general indicative statements of intent in much wider number of areas. Diversity of approach, while it seems to be the hallmark, potentially makes the later emergence of an Asian trade bloc centred on these agreements more problematical.

A second feature is their seeming brevity, and hence the inevitably vagueness of the texts involved (the Hong Kong and Macao Closer Economic Partnership Agreements (CEPA) have only thirteen pages of main text with additional annexes). Much seems to be left to subsequent joint agreement and mutual management of the trade relationship. A third feature is the absence (unlike the US agreements) of explicit and clear dispute resolution procedures with conciliation between the parties being relied upon. Other features include extensive lists of specific bilateral commitments in services (especially in the case of CEPA) which go beyond the form and type of commitments undertaken by most WTO members in the GATS. Another is extensive attention devoted to arrangements both for joint ventures and the operation of financial institutions in a joint regulatory environment in the Hong Kong Arrangement.

The focus of recent US bilateral initiatives is seemingly on gaining unilateral access for key service sectors in partner countries in return for accelerated bilateral tariff elimination (see Schott, 2004), and of recent EU bilaterals on wider diplomatic linkage to trade and competition policy (see Brenton, 2002) find no parallels in these emerging Chinese agreements. Instead, the emphasis for now is primarily on trade access for manufactures through bilateral tariff reduction/elimination and bilaterally scheduled commitments in services.

The majority of literature on regional trade agreements from economists continues to treat them all as relatively similar in structure, despite the fact that the reality is quite different. Here a third set of agreements, further differentiated from the already different US and EU regional agreements, seem to characterize early Chinese regional negotiation, and more agreements seem likely to follow. We first discuss the Hong Kong CEPA agreement, next the China–ASEAN agreement, and the Australia, New Zealand agreements, and then what seems to be emerging on other fronts. We conclude with a discussion of what the Chinese interest may be in further elaborating this network of treaty arrangements in the future.

2. The Closer Economic Partnership Arrangements with Hong Kong and Macao

China's Closer Economic Partnership Arrangement (CEPA) with Hong Kong was signed on June 29th, 2003, with the stated broad aims of promoting joint economic prosperity and development, and facilitating the further development of economic links between China, Hong Kong, and other countries (regions).[1] It contains 13 pages of text and 6 annexes. Its main content lies in progressive bilateral reduction or elimination of tariff and non-tariff barriers applying to goods trade, reducing bilateral restrictions on service trade, and various steps to further promote bilateral trade and investment. As a formal free trade agreement, the Hong Kong CEPA was notified to WTO on January 12th, 2004.[2] So far a working party has not been established and factual examination by the WTO Committee on Regional Trade Agreements has not yet started.

[1]See Preamble.

[2]See Notification From Parties, WTO WT/REG162/N/1, January 12, 2004, and Minutes of Meeting of the Council for Trade in Goods, WTO G/C/M/72, January 26, 2004.

Under the agreement Hong Kong maintains its current zero-tariff policy towards goods imported from the Mainland, with a staged tariff elimination for goods imported by China from Hong Kong. China agrees to introduce zero tariffs for a list of goods specified in Annex 1 as of January 1st, 2004.[3] Full elimination of bilateral tariffs will occur no later than January 1st, 2006. All goods have to meet CEPA rules of origin (details on these rules are in Annex 2). Imports claiming origin must also be accompanied by a valid Certificate of Origin. To acquire Hong Kong origin a good must have 30% value added in Hong Kong (this includes the value of raw materials, labour costs, component parts, and product development costs). Foreign companies in Hong Kong can export goods to China under CEPA if the products meet the added value requirement.

The Macao Closer Economic Partnership Arrangement is almost identical to the Hong Kong CEPA. The minor differences come from slightly different names of agencies and regulations in Hong Kong and Macao, and the lists of goods in Tables in Annexes 1 & 2 differ in some areas. Everything else is the same including the main text, Rules of Origin, and other requirements for entities operating in the Mainland. The date of signing the documents was October 17th, 2003, and the Macao CEPA has also been notified to WTO (in March 2004).

For non-tariff measures on goods, these agreements specify that neither party is to introduce new quotas or other barriers towards bilateral imports. Neither party will use any-dumping actions against the other. CEPA allows for safeguards actions in goods trade after written notice, but these safeguards measures are seemingly not fully specified.

Bilateral liberalization of trade in services is specified in Annex 4 of both CEPAs. They each list 18 services sectors and specific bilateral commitments in each of the sectors. The list includes (among others): management consulting, advertising, accounting, real estate and construction, logistics, freight forwarding, telecommunications, and legal services. The agreement applies to financial activities, banking, insurance, and securities, and opens financial markets in the Mainland to entities from Hong Kong. CEPA, for example, lowers the required minimum assets for Hong Kong banks that establish branches in China from 20 bn USD to 6 bn USD.

A significant innovation in these agreements is that they define a new services entity, "a Hong Kong service supplier" (Annex 5), which opens

[3]See Table 1 of Annex 1, 273 goods covering medicines, and toys, among others.

doors to Chinese markets for international companies who can utilize this entity.[4] Benefits from the bilateral scheduled commitments in services only apply to this entity. To qualify, such a company must be established in Hong Kong for no less than three years (five years for construction, banking, insurance, and related services), pay applicable profit taxes, have business premises (owned or rented) reflecting business activities in Hong Kong, and employ at least 50% of the staff locally from Hong Kong permanent residents. The intended business in China must be the same as the company's substantive business in Hong Kong, and documentation is required to establish this.

For the purposes of the agreement CEPA recognizes service companies acquired by an overseas company as a Hong Kong service company one year after the merger or acquisition takes place. Any qualifying Hong Kong company operating in China must have a Hong Kong Service Supplier Certificate issued in Hong Kong. Annex 5 excludes any overseas company registered in Hong Kong that is "specifically established for providing certain services to its parent company", e.g. representative offices and "mailbox companies".

Both CEPAs also provide for cooperation in tourism and mutual recognition of professional qualifications. In tourism the Mainland allows the residents of Guangdong to visit Hong Kong and Macao individually (at first on a trial basis in Dongguan, Zhongshan, and Jiangmen, then the entire province). The two countries also state their plan to promote bilateral tourism, jointly promoting programmes centred around the Pearl River Delta, and cooperate in raising the standard of services and protection of tourists. China and Hong Kong (Macao) aim to achieve mutual recognition of professional qualifications. Specific requirements and methodologies for qualification recognition are to be agreed through a consultative process with government authorities and professional bodies in the countries.

CEPAs contain trade and investment facilitation provisions under which China and Hong Kong (Macao) agree on seven areas of cooperation (trade and investment promotion, customs clearance facilitation, cooperation of small and medium sized enterprises, transparency in laws and regulations and others).

The overall coordination and implementation of each CEPA is the sole responsibility of a Joint Steering Committee who are to resolve disputes, and interpret provisions (Article 19). The Committee comprises senior

[4]The Macao CEPA has a similar Macao service supplier company construct.

representatives or officials nominated by the two countries who will meet at least once a year. Special meetings can be held upon 30 days notice or request by either side. The functions of the Steering Committee include supervising the implementation of CEPA, interpreting the provisions of CEPA, resolving disputes, drafting additions and amendments to the content of CEPA, and supervising the working groups. All decisions of the Committee must be made by consensus. Working groups of the Steering Committee are to be set up according to the needs of the parties and Liaison Offices are to be established both in the Chinese Ministry of Commerce and the Hong Kong Commerce, Industry and Technology Bureau (for the Macao CEPA, The Office of the Secretary for Economy and Finance of Macao Special Administrative Region Government).

In August, 2004, further details of the arrangement between China and Hong Kong going beyond what was in the original CEPA were agreed and took the form of a Record of Consultation on Further Liberalization under the Mainland and Hong Kong CEPA. This document states that progress on implementation of CEPA has been smooth and has had a positive impact on both economies, and then expands on the earlier agreement between the two sides.

In goods trade China agrees to apply zero tariffs to the next stage of goods imported from Hong Kong at the beginning of next year (2005). This includes 713 goods (and applies to both existing and planned production) covering food, chemical, mechanical and electronic products. Rules of origin for these goods (which maybe slightly different from those in the original CEPA) are to be concluded no later than October 2004.

In services trade China offers to further relax market access conditions for Hong Kong service suppliers (but without precisely specifying what relaxation is involved). This includes the 11 sectors already specified in the original CEPA, and eight new sectors including (among others): airport, information technology, job intermediaries, and marketing services. Most of these new commitments are to be implemented in January, 2005.

The reaction to and comment on both of the CEPAs has been that since Hong Kong (Macao) is already one of the most open economies in the world and does not apply any significant barriers towards goods and services imported from China, each CEPA is effectively a one-sided series of concessions by Beijing.[5] Before signing the agreement, only about 20%

[5]See *Business Asia*, July 14, 2003.

of all goods trade from Hong Kong to China were tariff free (it was 90% in 2004 after CEPA implementation).[6] To the extent that this is the case, one can argue that China gains little from the CEPAs on the trade front except for the freedom from anti-dumping actions by Hong Kong (Macao) against China.

But these CEPAs will likely have a larger impact on services trade and here joint interests come into play. In most of the specified sectors Hong Kong (Macao) service companies will gain improved access to Chinese markets and sooner than those from other countries waiting for the implementation of China's WTO accession commitments. China promotes Hong Kong service providers over third country competitors, and given the closeness of the relationship involved and with eventual reintegration this may be seen in China as in the Chinese interest. An issue skeptics might bring up is whether local regulations in China may anyway prove to be the binding restriction for Hong Kong companies operating in Mainland, and CEPAs provisions in reality will be of little importance.

China also may be planning to use the CEPAs to attract Hong Kong (Macao) professionals to its services markets so that they can then train Chinese workers.[7] New rules for individual tourists coming to the Mainland from Hong Kong are also seen as a way of bringing the bilateral relationship closer in addition to immaculate economic benefits. These CEPAs may be largely another step in Mainland–Hong Kong (Macao) integration without too much of an impact on the Chinese economy before China–WTO agreements come fully into force in 2007. They are nonetheless precedents for further Chinese regional agreements.

3. The ASEAN–China Agreement

China and ASEAN signed a Framework Agreement on Comprehensive Economic Cooperation in November, 2002. It is less concrete than the CEPAs and only sets out a broad framework for more detailed agreements that are to follow. It contains 21 pages of text and 4 annexes. Its main stated objectives are: economic, trade and investment cooperation, progressive liberalization of trade in goods and services, creation of a liberal and transparent investment regime, and closer economic integration within the region.[8]

[6] See *EIU ViewsWire*, September 30, 2003.
[7] See *China Staff*, February 2004.
[8] See Preamble.

Under the agreement the parties have agreed to work towards the establishment of a Free Trade Area (FTA) between China and ASEAN within 10 years, but precisely what this FTA will comprise and what its institutional underpinnings will remain, for now, unclear. What will be sought in CAFTA will be the elimination of tariffs and non-tariff barriers in goods trade, liberalization of services trade, promotion of bilateral investment within the FTA, and simplification of customs procedures and the establishment of mutual recognition arrangements. The China–ASEAN Agreement has not been notified to WTO, but the eventual CAFTA will presumably be.

Under the agreement, China and ASEAN FTA (CAFTA) with the original ASEAN 6 (Brunei, Indonesia, Malaysia, the Philippines, Singapore, and Thailand) is to be established by 2010 and, by 2015, with the newer ASEAN members (Vietnam, Lao PDR and Myanmar, Cambodia). Bilateral tariffs will be lowered to 0–5% on most goods, and non-tariff barriers are to disappear.

The goods subject to reduction/elimination, along with tariff rates and schedules (involving both a Normal and a Sensitive Track as per Article 3, Paragraph 4 of the agreement) and rules of origin are to be negotiated by the parties, and spelled in more detailed agreements to follow. Any bilaterally agreed safeguard arrangements and disciplines on subsidies, anti-dumping measures are to be based on existing GATT disciplines and are also to be elaborated.

As far as trade in services is concerned, the parties plan to negotiate progressive elimination of all discrimination in new and existing service restrictions (unless permitted under GATS). In the investment area, the parties are to liberalize their investment regimes, strengthen cooperation, and improve transparency of rules and regulations.

A key element in the 2002 ASEAN–China agreement is an Early Harvest Programme set to start in 2004 (Annex 1). The Programme will cut tariffs ahead of the planned establishment of the CAFTA in 2010 (it is also called a "trial move"). Eight categories of agricultural products (about 600 different goods) with exclusions are itemised in Annex 1. Depending on the product category involved, zero tariffs between China and ASEAN 6 under the Early Harvest Programme are to be in place at the latest by 2006, and not later than 2010 between China and the newer members of ASEAN.

The only ASEAN country not to participate in this Early Harvest Programme is the Philippines who argued that their agricultural sector could not withstand the liberalization (one issue is illegal imports of Chinese agricultural products in the Philippines). Additional goods can be added to this programme by negotiation (between China and individual ASEAN members).

The agreement also covers other areas of possible bilateral cooperation outside of trade in goods and services (Part 2). The parties agree to cooperate (in as yet unspecified ways) in agriculture, information and communications technology, human resources development, investment, Mekong River basin development, banking, finance, transport, energy development, and tourism. All discussions on cooperation are to take place in the ASEAN–China Trade Negotiation Committee. Cooperation will also cover promotion and facilitation of trade and investment through agreed standards (and conformity assessment); agreement on technical barriers to trade and non-tariff measures, customs cooperation; increasing the competitiveness of small and medium enterprises, promoting electronic commerce, capacity building, and technology transfer.[9]

Under CAFTA the Chinese markets covered by the early harvest programme will be opened for ASEAN countries ahead of the schedule negotiated for goods trade more broadly under China's WTO accession agreements. Trade between China and ASEAN continues to grow but still represents only 3% of exports and 5% of imports for the ASEAN 6. China will gain from more open markets for her manufacturers and a more stable supply of raw materials (ASEAN is China's fourth largest supplier).[10] The CAFTA may also bring faster liberalization within the ASEAN itself as non-tariff barriers affecting goods and services trade towards China are removed.

China's 2002 Framework Agreement with ASEAN was initially seen as largely symbolic, but that perception has changed as China has pushed strongly in negotiations on the Annexes to the Agreement. ASEAN is China's fifth largest trading partner, and China clearly hopes to strengthen her position in ASEAN markets. In China, the argument is made that CAFTA may be the first step for China in creating an economic counterforce to the US and Europe and may also help in any future negotiations on creating an all-Asian FTA.

Two-way trade between China and ASEAN increased by 40% in 2003.[11] In January 2004 it increased a further 15.4% year-on-year (6.4 billion USD).

---

[9]See Article 7, Paragraph 3.
[10]See M. Vatikiotis, *Far Eastern Economic Review*, July 1, 2003.
[11]See Bo Xilai in *China Daily*, September 5, 2004.

China's exports to ASEAN reached 8.1 billion USD in the first quarter of 2004 (up 31.9% year-on-year); imports increased to 13.8 billion USD (up 42.5%). China's imports of fruit and vegetables from ASEAN (where tariff cuts under the Early Harvest Programme occurred) increased by 38.7% year-to-year in the first six months of 2004; exports increased 33.9%.[12,13]

4. Chinese Regional Agreements with Australia and New Zealand

Besides the CEPA agreements and CAFTA China has also signed two broad initial framework agreements with Australia and New Zealand. These set out the emerging structure of trade, investment, and the wider economic relationship with two OECD countries in the region, and may indicate how China plans to proceed in regional agreements with other OECD countries.

4.1. *Australia*

A Trade and Economic Framework between Australia and China was signed in October, 2003. This sets out areas of future cooperation which aim to "achieve balanced and comprehensive trade and investment facilitation and liberalization".[14] The text is brief. It contains three pages and has two Annexes (Annex 2 is six pages long). Paragraph 2 and Annex 1 indicate the specific areas where the parties will promote strategic cooperation and seek to create favourable conditions for trade and investment.

In the areas of energy and mining, China and Australia state their wish to improve their joint regulatory and policy climate, cooperate in training, research and development, and promote business linkages and exchanges. Also, arrangements will be concluded on a Natural Gas Technology Partnership Fund to enhance mutual understanding in the field of clean energy.

In the area of textiles, clothing, and footwear, China and Australia commit to hold regular trade fairs and exhibitions, encourage the development of business links and contacts, and support joint ventures and joint development of brands.

[12] See Zhang Jin, *China Daily*, April 8, 2004.

[13] The first country to experience zero tariffs in China under the Early Harvest Programme was Thailand from June 2003 (went into force in October 2003). Thailand's exports of vegetables increased in the first quarter of 2004 by 38%, and fruit by 80%. Thailand's exports of fruit and vegetables accounted for over 60% of ASEAN's total exports to China in the first half of 2004.

[14] See Paragraph 1.

With regards to agriculture and quarantine inspection, China and Australia will cooperate further under existing agreements (e.g. the 1984 Agreement on Agricultural Cooperation and the 1984 Protocol on a Program of Cooperation in Agricultural Research for Development) and conclude other MOUs and Protocols (a Plant Quarantine Protocol on Australian Wheat and Barley Imports into China, a MOU on Cooperative Activities in Water Resources, and a MOU on Cooperation on Sanitary and Phytosanitary Matters).

They will also strengthen communication and consultation mechanisms regarding quarantine procedures to improve transparency and facilitate compliance and trade. The text is not detailed, but mentions a dialogue on quarantine management regulations, registration policies and other practices, consultation on food safety inspection and certification issues, and concrete actions to facilitate business and commercial linkages and exchanges.

Investment between the two countries will be enhanced through information exchanges, improved transparency and predictability of measures, and protection of investors and investments. The parties also commit to build institutional linkages between Australian and Chinese government agencies to promote cooperation and consultation.

In the services area, the parties plan to cooperate on education and training through mutual recognition of professional qualifications, joint labour services, and facilitation of travel for Chinese personnel to Australia. The parties also plan to work together on engineering, resources and mining development projects. There are few details but the possibility is raised of Chinese firms investing under contract in Australian projects in these fields.

In the areas of information and communications technology and e-commerce, the two countries plan to intensify their cooperation under an existing 1999 MOU. The countries will promote a dialogue between their customs agencies to simplify and facilitate trade, promote the development of e-commerce, and enhance cooperation in law enforcement. With regards to intellectual property, the countries state their wish to cooperate and to work together bilaterally, regionally and multilaterally. In matters of public health, the countries plan to cooperate under an existing 1993 MOU on Health Cooperation. The countries will also conclude a MOU on cooperation in food safety.

In the area of technical barriers to trade, the countries will seek to improve trade facilitation by concluding a bilateral understanding supplementing multilateral commitments for quality supervision, inspection and quarantine, as well as strengthening communication and consultation mechanisms. They will also strengthen cooperation in standards, certification and accreditation including exchanges between officials and experts, and conclude a mutual recognition agreement covering mechanical and electronic products.

The countries will also explore possibilities for improved facilitation of visa procedures for both work and business visas, support industry and business groups working on strengthening bilateral trade. In the anti-dumping area the countries plan to set up bilateral mechanisms for anti-dumping notification so that any conflicts can be better resolved through dialogue and consultation.

The Framework also stresses the importance of regular bilateral meetings, and their wish to strengthen the existing Joint Ministerial Economic Commission. Australia and China also agree to a Joint Feasibility Study in which the parties will explore the possibilities for a formal FTA.[15] This study is to provide an overview of recent trends in bilateral trade and economic relations, assess recent international trade policy developments and the possible implications for Australia–China trade and investment. It seeks to identify and describe existing barriers to trade and investment flows (in goods, services, and investment), and identify possible cooperation measures to promote trade and investment liberalization. It also aims to assess the impact of the removal and/or reductions of existing barriers in trade of goods and services, investment, and make recommendations and options for future action. The study is to be completed by the end of 2005. The Agreement also states that any future FTA talks can only proceed on an "equal basis". Before the FTA negotiations start, Australia will consider recognizing China as a market economy which is important to China in its dealings with anti-dumping measures in countries, such as the US, who use different procedures against exporters designated as non-market economies.

China is currently the second largest trading partner of Australia (China overtook the US last year), and Australia is China's ninth largest partner. In 2003 Australia had a trade surplus with China of over 13.5 billion USD reflecting exports of iron ore, copper, and petroleum.[16]

---

[15]See Annex 2.

[16]See *China Daily*, August 18, 2004.

4.2. *New Zealand*

China and New Zealand signed a Trade and Economic Cooperation Framework Agreement similar to that with Australia in May, 2004. In this agreement, the parties state their interest in seeking "comprehensive trade and investment facilitation and liberalization through all-round economic and trade cooperation"[17] and also agree on areas of further negotiation.

Paragraph 2 lists specific areas of "significant mutual economic potential" where the countries will promote strategic cooperation. Annex 1 contains the details. In the area of agriculture, animal husbandry, forestry, biosecurity, and food safety, the parties will strengthen cooperation and further development of Joint Commissions established in 2001. With regards to wool, development of trade will be promoted using the trade organizations in the countries. New Zealand also offers to help China through training and technological cooperation in these areas.

In the areas of science and technology, the parties will further develop an Agreement on Cooperation in Science and Technology signed in 2003. They will also seek to enhance cooperation between the two countries' research and innovation communities.

In technical barriers to trade, the parties plan to base their cooperation on the WTO/TBT mechanisms. The issue is how to strengthen communication and consultation on technical and inspection regulations and standards so that reductions in costs to business are achieved. The aim is to conclude a cooperative framework programme for quality supervision, inspection, standards and conformity assessment, and also to enhance arrangements for consultation between certification agencies to support recognition of each other's testing and certification requirements. It also aims to enhance cooperation in WTO-related training for Chinese personnel. The plan is to utilize the China–Australia–New Zealand Standard Wool Contract, establish liaison channels, enhance contacts and linkages, and adopt administrative measures to deal with outstanding issues.

In the areas of information and communication technology and e-commerce, the two countries will encourage cooperation through the development of a Memorandum of Understanding. In the services area the parties will seek to expand trade in services and explore possibilities for cooperation, especially in education, tourism, air services, and labour

[17] See Paragraph 1.

and professional services. In investment the parties aim to increase investment volumes by exchanging information, enhancing transparency and predictability, protecting investments and investors, and building institutional linkages to promote investment visits, B2B initiatives, conferences, and other innovations.

The agreement also covers environmental protection. The two countries agree to share information and cooperate on promoting environmental protection, resource management, and the protection of biodiversity. The countries also stress the importance of intellectual property rights and also plan to cooperate in this area.

Concerning customs cooperation, the countries plan to update the existing 1995 Cooperative Arrangement with new initiatives on trade facilitation and security. They will promote communication between customs administrations, electronic commerce strategies, and information sharing. They also recognize the importance of strengthened law enforcement and cooperation to prevent customs offenses. The countries plan to simplify application procedures for business visas, shorten processing times, and facilitate long term working visas for business travellers.

As with the Australian Framework Agreement there is stress on the importance of regular bilateral meetings between leaders and ministers. The countries will establish a Joint Ministerial Commission as a forum for a dialogue on joint trade and economic issues. China and New Zealand will also strengthen both the position and role of the Joint Trade and Economic Commission and other sectoral Joint Commissions.

Unlike Australia, New Zealand immediately recognizes China as a market economy and agrees not to implement any anti-dumping measures against China under the Sections 15 and 16 of the WTO accession protocol, and paragraph 242 of the Report of the Working Party on China's accession to the WTO. The parties commit (as with Australia) to undertake a Joint Feasibility Study[18] on a bilateral Free Trade Agreement and commence negotiations on establishing a FTA as soon as possible (possibly in early 2005).

China–New Zealand FTA negotiations will be the first China will start with a developed country, and there are clear reasons for China choosing New Zealand in this way. New Zealand has a one-China policy, recognized China early in the 1970s, and reached early agreement on China's accession

[18]See Annex 2.

to WTO.[19] New Zealand has also become the first developed country to recognize China as a market economy.

China is New Zealand's fourth largest trading partner, and the third largest purchaser of lamb and dairy, and fifth largest of forest products.[20] China–New Zealand trade was 1.8 billion USD in 2003, with over 30% growth year-to-year. For China an FTA with New Zealand is a precedent for other FTA negotiations China might conduct with other developed countries.[21]

5. Other Potential Chinese Regional Agreements

While formal agreements involving China are limited to the two CEPA agreements, ASEAN, Australia, and New Zealand, several others are seemingly in process with negotiations likely to be launched soon.

A key case is India. There is no official text of any pre-FTA agreement between India and China so far, but both countries appear to be moving towards FTA negotiations. In the past there have been disputes regarding borders issues between the countries, but it now seems that they share common interests in trade and also in WTO matters.

After the Indian Prime Minister's visit to China in June, 2003, a joint Declaration was signed. In the Declaration the two countries noted their mutual desire for good bilateral relations, and their common interests. In the area of trade, China and India plan to take measures consistent with the national laws and international obligations to remove impediments to bilateral trade and investment.[22] China and India have started discussing possible bilateral trade arrangement on preferential tariffs (more preferential than the MFN tariffs) on a range of products: including paper, steel, chemicals, and food. The list includes 217 Indian exports and 188 Chinese exports facing lower than average tariffs in the other market.[23] In June, 2003, the two countries agreed to form a Joint Study Group to explore the potential for expanded bilateral trade and cooperation.[24] The resulting India–China Group

[19]See Colin James, *Far Eastern Review*, April 22, 2004.
[20]See Chen Mingming, *The New Zealand Herald*, August 31, 2004.
[21]See Stuart McMillan, *The National Business Review*, July 2, 2004.
[22]See The India and China Declaration on Principles for Relations and Comprehensive Cooperation. June 23, 2003.
[23]See *Deccan Herald*, July 26, 2003.
[24]See S. Sethuraman, *The Kashmir Telegraph*, August 2003.

met in March, 2004, with the aim of preparing a five-year blueprint for enhanced bilateral trade and cooperation to present to the two governments.[25]

The first meeting discussed possibilities for both a comprehensive economic cooperation agreement and an India–China free trade agreement. The Group is to present its findings by the end of 2004.[26] A second meeting of the Joint Group was held in July, 2004, in New Delhi with the aim of fostering cooperation between the two business communities.[27]

China and Pakistan officially announced their plans for a Free Trade Agreement in early 2005. To provide a basis for the establishment of the FTA, the two countries agreed to negotiate an agreement on the Early Harvest Programme. The agreement was signed in April, 2005, after the two countries finalized their lists of products subject to zero tariffs under the EHP. The first phase of tariff reductions is set to begin in January, 2006, followed by the second phase two years later. The lists currently contain: home textiles, blended and synthetic fabrics, fruit (namely mango, oranges, dates), marble tiles, surgical goods, sports goods, industrial machinery, chemical raw materials, medicines and others. The lists are to be subsequently expanded to cover more goods. The two countries also decided to keep preferential tariffs on other products. The negotiations on the Rules of Origin for the future FTA are to be completed by September, 2005.

At the same time, China and Pakistan signed a Memorandum of Understanding on the creation of the FTA in which Pakistan agreed not to apply the anti-dumping rules contained in Articles 15 and 16 of the China's Protocol of Accession to the WTO and Paragraph 242 of the Report of the Working Party on the Accession of China to WTO, recognizing China as a market economy.

Chile and China officially announced in April, 2004, plans for a feasibility study regarding the possibilities for strengthening trade and economic cooperation, and a possible free trade agreement. The study is to evaluate the possible impacts of a free trade agreement between the two countries in different sectors and on overall economic relations. The group working on the study is composed of specialists from the Chinese Ministry of Foreign Affairs and Chilean DIRECON (General Directorate of

[25]See *Outlook India*, March 22, 2004.
[26]See P. S. Suryanarayana, *The Hindu*, March 24, 2004.
[27]See *India Daily*, July 26, 2004.

International Economic Affairs — government agency) with experts from ministries of finance, economics, agriculture, mining and transport, and the central bank.[28] The study will cover goods, services and investments; the study is to be presented not later than October, 2004. It is expected the negotiations towards the FTA between China and Chile will start this year during the November APEC meeting in Chile. Also, at this meeting Chile will probably announce their recognition of China's market economy status.

Chile is China's third largest trade partner in South America and due to large imports of copper and pulp, China has a trade deficit with Chile. Chinese exports to Chile are mainly limited to low-value manufactured goods (textiles and footwear). An FTA will help China further develop the Chilean market and creates the possibility of further penetration into South American markets.

There are opinions that China chose Chile as their first possible FTA partner in South America because Brazil is currently undergoing economic reforms and restructuring, and also because Chile is not as economically tied to the US as Mexico. Chile's economy depends heavily on foreign trade and 75% of Chile's foreign trade is currently covered by various FTAs (including Canada, the US, the EU, Norway, Finland, and Mexico).[29]

A further area of bilateral activity for China is South Africa. In June, 2004, China and South Africa issued a joint communiqué in which South Africa granted China market economy status. In the communiqué, China and South Africa also announced their plan to launch FTA negotiations. In the declaration, the two countries stated they would work on encouraging bilateral trade and investment and expanding cooperation in "areas of mutual economic interest".[30]

There are also bilateral activities with the Middle East. In July, 2004, China and the Gulf Cooperation Council (UAE, Bahrain, Kuwait, Oman, Qatar, and Saudi Arabia) announced in a joint communiqué that they had signed a Framework Agreement on Economic, Trade, Investment and Technological Cooperation. Under this, the two countries agree to encourage cooperation and technological exchanges, expand trade, and promote mutual investment. They also establish a joint committee for cooperation to implement the agreement and create a consultation

[28] See Press release, Ministry of Foreign Affairs of Chile, April 27, 2004.
[29] See Wang Li, *China Daily*, May 10, 2004.
[30] See China and Chile Joint Communique, June 29, 2004.

mechanism. Furthermore, China and the GCC agree to launch negotiations on a Free Trade Agreement (the dates have not yet been set).[31]

If established, a China–GCC FTA would be the second Chinese agreement with a regional group with the ASEAN agreement being the other. China's aim would be to benefit from secure oil imports from the Gulf countries and expand exports of garments, fabrics, and electronics to the region. China also seeks increased GCC investment in water and electricity supply, in the energy and mineral industry, transportation, communication, and closer cooperation in scientific and technological research.[32]

Elsewhere in Asia, Singapore and China have started consultations on a possible FTA after China concluded the ASEAN Agreement. Talks were scheduled to start in November, 2004, but now it seems that China wants to delay them following the Singapore Deputy Prime Minister's visit to Taiwan in September, 2004.[33]

6. Evaluating Regional and Multilateral Objectives in China's Trade Policy

In embarking upon negotiation of this ever-growing network of regional trade agreements China has followed a path similar to that chosen by the other large entities in the trading system (the US and the EU). A striking feature of the Chinese approach, however, is the speed at which this both has been and is being done given that accession to the WTO only occurred in 2002. Equally striking is the seeming difference in the structure of these regional agreements compared to those of the US and the EU. Recent US and EU bilateral agreements tend to follow a common template structure. Not only is the template different in the Chinese case, it is much more varied making the eventual emergence of an Asian trading bloc centred around these arrangements problematical. This seemingly reflects both a pragmatism in recognizing differences across partners, and also the clear linkages being established between seemingly conventional trade interests and China's interests in wider economic, diplomatic and strategic relationships. The approach seems to be one of pragmatic management of a series of bilateral relationships in a customized manner, in which conventional economic and trade agreements, such as tariff-based free trade

[31]See China and GCC Joint Communique, July 7, 2004.
[32]See Bo Xilai, Ministry of Commerce release, July 9, 2004.
[33]See *Agence France Presse*, August 3, 2004, and July 25, 2004.

areas of customs unions, are merged into broader, more encompassing relationship building rather than precise narrower legal text.

A natural question to ask is whether this course of action is in the Chinese interest. If China is so firmly committed to multilateralism and WTO disciplines as is often espoused, then why is China not content to leave the setting of its trade agreements with regional partners simply to WTO disciplines and process? And why negotiate in this varied way with different partners?

A first response to these questions is to note the conflicting interests of all larger powers in both multilateralisation in abstract, and in the WTO trading system in its present compromised multilateral guise. The incentive of the large powers, given the present system, is seemingly to both espouse and abide by WTO non-discrimination and MFN in their trade relationships with each other. This is to firm up non-discriminatory access to large markets and also to share in benefits negotiated by other large powers in third markets, while at the same time using their asymmetry in power to negotiate preferential agreements with local smaller partner countries. This suggests an inevitability to a two-tier international trading system of common multilateral disciplines involving all countries. It largely reflects the interests of large powers in their arrangements with each other, and regional disciplines going beyond multilateral arrangements and reflecting the dominant interest of a large power in any given smaller market. This seems the reality of the WTO system in place today.

If this position is accepted, along with an inherent asymmetry in power between large and smaller countries, then the coexistence of both multilateral WTO disciplines and a supplementary system of regional disciplines becomes an inevitability. From China's point of view, the issue is about what form of regional agreements should be negotiated, not whether they should be negotiated.

This leads naturally to the issue of whether the form of and modality for these negotiations fits China's interest. Seemingly in proceeding sequentially by country, and in first negotiating with Hong Kong where the form of agreement can be more easily shaped than in other cases and the precedent then used in subsequent negotiations, the approach seems to fit the national interest well. Precedent can be established in early simple cases, much like early US bilaterals with Singapore and Chile in their recent wave of negotiations. The twin objectives of building towards a regional structure in Asia, and in negotiating with entities other than the US and the EU, so as to enhance negotiating power with other large entities in the WTO seems to be the natural interest.

Using a structure of initial framework negotiation with sequential elaboration through further negotiation, more concessions may be eventually extracted, and learning as negotiations proceed seems to fit well. Equally, the absence of formalized dispute settlement, and reliance on conciliation would seem to fit the Asian way. And in customizing agreements to fit partner characteristics, prior elements of the relationship, and strategic considerations, the Chinese approach to bilateral commercial engagement seemingly displays a pragmatism less evident with the US and the EU.

Thus questions lie more with the coverage of these agreements. Compared to the regional agreements negotiated by the EU and the US, China's regional agreements are more centrally focused on the conventional WTO spheres of trade in goods and services. Other non-WTO areas such as special sectoral arrangements, possible tax harmonization, innovative dispute settlement, coverage of environment and non-trade matters, and financial integration (as they appear in NAFTA and the Treaty of Rome) are seemingly less central to these agreements in their present form. While this may change, it may for now reflect both the present structure of China's international economic engagement, and a desire to appear as WTO compatible as possible in these agreements (given the incomplete nature of China's WTO accession process). But as China's trade patterns and interest in her interaction with other economies evolve this may change. Thus in not being forward-looking in terms of coverage of future interests, these agreements may be less reflective of China's interests.

7. Concluding Remarks

This chapter discusses the emerging network of regional trade agreements that China is now involved in negotiating following her accession to the WTO in 2002. An initial and subsequently elaborated free trade agreement with Hong Kong has been concluded and notified to WTO. A similar agreement with Macao is in place. Initial agreements also exist with ASEAN, Australia, and New Zealand, and discussions are underway with India, South Africa, Singapore, the Gulf Cooperation Council, and others.

The chapter highlights the main features of these agreements: their relative brevity; the substantial differences between them; their focus on trade in goods and services rather than non-WTO matters; the absence of formal dispute resolution; and a negotiating style of initial agreements followed by subsequent elaboration rather than one-off treaty negotiation.

The chapter concludes with a discussion of how the Chinese national interest may be served by these agreements, arguing that asymmetries in size and power in the trading system seemingly produce an inevitable two-tier system of large power non-discriminatory arrangements reflected in common multilateral disciplines, and regional agreements negotiated by large powers with smaller countries going beyond these disciplines where the large power has the dominant interest. In this sense, the issue for China may not be whether they should have negotiated these agreements, but more on how they chose to do so and the implications for the future negotiations.

References

Agence France Presse (2004, July 25, and 2004, August 3). Available at http://www.singapore-window.org/sw04/040803af.htm and http://www.singapore-window.org/sw04/040725af.htm (accessed September 20, 2004).

Australian Government Department of Foreign Affairs and Trade (2003). *Trade and Economic Framework Between Australia and the People's Republic of China.* Available at http://www.dfat.gov.au/geo/china/fta/ (accessed October 2, 2004).

ASEAN Secretariat (2002). *Framework Agreement on Comprehensive Economic Cooperation Between the Association of South East Asian Nations and the People's Republic of China, 2002.* Available at http://www.aseansec.org/13197.htm (accessed September 5, 2004).

Bhattasali, D., S. Li and W. Martin (2004). *China and the WTO.* Washington D.C.: World Bank.

Bilal, S. (2003). *Preparing for the Negotiation of Preferential Trade Agreements with the EU: Preliminary Lessons from Some Developing Countries.* Available at the Social Science Research Network (SSRN): Working Paper Series.

Bo, X. (2004). Ministry of Commerce. Release, July 9. Available at http://english.mofcom.gov.cn/article/200407/20040700246161_1.xml (accessed October 2, 2004).

Brenton, P. and M. Manchin (2002). *Making EU Agreements Work: The Role of Rules of Origin.* CEPS: Working Document No. 183, March.

Caplan, J. (2004). CEPA: The Cure-all for a Recovering Economy, *China Staff,* 10(3): 26.

Chen, M. (2004). Golden Opportunity for Two Countries, *The New Zealand Herald,* August 31.

China Seeks Greater Trade Volume with ASEAN (2004). *China Daily.* Available at http://www.chinadaily.com.cn/english/doc/2004-09/05/content_371729.htm (accessed September 10, 2004).

Department of Foreign Affairs of South Africa (2004). *China and South Africa Joint Communiqué.* Available at http://www.dfa.gov.za/docs/2004/chin0629.htm (accessed September 29, 2004).

Free Trade Talks to Begin Next Year (2004). *China Daily.* Available at http://www.chinadaily.com.cn/english/doc/2004-08/18/content_366492.htm (accessed September 20, 2004).

Gift from Beijing (2003). *Business Asia*, 35(14): 3, July 14.

Hong Kong Economy: New Details Emerge of Hong Kong–Beijing Trade Pact (2003). *EIU ViewsWire*, September 30.

India–China Joint Study Group Holds First Meeting (2004). *Outlook India*, March 22.

India–China Preferential Trade Agreement Implementation Soon. (2003). *Deccan Herald*, July 26.

India, China to Discuss Free Trade Agreement at JDG Meet (2004). *India Daily*, July 26.

James, C. (2004). Deal With It. *Far Eastern Economic Review*, April 22.

Jin, Z. (2004). Programme Paves Way for Free Trade Deal with ASEAN, *China Daily*, April 8.

Kurzweil, M., O. von Ledebur and P. Salamon (2003). *Review of Trade Agreements and Issues.* Retrieved from ENARPRI: Working Paper No. 3, November.

Lardy, N. (Ed). (2002). *Integrating China into the Global Economy.* Washington D.C.: Brookings Institution Press.

Li, W. (2004). *China Daily*, May 10.

Long, Y. (2000). On the Question of Our Joining the World Trade Organization, *The Chinese Economy*, 38(1): 5–52.

Mallon, G. and J. Whalley (2004). *China's Post Accession WTO Stance.* Available at Cambridge, MA: National Bureau of Economic Research, Working Paper No. 10649.

McMillan, S. (2004). FTA with China: A Cautious but Necessary Approach, *The National Economic Review*, July 2.

Ministry of Commerce of the People's Republic of China, Department of International Trade and Economic Affairs (2005). *Agreement on the Early Harvest Programme for the Free Trade Agreement Between the Government of the People's Republic of China and the Government of the Islamic Republic of Pakistan.* Available at http://gis.mofcom.gov.cn/aarticle/af/dh/200504/200500400062422.html (accessed August 5, 2005).

Ministry of Commerce of the People's Republic of China, Department of International Trade and Economic Affairs (2005). *Memorandum of Understanding on the Free Trade Agreement and Other Trade Issues Between the Government of the People's Republic of China and the Government of the Islamic Republic of Pakistan.* Available at http://gis.mofcom.gov.cn/aarticle/af/dh/200405/20050400062513.html (accessed August 5, 2005).

Ministry of Foreign Affairs of Chile (2004). Press Release. Available at http://www.minrel.cl/prensa/Comunicados2004/27-09-04.htm (accessed September 16, 2004).

Ministry of Foreign Affairs of the People's Republic of China (2004). *China and the GCC Joint Communiqué.* Available at http://www.Fmprc.gov.cn/eng/wjdt/2649/t142542.htm (accessed October 2, 2004).

New Zealand Ministry of Foreign Affairs and Trade (2004). *Trade and Economic Cooperation Framework Between New Zealand and the People's Republic of China.* Available at http://www.mfat.govt.nz/foreign/Regions/northasia/nzchinafta/tecfmay04.html (accessed October 5, 2004).

Schott, J. (2004). *Free Trade Agreements: US Strategies and Priorities.* Washington D.C.: Institute for International Economics.

Sethuraman, S. (2003). India and China: On a path of cooperation. *The Kashmir Telegraph*, August.

Suryanarayana, P. S. (2004). India, China Discuss Economic Ties. *The Hindu*, March 25.

The Government of Hong Kong Special Administrative Region, Trade and Industry Department (2003). *Mainland and Hong Kong Closer Economic Partnership Agreement.* Available at http://www.tid.gov.hk/english/cepa/fulltext.html (accessed September 5, 2004).

The Government of Macao Special Administrative Region, Economic Services (2003). *Mainland and Macao Closer Economic Partnership Arrangement.* Available at http://www.economia.gov.mo/page/english/cepa_e.htm (accessed September 28, 2004).

Vatikiotis, M. (2003). China's Tight Embrace, *Far Eastern Economic Review*, July 1.

Wang J. (2004). China's Regional Trade Agreement (RTA) Approach: The Law, the Geopolitics, and the Impact on the Multilateral Trading System, *Singapore Yearbook of International Law*, Vol. 8. Singapore: National University of Singapore, Faculty of Law.

Whalley, J. (2003). Liberalization in China's Key Service Sectors Following WTO Accession: Some Scenarios and Issues of Measurement. Available at Cambridge, MA: National Bureau of Economic Research, Working Paper No. 10143.

CHINA IN THE WORLD TRADING SYSTEM*

John Whalley
University of Western Ontario
The Centre for International Governance Innovation (CIGI)
NBER and CESifo

This chapter discusses China's trade policy stance following WTO accession in 2002. The issues now for China are less the merits of WTO accession, and more how her global trade policies are cast given WTO membership. Three issues are taken up. The first is the extent to which WTO accession helps China in dealing with various key trade issues, including anti-dumping and textiles and apparel trade. The second is China's participation in regional trade agreements post WTO accession. The third is the implementability of China's accession commitments in key service areas (banking, insurance, telecoms).

1. Introduction

It is widely agreed that China's economy is undergoing major transformations as growth in the 7–9% range, which began in the late 1980s, continues on into the mid-2000s and potentially beyond. Central to this has been China's participation and involvement in both the global economy and, more broadly, the world trading system. China has gone from having small trade in the early 1980s to today being the world's third largest trading country (after the US and Germany). Export growth in recent years has been in the 30–40% range, and in 2003 already China accounted for nearly 10% of world trade. If these growth rates continue, by 2010, China would account for over 50% of world trade. China also accounts for around 60% of FDI flows from OECD to non-OECD countries and inward FDI for so-called platform production has been a central element in fuelling export

*This is a revised version of a paper presented to a CESifo Conference on "Understanding the Chinese Economy", June 10–11, 2005 held in Munich, Germany. I am grateful to Gerhard Illing, Agata Antkiewicz, Xu Dinghai, Xiaoyun Liu, and Shunming Zhang for help and comments.

growth.[1] China also runs large trade surpluses (reserves currently stand close to US$ 0.7 trillions), and the exchange rate regime has been a central issue in current trade policy debate with OECD countries pressing China to both revalue and float.[2]

China's involvement in the global economy has been accompanied by substantial and rapidly changing institutional arrangements, and China now faces a series of issues as she more clearly defines her position within the world trading system as it functions today. China acceded to the WTO in 2002, with implementation to be completed by 2007. Although now a member of the WTO and participating in Doha Round negotiations, China is faced with a range of trade policy issues that WTO accession did little to address, including growing use of dumping actions against her and the global textile and apparel regime following the end of the MFA. China is also now actively negotiating regional trade and broader economic cooperative agreements with a growing number of countries, and these are occurring surprisingly quickly following WTO accession.

In this chapter, I draw on three recent joint chapters of mine in this area (Whalley, 2003; Mallon and Whalley, 2004; and Antkiewicz and Whalley, 2005b) and discuss a series of issues arising with China's current and future participation in the global system. The first is China's stance on WTO and related global trade issues following her accession, asking how much WTO accession helps in dealing with access issues in areas such as anti-dumping and textiles and apparel. The second is China's emerging network of regional trade and economic cooperation agreements. The third is the implementability of her WTO accession terms in the key service areas (banking, insurance, telecoms).

As prefatory remarks to what follows in the chapter, I will state my own view that the structure of the Chinese economy still differs from that of OECD economies sufficiently that a simple minded application of Western neoclassical economic analysis to policy issues in China can mislead. Bill Gates (Gates, 2005) in a recent speech to the World Economic Forum suggested that China has created a "brand new form of capitalism" which he then proceeded to praise. I prefer, instead, to think of the Chinese economy as embodying a brand new form of communism (or communalism).

[1]See the recent discussion of inward foreign investment and growth in China in Whalley and Xin (2005). China's outward foreign investment activity is discussed in Antkiewicz and Whalley (2005a).

[2]See the discussion of this regime in Huang *et al.* (2005).

In this, central direction through planning has been effectively removed. But production units in the urban manufacturing sector remain largely communal in ownership and management structure (with many diverse forms including national, regional and municipal governments, and non-governmental entities such as research institutes, units of the military, and others).[3] Competition between communally owned units operates and can be aggressive, but many of these units make losses. Most of these units also involve management who seem to maximize size for personal network (guanxi) benefits rather than profits. The banking system has largely been used until recently as a mechanism for recapitalizing loss-making SOEs and has large non-performing loans.[4] Finally, individual economic behaviour in China is much more heavily reflective of group (family, village, town, province, country) interest over individual interest than is true of OECD economies.

In the trade area, recent analytical work (Whalley and Zhang, 2005) has highlighted the need to more carefully consider the behavioural response of state-owned enterprises (SOEs) and other communally managed enterprises to trade liberalization. Whalley and Zhang note the seeming absence of analytical literature as to how SOEs behave, and also note the wide variety of institutional forms in practice which exist in China. They develop two simple formulations and contrast them to the purely competitive structures used in existing modeling work on Chinese WTO accession such as Ianchovichina and Martin (2003). In their first formulation they treat enterprises as under control of politically appointed managers whose losses are recapitalized by the banking system. They assume credit rationing effectively freely allocates capital to enterprises and managers seek to maximize the size of enterprises rather than profit so as to secure personal benefits from networking (guanxi). They show how in this case with competitive labour markets (a strong assumption in China) enterprises hire labour up to the point where the wage equals the average rather than the marginal product of labour, and free trade in such a world is no longer best policy. In their second formulation they assume worker control, and with fixed membership and given wage rates treat enterprises as satisfying to meet an enterprise budget constraint with workers moonlighting or shirking from additional labour. In such a world a fall in a product price

[3]See Broadman (2001).

[4]See Bonin and Huang (2002) who suggest that perhaps 60% of loans to the banking sector are non-performing.

following trade liberalization increases output rather than reduces it as in the standard competitive model.

All of this makes understanding the Chinese economy difficult both for Chinese and non-Chinese. It also influences any discussion of China's participation in the world trading system. My own view is that the changes implied for China in both economic structure and more broadly in terms of social and cultural values are profound if the aim is to accommodate to the world economy with fully open trade and financial markets. Indeed this issue raised is as much how far the world will eventually integrate into China as this process progresses as much as it is how China will fully integrate into the broader world.

2. China's Post-Accession WTO Stance[5]

China's lengthy WTO accession process was concluded in 2002 with an agreement that involved tariff reductions and bindings in manufactures trade, termination of subsidies to most state-owned enterprises, reduction/elimination of export and production subsidies in agriculture, and for reaching market opening in banking, insurance, and telecoms. These commitments were to be implemented between 2002 and 2007.

There has been much discussion in the last few years of exactly what it was that took China into the WTO (or in Chinese eyes restored their GATT membership placed into suspension in 1950). Arguments range from the need to have the security of firm MFN benefits in place of previous insecure arrangements (and subject to periodic review and renewal), to the domestic uses by modernizers of WTO membership who wanted to see genuine market-based policy reform which would speed growth and reform and curb the power of provinces.[6]

At the conclusion of negotiations, parallel speeches from Chinese and EU/US negotiators talked from the Chinese side of a fair and balanced arrangement with restoration of normal trade relations (NTR), and from the EU/US side of a one-sided agreement in which China had made

[5]This section draws on Mallon and Whalley (2004).

[6]Long Yongtu, (the former chief Chinese negotiator on accession) (2000) argued, "We must let those [WTO] rules that stand at the core of the market economy, and which have to be obeyed, take firm roots in our society and country, so that our own market economy may become one that is truly orderly, efficient, honest and clean." See Long Yongtu, *The Chinese Economy*, 2000.

all the concessions with substantial commercial policy benefit to EU/US business interests.[7] Firmness of MFN benefits alone cannot seemingly explain the drive to accession since de facto China effectively received MFN benefits already, despite periods of Congressional agonizing in the US over human rights and labour standards. Long Yongtu, the former Chinese chief negotiator, identified the advantages to China as allowing the development of China's service sector, generating international acceptance for China's economy as a market economy, allowing China some say over the setting of multilateral global trade rules, and greater access to dispute settlement.[8]

But now in the WTO, China's interests lie both in using WTO disciplines and in writing new WTO trade rules in ways which most effectively guarantee access to large export markets in Europe and North America. Firmness of this access is also key to continuing to attract inward FDI to produce for export markets abroad. Thus, despite accession, China still faces a number of trade and WTO issues in the short- to medium-term, which affect both her access to foreign markets and the access she gives to foreigners to Chinese markets. Some of these directly involve WTO disciplines; others are broader reflecting the operation of the wider trading system.

2.1. *Anti-dumping*

China faces many critical challenges in the area of anti-dumping. Around 15% of anti-dumping actions worldwide now occur against China, since she is a dynamic grower of exports.[9] In addition, under US statute China is also currently classified as a non-market economy, provoking more stringent

[7]See the speech by Ambassador Charlene Barshefsky of the US Trade Representative to the Economic Club of Washington (March 16, 2000) describing what were portrayed as China's one-way concessions to US business interests. China's compliance with her WTO commitments is discussed in Stewart (2004).

[8]Yongtu, *The Chinese Economy*, 2000.

[9]In the period from July 1, 2002, to June 30, 2003, China was subject to 42 initiations of anti-dumping investigations, out of a total of 238, approx. 17.6%. See *WTO Annual Report 2004, Table II.5 Exporters Subject to Two or More Initiations of Anti-dumping Investigations 1 July 2002–30 June 2003* at 46 on WTO web site. In the preceding period, China was subject to 46 new initiations of a total 309. See *WTO Annual Report 2003, Table III.6 Exporters Subject to Two or More Initiations of Anti-dumping Investigations 1 July 2001–30 June 2002* at 83 on WTO web site. From 1995–2001 China was subject to 14% of total global anti-dumping actions (*People's Daily*, April 23, 2002). According to news reports, China has been subject to more than 200 anti-dumping cases since joining the WTO in 2001 (Oliver August, *Times Online*, June 3, 2004).

application of US dumping procedures.[10] China, in turn, has begun to intensify her own use of anti-dumping duties.[11]

WTO accession formally provides China with little additional defence against the use of anti-dumping measures against her. Article 6 of GATT 1994 effectively legitimizes the use of anti-dumping measures, and only constrains their use procedurally by specifying how domestic administrative tribunals should determine their use. It is thus hard to claim that WTO membership offers China any significant added benefits in dealing with this major access problem facing continued export growth. China may be able to push more aggressively for anti-dumping reform in the WTO, long seen as unacceptable to the US Congress even after China's WTO accession, but for now this still seems non-negotiable.

An issue China faces in this area is whether, realistically, it makes sense to fight anti-dumping actions if the legal and informational costs are high. Press reports in the *People's Daily* claim that China had won over 37% of anti-dumping cases in the ten years prior to accession,[12] but this was at a high cost in legal fees and other charges. If dumping actions against China are narrowly focused on particular products a simple strategy is simply to respond by producing and exporting other items. But if dumping actions continue against China and grow in coverage, at some point the export product range become sufficiently restricted that export performance suffers and potentially significantly.[13]

[10]Article 15 of the protocol on China's accession to the WTO allows other WTO members to treat China as a non-market economy in dumping and subsidy cases for 15 years after its entry. (*China Daily*, May 17, 2004). Under US anti-dumping laws, once a US trade authority deems a country a non-market economy it may disregard the prices of products exported from the country since they do not reflect supply and demand, and instead use costs in a third surrogate country to calculate dumping margins. At a hearing on June 3, 2004, the US Commerce Department said US deliberations over whether China is a market-based or state-controlled economy would take at least as long as deliberations on Russia (18 months). See Cheng Dawei, *China Daily*, May 17, 2004, and Doug Palmer, *Reuters*, June 3, 2004.

[11]China initiated 17 anti-dumping actions in the period of July 1, 2002, to June 30, 2003. See *WTO Annual Report 2003, Table 11.5: Summary of Anti-dumping Actions, 1 July, 2002 to June 30, 2003.* She initiated no actions in the previous year. China filed 24 anti-dumping cases in the period from 1997 to September 2003. See *People's Daily Online*, September 14, 2003.

[12]See *People's Daily Online*, March 29, 2002.

[13]China has also begun to use domestic anti-dumping procedures. Investigative procedures for imports have been implemented in March 2005, with initially two investigations. One is on stainless steel imports from Japan and Korea, and the other is on imports of Spandex from Singapore, Japan, Korea, and the US.

2.2. *Trade disputes*

China also faces a growing list of trade disputes, some of which some have the potential to spawn a significant number of new WTO dispute panels now that China is a WTO member. The list of potential disputes seen from the US is reflected in the latest USTR Foreign Trade Barriers Report. This report identifies a number of areas of potential US–China trade conflict, including import substitution policies in China in several product areas, such as fertilizer; automobile investment guidelines; tariffs on products that compete with sensitive domestic industries, such as motorcycles and electronic equipment; tariff classification and customs valuation procedures; Chinese border policies that give preferential treatment to non-US imports (such as Russian timber);[14] non-tariff barriers to trade in the form of regulations that set entry barriers to trade in services such as banking and insurance; unwarranted inspections of agriculture products; rules on biotechnology products, the use of sanitary and phytosanitary measures to control import volumes; and export subsidies on corn.[15]

WTO disciplines define clear rights for other WTO members when accessing China's markets for goods, services, and allowing the use of their intellectual property. Whether by more clearly defining such rights accession to the WTO has merely added to the list of disputes and hence the pressure for change in China, or whether the added clarity of rights for other WTO members works to accelerate trade and investment flows is unclear. China has thus to decide whether WTO trade disputes while superficially annoying from a practical view point, in reality speed modernization in China and confirm the arguments that took China into the WTO in the first place; or whether potential WTO disputes add new pressures on China to implement policy changes which she does not yet want to make.

On the offensive side of the trade dispute equation, China has thus far shown considerable reluctance to use her WTO membership to assert her rights. There have been no WTO trade panels initiated by China,[16] although China has been active in pressuring foreign governments on

---

[14] Russia is not a WTO member and so this practice by China is WTO compatible.

[15] See United States Trade Representative, *National Trade Estimate Report on Foreign Trade Barriers* (2004).

[16] Although China was the second of nine members to request a panel against the US on safeguards on imports of certain steel products. See *Request for a Panel against US Imports of Certain Steel Products*, April 2, 2002, on WTO website.

various trade matters such as the use of special safeguards in textiles and apparel in the US, Japanese farm measures affecting Chinese exports,[17] and EU environmental barriers on Chinese appliance exports.[18]

The one dispute that has thus far resulted in a formal WTO panel against China involves the treatment of imported semiconductor memory chips into the Chinese market. Under the Chinese national value-added tax, imported chips are subject to a value-added tax of 17%, but domestically produced chips are eligible for special tax rebates that lower the effective tax rate to between 3% and 6%.[19] The US allegation is that this practice is a violation of National Treatment (GATT 1994, Article 3). The EU and other suppliers (including Taiwan) have also notified an interest in the case to the WTO.[20] In July, 2004, after negotiations with the US, China agreed to remove the differential tax treatment of domestic and imported memory chips from April 1st, 2005.

Other emerging trade disputes involve financing packages offered by foreign auto producers in the Chinese market, which were initially disallowed on the grounds that China had yet to implement its WTO commitments re financial services;[21] and whether the current Renminbi exchange rate is a factor in China's significant trade surplus position and supports a GATT 1994 Article 23 nullification and impairment action by exporters to China.

China has recently concluded a bilateral agreement on imports of coking coal from the EU, reflective of an approach of using bilateral accommodation to defuse trade conflicts.[22] China's import quota in this area is to be sharply increased, although not removed as WTO disciplines would seem to imply. This case will likely lead to similar arrangements with

[17]See Meng Yan, *China Daily*, June 3, 2003. These complaints relate to a Japanese announcement to block imports of Chinese fowl and eggs in May 2003 after a flu virus was detected in exports originating in Guangdong.

[18]See *People's Daily Online*, February 17, 2004. This matter relates to a new EU directive on waste from electronic equipment that will impose a fee of 1 to 20 Euros on any colour TV or mobile phone exported to the EU.

[19]See *The Economist*, January 10, 2004, at 57.

[20]See *China — value-added tax on integrated circuits — Request to Join Consultations, Communication from the Separate Customs Territory of Taiwan, Phenghu, Kinmen and Matsu*, April 5, 2004 on the WTO website, and *China — value-added tax on integrated circuits — Request to Join Consultations, Communication from the European Communities*, March 30, 2004, on the WTO website.

[21]See Xiao Zhang, *China Daily*, November 14, 2003.

[22]See Dai Yan, *China Daily*, May 31, 2004.

other exporters of coking coal to the Chinese market, and possibly in other product areas.

2.3. *Textiles and apparel*

Key access related issues for China also arise in textiles and apparel trade. China is now the dominant exporter of apparel items from non-OECD countries; in value terms accounting for approximately 45% of non-OECD exports in 2002. Today China and India jointly account for the majority of apparel exports from non-OECD to OECD countries[23] with a large number of smaller suppliers in Asia, Eastern Europe, Central and Latin America with small shares of total trade which are still a large fraction of country exports.

Several issues arose with MFA termination at the end of 2004 as agreed in the Uruguay Round. This affected all MFA exporters, but the situation was especially critical for China. The central issue was whether free trade will really replace the MFA in the medium to longer term. Scenarios for a post-MFA elimination regime abounded from a growing wave of new anti-dumping petitions from domestic producers in OECD countries being used to force a new market sharing regime (as happened in steel in the mid-1900s), to the use of broader safeguard measures (GATT 1994, Article 19) by OECD countries on textile and apparel products.

The concerns in the US and also in the EU over labour adjustment from affected industry groups were clear and strongly stated.[24] A 2003 piece in *Asian Labour News* for instance, documented pressures in the US for use of new selective MFA transitional safeguards against apparel imports from non-OECD countries.[25]

MFA importers initially seemed content to allow the continuation of special selective safeguards as agreed in the Uruguay Round under the Agreement on Textiles and Apparel that terminated the MFA to define the regime. But as of March 1st, 2005, China implemented unilateral export taxes on a number of apparel export items, in part due to pressure from other low wage exporters who feared MFA elimination would erode their export market share, and China also instituted a new monitoring and

[23]See *Leading exporters and importers of clothing, 2002, Table IV.69*, WTO website. This is in sharp contrast to the 1980s, when Hong Kong, Taiwan and Korea accounted for 60% of such exports.
[24]See *The Standard* article, August 2, 2003.
[25]See *Asian Labour News* online article, November 19, 2003.

approval procedure for textile and apparel exports. In addition, refunds of value added tax on inputs for exported apparel items have been terminated. China was therefore following a policy of export restraint following MFA termination; a form of shadow MFA which presumably evolved due to the implicit threat of new anti-dumping and selective safeguard actions.

In June, 2005, the US imposed emergency safeguard restrictions on seven categories of Chinese imports which limit export growth to 7.5% over a transitional period of three years, justifying these as consistent with the safeguard provisions agreed to by China as part of the terms of China's WTO accession. China reacted by terminating the system of export taxes introduced in March, and restoring refunds of value added tax on inputs. China and the EU, however, subsequently came to an agreement under which China voluntarily limits export growth to 8–12.5% a year in categories of textile products until 2008. Categories include cotton cloth, t-shirts, flax yarn, bed sheets, tablecloths, and trousers. The US and China have more recently agreed on a new system of bilateral restraints on export growth in a range of items which limits growth to 10% a year until 2008.

A concern from other Asian exporters had been that China's share of quota restricted US and EU markets would grow sharply in the post MFA period, and other Asian exporters would suffer. Whalley (2005) documents the surges in Chinese apparel exports in the first few months of 2005 into US and EU markets prior to the introduction of safeguards by these importers. In aggregate, however, the surges are less dramatic as exports to Japan (a larger market for China than either the US or the EU) change little and exports to Hong Kong fall. Whalley also presents data which show that exports of other Asian exporters hold up surprisingly well, and there are larger losses in shares for non-Asian rather than Asian exporters to the US and the EU.

China's interest clearly lies in obtaining unhindered export access for this key area of Chinese trade through full and unhindered access to OECD export markets for textile and apparel exports. The belief is both that exports to OECD countries will grow even more rapidly under free access, and that higher cost production which has relocated to smaller countries in the region because of quotas on Chinese exports will relocate to China. The question for China is whether there is fresh leverage that can be used on this matter now that she is inside the WTO, which can be used to ensure true termination of restraints on these exports. China can also now use WTO membership to link her position on textiles and apparel to that on other WTO issues, including the remaining implementation of her accession terms.

2.4. *The domestic regulatory regime*

Challenges also arise for China with WTO accession through the extent of refocusing of the domestic regulatory regime that is implied in the medium term. Standards issues involving China's trade figure prominently in the USTR Foreign Trade Barriers reports, covering a lack of transparency in the certification process, lack of coordination among standards bodies and other agencies, burdensome requirements and long processing times for licenses.[26] US and EU companies frequently claim that achieving certification under China's Compulsory Certification system is time-consuming, difficult and costly, and that they are subject to redundant testing for cosmetics, pharmaceuticals, and several consumer electronic products, inconsistent application of sanitary and phytosanitary measures, and excessive or inappropriate food labeling requirements. An illustration of these problems is China's Wireless LAN encryption standards, which differ from internationally recognized standards and force international companies to work through the few Chinese manufacturers who possess the necessary algorithm to meet these standards.

According to Li Zhonghai, director of China's standardization watchdog, China now has 20,900 compulsory national standards covering safety, hygiene and environmental protection with more than 2,300 new national standards under creation. Only 44% of China's standards reflect agreed international standards (also according to Li Zhonghai) and the challenge is to modify remaining standards and elsewhere rewrite domestic regulatory standards relating to health, safety, electrical, product liability and other matters. Standards are widely agreed to be a central area of impact of domestic policy regimes on trade, and are little researched.

2.5. *China's negotiating position in WTO doha round negotiations*

Despite accessing the WTO in 2002, China has thus far not taken an especially active position in WTO Doha Round negotiations. These were already underway as China joined the WTO, and on the key Doha Round

[26]See United States Trade Representative, *National Trade Estimate Report on Foreign Trade Barriers* (2004) at 67–71.

issues of agricultural export subsidies, agricultural supports, industrial tariffs, and implementation of Uruguay Round commitments China had relatively little to contribute as these are all matters covered in some detail by China's accession terms. The Chinese approach has thus been one of watching and participating in a less active way than might have been anticipated ex ante following accession.

The issues are thus what a more activist involvement in WTO negotiation might lead to in a post Doha Round environment. The WTO has been widely portrayed in China as a central plank in China's developmental strategy (despite the recent work of Rose, 2004, which claims that the WTO has made little difference to World Trade), and how WTO membership can now more actively be used for this purpose is the issue.

3. China's New Regional Trade Agreements[27]

Another key area for Chinese trade policy post WTO accession involves China's regional trade agreements, which have been aggressively pursued since 2002. Regional trade agreements or initial frameworks of agreements are now in place for China with Hong Kong, Macao, ASEAN, Australia, and New Zealand. Discussions on possible further FTAs with India, Chile, Singapore, South Africa, and the Gulf Cooperation Council are underway. Possible direct or indirect arrangements involving Korea and Japan are also the subject of speculation.

China, like other large powers in the trading system (the US and the EU) has clear incentive to commit to multilateral disciplines in the WTO as a way of gaining non-discriminatory access to large markets and head off discrimination against her either in both these or smaller third country markets by fellow large powers. But closer to home (and as with the US and the EU) China has equally clear incentive to negotiate supplemental regional arrangements which deal with interests in local markets in ways which go beyond WTO disciplines. The US with NAFTA, and the EU with accession and other agreements have encountered similar incentives with similar results.

There are several striking features of China's emerging network of agreements which differentiate it both from the one-off negotiation of

[27] This section draws on Antkiewicz and Whalley (2005b).

NAFTA by the US in 1991 and the process of ever deeper EU integration initiated by the 1957 Treaty of Rome. The first is their diversity, and both of form and coverage. For example, the agreement with Hong Kong is concrete and focuses on both goods trade and cross border investment and financial activities, while the agreements with Australia and New Zealand largely provide general indicative statements of intent in a much wider number of areas. This diversity of approach affects the prospects for an eventual emergence of a trade bloc centred on these agreements.

A further feature is their seeming brevity, and hence the inevitably vagueness of the texts involved (the Hong Kong and Macao Closer Economic Partnership Agreements (CEPA) have only thirteen pages of main text with additional annexes). The negotiation of regional trade agreements for China seemingly represents as much a process of ongoing trade management, as agreement on a single legal text which defines rights and obligations. Much seems to be left to subsequent joint agreement and mutual management of the trade relationship. Finally noteworthy are the extensive lists of specific bilateral commitments in services (especially in the case of CEPA) which go beyond the form and type of commitments undertaken by most WTO members in the GATS, and the substantial attention devoted to arrangements both for joint ventures and the operation of financial institutions in a joint regulatory environment in the Hong Kong Arrangement.

3.1. *The closer economic partnership arrangements with Hong Kong and Macao*

China's Closer Economic Partnership Arrangement (CEPA) with Hong Kong was signed on June 29th, 2003, with aim of promoting joint economic development, and further developing links between China, Hong Kong, and other countries (regions). The Macao Closer Economic Partnership Arrangement which followed shortly after is almost identical to the Hong Kong CEPA. Minor differences are slightly different names of agencies and regulations in Hong Kong and Macao, and the lists of goods in Tables in Annexes 1 & 2 differ in some areas.

The Hong Kong CEPA contains 13 pages of text and six annexes. Its main content lies in progressive bilateral reduction or elimination of tariff and non-tariff barriers applying to goods trade, reducing bilateral restrictions on service trade, and various steps to further promote bilateral trade and investment. The Hong Kong CEPA was notified to WTO on January 12th, 2004.[28]

China agrees to introduce zero tariffs for a list of goods specified in Annex 1 as of January 1st, 2004,[29] and full elimination of bilateral tariffs is to occur no later than January 1st, 2006. All goods have to meet CEPA rules of origin (these rules are set out in Annex 2). To acquire Hong Kong origin a good must have 30% value added in Hong Kong (this includes the value of raw materials, labour costs, component parts, and product development costs). Foreign companies in Hong Kong can export goods to China under CEPA if the products meet the added value requirement.

The agreement also specifies that neither party is to introduce new quotas or other barriers towards bilateral imports, and neither party will use anti-dumping actions against the other. CEPA allows for safeguards actions in goods trade after written notice, but these safeguards measures are not fully specified.

Bilateral liberalization of trade in services is specified in Annex 4 of both CEPAs. 18 services sectors are listed with specific bilateral commitments in each. The list includes (among others): management consulting, advertising, accounting, real estate and construction, logistics, freight forwarding, telecommunications and legal services.

The agreement applies to a range of financial activities, banking, insurance, and securities, and opens financial markets in the Mainland to entities from Hong Kong. CEPA for example lowers the required minimum assets for Hong Kong banks that establish branches in China from 20BN USD to 6BN USD. A significant innovation in these agreements is that the definition of a new services entity, "a Hong Kong service supplier" (Annex 5), which opens doors to Chinese markets for international companies who can utilize this entity.[30] Benefits from the bilateral scheduled commitments in services only apply to this entity. To qualify, such a company must be established in Hong Kong for more than three years (five years for construction, banking, insurance, and related services), pay applicable profit taxes, have business premises (owned or rented) reflecting business activities in Hong Kong, and employ at least 50% of the staff

[28]See Notification From Parties, WTO WT/REG162/N/1, January 12, 2004, and Minutes of Meeting of the Council for Trade in Goods, WTO G/C/M/72, January 26, 2004. So far a working party has not been established and factual examination by the WTO Committee on Regional Trade Agreements has not yet started.
[29]See Table 1 of Annex 1, 273 goods covering medicines, and toys, among others.
[30]The Macao CEPA has a similar Macao service supplier company construct.

locally from Hong Kong permanent residents. The intended business in China must be the same as the company's substantive business in Hong Kong, and documentation is required to establish this.

For the purposes of the agreement CEPA also recognizes service companies acquired by an overseas company as a Hong Kong service company one year after the merger or acquisition takes place. Any qualifying Hong Kong company operating in China must have a Hong Kong Service Supplier Certificate issued in Hong Kong. Annex 5 excludes any overseas company registered in Hong Kong that is "specifically established for providing certain services to its parent company", e.g. representative offices and "mailbox companies".

Both CEPAs also provide for cooperation in tourism and mutual recognition of professional qualifications, and both CEPAs contain trade and investment facilitation provisions under which China and Hong Kong (Macao) agree on seven areas of cooperation. The overall coordination and implementation of each CEPA is under a Joint Steering Committee who are to resolve disputes, and interpret provisions (Article 19).

In August, 2004, further details going beyond what was in the original CEPA were agreed, taking the form of a Record of Consultation on Further Liberalization under the Mainland and Hong Kong CEPA. In goods trade China agrees to apply zero tariffs to the next stage of goods imported from Hong Kong at the beginning of next year (2005). This covers 713 goods (and applies to both existing and planned production) covering food, chemicals, mechanical and electronic products. Rules of origin for these goods (which can differ from those in the original CEPA) are to be concluded no later than October 2004. In services trade China will further relax access conditions for Hong Kong service suppliers (no details are provided). This includes 11 sectors specified in the original CEPA, and eight new sectors including (among others): airport, information technology, job intermediaries, and marketing services. These new commitments were to be implemented in January, 2005.

3.2. *The ASEAN — China agreement*

A China and ASEAN Framework Agreement on Comprehensive Economic Cooperation was concluded in November, 2002, but is less concrete than the CEPAs. It sets out a broad framework for more detailed agreements that are to follow in 21 pages of text and four annexes. The parties agree to work towards the establishment of a Free Trade Area (FTA) between China and ASEAN within ten years, but precisely what this FTA will comprise and what its institutional underpinnings are for now unclear. What will be sought will be elimination of tariffs and non-tariff barriers in goods trade, liberalization of services trade, promotion of bilateral investment, and simplification of customs procedures and the establishment of mutual recognition arrangements. A China and ASEAN FTA with the original ASEAN 6 (Brunei, Indonesia, Malaysia, the Philippines, Singapore, and Thailand) is to be established by 2010 and by 2015 with the newer ASEAN members (Vietnam, Lao PDR and Myanmar, Cambodia). Bilateral tariffs will be lowered to 0–5% on most goods, and non-tariff barriers are to disappear.

The goods subject to reduction/elimination, along with tariff rates and schedules and rules of origin are to be negotiated by the parties, and spelled in more detailed agreements to follow. An element in the 2002 ASEAN–China agreement is an Early Harvest Programme set to start in 2004 (Annex 1) which cuts tariffs ahead of the planned establishment of the FTA in 2010. Any bilaterally agreed safeguard arrangements and disciplines on subsidies, anti-dumping measures are to be based on existing GATT disciplines and are also to be elaborated.

In trade in services, the parties plan to negotiate progressive elimination of all discrimination in new and existing service restrictions (unless permitted under GATS). In the investment area, the parties are to liberalize their investment regimes, strengthen cooperation, and improve transparency of rules and regulations.

The agreement also covers other possible areas of cooperation outside of trade in goods and services in as yet unspecified ways in agriculture, information and communications technology, human resources development, investment, Mekong River basin development, banking, finance, transport, energy development, and tourism. Cooperation will also cover promotion and facilitation of trade and investment through agreed standards (and conformity assessment); agreement on technical barriers to trade and non-tariff measures, customs cooperation; increasing the competitiveness of small and medium enterprises; promoting electronic commerce, capacity building, and technology transfer.[31]

Trade between China and ASEAN continues to grow but still represents only 3% of exports and 5% of imports for the ASEAN 6. China will gain

[31] See Article 7, Paragraph 3.

from more open markets for her manufacturers and a more stable supply of raw materials (ASEAN is China's fourth largest supplier).[32] The FTA may also bring faster liberalization within the ASEAN itself as non-tariff barriers affecting goods and services trade towards China are removed.

3.3. *Chinese regional agreements with Australia and New Zealand*

Besides the CEPA and ASEAN agreements, China has also signed two broad framework agreements with Australia and New Zealand which may indicate how China plans to proceed in regional agreements with other OECD countries.

A Trade and Economic Framework between Australia and China was signed in October, 2003, which sets out areas of future cooperation which aim to "achieve balanced and comprehensive trade and investment facilitation and liberalization".[33] The text is brief, containing three pages and two Annexes (Annex 2 is six pages long). Paragraph 2 and Annex 1 indicate the specific areas where the parties will promote strategic cooperation and create favourable conditions for trade and investment: In energy and mining, China and Australia state their wish to improve their joint regulatory and policy climate, cooperate in training, research and development, and promote business linkages and exchanges. Also, arrangements will be concluded on a Natural Gas Technology Partnership Fund to enhance mutual understanding in the field of clean energy. In textiles, clothing, and footwear China and Australia commit to hold regular trade fairs and exhibitions, encourage the development of business links and contacts, and support joint ventures and joint development of brands. In agriculture and quarantine inspection China and Australia will cooperate further under existing agreements[34] and conclude other MOUs and Protocols.[35] The two countries will also strengthen communication and consultation mechanisms regarding quarantine procedures. The text is not detailed, but mentions a dialogue on quarantine management regulations,

---

[32]See M. Vatikiotis, *Far Eastern Economic Review*, July 1, 2003.
[33]See Paragraph 1.
[34]The 1984 Agreement on Agricultural Cooperation and the 1984 Protocol on a Program of Cooperation in Agricultural Research for Development.
[35]A Plant Quarantine Protocol on Australian Wheat and Barley Imports into China, a MOU on Cooperative Activities in Water Resources, and a MOU on Cooperation on Sanitary and Phytosanitary Matters.

registration policies and other practices, and consultation on food safety inspection and certification issues.

In the services area, the parties plan to cooperate on education and training through mutual recognition of professional qualifications, joint labour services, and facilitation of travel for Chinese personnel to Australia. The parties also plan to work together on engineering, resources and mining development projects. There are few details but the possibility is raised of Chinese firms investing under contract in Australian projects in these fields. Investment between the two countries will be enhanced through information exchanges, improved transparency and predictability of measures, and protection of investors and investments. The parties also commit to build institutional linkages between Australian and Chinese government agencies to promote cooperation and consultation.

In the area of technical barriers to trade, the countries will seek to improve trade facilitation by concluding a bilateral understanding supplementing multilateral commitments for quality supervision, inspection and quarantine, and strengthening communication and consultation mechanisms. They will also strengthen cooperation in standards, certification and accreditation including exchanges between officials and experts, and conclude a mutual recognition agreement covering mechanical and electronic products. In information and communications technology and e-commerce, the two countries plan to intensify their cooperation under an existing 1999 MOU. The countries will also explore possibilities for improved facilitation of visa procedures for both work and business visas, support industry and business groups working on strengthening bilateral trade, and in the anti-dumping area the countries plan to set up bilateral mechanisms for anti-dumping notification so that any conflicts can be better resolved through dialogue and consultation.

Australia and China have also agreed to a Joint Feasibility Study in which the parties will explore a formal FTA. This study will provide an overview of trends in bilateral trade and wider economic interaction, assess recent international trade policy developments and possible implications for Australia–China trade and investment. It will also identify and describe existing barriers to trade and investment flows (in goods, services, and investment), possible cooperation to promote trade and investment liberalization, assess the impact of the removal and/or reductions of barriers in trade of goods and services, investment, and make recommendations for future action. The study is to be completed by end of 2005. Before the FTA negotiations start, Australia will consider recognizing China as a market economy which is important to China in its dealings with anti-dumping measures in countries (such as the US) who use different procedures against exporters designated as being from non-market economies.

China and New Zealand also signed a Trade and Economic Cooperation Framework Agreement in May, 2004, which is similar to that with Australia. In this, the parties state their interest in seeking "comprehensive trade and investment facilitation and liberalization through all-round economic and trade cooperation" and also agree areas of further negotiation.

Specific areas of "significant mutual economic potential" where the countries will promote strategic cooperation are listed. In agriculture, animal husbandry, forestry, biosecurity, food safety, the parties will strengthen cooperation and further development of Joint Commissions established in 2001. In wool, trade will be promoted using trade organizations in the countries. New Zealand also offers to help China through training and technological cooperation in these areas. In science and technology, the parties will further develop an Agreement on Cooperation in Science and Technology signed in 2003. They will also seek to enhance cooperation between the two countries research and innovation communities.

In the area of technical barriers to trade, the parties plan to cooperate using the WTO/TBT mechanisms. The issue is how to strengthen communication and consultation on technical and inspection regulations and standards so that reductions in costs to business are achieved. The aim is to conclude a cooperative framework programme for quality supervision, inspection, standards and conformity assessment, and also to enhance arrangements for consultation between certification agencies to support recognition of each other's testing and certification requirements.[36]

In information and communication technology and e-commerce, the two countries will cooperate by developing a memorandum of understanding. In services the parties will expand trade in services and explore possibilities for cooperation, especially in education, tourism, air services, and labour and professional services. In investment the parties aim to increase investment by exchanging information, enhancing transparency and predictability, protecting investments and investors, and building institutional linkages

[36]The aim is also to enhance cooperation in WTO-related training for Chinese personnel. The plan is to utilize the China–Australia–New Zealand Standard Wool Contract, establish liaison channels, enhance contacts and linkages, and adopt administrative measures to deal with outstanding issues.

to promote investment visits, B2B initiatives, conferences, and other innovations.

As with the Australian Framework Agreement there is stress on the importance of regular bilateral meetings between leaders and ministers. The countries have established a Joint Ministerial Commission as a forum for a dialogue on joint trade and economic issues. China and New Zealand will strengthen the role of their Joint Trade and Economic Commission and other sectoral Joint Commissions.

Unlike Australia, New Zealand has immediately recognized China as a market economy[37] and agrees not to implement any anti-dumping measures against China under the Sections 15 and 16 of the WTO accession protocol, and paragraph 242 of the Report of the Working Party on China's accession to the WTO. The parties commit (as with Australia) to undertake a Joint Feasibility Study[38] on a bilateral Free Trade Agreement and commence negotiations on establishing a FTA as soon as possible (possibly in early 2005). China–New Zealand FTA negotiations will be the first China will have with a developed country, and there are good reasons for China choosing New Zealand in this way. New Zealand has a one-China policy, recognized China early in the 1970s and reached early agreement on China's accession to WTO.[39]

3.4. *Other potential Chinese regional agreements*

While formal agreements involving China are limited to the two CEPA agreements, ASEAN, Australia, and New Zealand, several others are either in negotiation or proposed. One example is India. There is no official text of any pre-FTA agreement between India and China thus far, but both countries appear to be moving towards FTA negotiations. In the past there have been disputes regarding borders issues between the countries, but it now seems that they now share common interests in trade and also in WTO matters.

A joint Declaration was signed after the Indian Prime Minister's visit to China in June 2003. In the Declaration the two countries, China and India indicate their plan to use measures consistent with the national laws and international obligations to remove impediments to bilateral trade and

[37]New Zealand is the first developed country to recognize China as a market economy.
[38]See Annex 2.
[39]See Colin James, *Far Eastern Review*, April 22, 2004.

investment.[40] China and India have started discussing a possible bilateral trade arrangement on preferential tariffs (more preferential than the MFN tariffs) on a range of products: including paper, steel, chemicals, and food. The list includes 217 Indian exports and 188 Chinese exports facing lower than average tariffs in the other market.[41] In June, 2003, the two countries agreed to form a Joint Study Group to explore the potential for expanded bilateral trade and cooperation.[42] The resulting India–China Group met in March, 2004, with the aim of preparing a five-year blueprint for bilateral trade and cooperation.[43]

Another example is Chile. Chile and China announced plans for a feasibility study in April, 2004, on possibilities for strengthened trade and cooperation, and a possible free trade agreement. The study is to evaluate a free trade agreement between the two countries in different sectors and on overall economic relations and will cover goods, services and investments. Negotiations between China and Chile are expected to start later this year on an FTA, and at this time, Chile may well announce their recognition of China's market economy status.

A further area of bilateral activity for China is South Africa. In June, 2004, China and South Africa issued a joint communiqué in which South Africa granted China market economy status. In the communiqué, China and South Africa also announced their plan to launch FTA negotiations. In the declaration, the two countries stated they would work on encouraging bilateral trade and investment and expanding cooperation in "areas of mutual economic interest".[44]

There are also bilateral activities with the Middle East. In July, 2004, China and the Gulf Cooperation Council (UAE, Bahrain, Kuwait, Oman, Qatar, and Saudi Arabia) signed a Framework Agreement on Economic, Trade, Investment and Technological Cooperation. Under this, the two countries agree to encourage cooperation and technological exchange, expand trade, and promote mutual investment. They also establish a joint committee on cooperation to implement the agreement and create a consultation mechanism.

---

[40]See *The India and China Declaration on Principals for Relations and Comprehensive Cooperation*. June 23, 2003.
[41]See *Decan Herald*, July 26, 2003.
[42]See S. Sethuraman, *The Kashmir Telegraph*, August 2003.
[43]See *Outlook India*, March 22, 2004.
[44]See China and Chile Joint Communique, June 29, 2004.

China and the GCC have also agreed to launch negotiations on a Free Trade Agreement (the dates have not yet been set).[45] If established a China-GCC FTA would be the second Chinese agreement with a regional group, the ASEAN agreement being the other. China's aim would be to benefit from secure oil imports from the Gulf countries and expand exports of garments, fabrics, and electronics to the region. China also seeks increased GCC investment in water and electricity supply, energy and mineral industry, transportation, communication, and closer cooperation in scientific and technological research.[46]

Elsewhere in Asia, Singapore and China have started consultations on a possible FTA after China concluded the ASEAN Agreement. Talks were scheduled to start in November, 2004, but were delayed following the Singapore Deputy Prime Minister's visit in Taiwan in September, 2004.[47]

China has therefore already moved some distance down the regional negotiation path, proceeding pragmatically in different ways with different partners. Also, these negotiations seemingly represent progressive engagement and the development of intercountry relationships as much as precise text with clearly defined and precisely articulated commitments. Agreements go well beyond trade and services, and cover many areas of cooperation not touched on in WTO agreements.

4. China's WTO Commitments and Key Service Sectors[48]

In this section, I discuss the policy changes that WTO accession implies in key service categories in China (banking, insurance, and telecoms). The commitments in these areas are deep and wide ranging. Over the five years from 2002 to 2007 China committed to open all of her service markets to full international competition from foreign service providers in a series of key areas: distribution, telecommunications, financial services, professional business and computer services, motion pictures, environmental services, accounting, law, architecture, construction, and travel and tourism. Barriers to entry in the form of discriminatory licenses to operate were removed and conduct barriers in the form of differential regulation for domestic and foreign entries were removed. China also agreed to undergo a special Trade Policy Review Mechanism (TRM) exercise in the WTO, under which

[45] See China and GCC Joint Communique, July 7, 2004.
[46] See Bo Xilai, Ministry of Commerce release, July 9, 2004.
[47] See Agence France Presse, August 3, 2004, and July 25, 2004.
[48] This section draws on Whalley (2003).

the WTO's 16 subsidiary bodies and committees reviewed the country's progress on implementation each year for the next eight years. If fully implemented these commitments amount to major new market openings in China in terms of access for foreign suppliers for core intermediation services.

However, the starting point for implementing these policy changes also seems so highly restricted that doubts have been raised about the feasibility of implementing such changes over such a short time, even if threats of eventual retaliation from WTO partners speeds things along. WTO members are monitoring the implementation of China's WTO commitments, and following dispute settlement might retaliate in the future were these agreed changes not to be implemented.

4.1. *Banking* [49]

China has committed herself to full market access for foreign banks within five years. The current regime is restrictive of foreign banks who are not allowed to conduct local currency (Renminbi) business with foreign businesses or individuals. Geographical restrictions also apply to the establishment of foreign banks. These restrictions will go, and China will allow internal branching and provide national treatment for all newly allowed activities by foreign entities. Local currency business will be allowed with Chinese enterprises two years after WTO accession, and with Chinese individuals five years after.

Foreign financial institutions were permitted to provide foreign currency services in China immediately following Chinese accession to the WTO and without any restrictions as to clients or location. However, the Renminbi (or foreign exchange certificate), the local currency, remains inconvertible. Local currency business is to be opened up in step by step fashion over five years (until 2007). China will also open foreign banking business in local currency in twenty cities in five groups within four years of accession. Foreign financial institutions will be allowed to provide retail banking services everywhere in local currency, and to all Chinese clients. Foreign institutions will also be allowed to provide intermediary and advisor services freely, including deposit services, financial lending services, merger and acquisition advice, and securities investment advice.

[49] See also the detailed discussion of China's banking sector and the implications of WTO accession in Bhattasali (2002).

A number of foreign or joint venture banks have already received licenses as part of the implementation of China's WTO commitments. As of 2003, as Whalley (2003) documents, these already included the Bank of East Asia, Citibank, Hang Seng, HSBC, and Standard Chartered. A more extensive recent list is provided by Hope and Hu (2005). Rights to offer Renminbi lending to foreign companies and individuals have also been extended beyond regional pilot programmes, and when China's WTO commitments are fully implemented the aim is that the entire Chinese banking sector will then be fully open to foreign competition. However, the initial starting point for these reforms is so far away from the planned termination point (in part because the role of the Chinese banking sector in the past differs sharply from that of an OECD economy), that doubts have inevitably been expressed as to China's ability to fully implement the commitments.

Prior to the economic reforms of the 1990s China had a planned economy with development of heavy industry as the priority for its economic development.[50] Financial markets did not exist and the People's Bank of China (PBOC) was the single financial institution. It acted both as a central bank and as a provider of banking services via deposits and loans, but loans were made almost exclusively to state-owned enterprises. While the Chinese banking system today has a wider range of financial institutions with the PBOC now acting solely as a central bank, the function of the banking system still reflects the earlier structure.

At the top tier of the Chinese Banking System (the largest part of the system) are four large state banks: China Industry and Commerce Bank, China Agriculture Bank, Bank of China, and China Construction Bank. They are under no explicit mandate to lend heavily to state entities, but do so on the grounds that such loans are safe (i.e. they are state to state loans), even though recipient enterprises lose money and cannot directly service their debt. The expectation is that the state (via the banking system) will bail out loss-making enterprises and the loans involved will eventually be repaid.

A second tier involves locally-owned banks, such as the Shanghai Bank, and the Shenzhen Development Bank. These operate in similar ways to the state-owned banks, but are under different political control (typically provincial or citywide). A third tier consists of three major

[50]See Lin, Cai, and Li (1998) for a discussion of this evolution.

policy-based regional shareholder commercial banks: the Construction Agricultural Development Bank, the Import/Export Bank, and the Bank of China (foreign currency bank). A fourth tier involves mixed individual enterprise-owned banks. Ownership here includes state-owned enterprises, local enterprises, and local governments. Few of these banks issue securities which are traded on stock markets. Currently there are only four banks for whom trading takes place and this is in class A shares (these are only allowed to be held by Chinese residents).

State-owned enterprises remain the largest borrower from the banking system,[51] and four large state-owned banks conduct most of this business. Relatively few individuals have bank accounts. Personal assets (houses, autos) when acquired are usually paid for in full. Financing of these usually reflects informal credit (loans from family or friends). State-owned enterprises also typically lose money, and state-owned banks have major difficulties with non-performing loans. Official estimates put these as high as 25% of loans outstanding, but unofficial estimates are as high as 50–60% of loans outstanding (see Zhang, 1999; Yuan, 2000; and Bonin and Huang, 2001). The Central Bank thus recapitalizes the state banks who in turn lend money to loss-making state-owned enterprises.

Participation by foreign financial institutions in this banking system is limited, but is developing. According to Lin (2001), by early 2000 foreign banks and financial institutions had already established 191 representative offices and subsidiaries in 23 city locations in China with total assets of $36 billion.[52] Foreign banks have also recently been allowed to upgrade their representative offices to branches and to conduct local currency business in certain areas. Even more recently, foreign financial institutions have acquired minority share ownership in smaller mixed-ownership banks. For instance, Newbridge Financial has acquired a 15% interest in Shenzhen Development Bank, and Citicorp has taken a 5% interest in Pudong Development Bank.[53]

To complete the implementation of China's WTO accession commitments by 2007 seemingly more major changes need to occur, and if enacted would also likely substantially change the structure of the Chinese economy (also see Lin, 2000). Foreign entry into banking services could

[51] See the description in Broadman (2001).

[52] Bhattasali (2002) reports the same data.

[53] Hope and Hu (2005) provide more recent data involving 13 Chinese domestic banks and foreign strategic partners.

provide strong competition for local banks who are not only believed to be inefficient but also saddled with large non-performing loans. Some believe that the local banking industry could be greatly impacted by such changes and such change may not easily be able to be accommodated. Others argue that an incentive will remain for China to keep the Renminbi inconvertible so that foreign banks will have limited initial access to Renminbi deposits and hence will be unable to make local currency loans. Another argument sometimes heard is that only the local Chinese banks fully understand how business is done in China, and hence local banks will keep most of their market share, especially in more remote rural areas.

Also, subsidies to state-owned entities are to be terminated as part of the WTO accession process, and loan activities based on an expectation they will continue to be paid must also seemingly change. China's WTO commitments thus need to be seen in their totality as they affect banking services, both as they relate directly to the banking sector and to the real side of the economy. Given the scope of China's WTO commitments the banking system seemingly must evolve from a structure which *defacto* recapitalizes loss-making state-owned enterprises towards a more conventional OECD style commercial banking system largely offering intermediation. For this to happen the real side of the economy must seemingly also undergo substantial change along with the banking sector.

4.2. *Insurance*

In insurance, few foreign insurers operate in the Chinese market, and prior to WTO accession China reserved the right to limit operations by city and to terminate any rights granted to foreign entities. Most insurance activity in China is business related. There is relatively little personal life or house insurance, although the car insurance market is growing rapidly with the growth of autos. Under its WTO commitments, China agrees to limit licenses only on prudential grounds with no limits on the number of licenses issued. China will progressively eliminate geographical restrictions on licenses within three years, and will also allow internal brokerage. The situation in insurance differs considerably from that in banking, and implementation of WTO commitments in this area will likely be easier to achieve.

The tiering of insurance companies differs from that in the banking sector since there is no insurance analogue to the central bank. First comes wholly state-owned insurance companies who are nonprofit, and account for around 70% of Chinese insurance business; the largest being Peoples Insurance and Life. Next comes joint share insurance companies owned by state-owned enterprises of which the largest is Pacific. Then comes joint venture insurance companies of various forms, followed by wholly foreign-owned companies directly offering insurance services, largely to Chinese companies. The latter are typically branches of foreign insurance companies.

Unlike in banking, foreign entry to China's insurance market is already allowed through licensing, and though building from a small base an entry point has already been established for foreign insurance providers. In insurance the main barriers to foreign activity seem not to be policy related but are more market driven.[54] Licenses for life insurance operations have been granted on a city basis to American International and Sun Life.

However, the Chinese market is seen by foreigners as complicated because (for foreign companies) of unusual organizational forms, legal and other arrangements, differing business customs, and the need for Chinese language skills to conduct business. Since foreign insurance companies seem to find it hard to do business in China entry by them into the market has been difficult and foreigners do not always accept licenses to operate, even when applied for and offered. According to Chinese insurance providers, many opportunities for joint ventures have not been taken up by foreign entities even though there are no formal barriers.

In insurance, unlike banking, foreign entry to the Chinese market is both already possible and allowed, but foreigners seemingly do not take up new entry opportunities quickly. As a result, the terms of WTO accession in insurance seemingly pose fewer problems for China than in banking since the market seems formally open to foreigners, even if appearing *defacto* closed. As a result WTO accession in insurance may pose fewer adjustment pressures for China than in banking.

4.3. *Telecoms*[55]

In telecoms, as part of China's WTO commitments, China's Ministry of Information Industry (MII) has agreed to new rules for basic and value-added services in telecoms which allow for more foreign ownership and less

[54] This may be more the perception on the Chinese side than that of OECD trade negotiators, but is as communicated to me on a recent visit in China.

[55] Also see the discussion of the telecoms situation in Pangestu and Mrongowius (2002).

geographical restriction of licenses. This will limit the ability of dominant local carriers to keep rates high and depress demand for telecommunications services and electronic commerce.

Seven operators are currently licensed in China reflecting a regulatory structure inherited from prior reforms in 1999. The most significant entity in the sector is China Telecom (CT) originally part of the Ministry of Posts and Telecommunications and established as a separate entity in 2000. CT controls 99% of China's main fixed line phone capacity. Next comes China Unicom, the major mobile phone operator, established in 1994. Then come a series of enterprises with regulatory approval to operate in various telecom markets. These include a satellite operator ChinaSat, a broadband IP network developer China Netcom, as well as China Telecommunications Broadcast Satellite Corporation, Jitong, and China Railways Communications.

As part of WTO accession China has also signed the WTO Telecommunications Agreement which requires free entry to the Chinese market for foreign service providers by 2007. This would place China on a par with the larger OECD economies where in recent years foreign providers frequently and freely access foreign markets and large rate reductions have occurred.

The current situation is that *defacto* two large state-owned providers (China Unicom, and Telecom China) dominate the market and there is both rate and entry regulation. This structure applies both for basic (hardwire and mobile) telecom services and for peripheral add-on services. Rates are set at above international levels and profits of these utilities are a significant revenue source for both national and provincial governments.

The main commitments stemming from China's WTO accession in this area involve market access (via rights to establish) and national treatment. Foreign investment will be allowed in the sector, but with initially geographical restrictions and limits placed on ownership levels. Geographical restrictions are to be removed and the foreign ownership limit is to be raised to 49% for most services in two years for value-added services, five years for mobile telephones, and six years for international services.

Different issues arise in telecoms compared to banking and insurance. One is the revenue implication of foreign telecom entry for national and provincial governments since both benefit by participating in regulated utilities either directly or indirectly under their management. Another is the costs to consumers in switching when new entry occurs.

4.4. *Implementability of China's WTO service commitments*

China's WTO commitments in these service areas (and particularly banking) are so extensive that they have inevitably lead to questions about both the feasibility and likelihood of full implementation. Once in place WTO commitments become subject to dispute settlement and enforcement through retaliation. Whether China can retain enough autonomy to keep the unique economic structure it now has, and whether political opposition will ensue and in some way limit their full implementation is an issue.

On the infeasibility side, concerns usually focus on the possible disappearance of much of domestic industry in these service categories under WTO implementation[56] and the potential unacceptability if this were it to happen (and the political impact of the resulting labour market dislocation) as well as the perceived strategic need for domestic service industries (as argued by Brazil for their own banking sector in the WTO, for instance). Believers in such liberalization stress the benefits to China from the gains from free trade, but such benefits even if achieved will likely not remove opposition to change. A conjecture that has been advanced is that Chinese negotiators either were not really fully aware of what they were committing to, or if so aware believed there was some form of escape still available through other unconstrained regulation (perhaps new licenses of some form). Those taking this line argue that all these pressures will likely eventually force some kind of *defacto* renegotiation of accession terms or a slowing of implementation, even though other country WTO members would likely take the line that renegotiation is impossible since the commitments involved are all set out in firm contractual form.

On the feasibility side, the arguments are that services liberalization in China is to be implemented as part of WTO commitments and fits into a wider developmental strategy of SOE containment and achieving of efficiency gains and resource allocation improvements. The claim is that domestic service industries can compete in an internationally freer environment. One possible supporting mechanism sometimes suggested involves other policy elements in the equation which will shield Chinese industry from adjustment (such as an inconvertible Renminbi in the case of banking). Since implicit threats to pursue WTO dispute settlement and retaliation (if necessary) characterize the position of US and other OECD

---

[56]The likelihood of this in the banking sector is discussed by Bhattasali (2002).

country WTO negotiations (in public at least), the argument is that China will have no choice but to implement their commitments in these key service areas. Question marks thus remain both over China's objectives in negotiating WTO services liberalization, her ability to implement it and the resolve of foreigners to push it through.

5. Concluding Remarks

China is so large in population terms and, along with India, growing so rapidly that the global economy over the next few decades will be significantly influenced by what is happening in China. China's trade is a central part of the equation; how China responds to the challenges she faces both in and outside the WTO will affect future global performance and is of importance to all, whether inside or outside of China.

In contrast to other global economic powers China stands in contrast in seemingly building its current developmental strategy centrally around her accession to the WTO and implementation of accession terms. Outside China, the WTO does not seemingly enter domestic policy discussion in this central way and there is even considerable pessimism as to the WTO's prospects. For China, the issue is whether delivery on the internal claims made for WTO accession is feasible.

On access issues, I argue that the WTO seemingly yields China less than the rhetoric that was suggested of Chinese accession at the time citing the areas of anti-dumping and textiles and apparel trade. I also highlight the emerging network of regional trade agreements that China is now involved in negotiating following her accession to the WTO in 2002. The issue is how the Chinese national interest may be served by these agreements, given that asymmetries in size and power in the trading system seemingly produce an inevitable two tier system of large power non-discriminatory arrangements reflected in common multilateral disciplines and regional agreements negotiated by large powers with smaller countries going beyond these disciplines where the large power has the dominant interest.

I finally discuss China's WTO accession commitments in the areas of banking, insurance, and telecoms. Whether China will be able to fully implement these commitments over the implementation period from 2002 to 2007 and with what effect are issues highlighted.

The central role that China is now playing in the global economy is highlighted by her large and rapidly growing trade share, the adjustment problems this is raising in the OECD and elsewhere (but with the commitment gains to OECD consumers), and the role of export platform inward FDI in fuelling this trade growth. China is both completing WTO accession implementation and exploring her options on global trade policy as this order process unfolds. If these trends continue the challenge for the world outside China is as much to integrate into China, as it is for China to integrate into the world.

References

Antkiewicz, A. and J. Whalley (2005a). Recent Chinese Buy Outs: Possible Implications for Global Economic Architecture, mimeo.

Antkiewicz, A. and J. Whalley (2005b). China's New Regional Trade Agreements, *The World Economy*, 28(10): 1539–58.

Australian Government Department of Foreign Affairs and Trade (2004). *Australia–China Free Trade Agreement Feasibility Study*. Available at http://www.dfat.gov.au/geo/china/fta/ (accessed June 24, 2004).

Bach, C., W. Martin and J. Stevens (1996). China and the WTO: Tariff Offers, Exemptions and Welfare Implications, *Weltwirtschaftliches Archiv*, 132(3): 409–31.

Barshefsky, Ambassador Charlene (2000). *American Trade Policy and China's WTO Accession, Speech to the Economic Club of Washington, March 16, 2000.* Hong Kong: US Consulate website. Available at http://hongkong.usconsulate.gov/uscn/trade/general/ustr/2000/0316a.htm (accessed June 30, 2004).

Bhattasali, D. (2002). *Accelerating Financial Market Restructuring in China*, Washington, DC: The World Bank, mimeo.

Bhattasali, D., S. Li and W. Martin (2004). *China and the WTO: Accession, Policy Reform, and Poverty Reduction Strategies.* Washington DC: The World Bank.

Bonin, J. P. and Y. Huang (2002). Foreign Entry into Chinese Banking: Does WTO Membership Threaten Domestic Banks? *The World Economy*, 25(8): 1077–1093.

Broadman, H. E. (2001). The Business(es) of the Chinese State, *The World Economy*, 24(7): 849–875.

Hope, N. and F. Hu (2005). Can Foreign Entry Transform China's Banking System. Stanford Institute for Economic Policy Research, Stanford University, Policy Brief, November.

Huang, H., Y. Wang, J. Whalley and S. Zhang (2005). A Trade Model with an Optimal Exchange Rate Motivated by Current Discussion of a Chinese Renminki Float. CESifo WP No. 1471, Munich.

Ianchovichina, E. and W. Martin (2004). Economic Impacts of China's Accession to the WTO, in Bhattsali, D., S. Li and W. Martin (eds.), *China and the WTO*. Oxford University Press, for the World Bank.

Ianchovichina, E. and W. Martin (2003). Economic Impacts of China's Accession to the World Trade Organization. Washington DC: The World Bank, Policy Research Working Paper No. 3053.

Lardy, N. R. (1998). *China's Unfinished Economic Revolution.* Washington DC: The Brookings Institution Press.

Lardy, N. R. (2002). *Integrating China into the Global Economy.* Washington DC: The Brookings Institution Press.

Lin, J. Y. (2001). WTO Accession and Financial Reform in China. *The Cato Journal*, 21(1): 13–18.

Lin, J. Y. (2000). What is the Director of China's Financial Reform?, in Went Cai and Feng Lu (eds.) *China Economic Transition and Economic Policy.* Beijing, China: Peking University Press, 296–301.

Lin, J. Y., Fang Cai and Zhou Li (1996). *The China Miracle: Development Strategy and Economic Reform.* Hong Kong: Chinese University Press.

Pangestu, M. and D. Mrongowius (2002). *Telecommunications in China: Facing the Challenges of WTO Accession.* Washington, DC: The World Bank, mimeo.

Rose, A. (2004). Do We Really Know that the WTO Increases Trade? *American Economic Review*, 94(1): 98–114.

Schott, J. J. (ed.) (2004). *Free Trade Agreements: US Strategies and Priorities.* Washington, DC: Institute for International Economics.

Stewart, T. P. (2004). *China's Compliance with World Trade Organization Obligations: A Review of China's 1st Two Years of Membership.* A Report for the US-China Economic and Security Review Commission. Washington DC: USCC. Available at http://www.uscc.gov/researchreports/2004/04annual_report.PDF (accessed June 30, 2004).

United States Trade Representative (2004). *2003 National Trade Estimate Report on Foreign Trade Barriers.* Washington DC: USTR. Available at http://www.ustr.gov/reports/nte/2003 (accessed June 23, 2004).

Walmsley, T. L. and T. W. Hertel (2001). China's Accession to the WTO: Timing is Everything. *The World Economy*, 24(8): 1019–1049.

Wang, Jiangyu (2004). China's Regional Trade Agreement (RTA)Approach: The Law, the Geopolitics, and the Impact on the Multilateral Trading System. *Singapore Year Book of International Law*, 8: 119–147.

Whalley, J. (2003). Liberalization in China's Key Service Sectors Following WTO Accession: Some Scenarios and Issues of Measurement. Cambridge, MA: National Bureau of Economic Research Working Paper No. 10143.

Yongtu, Long (2000). On the Question of Our Joining the World Trade Organization. *The Chinese Economy* 33(1): 5–52.

Yuan, Gangming (2000). An Empirical Analysis of Non-performing Loans in China's SUEs. *Economic Research Journal* (Tan Ji Yan Jiu), 5: 12–20.

Zhang, S. and J. Whalley (2005). Modelling Behavioural Responses to Trade Liberalization in China Capturing SOE Behaviour, mimeo.

CHINA'S POST-ACCESSION WTO STANCE

Glenda Mallon
Centre for International Governance Innovation (CIGI)
Waterloo, Canada

John Whalley
University of Western Ontario; CIGI and NBER

We discuss China's stance in the WTO post-accession, noting the many issues with the implementation of China's accession terms by 2007. We evaluate how much benefit China can realistically receive from WTO membership given the current problems with dumping actions against China and trade restrictions against textile and apparel exports. We discuss emerging WTO and non-WTO trade disputes involving China, and China's now-extensive regional trade initiatives that have raised issues of multilateral regional balance in China's trade policy strategy.

1. Introduction

Prior to the completion of the lengthy negotiations on Chinese WTO accession,[1] there was extensive debate inside China on the merits of this step from a Chinese perspective. This debate has continued, despite the initiation of implementation of the terms of accession now due to be completed by 2007. The talk in China today is of post-WTO China; and every new policy initiative is discussed not only in terms of its WTO compatibility, but also in terms of its ability to contribute to the implementation of the accession process and the eventual harnessing of China's WTO benefits. The completion of accession negotiations was been hailed internally as a milestone in China's economic development, with claims of significant additions to growth potential, and a new policy environment underpinned by the single most important policy departure

[1]These concluded with the adoption of the report by the WTO working party on Chinese Accession on November 10, 2001.

since Deng Xiao Ping's introduction of the responsibility system in 1976. At the same time, WTO accession has been criticized by detractors as establishing too quickly a western style market-oriented environment in China, which will likely lead to greater inequality and over-centralization, and has resulted in China giving away too many WTO bargaining chips which could have been more effectively used in later global negotiations.

From outside, this discussion inside China seems orthogonal to recent discussion of the WTO elsewhere. Globally, there has until recently been pessimism about prospects for the completion of the Doha Round in 2005,[2] rejection of the WTO and global institutions by anti-globalization protesters, a sense of an overburdened and, at times, atmosphere-poisoned dispute settlement process in the WTO whose credibility is in some eyes increasingly becoming tarnished.[3] This pessimism is also compounded by the acceleration of a seemingly post-Uruguay Round headlong rush into Bhagwati's spaghetti bowl of overflowing and inconsistent regionalism, with multiple US and EU regional initiatives, and many other bilateral or small new group arrangements. The point of departure for this paper relative to the substantial literature on the possible impacts of Chinese accession[4] is to instead focus on China's WTO situation in the post-Uruguay, pre-Doha Round completion period.[5] We focus less on accession and more on issues surrounding China's participation in the WTO post-accession.

Despite being a large entity with an ever-more sophisticated delegation in Geneva and an active trade ministry, China has been largely content to

---

[2]A significant change in atmosphere has occurred only recently. In June 2004, the G-8 countries following an EU initiative mutually agreed to terminate export subsidies in agriculture, removing a central impediment to forward progress in the agriculture negotiations in the Round. The EU have also removed all requests for a negotiation in competition policy and investment. The G-8 claim is that this will enable progress to be made in July on a final package, but developing countries remain cautious. See Colitt (2004), and Williams (2004).

[3]The atmosphere in dispute settlement has been adversely affected by critical US–EU cases regarding bananas and growth hormones, where due to the time limits on process agreed to in the Uruguay Round, multiple panels were spawned by a single initial dispute, and the reports of one panel were never finally accepted by all parties. Other US–EU trade disputes such as steel have also contributed to this atmosphere. See for example, Cooper (2001), *Wall Street Journal* or Hecht (2000), *Law and Policy in International Business* (2000).

[4]See, for example, Ianchovichina and Martin (2003) and Yang (2003).

[5]As such, this seems to go beyond the discussion in Lardy (2002) and World Bank (1997).

observe and try to better understand WTO process, rather than actively promote new initiatives. As 2007 approaches, however, there is the question of what China actually should and can do in the WTO.

We ask a series of questions to help focus our discussion. We ask how important is the WTO membership to China in terms of yielding traditional access benefits to markets around the world if accession terms yield China little on dumping, and textiles and apparel? Is the Chinese interest more in the quality of access or security of access that China already has? If the latter, what extra advantages does WTO membership offer China on this front? Does WTO membership help in trade disputes or merely serve to generate new ones?

In our discussion, we focus less on the use of the WTO as a masthead to cement and underpin domestic policy reform, which was seemingly a major factor in the Chinese decision to seek accession. Instead, we discuss a series of key short- to medium-term trade access issues. These include anti-dumping actions against China, a prospective new global trade regime in textiles and apparel following the end of the Multifibre Arrangement, and a growing list of trade conflicts both inside and outside the WTO. Here, we ask what WTO membership can potentially do for China in these areas. We also ask how regional and multilateral trade strategies for China can best be commingled, and conclude with a discussion of how China's interests in the WTO overlap with those of other large emerging economies (India, Brazil, and Russia) and the plurality of poorer medium- to small-countries who can formally outvote all in the WTO.

The two central arguments we make are firstly that China's WTO membership seemingly changes little about the two central access issues of anti-dumping and textiles and apparel. We also argue that the complexity of both the WTO agreements inherited on accession (around 26,000 pages of text for the Uruguay Round decisions) and of current Chinese policy instruments could give rise to many new trade disputes involving instruments of policy not previously encountered by the WTO.

We further argue that China has split interests in future trade arrangements. China has a global interest in using strong multilateral trade rules, similar to that of Japan in the 1960s, to allow relatively unhindered access to the EU and North American markets to fuel continued export growth. Regionally and locally, China can exert power in regional or bilateral negotiations to obtain preferential access to rapidly growing regional markets. However, this is inconsistent with both the spirit and letter of multilateral rules. We suggest that finding a way to combine these two interests in securing market access interests will be central to China's trade growth over the next few decades.

China is well placed strategically to exert great influence over developments in the trading system in the next few decades, if she chooses to exercise strong leadership among emerging powers in fora such as the G20. How the WTO will be changed by Chinese membership, and whether China's accession terms may eventually be (*de facto*) renegotiated slightly, are the final issues we discuss.

2. China's Interest in the WTO

There has been much discussion in the last few years of what exactly it was that took China into the WTO (or in Chinese eyes, restored their GATT membership that was suspended in 1950).[6] Arguments range from the need to have the security of firm MFN benefits in place of previous insecure arrangements (and subject to periodic review and renewal), to the domestic uses of WTO membership by modernizers who wanted to see genuine market-based policy reform which would speed growth and reform as well as curb the power of provinces.[7]

In our view, there was a deeper WTO accession debate in China that should be seen as part of a longer historic discussion of China's relationship with the outside world, albeit one significantly coloured by Chinese engagement with the European powers in the late 19th century. The central issue is whether China was being threatened by the outside world and should therefore turn inwards, or whether the outside world (and the WTO) was a source of opportunity and modernity that China should embrace. The broad question debated was thus the one of engagement with versus isolationism from the world community, rather than the precise terms of accession to the WTO. The central argument in favour of accession was that China should pursue modernization and take its rightful place among the leading world powers in global institutions, and that WTO accession was the vehicle for this.

[6]On March 6, 1950, Taiwanese authorities notified the UN Secretary General of its decision to withdraw from the GATT. See: University of Toronto website: *China's Accession to the WTO: A Chronology of Major Events between China and the GATT/WTO*.

[7]According to Long Yongtu, the former chief Chinese negotiator on accession: "We must let those [WTO] rules that stand at the core of the market economy, and which have to be obeyed, take firm roots in our society and country, so that our own market economy may become one that is truly orderly, efficient, honest and clean." See Long (2000).

For the larger powers negotiating with China (especially the US and the EU) the accession process was in contrast seen primarily as an opportunity to pursue commercial policy interests rather than being about engagement or isolationism. How could greatly improved access to a rapidly growing and potentially huge — if not dominant — market be secured, and at minimal cost in terms of formal reciprocal WTO commitments made to China? At the time of the conclusion of accession negotiations, parallel speeches from Chinese and EU/US negotiators spoke from the Chinese side of a fair and balanced arrangement with the restoration of normal trade relations (NTR), and from the EU/US side of a one-sided agreement in which China had made all the concessions at a great commercial policy benefit to EU/US business interests.[8]

It has been written elsewhere that the terms of accession for China to the WTO are breathtaking in scope. This is the case particularly in key service areas (banking, telecoms, insurance) where the most radical liberalization commitments anywhere in the world were undertaken with China surrendering most of its future bargaining chips, and receiving little or no reciprocal benefits in return.[9] It is now questionable as to whether China can fulfil these commitments by 2007.

One might therefore ask why China was so concerned to achieve the accession outcome that ensued. Firmness of MFN benefits alone cannot, in our view, explain much since China was already a de facto recipient of MFN benefits, despite periods of Congressional agonizing in the US over human rights and labour standards. Yongtu identifies the advantages to China as allowing the development of China's service sector, generating international acceptance for China's market economy, allowing China some say in the setting of multilateral global trade rules, and greater access to dispute settlement.[10] Further, other countries (Taiwan being the extreme case) seem to have achieved remarkable long-term export growth without formal WTO membership.

But now in the WTO, China's interests will lie both in using WTO disciplines and in writing new WTO trade rules in ways which most effectively guarantee access to large export markets in Europe and North

---

[8]See the speech by Ambassador Charlene Barshefsky of the US Trade Representative to the Economic Club of Washington (March 16, 2000) describing what were portrayed as China's one-way concessions to US business interests. China's compliance with its WTO commitments is discussed in Stewart (2004).

[9]See Whalley (2003).

[10]Long (2000).

America. In approaching the accession decision, a central question for China should have been how far these objectives could have been achieved inside the WTO rather than outside a system of WTO multilateral trade rules, and how the terms of accession should be crafted instead of broader security-related issues of global engagement.

If Chinese growth today rests on continued manufactured export growth fuelled by inward foreign investment, then this trade growth must in turn rest on relatively free and secure access to large markets abroad. This parallels Japan's interests in the 1960s and 1970s. Japan has long been considered one of the major gainers from the post-war GATT system, since the GATT delivered relatively free and nondiscriminatory access to key export markets during a period of sharp export growth. The question is how China can make use of WTO membership to keep markets in Europe and the US open, and tap into increasingly important export markets in middle- to lower-income countries. Are there real and important opportunities, or does WTO membership offer relatively little, especially in key areas such as anti-dumping laws and textiles and apparel trade?

Our discussion thus points to a strong Chinese interest both in effective WTO dispute settlement and ongoing WTO negotiation to improve access terms.[11] It also raises the question of how these fora can be best utilized by China. Should China actively pursue WTO disputes to open up markets abroad, or is the prospect instead one of numerous complaints against China fuelled by WTO membership — which, once in the WTO, China must deal with? Further, these issues may be approached from a Western neo-classical perspective, which is still not fully compatible with China's chosen development route.

The Chinese interest in strong multilateral rules also creates a further dilemma. How can this interest be balanced with China's regional and more local interests to gain China preferential market access closer to home through using market power in bilateral or regional negotiations? And what of concessions on access to the Chinese market made to foreigners as a result of WTO accession, and Chinese concerns over the non-trade areas such as intellectual property, environment, labour standards and competition policy?

Finally, there are strategic issues for China which involve national security interests and their links to trade and commerce, which are

[11]See also the discussion in Martin (2002).

not discussed here. Can WTO membership cement China's key security relationships? Does joint WTO membership for both China and Taiwan pose new problems or create fresh opportunities? Does WTO membership help or hurt relations with the US and Europe? Does it allow for new leadership opportunities in middle- to lower-income countries which would otherwise not be available?

3. Some Key Short- to Medium-Term Trade and WTO Issues for China

China is now facing a number of trade and WTO issues in the short- to medium-term that are affecting both her access to foreign markets and the access granted to foreigners to Chinese markets. Some of these directly involve WTO disciplines; others are broader, reflecting the operation of the wider trading system. If Chinese WTO membership is not perceived to help very much in dealing with these problems, internal political commitment to WTO participation and even domestic policy reform might be weakened. Equally, how China maneouvres within the WTO process will affect global outcomes, China's future trade performance and ultimately, global economic performance.

3.1. *Textiles and apparel*

Near the top of the list of key access-related issues for China is the textiles and apparel trade and the prospective termination of the Multi Fibre Arrangement (MFA). China is now the dominant exporter of apparel items from non-OECD countries; in 2002 value terms accounting for approximately 45% of non-OECD exports. Today, China and India jointly account for the majority of apparel exports from non-OECD to OECD countries,[12] with a large number of smaller suppliers in Asia, Eastern Europe, Central and Latin America with small shares of total trade (but are still a large fraction of country exports). Sri Lanka, for instance, had 53% of total exports in textiles and apparel products in 2002,[13] and these products were 95% and 93% of Bangladesh's and Laos's manufactured goods exports in 2000 respectively.[14]

[12]See WTO (2003b). This is in sharp contrast to the 1980s, when Hong Kong, Taiwan and Korea accounted for 60% of such exports.
[13]See WTO (2004d).
[14]See *Evolution of Trade in Textile and Clothing Trade, Worldwide Trade Figures and Structural Data*, on Europa website.

Since 1974, global trade in textiles and apparel has been restrained by the MFA,[15] which followed the original Short and Long-Term Arrangements on Cotton Textiles first negotiated by the US with key Asian exporters (Japan, Hong Kong, Taiwan and Korea) in 1962.[16] After four rounds of MFA renewal were mutually agreed to by both importing and exporting countries, WTO members agreed to terminate the MFA at the end of 2004 in the 1994 Uruguay Round decisions, using a complex 10-year transitional process to achieve elimination.[17]

The MFA operates with agreed growth rate quotas on exports, complex rules of origin, transshipment rules, a monitoring and a consultation mechanism (a calls system), with 44 exporters and eight North American and European importers. It is widely agreed that the MFA has slowed and restrained export growth in textile and apparel products over the years, even though export shares from non-OECD countries have increased considerably.

Several issues now arise with its termination, which affects all MFA exporters, especially China. One is whether free trade will really replace the MFA. Scenarios for a post-MFA elimination regime abound, from a wave of new anti-dumping petitions from domestic producers in OECD countries that are being used to force a new market-sharing regime (as with steel in the mid-1900s) to the use of safeguard measures (GATT 1994, Article 19) by OECD countries on textile and apparel products.

The view of most developing exporter countries is that there has only been token implementation of transitional arrangements by OECD countries so far, along with a tightening of the application of MFA rules as the MFA is being eliminated. Concerns in the US and the EU over labour adjustment from affected industry groups are clear and strongly stated.[18] A recent piece in *Asian Labour News*, for instance, documents pressures

[15]The Arrangement Regarding International Trade in Textiles (the Multi Fibre Arrangement) came into effect on January 1, 1974.
[16]The Short Term Arrangement on Cotton Textiles was negotiated in 1961, and subsequent a long term arrangement negotiated in 1962. See Thongpakde and Pupphavesa (1999).
[17]A paradox of this outcome was that the MFA was an arrangement mutually agreed to by developing countries that could have unilaterally terminated the agreement by their own decision not to agree to a renewal.
[18]See US Fears Massive Job Losses as Controls Lifted (2003, August 2). *The Standard.*

in the US for the use of new selective MFA transitional safeguards against apparel imports from non-OECD countries.[19]

China's interest is clearly in obtaining unhindered export access in this key area of Chinese trade performance, through full access to OECD export markets for textile and apparel exports. The belief is both that exports to OECD countries will grow even more rapidly under free access and that higher cost production, which has relocated to smaller countries in the region because of quotas on Chinese exports, will relocate to China. How China deals with these issues inside and outside the WTO could well be critical to China's medium-term trade growth. One question is whether China has fresh leverage now that she is inside the WTO, which she can use to ensure smooth and effective termination of restraints on these exports. Or perhaps it is the case that WTO membership makes little difference to the situation, since China was a MFA member both before and after WTO accession. If the former, does China have more effective formal and informal leverage with other interested parties such as India, so as to act together in any subsequent negotiations (such as market sharing arrangements)? Also, can China use WTO membership to link its position on textiles and apparel to that on other issues, including the remaining implementation of its accession terms? One scenario that has been raised is that China may only agree to new global arrangements in textiles and apparel if there is mutual agreement from OECD countries to slow the accession implementation process in services areas such as banking.

3.2. *Anti-dumping*

China also faces many critical challenges in the area of anti-dumping. Around 15% of anti-dumping actions world wide now occur against China, since she is a dynamic grower of exports.[20] In addition, under US statute

---

[19]US Invokes 'Safeguard' on Textile Imports, (2003, November 19). *Asian Labour News*.

[20]In the period from July 1, 2002 to June 30, 2003, China was subject to 42 initiations of anti-dumping investigations, out of a total of 238, approx. 17.6%. See *WTO Annual Report 2004, Table 11.5 Exporters Subject to Two or More Initiations of Anti-dumping Investigations 1 July 2002–30 June 2003* at 46 on WTO web site. In the preceding period, China was subject to 46 new initiations of a total 309. See *WTO Annual Report 2003, Table 1I1.6 Exporters Subject to Two or More Initiations of Anti-dumping Investigations 1 July 2001–30 June 2002* at 83 on WTO web site. From 1995–2001 China was subject to

China is also currently classified as a non-market economy, provoking more stringent application of dumping procedures.[21] China, in turn, has begun to intensify her own use of anti-dumping duties.[22]

One issue China faces in this area is whether, realistically, it makes sense to fight anti-dumping actions if the legal and informational costs are high? *People's Daily* indicates that China had won over 37% of cases in the prior 10 years,[23] but at a high cost in legal fees and other charges. The current view in some circles in China is that if dumping actions against China are narrowly focused on particular products the simplest strategy is simply to respond by producing and exporting other items. But if dumping actions continue against China, at some point the export product range become sufficiently restricted that export performance suffers significantly.

WTO accession formally provides China with little defence against the use of anti-dumping measures against it. Article 6 of GATT 1994 effectively legitimizes the use of anti-dumping measures, and only constrains their use procedurally by specifying how domestic administrative tribunals should determine their use. It is therefore unlikely that WTO membership offers China any significant added benefits in dealing with this major access problem facing its continued export growth. China may be able to push more aggressively for anti-dumping reform in the WTO, long seen as unacceptable to the US Congress even after China's WTO accession. For now, however, this remains non-negotiable.

14% of total global anti-dumping actions (*People's Daily*, April 23, 2002). According to news reports, China has been subject to more than 200 anti-dumping cases since joining the WTO in 2001 (Oliver August, *Times Online*, June 3, 2004).

[21] Article 15 of the protocol on China's accession to the WTO allows other WTO members to treat China as a non-market economy in dumping and subsidy cases for 15 years after its entry. (*China Daily*, May 17, 2004). Under US anti-dumping laws, once a US trade authority deems a country a non-market economy it may disregard the prices of products exported from the country, since they do not reflect supply and demand, and instead use costs in a third surrogate country to calculate dumping margins. At a hearing on June 3/04, the US Commerce Department said US deliberations over whether China is a market-based or state-controlled economy would take at least as long as deliberations on Russia (18 months). See Cheng Dawei, *China Daily*, May 17, 2004, and Doug Palmer, *Reuters*, June 3, 2004.

[22] China initiated 17 anti-dumping actions in the period of July 1, 2002 to June 30, 2003. See *WTO Annual Report 2003, Table 11.5: Summary of Anti-dumping Actions, 1 July 2002 to June 30, 2003.* She initiated no actions in the previous year. China filed 24 anti-dumping cases in the period from 1997 to Sept 2003. See *People's Daily Online*, September 14, 2003.

[23] See *People's Daily Online*, March 29 2002.

3.3. *Services*

In the key service areas of banking, insurance and telecoms, China faces the tasks of implementing far-reaching commitments made in 2001, and manoeuvring on the access front with few service-related bargaining chips, since they were effectively surrendered when China accepted its WTO accession terms. Elsewhere, we have discussed these issues and raised questions about the credibility and implementability of China's commitments in this area.[24]

In banking, China has agreed to remove all geographical restrictions on licences, and also to grant them in a non-discriminatory manner to both domestic and foreign entities, and to extend them to all types of business (including in banking to both domestic and foreign currency transactions). If fully implemented, these commitments will effectively undermine the present fixed exchange rate remnimbi regime, and also restrain the current practice of using state-owned banks in part as recapitalization agencies for loss generating state-owned enterprises (SOE). There has been speculation that the end of such practice will significantly weaken Chinese trade performance, since effective subsidization of SOEs through these devices has fuelled her trade growth.

In insurance, China's main commitment is to non-discriminatory licensing for insurance providers and to also grant licenses free of any geographical restriction. During accession negotiations, foreign negotiators believed that this would effectively open the Chinese insurance market to foreign providers. For now, however, there are more indications of infrequent issuance of licenses to either domestic or foreign providers and hence, more cartelization of the Chinese insurance markets. In telecoms, the commitments relate again to the use of non-discriminatory licensing combined with significant liberalization in terms of foreign currency.

The WTO challenges for China in these service areas involve both the scope of the commitments and the extent of change they imply for the operation of the Chinese economy. A major and radical change is in store for the Chinese banking system if these commitments are fully implemented. If these measures are fully implemented by 2007, China will have one of the most open key service markets of any large global economy. All of this will have been agreed to with no negotiating *quid pro quo* in terms of access

---

[24]See Whalley (2003).

to foreign service markets and with potential significant labour adjustment loss, although these currently appear to be unquantified.

In this area, China must try to find a way to implement what seem to be over-negotiated commitments, or try to obtain some formal concession in the WTO (perhaps for concession in non-service areas) to slow the implementation of the commitments.

3.4. *Trade disputes*

China also currently faces a list of trade disputes, of which some have the potential to spawn a significant number of new WTO dispute panels. The list of potential disputes seen from the US is reflected in the latest USTR Foreign Trade Barriers Report. This itemizes import substitution policies in China in several product areas, such as fertilizer; automobile investment guidelines; tariffs on products that compete with sensitive domestic industries, such as motorcycles and electronic equipment; tariff classification and customs valuation procedures; Chinese border policies that give preferential treatment to non-US imports (such as Russian timber);[25] non-tariff barriers to trade in the form of regulations that set entry barriers to trade in services such as banking and insurance; unwarranted inspections of agriculture products; rules on biotechnology products, the use of sanitary and phytosanitary measures to control import volumes; and export subsidies on corn.[26] Thus far, only one of these disputes has resulted in a formal panel proceeding (the chips case), but others seem poised to be added to the list. China has settled some of her emerging disputes through bilateral accommodation, but the issue for China is how far to move in this direction to accommodate such a procedure.

WTO disciplines define clear rights for other WTO members when accessing China's markets for goods and services, and allowing the use of their intellectual property. It is unclear whether the definition of such rights for China's accession will merely add to the list of disputes and pressure for change in China, or if the added clarity of rights for other WTO members will accelerate trade and investment flows. Free traders typically argue that many or most of the changes that China may be pressured to make under threat of WTO process are in China's interest anyway, since they allow China to more fully harness the gains from trade. However,

[25]Russia is not a WTO member and so this practice by China is WTO compatible.
[26]See United States Trade Representative (2004).

China's developmental strategy thus far has not been fully reflective of an unrestricted market approach, and the more rapid change that is probably implied by the outcome to these disputes may not be seen as a policy compatible with China. China has thus to decide whether WTO trade disputes will ultimately help hasten China's modernization, or are simply a confirmation of the arguments that took China into the WTO in the first place. On the other hand, potential WTO disputes may pressure China into implementing policy changes which she does not yet want to make.

On the offensive side of the trade dispute equation, China has thus far been reluctant to use her WTO membership to assert her rights. There have been no WTO trade panels initiated by China,[27] although China has been active in pressuring foreign governments on various trade matters such as the use of special safeguards in textiles and apparel in the US, Japanese farm measures that affect Chinese exports,[28] and EU environmental barriers on Chinese appliance exports.[29]

The one dispute thus far that has resulted in a formal WTO panel against China involves the treatment of imported semiconductor memory chips into the Chinese market. Under the Chinese national value-added tax, imported chips are subject to a value-added tax of 17%, but domestically produced chips are eligible for special tax rebates that lower the effective tax rate to between 3% and 6%.[30] The US allegation is that this practice is a violation of National Treatment (GATT 1994, Article 3), and the EU and other suppliers (including Taiwan) have also notified an interest in the case to the WTO.[31]

Other emerging trade dispute issues involving China relate to financing packages offered by foreign auto producers in the Chinese market, which were initially disallowed on the grounds that China had yet to implement its WTO commitments with regard to financial services;[32] and whether the current remnimbi exchange rate is a factor in China's significant trade

[27] Although China was the second of nine members to request a panel against the US on safeguards on imports of certain steel products. See WTO (2002).

[28] See Yan (2003). These complaints relate to a Japanese announcement to block imports of Chinese fowl and eggs in May 2003 after a flu virus was detected in exports originating in Guangdong.

[29] See *People's Daily Online* (2004). This matter relates to a new EU directive on waste from electronic equipment that will impose a fee of 1 to 20 euros on any colour TV or mobile phone exported to the EU.

[30] See *The Economist* (2004).

[31] See WTO (2004c).

[32] See Zhang (2003).

surplus position, and represents a GATT 1994 Article 23 nullification and impairment case.

China has recently concluded a bilateral agreement on imports of coking coal from the EU, reflective of an approach of using bilateral accommodation to defuse trade conflicts.[33] China's import quota in this area is to be sharply increased, although not removed as WTO disciplines would seem to imply. This case will likely lead to similar deals with other exporters of coking coal to the Chinese market, and possibly similar deals in other product areas.

3.5. *The domestic regulatory regime*

A final challenge for China that WTO membership entails is the extent of refocusing of the domestic regulatory regime in the medium term. Standard issues involving China's trade figure prominently in the USTR Foreign Trade Barriers report including a lack of transparency in the certification process, a lack of coordination among standards bodies and other agencies, burdensome requirements and long processing times for licenses.[34] US companies claim that achieving certification under China's compulsory certification system is time-consuming, difficult and costly, and that they are subject to redundant testing for cosmetics, pharmaceuticals, and several consumer electronic products, inconsistent application of sanitary and phytosanitary measures, and excessive or inappropriate food labeling requirements.

An illustration of these problems is China's wireless LAN encryption standards, which differ from internationally recognized standards and force international companies to work through the few Chinese manufacturers who possess the necessary algorithm to meet these standards. According to Li Zhonghai, director of China's standardization watchdog, China now has 20,900 compulsory national standards covering safety, hygiene and environmental protection with more than 2,300 new national standards under creation. Only 44% of China's standards reflect agreed international standards (also according to Li Zhonghai) and the challenge is to modify remaining standards and elsewhere rewrite domestic regulatory standards. Such standards relate to health, safety, electrical, product liability and other matters. Standards are widely agreed to be a central area of impact of

[33]See Yan (2004).
[34]See United States Trade Representative (2004), 67–71.

domestic policy regimes on trade, and are not extensively researched. The issues in this area in the Chinese case seem to be quantitatively even larger than those for other economies.

4. Regionalism, China's Trade Policies and the WTO

It is in the area of regional trade agreements that some of the most central trade issues arise for China with her WTO participation. Thus far, China has formally initiated two regional agreements; an agreement with ASEAN and a bilateral agreement with Hong Kong under a Closer Economic Partnership Agreement (CEPA),[35] but others seem likely to follow.

The ASEAN agreement concluded in 2002 is a broad framework agreement with a specified bilateral tariff elimination list to be implemented by 2010.[36] This agreement has yet to be finalized and hence registered with the WTO, where a working party will be established to consider it. *China Daily* reports that initial negotiations for a China–ASEAN FTA are expected to conclude before June 30 2004,[37] with the conclusion of the broad terms of the trade agreement. Current negotiations are focused on rules of origin, trade of goods and trade of services and investment. An early harvest program that was launched on January 1, 2004 has resulted in preferential tariffs on more than 500 mostly agricultural goods.[38] Agriculture, information and communication technologies, human resources development, mutual investment and the development of the Mekong River have been identified as priorities for cooperation.

The CEPA agreement is a tariff elimination agreement. Tariff elimination will occur by 2006. The two parties mutually agree to forgo the use of antidumping and countervailing duties against each other. Safeguards are allowed under a prior written notice arrangement. It also has significant additional provisions in a number of areas. One is in financial services, since it allows Hong Kong banks to acquire ownership and control of Chinese banks; the foreign acquisition of Hong Kong banks is a potential gateway for foreign entry into the Chinese banking market. The CEPA commits the

[35] See Mainland and Hong Kong Closer Economic Partnership Arrangement (2003).

[36] The Framework Agreement on China–ASEAN Comprehensive Economic Cooperation was signed in November 2002, with a proposed free trade area involving 1.7 billion people. Trade between China and ASEAN in the first 10 months of 2002 alone was worth almost US$43.46 billion, by 2005 this number is expected to reach US$63 billion. See People's Daily Online (2002c).

[37] See Yan (2004b).

[38] *Ibid.*

mainland and the Hong Kong Special Administrative Region to progressive removal of bilateral service trade restrictions.

The provisions in the financial cooperation provisions (Article 13 of CEPA) support mainland banks in developing network and business activities in Hong Kong and the "full utilization of financial intermediaries in Hong Kong during the process of reform, restructuring and development of the financial sector in the Mainland".[39] There is agreement on cooperation in tourism and the mutual recognition of professional qualifications, and trade and investment facilitation.

Compared to recent regional trade agreements involving OECD countries, the CEPA is notable for its brevity (and hence, significant degree of vagueness) and its absence of an additional dispute resolution mechanism beyond what the WTO process entails. Disputes are to be resolved "through consultation in spirit of friendship and cooperation",[40] and all decisions of the CEPA steering committee are to be by consensus.

The CEPA has been notified to the WTO, even though China and Hong Kong are two separate WTO members. As the first regional agreement to be concluded by China, this seems to set the precedent for others that will follow, potentially including some parts of the China–ASEAN agreement. Other possible regional partners for China include Korea, Australia–New Zealand, India and even Japan.

On other fronts, the *Financial Times* reported in 2003 that China and India had agreed to coordinate their WTO positions on a range of issues including essential medicines, agriculture and investment.[41] In June 2003, the Indian Prime Minister visited China and agreed to form a joint working party to study bilateral economic cooperation and lay the way for a possible bilateral free trade agreement.[42] Australia and China have jointly released an Australia–China Free Trade Agreement Feasibility Study,[43] Singapore has begun talks on a free trade deal with China,[44] New Zealand has agreed to a formal bilateral trade framework with China,[45] and China, Japan and South Korea have met to discuss regional trade issues.[46]

---

[39] CEPA agreement, Article 13, Section 3.
[40] CEPA agreement, Article 19, Section 5.
[41] See De Jonquieres (2003).
[42] See Vatikiotis and Hiebert (2004).
[43] See Australian Department of Foreign Affairs and Trade (2004).
[44] See Chen (2004).
[45] See James (2004).
[46] See English News Service (2004) and Donnan and Ward (2003).

For China, as for the US and the EU, the incentive is to adhere to strong multilateral WTO disciplines as a way of securing access to larger markets on non-discriminatory terms, while seeking regional arrangements going beyond WTO rules with smaller entities giving China preferential regional access to smaller markets. The current US regional agreements stress preferential access in services, while EU agreements stress partnership and commonality in legal structure. As a large manufactured goods exporter, China's regional agreements for now stress preferential access in these areas, and so the structure of China's regional agreements will likely continue to differ significantly from those of other large trade entities. Cultural differences will also be reflected in areas such as dispute settlement, where an Asian consensus will likely be stressed. For China, however, the issue will remain one of balance between WTO and regional trade objectives.

5. China, the Doha Round, Trade Relations with Other Emerging Large Middle Income Powers and Global Architecture

While China is now a key player in the WTO process, China is not alone in both having negotiating power and being able to exercise this in her own interests in WTO process. How far China goes in exercising her influence jointly with other emerging middle-income powers such as India, Brazil and Indonesia, and powers yet to join the WTO such as Russia will be important.

On the one hand, these are economies in competition with China for export growth-driven access to large markets in the EU and the US. But on the other hand-the commonality of interest suggests that substantial opportunities exist for collaborative activity between China and these other countries, both within the WTO and outside. These are also more rapidly-growing markets than in the OECD and are increasingly areas of significant export importance to China.

In the short term, Chinese interests in the WTO Doha Round are key. Optimism or pessimism on its outcome will play a role, as will China's interest in exercising leadership among the emerging large middle income powers in its conclusion. Agriculture and the export subsidization, which until recently divided the EU and the US, is one issue. But issues of implementation of Uruguay Round decisions will preoccupy smaller and poorer countries, and related matters of clarifying the interpretation of special and differential treatment also arise.

China is also a country with a large, rapidly-growing economy effectively outside of the global institutional apparatus of the WTO, the World Bank, and the IMF for nearly 50 years, and formally joined this structure in 2001. For now, China has been content to observe and move cautiously, but over time fundamental issues will arise for China as to how accepting it should be of this structure and where and how rapidly she should push for change, and with whom.

The WTO/WB/IMF triad to a large degree reflects the response of the US and the European powers to the immediate post-World War II concerns of achieving international economic stability and laying the preconditions for growth in the immediate post-1945 period. The aim was to prevent a return to the 1930s and the depression and economic dislocation that occurred (especially in Central Europe) after the World War I. The IMF was to guarantee a fixed exchange rate regime, the World Bank was to yield concessional financing for infrastructure in developing countries, and the ITO (and later the GATT and the WTO) was to be the vehicle to establish rules for the use of trade policy so as to facilitate trade growth globally.

But the world of today is no longer that of the 1940s, and while these agencies have changed over the years, whether they fully respond to the global challenges of today, especially as seen by China, is key. In the long term, the key issue for China is whether it should also be a prime global mover for a whole new global institutional economic architecture.

Such an architecture could concentrate on issues of major concern to China more effectively then global institutions do at present. One area is that of global labour mobility, with restrictions in OECD countries on the free flow of cheap Chinese labour abroad. Another is the issue of certification procedures for the use of considerably cheaper Chinese services (medical services in China for instance) in place of OECD service provisions. Other key issues involve the environment, anti-trust, banking regulation and how they are dealt with globally.

6. Concluding Remarks

The paper looks beyond recent debate both in and outside China as to both the merits of and possible impacts from China's accession to the WTO (to be implemented between 2002 and 2007), and discusses China's stance in the WTO in the post-accession period. China is now in the WTO; how to use WTO membership to serve China's trade interest is the issue, not an accession process already negotiated. Chinese growth has already changed the global economy, and our belief is that Chinese membership of the WTO will ultimately change both global economic performance and the shape of global economic institutions. We are at the start of this process, and here we try to raise a series of issues for wider debate.

China is so large in population terms and, along with India, growing so rapidly that change in the global economy is now reflective of what is happening in China. Trade is a central part of this change; how China responds to the challenges she faces both in the WTO and outside will affect future global performance and is of importance to us all, whether inside or outside China. We ask how much difference formal WTO membership realistically makes to China's conduct of commercial diplomacy, especially in key areas such as textiles and apparel, anti-dumping, and handling emerging trade disputes. We also ask what this implies for China's interests in a possible new global economic architecture.

China now stands in contrast to nearly all the major economic powers in building its latest developmental strategy around its accession to the WTO and implementation of accession terms. Outside China, the WTO does not enter domestic policy formation in this central way and there is much pessimism as to the WTO's prospects. On access issues, seemingly the WTO yields China less than the rhetoric of Chinese accession suggested and China's new-found regional strategy is in part a manifestation of this. Whether the WTO will occupy the same central role in Chinese policy making in future years now seems to be in doubt.

References

August, O. (2004). Change of Beijing's Status May Cost US Billions. *The Times Online*. http://business.timesonline.co.uk/article/0,,13129-1132617,00.html.

Australian Government Department of Foreign Affairs and Trade (2004). *Australia-China Free Trade Agreement Feasibility Study*. http://www.dfat.gov.au/geo/china/fta/.

Bach, C., W. Martin and J. Stevens (1996). China and the WTO: Tariff offers, exemptions and welfare applications, *Welt schaftfiches Archiv*, 32(3) 409–31.

Barshefsky, C. (2004). *American Trade Policy and China's WTO Accession*. Speech to the Economic Club of Washington, March 16, 2000. http://hongkong.usconsulate.gov/uscn/trade/general/ustr/2000/0316a.htm.

Business: Broken China; The Chip Industry (2004, January 10). *The Economist*.

Chen, Q. (2004). Singapore Working on Free Trade Deal with China. *China Daily*. March 1.

Cheng, D. (2004). China Deserves Market Economy Status, *China Daily*, May 17.

China Files 24 Anti-dumping Cases since 1997: Official (2002, September 14). http://english.peopledaily.com.cn.

China Takes a Swipe at Major Trading Patters Claims Discriminating Barriers. (2004, May 20) *EU Business.*

China Won 37.5% Anti-dumping Cases in Past Ten Years, (2002, March 29). http://english.peopledaily.com.cn/200203/29/print20020329_93087.html.

China, ASEAN Economic, Trade Ties Speed Up (2002, December 17). http://english.peopledaily.com.cn.

China, a Country Suffering Most From Anti-dumping Cases (2002, April 23). http://english.peopledaily.com.cn.

China: US Invokes 'Safeguard' on Textile Imports. (2003, November 19). http://www.asianlabour.org/archives/000022.html.

Colitt, R. (2004). Trade Groups Pledge over Farm Talks Rules, *Financial Times,* June 15.

Cooper, H. (2001). US, EU End Trans-Atlantic Banana War — Chiquita Imports to Climb in Return for Lifting Tariffs on Europe Goods, *Wall Street Journal.* April 12.

De Jonquieres, G. (2003). China and India to Co-ordinate Trade Policy, *Financial Times.* July 1.

Donnan, S. and A. Ward (2003). East Asian Trio Stops Short of Free Trade Pact, *Financial Times*, October 8.

EU Environmental Barriers to Chinese Appliances (2004, February 17). http://english.peopledaily.com.cn.

Evolution of Trade in Textile and Clothing Trade, Worldwide Trade Figures and Structural Data. (2003). http://trade-info.cec.eu.int/textiles/conf_docs.cfm.

Hecht, J. C. (2000). Operation of WTO dispute settlement panels: Assessing proposals for reform, *Law and Policy in International Business*, 31(3): 657–664.

Hong Kong Trade and Industry Department (2003). *Mainland and Hong Kong Closer Economic Partnership Agreement* (CEPA). http://www.tid.gov.hk/english/cepa/fulltext.html.

Ianchovichina, E. and W. Martin (2003). Economic Impacts of China's Accession to the World Trade Organization. *Policy Research Working Paper No. 3053.* Washington DC: World Bank.

James, C. (2004). Deal With It. *Far Eastern Review* 167(16): 20.

Japan, China, S. Korea to Boost Investment, Trade (2004, June 8). *Jiji Press.*

Lardy, N. (ed.) (2002). *Integrating China into the Global Economy.* Washington DC: Brookings Institution Press.

Long, Y. (2000). On the Question of Our Joining the World Trade Organization. *The Chinese Economy*, 38(1): 5–52.

Martin, W. (2002). Implications of reform and WTO accession for China's trade policies, *Economics of Transition*, 9(3): 717–42.

Palmer, D. (2004). China Market Economy Bid Could Take Years — US. *Reuters.* June.

Stewart T. P. (2004). *China's Compliance with World Trade Organization Obligations: A Review of China's 1st Two Years of Membership.* Washington DC: USCC. http://www.uscc.gov/researchreports/2004/04annual_report.PDF.

Thongpakde, N. and W. Pupphavesa (1999). *Returning Textiles and Clothing to GATT Disciplines.* Washington, DC: World Bank.

US Fears Massive Job Losses as Controls Lifted (2003, August 2). The Standard Online. http://www.thestandard.com.hk/news_detail_frame.cfm?articleid=40801&intcatid=1.

United States Department of State (2004). *Statement from Commerce Secretary Donald L. Evans on America's Economic Relationship with China.* http://usinfo.state.gov/ei/Archive/2004/Apr/30-591232.html.

United States Trade Representative (2004). *2003 National Trade Estimate Report on Foreign Trade Barriers.* Washington DC: USTR.

University of Toronto. *China's Accession to the WTO, Chronology of Major Events between China and the GATT/WTO.* http://www.library.utoronto.ca/east/students01/cheung_bessie/road_map.html (accessed June 24, 2004).

Vatikiotis, M. and M. Hiebert (2004). Dancing Elephants, *Far Eastern Economic Review*, 167(17): 12–15.

Whalley, J. (2003). Liberalization in China's Key Service Sectors Following WTO Accession: Some Scenarios and Issues of Measurement. Working paper 10143. Cambridge, Ma.: National Bureau of Economic Research.

Williams, F. (2004). Talks on Farm Subsidies Enter Final Phase, *Financial Times.* June 23.

World Bank (1997). *China Engaged: Integration with the World Economy.* Washington DC: World Bank.

World Trade Organization (2002). Request *for a panel against the US on Safeguards on Imports of Certain Steel Products.* Document WT/DS252/1. Geneva: World Trade Organization.

World Trade Organization (2003a). *Annual Report 2002.* http://www.wto.org/english/res_e/booksp_e/anrep_e/anrep03_e.pdf.

World Trade Organization (2003b). International Trade Statistics 2003: Leading exporters and importers of clothing, 2002, Table IV.69. http://www.wto.org/english/res_e/statis_e/its2003_e/section4_e/iv69.xls.

World Trade Organization (2004a). *Annual Report 2003.* http://www.wto.org/english/res_e/booksp_e/anrep_e/anrep04_e.pdf.

World Trade Organization (2004b). *China — Value-added Tax on Integrated Circuits — Request to Join Consultations, Communication from the European Communities.* Document WT/DS309/2. Geneva: World Trade Organization.

World Trade Organization (2004c). *China — Value-added Tax on Integrated Circuits — Request to Join Consultations, Communication from the Separate Customs Territory of Taiwan, Phenghu, Kinmen and Matsu.* Document WT/DS309/5. Geneva: World Trade Organization.

World Trade Organization (2004d). *Trade Policy Review: Sri Lanka, Report by the Secretariat*, document (04-0329). http://www.wto.org/english/tratop_e/tpr_e/tp228_e.htm.

Yan, D. (2004a). EU, China Reach Deal on Coke Supply, *China Daily* (North American edition). May 31.

Yan, D. (2004b). FTA Talks to Conclude Ahead of Schedule, *China Daily* (North American edition). May 21.

Yan, M. (2003). Unfair Measures Condemned, *China Daily* (North American edition). June 3.

Yang, Y. (2003). China's Integration in the World Economy: Implications for Developing Countries, *IMF Working Paper WP/03/245.* Washington DC: International Monetary Fund.

Zhang, X. (2003). Financing Rules Announced, *China Daily* (North American edition). November 14.

Part III

China's Tax System

THE UNIFIED ENTERPRISE TAX AND SOEs IN CHINA

John Whalley
University of Western Ontario, Canada and NBER

Li Wang*
Chinese Academy of Social Sciences
University of Western Ontario, Canada

Currently proposals are actively circulating in China to move to a unified enterprise tax structure with similar tax treatment of state-owned enterprises (SOEs), other private enterprises (OPEs) and foreign investment enterprises (FIEs). FIEs presently receive significant tax preferences through a sharply lower tax rate, tax holidays and other provisions. Here we use analytical representations of SOE behavior, which differ from that of the competitive firm, to argue that a unified tax structure may not be a desirable tax change and that typically a higher tax rate on SOEs is called for on efficiency grounds. Using a worker control model with endogenously determined shirking, taxes on SOEs reduce shirking and a reduced SOE tax rate under a unified tax relaxes discipline on SOEs and losses result. Our results indicate a 0.26% of GDP welfare loss using 2004 data from a unified tax, and larger loss relative to an optimal tax scheme. Alternatively, if we use a managerial control model variant, we find a 0.19% welfare loss from a unified tax, and larger losses relative to initial higher SOE tax rates.

1. Introduction

A central element in China's recent strong growth performance has been large inflows of foreign direct investment (FDI),[1] and a key factor in attracting foreign investment has been substantial tax preferences. The

*Financial support from SSHRC and a CIGI Post-doctoral Fellowship held by the second author makes this paper possible and is greatly appreciated.

[1]Xin and Whalley (2006) report in a recent growth accounting study on China that Foreign Investment Enterprises (FIEs), a special legal form that embodies most FDI, now account for over 20% of GDP, nearly 50% of manufacturing output, and over 50% of exports. Simultaneously, however, they only account for 3% of employment and

tax preferences currently given to FIEs are complex. If they are in special economic zones, national hi-tech industrial zones and national grade economic and technical development zones, they pay a reduced enterprise tax rate of 15% compared to the general rate of 30%. FIEs in coastal regions and all provincial capitals pay 24%. FIEs also receive extensive tax holidays with a full exemption for two years, a 50% exemption for the next three years and (if in particular geographical zones) a tax reduction of 15–30% for a further 3–5 years. In addition, local governments frequently exempt them from local surcharges applied to other enterprises of 3% of taxable income, and taxable income can again be reduced if income is reinvested. There is also differential tax treatment of wages paid to employees between FIEs and other enterprises. There are no formal estimates of effective tax rates on Chinese enterprises comparable to those for OECD economies, but instead indications that widely circulate that FIEs on average may face tax rates in the 10–15% range, while non-FIEs face tax rates of between 22% and 28%.[2] The proposal is for a unified and single equal yield tax rate to apply to all enterprises and for tax preferences towards FIEs to be removed.

The feature of China's economy we focus on here in the design of a unified tax is state-owned enterprises (SOEs) whose behavior departs from that of competitive firms due to either worker or managerial control. SOEs dominated the Chinese economy before China's economic reform process began in the late 1970s. From the early 1980s a management contract system was implemented for SOEs to improve their efficiency within the state ownership structure. But in 2004, SOEs and collective enterprises still accounted for 42.4% of value added of all enterprises in the industrial sector and 46.2% of employment. They also had lower productivity than other types of firms in the Chinese economy.

Here we argue that although in tax policy models used in OECD countries a change to a unified tax may appear desirable since all firms are similar, things are less clear in a tax model of China which incorporates analytical representations of SOE behavior. We consider two simplified treatments of SOE behavioral response which build on models used in Whalley and Zhang (2006). In one, which we term a worker control model, enterprises are assumed to receive capital allocated through the banking system via credit rationing with any losses incurred subsequently

have labor productivity nearly eight times that of the rest of the economy (admittedly including agriculture).

[2]See footnote 4 on page 182.

recapitalized. In essence, capital is freely allocated to SOEs through this mechanism. Workers are guaranteed jobs at fixed wages, and the enterprise must meet a budget constraint which implies that the value of output must cover the wage bill plus any surplus required by the state. Shirking is thus endogenously determined as workers collectively engage in satisfying behavior. Hence, a tax on enterprise income (on the surplus) acts to reduce shirking and raise output.

In the other, which we term a managerial control model, enterprises are controlled instead by managers, who again receive credit allocated recapitalizable loans (effectively capital at zero cost). With political appointed managers, we assume managers act so as to maximize their own political and business connections and maximize the size of enterprises rather than profit. This implies average product pricing of labor, and enterprises which are too large relative to Pareto efficiency. Taxes on any required surplus in this case reduce the enterprise size, and a higher tax rate on SOEs compared to other enterprises is again preferred.

We explore the influence of these effects on tax design using calibrated general equilibrium models of the Chinese economy capturing four sectors with each assumed to produce heterogeneous outputs using capital and labor as inputs. The four sectors are an agriculture producing sector, a sector with SOEs, one with FIEs and one with other private enterprises. We use the two different formulations of SOE behavior described above in alternative model variants. We use data for 2004 from the Chinese Statistics Yearbook for calibration, and assume values for key unobservables in the base year (such as the level of shirking in SOEs in the worker control model).

We conduct a series of counterfactual experiments with these models. We then investigate model outcomes when moving to a uniform tax treatment across all four sectors (relative to the current tax treatment of preference to FIEs) which preserves government tax yield. In both worker and managerial control models losses occur. We then evaluate losses relative to higher initial tax rates on SOEs and find that the losses involved are even larger.

The theme that emerges from our analysis is that tax changes that do not take account of the special role and behavior of SOEs in China can potentially mislead. Uniform tax treatment across all non-SOE sector enterprises may be desirable, but not across all enterprises. Lowered tax rates on SOEs effectively relax discipline on them, moving resource allocation further away from a Pareto efficient allocation.

2. The Unified Tax Reform Proposal in China

Two decades ago, the main source of tax revenue for the national government in China was taxes collected from enterprises, which were almost entirely owned by the national government (see Brean, 1998, for a discussion of the evolution of Chinese tax policy). This heavy revenue dependence of the government on the state-owned sector distorted government decision-making and caused the government to favor this heavily taxed sector through prioritized bank loans and preferential regulation. In the beginning of the 1990s, however, the Chinese Government set out a long-term tax reform plan, which included "unification of taxation management, equity of tax burden, simplification of tax system, reasonalization of revenue distribution relations and guarantee of the financial revenue". The aim was to improve economic efficiency, as well as to promote social fairness. This plan remained, however, as a long term goal and was not implemented in concrete form.

As Table 1 shows, after the tax reforms of the 1990s, the structure of Chinese government revenue changed substantially. Not only was there growth in tax revenues as a fraction of GDP, but also a shift away from enterprise taxes towards other tax sources (especially the VAT). To attract FDI during this period, tax preferences were given to almost all foreign enterprises resulting in a dual-track enterprise income tax system. First in 1991 and later in 1994, laws for separate corporate income taxes for foreign and domestic enterprises were enacted.[3] Under this system, most FIEs paid taxes at a rate of 15%, while other types of enterprises paid tax at a 30% rate. To qualify FIEs had to be in special economic zones, hi-tech industrial zones and national grade economic and technical development zones. FIEs in coastal regions and in all provincial capitals paid taxes at a 24% rate. FIEs additionally received complete tax holidays for the first two years,

[3]The two laws are "Income Tax Law of the People's Republic of China for Enterprises with Foreign Investment and Foreign Enterprises" which was enacted in 1991 and "Income Tax Law of the People's Republic of China for Enterprises" which was enacted in 1994.

[4]Prior to 2001, data is only separately available for tax revenues from SOEs, and after 2001, only available for all enterprises and FIEs according to Chinese Statistical Yearbook. Tax revenue data for SOEs and FIEs in 1999 and 2000 are taken from Ministry of Finance, PRC and can be accessed at www.mof.gov.cn.

[5]Shares in this column and last column in this table are calculated by the authors using data published by Ministry of Finance, PRC. http://www.chinatax.gov.cn/data99-04.jsp.

Table 1. National Government Revenue and Enterprise Tax Revenues in China.

	Total national government revenue (billion RMB)	Total tax revenue (billion RMB)	Enterprise tax revenue from SOEs[4] (billion RMB)	Enterprise income tax from all enterprises (billion RMB)	Share of enterprise tax revenue from SOEs and OPEs[5] (%)	Share of enterprise tax revenue from FIEs (%)
1985	200.5	134.5	69.6			
1986	212.2	139.8	69.2			
1987	219.9	147.6	66.5			
1988	235.7	171.4	67.6			
1989	266.5	202.7	70.0			
1990	293.7	210.6	71.6			
1991	314.9	225.9	73.1			
1992	348.3	257.6	72.1			
1993	434.9	357.7	67.9			
1994	521.8	441.9	70.8			
1995	624.2	515.9	87.8			
1996	740.8	594.1	96.8			
1997	865.1	823.4	96.3			
1998	987.6	926.3	92.6			
1999	1144.4	1068.6	81.1	122.7	82.3	17.7
2000	1339.5	1258.2	99.9	177.1	81.6	18.4
2001	1638.6	1530.1		263.1	80.5	19.5
2002	1890.4	1763.6		308.3	76.2	23.8
2003	2171.5	2001.7		291.9	76.9	23.1

Source: 1. Chinese Statistical Yearbook 2005 and 1996.
2. State Administration of Taxation, PRC.

a 50% exemption for the next three years, and an exemption from a 3% local surcharge collected by municipalities, and retained earnings were more lightly taxed. Also, FIEs could fully deduct wage costs while other enterprises could only deduct 40% of wage costs. Converting these tax preferences into effective tax rates by enterprise type is treacherous, as the effective tax rate varies with the time profile of returns to investment (most FIEs make no profit in their first two years, for instance), their location, their financing, and labor costs. There are no estimates of effective tax rates for Chinese enterprises comparable to those of OECD economies (such as in Fullerton and King, 1984, and the studies which have followed), but various Chinese sources put the capital tax rates faced by FIEs in the range of 10%–14%, while for the non-FIEs a range of 22–28%[6] is widely used.

In the modeling work report below, we use a tax rate FIEs of 14% and on other sectors of 24%, which we then replace by a single rate unified tax across all enterprises. In 2004, 23% of total enterprise taxes were paid by FIEs, and 77% were paid by the other types of enterprises (See Table 1), even though FIEs accounted for a significantly larger part of the total return to capital.

With more than two decades of reform completed and accession to the WTO accomplished, under China's so-called "Gradual Therapy" the

[6]Different sources provide different estimates which lie in these ranges. Effective tax rates will differ by the life of assets, location of investments and finance. See the articles from (1) Embassy of the People's Republic of China in the United States of America: in the article: "China to Unify Corporate Income Tax Systems", which says: "The actual income tax rate has remained at 14% for overseas-funded businesses, much lower than the 24% rate for domestic firms, since China formulated the preferential policy for overseas-funded enterprises in mid–1980s in a bid to lure foreign investment". The article can be accessed at http://www.china-embassy.org/eng/gyzg/t231590.htm; (2) Hong Kong Trade Development Council: in "Drafting of Unified Enterprise Income Tax Completed" says: "At present, domestic enterprises in China are subject to a nominal income tax rate of 33% while the actual rates applied to FIEs and foreign enterprises range from 15% to 24%". The article can be accessed at http://www.tdctrade.com/alert/cba-e0304a-2.htm; (3) Development Research Center of State Council, PRC (2006, in Chinese). In the article: "When Can We Unify Enterprise Income Tax?", it says: "In 2004, domestic enterprises in China are subject to an actual income tax rate of 26.29% while the actual rates applied to FIEs and foreign enterprises is just around 13.87"%". This article can be accessed at: http://www.drcnet.com.cn/temp/20061114/gylt_7.html; (4) Peoples Daily (in Chinese): in the article "Why Is It So Difficult in Unifying Enterprise Income Tax" says "According to experts' evaluation, while domestic enterprises in China are subject to an actual income tax rate of 23% the actual rates applied to FIEs and foreign enterprises is just around 10%". This article can be accessed at http://finance.people.com.cn/GB/1045/3860233.html.

government position now is that FDI inflows are mainly attracted by non-tax factors. These include China's economic environment, a growing domestic market, low wage rates, well trained and hard working labor, a market system and a stronger judicial system. With tax preferences seen as less important, the government proposal is thus to unify enterprise tax rates and to remove what are seen as distortions associated with the various incentive schemes for FIEs.

The most recent proposal on unified tax reform has been discussed by members of the Standing Committee of the National People's Congress. At the end of December, 2006, they deliberated a draft of a new corporate income tax law which includes following.[7] (1) The draft bill suggests a unified tax rate of 25% for both domestic and foreign-funded businesses. (2) For small business enterprises, according to the draft law, the income tax for small businesses will be 20%. Depending on what region and what industry they are active in, small businesses now pay either 18% or 27%. (3) The bill allows domestic companies to deduct employees' full salaries from taxable income as foreign companies now do. (4) There will be transitional measures for FIEs under which the current two-year full tax exemption and three-year partial tax exemption for foreign manufacturers will be removed and export-oriented foreign-funded businesses will no longer enjoy an additional 50% tax reduction. But existing FIEs will continue to receive tax preferences for five years after the new law is implemented and will only gradually face increased income taxes. The bill also extends some existing tax preferences. For instance, all hi-tech companies will enjoy a 15% tax rate to stimulate innovation, while at present only those in state hi-tech zones enjoy this privilege. Investments in equipment for environmental protection and water conservancy purposes and for production safety will be able to be used to offset taxes payable. The new enterprise tax structure is expected to take effect in 2008 if the bill is adopted by the NPC plenary session in March, 2007.

3. General Equilibrium Models of China Incorporating SOE Behavior

An immediate reaction to any proposal to analyze the efficiency and distributional impacts of the unified tax proposal is to use competitive

[7]The draft can be accessed at China Daily: http://www.chinadaily.com.cn/china/2006-12/25/content_766418.htm and Ministry of Finance, PRC, at www.mof.gov.cn.

equilibrium models of tax policy changes that are well documented in the literature; beginning with Harberger (1962) and further developing in Shoven and Whalley (1972, 1984).[8] Some representation of the applied tax rates before and after the change would be used, and transitional arrangements would be ignored. Typically, constant returns to scale goods and factor production functions are assumed in these for competitive firms, with demands generated from utility maximization. For simplicity, we redistributed tax revenues to consumers in lump-sum form. Market clearing in goods and factors then characterizes equilibrium. For a closed economy, this occurs in both goods and factor markets, with both goods and factor prices being endogenously determined. For a small open economy which is a taker of goods prices, only factor prices are endogenously determined with factor market cleaning. Taxes on both goods and factors along with income taxes in multi-consumer variants change equilibrium behavior, and distorting taxes impose welfare costs usually captured in Hicksian measures such as the equivalent or compensating variation. The sum of Hicksian measures across consumers is usually taken as the aggregate welfare measure of impact. The presumption in a standard competitive model is that unified and common tax treatment across all sectors is welfare preferred.

However, if there are different behaviors by type of enterprise, and SOEs behave differently from competitive firms, things are less clear. To explore how this applies to the unified tax proposal we can thus consider similar models, but with the added element of explicit representation of the SOE sector in alternative form. To do this, we consider agriculture and manufacturing sectors to represent the Chinese economy, but we subdivide manufacturing into three different subsectors: foreign-invested enterprises, other private enterprises; and state-owned enterprises,[9] each producing a distinct output.

[8]See Lockwood, Ben and E. Ahmad, R. Singh (2005) for the use of such a model to analyze Chinese VAT reforms which would combine what is effectively now a manufacturing level VAT at 17% and a turnover tax on services at 3%.

[9]In the Chinese Statistical Yearbook, value-added data for manufacturing is given for 10 different types of enterprises: Manufacturing 1 = State-Owned Industry, Manufacturing 2 = Collective-Owned Industry, Manufacturing 3 = Co-operative Enterprises, Manufacturing 4 = Joint Ownership Enterprises, Manufacturing 5 = Limited Liability Co-operations, Manufacturing 6 = Share Holding Enterprises, Manufacturing 7 = Private Enterprises, Manufacturing 8 = Other Enterprises, Manufacturing 9 = Enterprises with Funds from Hong Kong, Macao, and Taiwan, and Manufacturing 10 = Foreign-Funded Enterprises. We treat the first two as the SOE manufacturing subsector,

For the first three subsectors, we consider a sectoral production function of the form.

$$Y_i = F_i(K_i, L_i) \quad i = AGR, FIE, OPE \tag{1}$$

where Y_i refers to output, K_i and L_i are capital and labor inputs.

We assume CES forms, but we can alternatively use Cobb-Douglas or some other variant. Both capital and labor in these sectors are treated as intersectorally mobile among the three sectors, but internationally immobile with factors hired up to the point that their marginal value product equals the corresponding factor price (the wage or rental rate).

We then consider two alternative variants of submodels for the SOE sector, even though in reality the Chinese SOE sector is highly complex with a variety of arrangements, and any simplification is inevitably an abstraction from a more diverse and complex reality. Each variant assumes different forms of control and optimizing behavior. It is difficult to consider these two forms simultaneously in a single model since different optimizing behavior is assumed in each, and so we separately consider two different model variants each of which point in the same direction for tax policy implications.

3.1. *Worker control SOE submodel*

We designate the first of these as a worker control SOE submodel, and this can be thought of as reflective of traditional SOEs in the 1970s. In this formulation of SOE behavior we assume workers have both job and wage guarantees with the membership of the enterprise fixed. We model the sector in the form of a single representative enterprise.

We assume that capital is allocated to the SOE sector by credit rationing through a state-controlled banking system, and that any losses incurred by banks on loans through non-repayment of interest and principal are recapitalized by the central bank. We assume that SOEs behave as if loans need not be repaid, and as such, capital is freely allocated to enterprises once rationed credit is assigned. Members of the enterprise collectively decide on enterprise output, but must meet an enterprise budget constraint which covers wages plus any surplus to be returned to the state.

---

3 to 8 are aggregated as other private enterprise subsector (OPEs), and the latter two as the foreign investment subsector (FIEs).

After meeting the enterprise budget constraint, workers can either shirk (enjoy the leisure) or pursue second jobs by moonlighting.

This is a strong simplification since from the 1990s on, there has been progressive discipline applied to state-owned enterprises and major efforts to reduce the size of SOE non-performing loans in the banking system. Today in China many of the large SOEs in banking, telecoms, petrochemicals and other sectors are highly profitable, but the simplicity of the formulation serves our end of demonstrating the need to differentiate tax policy toward SOEs.

We consider a single representative SOE and write the SOE production function as:

$$Y_{\text{soe}} = A(\lambda \overline{L})^{1-\alpha} \tag{2}$$

where Y_{soe} is output, $\bar{L}$ is the enterprise membership, and λ denotes the degree of effort extended by workers ($\lambda = 0$ implies complete shirking; $\lambda = 1$ implies full effort). α ($\alpha < 1$) is an exponent giving decreasing returns to labor input, and A is an efficiency parameter.

The collective budget constraint for enterprise members is:

$$P_{\text{soe}} Y_{\text{soe}} = \overline{wL} + S_{\text{soe}} \tag{3}$$

where S_{soe} represents the surplus to be returned to the state.

From the production function, λ (the degree of effort) increases as Y_{soe} increases. Simple substitution of (2) into (3) implies that a tax imposed on S_{soe} as an enterprise income tax will increase Y_{soe} and hence λ.

We complete the model in the following way. We consider households to have preferences defined over both the four goods in the model and leisure but differently treat workers in SOEs and other enterprises. SOE workers collectively decide on their level of shirking so as meet the enterprise budget constraint and so do not make labor supply decision based on utility maximizing behavior. For SOE members, leisure enters preferences but leisure consumption is implied by the satisfying behavior of them collectively meeting their enterprise budget constraint which is necessary for workers to retain their job. SOE members thus optimize over the consumption of goods, but satisfice in their leisure and labor supply behavior.

Because of this behavior in the SOE sector we partition consumers into those working in SOEs and elsewhere. For the former (SOE workers) utility maximization takes the form:

$$\max U(X_1, \ldots, X_4, (1-\lambda)\bar{L}) \tag{4}$$

$$\text{st.} \sum_{i=1}^{4} (P_i X_i) = \overline{\omega L} + R_{\text{soe}}$$

where $(1 - \lambda)\bar{L}$ is shirked labor and defines the amount of leisure entering preferences. In this structure, since workers satisfice in their shirking behavior in order to retain their SOE jobs, leisure is not derived from conventional first order conditions. R_{soe} is government revenues redistributed to workers in the SOE sector.

For the non-SOE workers utility maximization takes the more conventional form:

$$\max U(X_1, \ldots, X_4, Le) \tag{5}$$

$$\text{st.} \sum_{i=1}^{4} P_i X_i = \omega(L - Le) + r\overline{K} + R_{\text{non-soe}}$$

where L represents their labor endowment, Le is leisure consumption, $\overline{K}$ is the economy wide endowment of capital used in the three non-SOE sectors and $R_{\text{non-soe}}$ is government revenues redistributed to workers in the non-SOE sector.

Equilibrium in this model version implies clearing in all goods markets, factor market clearing in capital and labor across the three non-SOE sectors and government budget balance with tax collection equaling revenue distributed. Taxes can be applied to either or both of goods and factors. Because of the differential treatment of the SOE sector, taxes on capital income applied to SOEs as a tax on their surplus to be transferred to the state will increase output and lower shirking. However, because of the presence of leisure in preferences it will not to be optimal to tax S_{soe} so as to force λ to 1. An optimal tax scheme will typically involve a tax rate on the SOE sector different from that on the non-SOE sector, and depending on the configuration of initial tax rates a move to a unified tax may no longer be desirable.

3.2. *Managerial control SOE model*

In our second SOE model variant, we assume managerial rather than worker control. Capital is again assumed allocated freely to the SOE by credit rationing with a recapitalization mechanism as before, but now managers not workers decide on the output level of the firm. In this case both employment and shirking are assumed monitorable by management and hence shirking is absent. We assume managers are politically appointed and pursue personal gain rather than state enterprise profit, and so they seek to maximize the size of the enterprise so as to yield maximal personal network benefits rather than profit. If there is no surplus to be returned to the state by the SOEs, this implies hiring labor up to the point that the wage paid to labor equals average rather than marginal product.

In this model variant we assume all four sectors including SOEs have constant returns to scale production functions, but capital used by the SOEs is fixed to reflect capital allocation to this sector by rationed credit.

$$Y_i = F_i(K_i, L_i) \quad i = AGR, FIE, OPE \tag{6}$$

$$Y_{\text{soe}} = F_{\text{soe}}(\bar{K}_{\text{soe}}, L_{\text{soe}}). \tag{7}$$

There is again a surplus to be paid to the state and this surplus can offset the distortion in average product pricing of labor that makes the size of the enterprise too large relative to Pareto efficiency. If the size of the surplus is below that which fully offsets this distortion, a higher enterprise tax on the SOEs will be desirable.

For the three non-SOE sectors:

$$w_i = P_i \frac{\partial Y_i}{\partial L_i} \quad r_i = P_i \frac{\partial Y_i}{\partial K_i} \quad i = AGR, FIE, OPE \tag{8}$$

but for the SOE sector, given size maximizing behavior by managers:

$$w_{\text{soe}} = \frac{P_{\text{soe}} Y_{\text{soe}} - S_{\text{soe}}}{L_{\text{soe}}} \tag{9}$$

where S_{soe} is the surplus returned to the state, and P_i and P_{soe} are output prices. Equilibrium is given by clearing in goods market and the capital market across the three non-SOE subsectors and for labor across all four sectors. Here a tax on S_{soe} will reduce Y_{soe} and L_{soe} and hence can help correct a distortion in labor markets associated with average rather than marginal product pricing of labor if the original value of S_{soe} is below what is required.

In this model variant, as in the worker-controlled model, taxes on SOE will optimally be set in ways which are different from those of other enterprises. A move to a unified tax may or may not improve things.

4. Model Calibration and Results

We have calibrated the two model variants set out above to a benchmark data set for China for 2004 which separately identifies SOEs, FIEs and OPEs in manufacturing. We assume CES functions for the three non-SOE subsectors, AGRI, FIE and OPE. For the SOE sector in the worker-controlled case we have the decreasing returns function (2), and in the managerial control variation case we use a CD function, which implies a similar treatment to that of worker control model. We use the resulting model parameterizations in counterfactual equilibrium analyses of moves both to a unified tax scheme across all enterprises and also of an optimal tax structure with a separate tax rate on SOEs.

The elements of the benchmark equilibrium data set we have constructed are set out in Table 2. This data set is in value form, and we use the units convention set out in both Harberger (1962) and Shoven and Whalley (1972, 1974, 1992) of defining units for output and factors, as the amount selling for 1 billion RMB in the base case for the output of the agriculture, FIE and the other private enterprise sectors. The parameter for leisure in each household is assumed to be 0.2 as we have no direct

Table 2. 2004 Benchmark Equilibrium Data Set for China Incorporating SOEs.

	Value added[10] (billion RMB)	Value of labor input[11] (billion RMB)	Value of capital input[12] (billion RMB)	Surplus return to the state (billion RMB)		Tax rate on capital (%)
				Worker control	Manager control	
AGRI	2076.8	1336.5	740.3			24%
FIEs	1524.1	189.0	1335.1			14%
OPEs	1635.2	920.7	714.5			24%
SOEs	2321.3	1210.6	1110.7	1110.7	1110.7	24%

Source: Chinese Statistics Yearbook 2005.

[10]Data in this column are from NBS "Chinese Statistics Yearbook 2005".
[11]Wage and employment data are from NBS "Chinese Statistics Yearbook 2005". The value of labor input is calculated by the authors using wage times employment.
[12]This is calculated by residual and is gross of tax.

observation on leisure consumption. We later change this value in sensitivity analysis.

For the SOE sector, a different calibration treatment is needed. In the worker control case, we assume a value of the SOE wage W_{soe} equal to 0.75 as this is unrelated to the market clearing wage in the rest of the economy. We also again assume a share parameter on leisure in preferences of 0.2. Setting a value using the share of labor input to total value-added for α then implies a value for A. In the managerial control case, the use of labor inputs do not correspond to first order conditions for profit maximization and these are replaced in calibration by the average product condition. The share parameter on labor in the CD production function for the SOE sector in this model variant is set using the share of labor input to total value-added and A is calculated using the production function. For non-SOE sectors, we use a conventional calibration in generating parameters for the CES functions. Demand side parameters are also generated by conventional calibration, with the exception of leisure parameters as noted above. We draw on the GTAP data base (see Betina, 2005) for elasticity parameter estimates. The resulting model parameterizations are reported in Table 3.

Table 3. Model Parameterizations Generated by Calibration to the 2004 Benchmark Dataset.

	Worker control			Managerial control		
Production	A[13]	α	σ	A	α	σ
Agriculture	1.739	0.922	0.24[14]	1.739	0.922	0.24
FIE	1.525	0.175	1.26	1.525	0.175	1.26
OPE	1.987	0.550	1.26	1.987	0.550	1.26
SOE	57.476	0.521		57.476	0.521	

	Worker control		Managerial control	
Preferences	SOEs	Non-SOEs	SOEs	Non-SOEs
Agriculture	0.166	0.166	0.166	0.166
FIE	0.213	0.213	0.213	0.213
OPE	0.179	0.179	0.179	0.179
SOE	0.242	0.242	0.242	0.242
Leisure	0.200	0.200	0.200	0.200

[13]The CES production function used in the Agri, FIE and OPE sectors is $Y = A * [\alpha * L^{(\sigma-1)/\sigma} + (1-\alpha)^* K^{(\sigma-1)/\sigma}]^{\sigma/(\sigma-1)}$.

[14]These elasticity parameters are taken from GTAP database for China. See Betina *et al.* (2006).

5. Some Results

We have used the resulting model parameterizations in two different types of counterfactual equilibrium analyses. In one, we assess the impacts of moving to a unified enterprise tax scheme. In the other, we iteratively vary the SOE tax rate to compute an optimal tax scheme with a separate tax rate on SOEs and equal yield but common tax rates on all other enterprises. Results are set out in Tables 4 and 5, and in Figs. 1 and 2.

In both cases in Table 4 moving to a unified enterprise produces a welfare loss of 0.256% of GDP in the worker control model and 0.192% of GDP in the managerial control case. These indicate that the current uneven tax structure is welfare preferred to a unified tax structure in a model where SOE behavior is differently modeled from that of competitive firms elsewhere in the economy. The equal yield tax rates also differ in the two cases because of the differences in SOE output response. An equal yield tax rate of 19.0% applies for the worker control model, but 18.7% for the managerial control model. These tax rates also differ sharply from the 25% rate proposed in the recent draft law. This difference in equal yield tax rate reflects the different output response for SOE in the two model variants. In the case of the worker control model, a lowered tax rate applies to the

Table 4. Model Results from Moving to A Unified Enterprise Tax in China.

	Worker control	Managerial Control
Equal yield unified tax rate (%)	19.000	18.7
Aggregate welfare (EV as % of GDP)	−0.256	−0.192
Impact on output (% change)		
Agriculture	0.940	0.042
FIE	−2.372	−2.467
OPE	1.947	1.401
SOE	−2.061	1.115
Impact on capital (% change)		
Agriculture	4.568	5.053
FIE	−2.639	−2.633
OPE	3.117	3.027
SOE	0.000	0.000
Impact on labor (% change)		
Agriculture	0.565	−0.471
FIE	−1.925	−2.198
OPE	0.744	−0.241
SOE	0.000	2.152
λ (degree of effort)	−3.918	

Note: All data are reported as % changes compared to the benchmark data except for the equal yield unified tax rate.

Table 5. Impacts of Varying Leisure Shares and the Size of Surplus of SOEs in Benchmark Data on the Welfare Impact of Unified Tax Schemes.

	Hicksian equivalent variation as % of base case income Move to unified tax scheme	
Leisure Share	Worker control	Managerial control
0.05	−0.524	−0.061
0.10	−0.414	−0.104
0.15	−0.322	−0.148
0.20	−0.256	−0.192
0.25	−0.216	−0.235
0.30	−0.209	−0.279
0.40	−0.296	−0.366
0.50	−0.508	−0.453
Modified size of the SOE surplus relative to base case data		
0.25	−0.326	−0.012
0.50	−0.258	−0.072
0.75	−0.234	−0.155
1.00	−0.256	−0.192
1.25	−0.289	−0.213
1.50	−0.335	−0.155
1.75	−0.390	−0.089
2.00	−0.436	−0.031

surplus paid to the state which relaxes the budget constraint on SOEs. This increases shirking which in turn reduces output. In the case of the managerial control model, the smaller tax on the surplus paid to the state implies that the average product of labor can now fall which in turn implies an increase in output.

These output changes have corresponding changes in factor use by sector, which are also reported in Table 4. The FIE use of capital falls in both models, reflecting the higher tax rate on capital in this sector under a unified tax. Labor input in this sector falls too, but less than in the case of capital. The output fall in FIEs is intermediate to the two, being a weighted average of the change in the use of the two inputs.

In the agriculture and other private enterprise sectors, capital use expands in both cases reflecting the lowered tax rate on capital in these two sectors. However, different results between models apply for labor use. In the worker control case labor use expands in the two non-FIE sectors since it is in fixed supply for the three non-SOE sectors, and FIE labor use falls. In the managerial control case it contracts given the significant increase in labor use in the SOE sector.

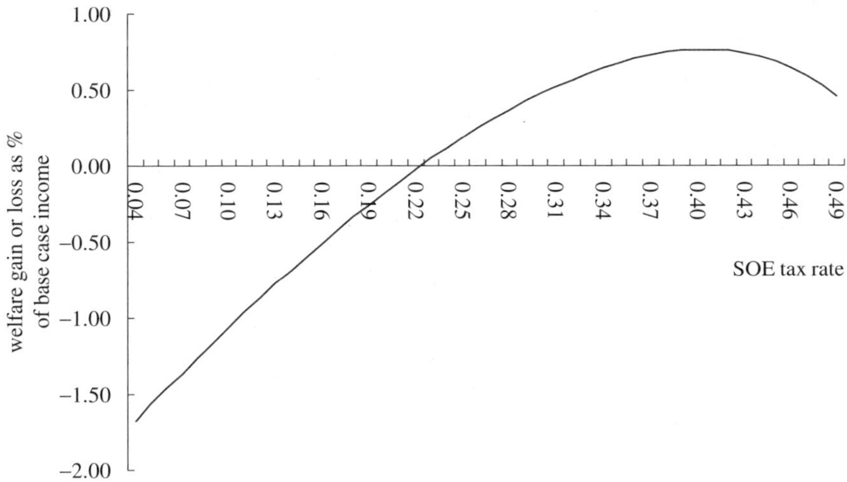

Fig. 1. Welfare gain or loss in worker control model as function of a SOE tax rate.

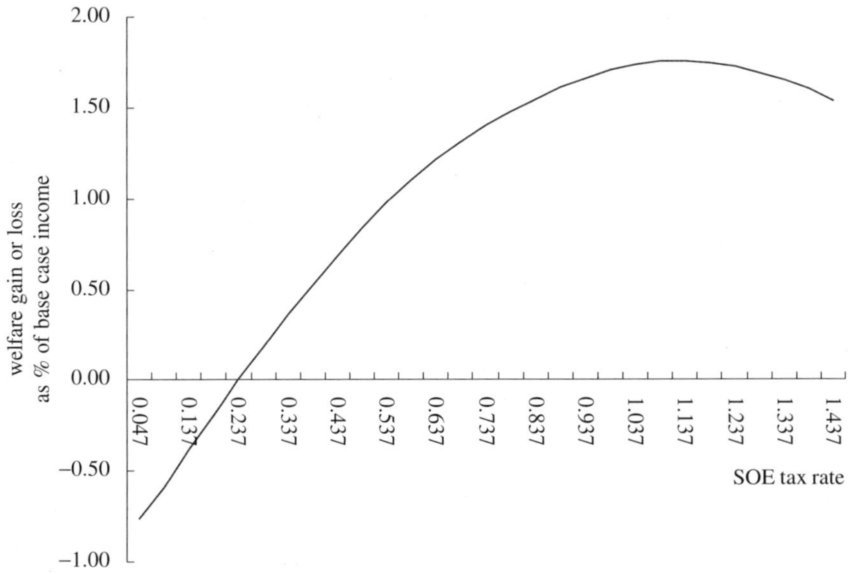

Fig. 2. Welfare gain or loss in managerial control model as a function of SOE tax rate.

In Table 5 we parametrically vary both the setting of leisure share parameters in the utility functions both for SOE workers and for non-SOE workers, and the size of SOE surplus in the benchmark data. When we vary leisure parameters between 0.05 and 0.5, in each case we recompute the welfare gain for the worker control and managerial control cases. Results show that varying shares of leisure in utility functions does not change the sign of welfare measures in a unified scheme. This finding supports the results reported in the Table 4 and show that the sign of the model's results regarding a move to a unified tax are robust with respect to these parametric changes. In the worker control case, the size of the welfare loss under a unified tax scheme is a "reverse U shape" in the change in the leisure parameters. In the managerial model case, the welfare loss under a unified tax scheme falls continuously as the share increases.

We have also modified the size of the SOE surplus relative to base case data in sensitivity analysis by both reducing and increasing its size. The results here for the two models indicate again that varying the surplus does not change the sign of the welfare effect under a unified scheme. The welfare loss under a unified tax scheme has a maximum value at 0.75 times benchmark surplus in the worker control model and modifying the surplus shows a "reverse-U" impact on welfare. The relationship between the two variables has a "U-shape" in Managerial Control variant, with a minimum welfare gain when surplus is 1.25 times benchmark. This implies that the surplus can offset the distortion in average product pricing of labor in this model as we have discussed above.

In Figs. 1 and 2 we set out results of computations designed to show how the welfare impacts of tax changes vary if the value of the SOE tax rate is set separately from that for all other sectors. In these computations, uniform tax rates apply only to the three non-SOE sectors, and a separate tax rate is used for the SOE sector. Figure 1 implies that any SOE tax rate set above 0.23 implies a welfare gain, with a maximum welfare gain at a tax rate of 0.40. This maximum occurs since a higher SOE tax rate in the worker control model will discipline shirking and increase output, but the progressively smaller value implied for leisure when entered into preferences lowers utility. The common unified tax rate of 19% in Table 4 implies a welfare loss as shown in the diagram. Similarly, results in Fig. 2 show that any SOE tax rate set above 0.227 implies a welfare gain, with a maximum welfare gain at a tax rate of 1.107 on the SOE surplus. This sharply higher rate implies negative capital taxes on the three non-SOE sectors, which is extreme.

6. Concluding Remarks

In this chapter we consider the potential impacts of a move to a unified enterprise tax in China in a model in which the behavior of state-owned enterprises (SOEs) is differently modeled for that of other enterprises in both manufacturing and non-manufacturing. The unified tax has been debated for some years as a way of removing large tax preferences to Foreign Invested Enterprises (FIEs), and currently draft implementing legislation is under review. The point of our paper is to argue that while moving to unified treatment across all enterprises in a simple competitive world seems to be sound policy, once different enterprise behavior by subsector enters things are less clear. We use two different submodel variants of SOE behavior embodied in a general equilibrium model of China; one we term worker control and the other managerial control. In the former, workers satisfy in meeting an enterprise budget constraint and otherwise shirk. In the latter, managers seek to maximize the size of the enterprise rather than profits to gain maximal personal networking benefits. In both model variants capital is assumed allocated by rationed credit, with any losses on loans recapitalized by the central banks to state banks.

In both of these model forms, a move to a unified tax which removes tax preferences to foreign invested enterprises (FIEs) and raises FIE tax rates while lowering others is a welfare losing change. This is because a lowered tax rate on SOEs departs further from what in the model is an optimal tax rate on SOEs given their assumed behavior. There is also a difference in the value of the equal yield tax rate between the models due to different SOE output responses in two model variant.

In reality a move to a unified tax would involve other behavioral response, which would further modify impacts. One is the impact of higher FIE tax rates on inward FDI. Another is the impact of these tax rate changes on capital accumulation and investment. But our theme, that different and separate modeling of SOE behavior can modify the policy prescription for tax reform in China is striking and likely robust to more complicated formulations.

References

Betina, V. D., R. A. McDougall, and T. W. Hertel (2006). "GTAP Version6 Documentation: Chapter 20 'Behavioral Parameters'" Available at https://www.gtap.agecon.purdue.edu/resources/download/2906.pdf.

Brean, D. J. S. (1998). Taxation in Modern China, Routledge, New York.

Harberger, A. (1962). "The Incidence of the Corporation Income Tax." *Journal of Political Economy*, 70: 215–240.

Lockwood, B., E. Ahmad and R. Singh (2005). "Financial Consequences of The Chinese VAT reform", *International VAT Monitor*, 16: 181–187.

National Bureau of Statistics, PRC. "Chinese Statistics Yearbook" series, Chinese Statistics Publishing House.

Shoven, J. B. and J. Whalley (1972). "A General Equilibrium Calculation of the Effects of Differential Taxation of Income from Capital in the US", *Journal of Public Economics*, 1: 281–321.

Shoven, J. B. and J. Whalley (1984). "Applied General Equilibrium Models of Taxation and International Trade: An Introduction and Survey", *Journal of Economic Literature*, 22: 10007–51.

Whalley, J. and S. Zhang (2006). "State-Owned Enterprise Behaviour Responses to Trade Reforms: Some Analytics and Numerical Simulation Results Using Chinese Data" NBER working paper No. 12780.

King, M. A. and D. Fullerton (ed, 1984). "The Taxation of Income From Capital: A Comparative Study of the United States, the United Kingdom, Sweden, and West Germany", University of Chicago press for NBER.

EVALUATING THE IMPURE CHINESE VAT RELATIVE TO A PURE FORM IN A SIMPLE MONETARY TRADE MODEL WITH AN ENDOGENOUS TRADE SURPLUS

John Whalley
University of Western Ontario, Canada and NBER

Li Wang*
Chinese Academy of Social Sciences
University of Western Ontario, Canada

China's VAT, while seemingly conventional, has two major impurities. One is that a separate export rebate system exists where rebate rates are linked from rates paid on creditable inputs. The other is the use of an income base for which there is no crediting of taxes on capital good, rather than the more conventional consumption base with expensing of investment expenditures. Here we argue that in a conventional competitive model both impurities would typically involve a welfare loss, but if we use a numerical calibrated equilibrium model with a monetary structure capturing by these Chinese features in which the trade surplus is endogenously determined and the exchange rate is exogenously set, things are different. These impurities effectively act as added taxes on domestic production (lowered export rebate rates, taxes on a larger VAT base) and tax exporting. Tax exporting reduces exports which lowers the surplus and accumulation of foreign currency. In a static model, a reduced surplus is welfare improving. Using 2002 data, we thus find that China's impure VAT system yields welfare gains in contrast to what a conventional model would show. These results are important since there are arguments being made inside and outside China for changes to be made and move closer to a pure VAT. Our results suggest that unless there are wider changes first in macro-structure, such changes may not be welfare preferred.

1. Introduction

China since 1994 has had a Value-Added Tax (VAT) which seems conventional by international standards, but on closer inspection is

*Financial support from the SSHRC and CIGI Post-doctoral Fellowship held by the second author makes this paper possible and is greatly appreciated. We are grateful to Jim Davies for comments.

nonstandard and impure in some key areas. Export credits are not always given, and are used as a stabilization device on an on/off basis in certain key sectors (textiles and apparel). The tax is administrated on an income basis in most sectors, but on a consumption basis in such areas as light industry. In addition, the tax is effectively restricted to a manufacturing level with a lower rate turnover tax on key service sectors.

Here we argue that in a conventional competitive monetary framework such features of the VAT are distortionary and impose welfare costs. However, in a world of fixed exchange rates, non-accommodative monetary policy and endogenous trade deficits (as currently in China), this need not be the case. We use a simple single period monetary general equilibrium model with fixed exchange rates and endogenous trade surplus which we calibrate to 2002 Chinese data and show the impure Chinese VAT to be welfare improving compared to the classical neutral tax since it reduces the trade surplus.

Essentially the argument advanced is that in classical public finance analysis of the VAT, departures from a pure destination-based consumption form would be regarded as distortionary and imposing welfare costs. However, in a model where the trade surplus is endogenously determined given the exchange rate and non-accommodative monetary policy, such policies may instead be welfare improving compared to a pure VAT through these trade effects because they increase production costs for exports and lower the size of the trade surplus. We also show how changes in export rebate rates and exchange rate policy can be substitute instruments in terms of macro impacts on trade flows. There effects can clearly be offset by others excluded from the model. For instance, a labor leisure choice will change the analysis of an income base versus a consumption base because with a large base equal yield rates will be lower under an income tax and distortions of labor supply reduced. We concentrate only on the trade effects of the impure base and their interaction with the surplus.

We first discuss the Chinese VAT, as emphasized above, as well as the two elements of impurities we emphasize how they operate and have evolved over time. Interactions with trade performance and exchange rate policy are also highlighted. We then present a monetized general equilibrium trade model in which the trade surplus is endogenously determined given exchange rate and monetary policies. Production structures in the model capture intermediate production and value-added functions for a model calibrated to 2002 Chinese data covering ten sectors and capturing both China's key items of foreign trade and products/sectors where impurities in tax VAT treatment arise both in export rebates and the use of an income basis. The model is then calibrated to base case data for 2002 and generate a supporting parameterization for trade, consumption, the trade surplus and production in the presence of VAT impurities. We then compute an equilibrium in the absence of these impurities, by money to a pure VAT and jointly show welfare losses arise. We suggest that relative to a pure VAT these impurities both allow for tax exporting effects which reduce the size of the surplus and yield a welfare gain. We also show how a structure giving no rebates is equivalent to a Renminbi revaluation, suggesting equivalence and interplay between these instruments. The broader theme of the results is that particular features of policy structure in China which may strike those versed in classical theory as odd may make good sense given the overall policy system within which elements reside.

2. China's Impure VAT

China introduced the Value-Added Tax (VAT) in 1994 as part of a general tax reform. It replaced a preexisting cascading whole sale turnover tax, and was seen both at home and abroad as a major improvement in terms of removing tax distortions and providing a stable revenue source. The VAT has since emerged as the major and secure revenue source underpinning the finances of the Chinese state. It has a standard tax rate of 17%, which is largely restricted to manufactures and is supplemented by a low rate (3%) turnover tax on key service items. The lower 13% rate applies to a range of products (agriculture, vegetables, heating and natural gas, chemicals, fertilizer, metals and coal, see Table 1).

China's VAT is administered by the State Administration of Taxation (VAT on imports is collected by customs) and VAT tax revenues shared between the central government and local governments who receive roughly 25% of revenue. The VAT coexists at enterprise level with a consumption tax whose rates range from 3–17% on all taxable items, and a business tax at rates of 3–20% on taxable items, as well as enterprise income taxes. These additional taxes apply to domestic sales and imports and cover areas both where the VAT is difficult to collect and luxury-oriented consumption items such as cars. Among all Chinese taxes, the VAT is the most important revenue source.

The Chinese VAT, however, has evolved in ways which are quite different from VATs elsewhere, being used both as a stabilization device and an incentive mechanism for policy objectives such as location of

Table 1. China's VAT Taxable Items and Rates.

Coverage of collection	Rate
Exports of goods(except otherwise reduced by limited export rebates)	0%
Agriculture, forestry, animal husbandry, aquatic products; Edible vegetable and grain products; Tap water, heating, cooling, hot air supply, hot water, gas, liquefied petroleum gas, natural gas, coal/charcoal products for household use; Book, newspapers, magazines Feeds, chemical fertilizers, agricultural chemicals, agricultural machinery and plastic converting film for farming; Selected metal mineral products, Selected non-metal mineral products, coal.	13%
Crude oil, mine salt and goods other than those listed above; Taxable services.	17%

Source: Ministry of Finance, China "Provisional Regulations of the People's Republic of China on Value-Added Tax".

firms and area of economic activity (such as high technology products). Specifically, though the tax is formally administered (as in most countries) on a destination basis, rebates of input taxes are variable by sector and commodity, and also used in an on/off manner for stabilization purposes. This is especially the case in the textiles and clothing sector where export tax credits are terminated periodically when export growth rates seem too high, and become the source of international pressure. One of China's actions following the termination of the Multi Fiber Arrangement (MFA) in 2005 was to reduce export rebates as a way of slowing the export surge of newly quota-free products to the US and other developed country markets. China has also an announced formal policy of limited export rebates for VAT which varies by product and which changed in 2003, 2005 and more recently in 2006.

The tax is also administered on an income base which does not allow the expensing of purchases of capital goods. This contrasts with the consumption base used in most other countries under which expensing is allowed. Recent tax changes have introduced elements of a consumption basis by region and by sector, and so now a mixture of the two bases operates.

Earlier VAT literature on a switch from destination to origin taxation shows such a switch at given tax rates may have no real effects because adjustments of exchange rate and price levels may offset tax effects (Whalley, 1979; Krugman, 1980; Grossman, 1980). Substituting the origin principle (tax on exports, no tax on imports) for the destination principle (tax on import, no tax on export) thus should have no affects on real trade. Since a tax on exports is equivalent to a tax on imports, compensating exchange rate and price level adjustments simply restore the original equilibrium. Generally, full price flexibility in a competitive economy, is taken to imply that a comprehensive uniform-rate VAT yields this equivalence in practice. Lockwood (Lockwood *et al.*, 1994a, 1994b) extends his analysis to imperfect extends competitive economy, money economy and when transport cost is taken into account. They find, under assumptions that are different from the earlier literature, that nonequivalence may apply and distortionary policies can influence the economy in various ways.

Besides this equivalence, literature also notes that the administration of the origin principle is difficult. If exports are to be taxed, export values must be verified to ensure that all domestic value-added is included in the base. Arm's length pricing rules from the application of separate accounting principles under the corporate income tax would have to be adopted. National tax credits, would have to be attached to imports at amounts equal to the product of the domestic VAT rate and arm's length import values to ensure that they would not be taxed in domestic stages of production or distribution. Thus, in contrast to the assumptions made in earlier literature, the proper treatment of exports and imports under the origin principle seemingly requires the maintenance or re-establishment of border controls.

Equally, tax effects of the VAT are typically analyzed assuming that the trade balance is exogenous if international trade is taken into account. The unrealism of this assumption in the Chinese case is especially troublesome since trade balance is a major element in the structure and reflects exchange rate and monetary policies. Here we start from the classical neutrality literatures Whalley (Whalley, 1979) and Lockwood (Lockwood, 1994a, 1994b) and introduce monetary non-neutralities in analyzing how under a fixed exchange regime, when the trade surplus is endogenously determined, features of VAT structure traditionally regarded as impure can nonetheless be welfare preferred.

3. Export Rebates

The first impurity in China's VAT that we discuss are limits placed on the rebate of input tax credits as they relate to export. Exports are zero-rated as in conventional VATs, but export rebates of inputs credits are restricted in various ways and rebate rates differ from rates. There are both general policies by product and sector (which change over time) as to the amount of rebate allowed, and specific responses to trade pressures from importing countries (as in apparel) that temporarily suspend rebates.

The origins of this system lie in the 1994 tax system and the introduction of the VAT when full rebates were planned and the government earned a certain amount of revenue for rebates. Due to sharp export growth, and bogus invoices and rebate claims, much of the claimed 1994 rebates had to be deferred. In 1995, the government budget could again not cover requested rebates (which were double the budget), and the government changed the rebate rate. The rebate rate was set at 14% on items taxable at 17%, 10% for items taxable at 13%, and 3% on a small range of items. A year later the government once again could not cover the requested rebates, and rebate rates fell further to 10% from 14% and to 6% from 10%. Table 2 lists refund rates currently used in China.

Between 1991 and 1995, rebates accounted for 7–10.5% of government expenditures. The growth rate of export rebates in 1996 was 50.5% in part due to rapid export growth from foreign-invested enterprises, but also due to fraud and invalid VAT invoices. The share of VAT revenues going to local governments (who did not contribute to rebates before 2003) compounded the problem.

Also, as China's exports grew in the late 1990s, and the share of processing trade involving imported components also grew, more than half of China's exports came from export processing zones where imports entered both duty-free and free of VAT. This created a strong incentive for local firms to convert to processing trade from general trade, since they were

Table 2. Structure of Current China Export Rebates (2005).

Items	Export rebate rate
All non-metal mineral products (except cement and mine salt) include crude oil, coal, natural gas, wax etc. Selected wood products, paper, leather, wool	0%
Some products using agriculture product as material include wheat, maize, flour	5%
Steel	8%
China, selected leather product and cement, glass	8–11%
Selected metal mineral products	5–11%
Textile, furniture, plastic, few wood product	11%
Important equipment, selected IT products and government preferential export product	17%

Source: Taxation Administration of China.

still eligible for export rebates. These fiscal problems of processing trade, tax revenue assignment to local governments, and false involves again forced the central government to limit export tax rebates.

Export rebates have thus evolved in ways which are unrelated to input taxes paid on materials as in a conventional credit-invoice VAT, and schedules of allowable rebates are announced which are changed from time to time. These are then supplemented by ad hoc product-specific announcements to change or terminated rebates usually as a result of pressure (actual or perceived) to slow exports growth to key markets abroad.

These refunds work in the following way. The enterprise first pays VAT to the government ignoring that export products. Each enterprise engaged in export activity calculates its VAT liabilities as

$$T_i = tS_i - tM_i - R_i$$

where T_i are taxes payable, t is the VAT rate, S_i are sales of enterprise i, M_i are material inputs of firm i, and R_i is the refundable VAT on exports sales. Refunds, in turn, are calculated as:

$$R_i = E_i r_i$$

where E_i are export sales, r_i is the refund rate (as per cent in Table 2). $t \geq r_i \geq 0$, and if

$$r_i = 0$$

no refund on all export sales applies. This rebate differs from a credit-invoice VAT in applying to the full value of exports, not just the material input component, but if added materials are used to produce export non-export VAT is correspondingly reduced.

The net result of this structure is a series of export rebates at varying rates across products and sectors which are little connected to the taxes paid on material inputs, with effects both on trade patterns and trade volumes. And in a model with monetary non-neutralities the endogenously determined trade surplus is affected, and changes in rebate rates can be partial substitute instruments for exchange rate realignment. This latter linkage has been much discussed in China.

The second element of impurity in the Chinese VAT relates to the use of an income basis for the tax in contrast to the more conventional consumption base used in most countries, where capture good purchases are expensed under the VAT. Fixed assets for Chinese VAT purposes include machines and transport equipment; effectively all capital equipment used in production regardless of whether the equipment was imported or purchased domestically. This implies input taxes apply to capital goods through the production process.

This treatment is however in transition. In January, 2004 a pilot program was launched covering eight sectors (including oil, chemical and autos) in three provinces (Heilongjiang, Jilin and Liaoning) to evaluate the application of VAT on a consumption basis by allowing deductions for capital goods. Also, as part of the 11th 5-year-plan in 2005, VAT the input credits for capital goods are extended to the production of high technology goods. A mixed income/consumption basis is thus evolving. Both of these impurities represent a considerable departure from a classical pure form of VAT.

4. Modeling the Effects

We first discuss the impacts of changes in VAT structure in standard classical models, and then subsequently discuss models which depart from this form by explicitly capturing monetary non-neutralities and allowing for the endogenous determination of the trade surplus. In this latter class of models, tax structures which reduce exports will tend to reduce the surplus, and this reflects central bank accumulation of foreign currency to support a fixed exchange rate (with inconvertibility). This will be the welfare improving static model. While simple, this formulation is clearly closer to the contemporary situation in China and in such a model an impure VAT may dominate a pure VAT by generating a smaller trade surplus. Thus, given China's current macro policy posture, an impure VAT may dominate a pure VAT.

4.1. *The standard classical case*

In a classical world it is relatively easy to demonstrate the neutrality of either a consumption (destination) or origin (production) broadly based VAT levied at a single rate. For simplicity, we can consider two countries with two producers and two factors.

The production function for each good in each country can be written as

$$Y_i^j = g_i^j(K_i^j, L_i^j) \quad i = \text{sector},\ j = \text{country} \tag{1}$$

where Y_i^j is the output, K_i^j and L_i^j are the use of capital and labor input. g_i^j is assumed CRS.

First order conditions imply the following, where factor prices are w_i^j, r_i^j and goods prices are p_i^j:

$$w_j = p_i^j \frac{\partial g_i^j}{\partial L_i^j}$$

$$r_j = p_i^j \frac{\partial g_i^j}{\partial K_i^j}.$$

The demand side for each economy reflects utility maximizing behavior for a single representative agent, that is:

$$\max U^j(D_i^j, M_i^j) \tag{2}$$

$$\text{st.} \sum_i \left(pd_i^j D_i^j + pm_i^j M_i^j\right) = \sum_i p_i^j Y_i^j - S^j \quad j = 1, 2$$

where D_i^j and M_i^j are domestic and imported goods i in j country, and PD_i^j and pm_i^j are prices of the these goods in country j.

Equilibrium in this economy is given by market clearing prices for goods and factors such that

$$D_i^i + M_i^j = Y_i^i \quad i = 1, 2 \quad j = 1, 2 \quad i \neq j \tag{3}$$

and

$$\sum_{i=1}^{2} L_i^j = \overline{L}^j \quad j = 1, 2$$

$$\sum_{i=1}^{2} K_i^j = \overline{K}^j \quad j = 1, 2$$

where $\overline{K}^j$ and $\overline{L}^j$ are endowments of capital and labor in country j.

Defining the net trade, import M_i^j is the difference between domestic demand and output, and export E_i^j is the difference between output and domestic household demand.

$$\begin{aligned} M_i^j &= \max((X_i^j - Y_i^j), 0) \\ E_i^j &= \max((Y_i^j - X_i^j), 0). \end{aligned} \tag{4}$$

If it follows directly from the budget constraint that balanced trade holds, we have

$$\sum_i p_i^j M_i^j = \sum_i p_i^j E_i^j. \tag{5}$$

If we then consider a monetized extension of this model where prices are denominated in terms of domestic currency with an exchange rate e between the two domestic moneys, then cross country arbitrage between the country specific prices with no tax distortion in trade yields:

$$p_i^1 = ep_i^2 \quad i = 1, 2 \tag{6}$$

If, in turn, we consider only transactions demand for money in each country with unitary velocity and exporters being paid in their own country currency, we have a transactions demand for money in each country. In equilibrium

$$\sum_i (pd_i^j D_i^j + pm_i^j M_i^j) = \overline{m}_j \quad j = 1, 2 \tag{7}$$

where $\overline{M}^j$ is the money stock in country j.

In this model, money is neutral in the sense that once domestic money stocks are specified, then an equilibrium exchange rate is determined independently of the real side. If instead e is fixed at $\overline{e}$, then the relative domestic money stocks $\overline{m}_i/\overline{m}_j$ need to accommodate to $\overline{e}$ so as to support it as an equilibrium exchange rate.

The neutrality of movements between a broadly based VAT administered on a destination (consumption) or origin (production) basis, or indeed between no VAT and a VAT for this economy follows directly. If we define $\hat{p}_i^j$ as the consumer price of good i in country j and p_i^j as the producer price under both a production and a consumption tax, then:

$$\hat{p}_i^j = (1 + t)p_i^j \tag{8}$$

and the household budget constraint changes to

$$\sum_i (\hat{pd}_i^j D_i^j + pm_i^j M_i^j) = \sum_i p_i^j Y_i^j + R^j \tag{9}$$

where $R_j = \sum_i p_i^j t Y_i^j$, refers to tax revenue in country j.

The differences in tax structure between an origin and destination based tax in country j appears in the cross country international arbitrage conditions. Under an origin-based tax on production:

$$\hat{p}_i^1 = ep_i^2 \quad \text{import (not taxed)} \tag{10}$$

$$\hat{p}_i^2 = \frac{(1+t)p_i^1}{e} \quad \text{export (taxed in country } j).$$

In the origin case, if all p_i^j fall by $\frac{1}{1+t}$, or if e increases by $(1+t)$, the same equilibrium will prevail both in a no tax case, and under an origin or destination basis tax. Taxes and their bases are neutral in effect.

4.2. *Non-accommodative monetary policy, and fixed exchange rate case*

If, however, as in China the monetary regime is non-accommodative to the fixed exchange rate chosen and the surplus (and accumulation of reserves) are endogenously determined the neutrality propositions above for broadly based taxes breakdown. In this case, an impure VAT can be welfare preferred to a pure VAT. This can occur, for example, if for a given statutory rate there is a smaller surplus associated with the impure VAT compared to the pure VAT.

To analyse this case, we assume a fixed exchange rate $\overline{e}$ chosen by Country 1 who is willing to support the rate with reserve accumulation which implies trade surpluses. We thus assume that monetary policy in Countries 1 and 2 as represented by $\overline{m}_1/\overline{m}_2$ is non-accomodative of $\overline{e}$, and a trade surplus (deficit) results in Country 1 (2).

In this case, the budget constraints for each country in the no tax case are given by

$$\sum_i p_i^1 X_i^1 = \sum_i p_i^1 Y_i^1 - S^1 \tag{11}$$

$$\sum_i p_i^2 X_i^2 = \sum_i p_i^2 Y_i^2 + D^2$$

where S^1 represents the endogenously determined trade surplus in 1 in the currency of j. S^1, in turn, is

$$S^1 = \sum_i p_i^1 E_i^1 - \sum_i p_i^1 M_i^1. \tag{12}$$

And the corresponding trade deficit D^2 in Country 2 is:

$$D^2 = \sum_i p_i^2 M_i^2 - \sum_i p_i^2 E_i^2. \tag{13}$$

In equilibrium, $S^1 = D^2$, and in this case, money demand functions change to reflect the surplus and become

$$\sum_i p_i^1 X_i^1 = \overline{m}^1$$

$$\sum_i p_i^2 X_i^2 + S^j = \overline{m}^2.$$

The surplus thus is accommodated in the model by the central bank in country i accumulating currency of i equal to S^i $(=eS^j)$.

In this world, a consumption-based VAT will be similar to the classical case in that arbitrage across countries will still imply that

$$\hat{p}_i^1 = e(1+t)p_i^2 \quad \text{(imports taxed)} \qquad (15)$$

$$\hat{p}_i^2 = \frac{p_i^1}{e} \quad \text{(export not taxed)}$$

and so no adjustment is needed in either p_i^j or e to achieve the same equilibrium. However, a tax structure that reduces S will typically be welfare preferred for country j, and so an impure VAT in these cases can yield welfare benefits.

The case of a production-(origin) based VAT will also no longer be equivalent to a destination basis VAT on consumption. In these cases, the international arbitrage conditions are as before, that is:

$$\hat{p}_i^1 = ep_i^2 \quad \text{import (not taxed)} \qquad (16)$$

$$\hat{p}_i^2 = \frac{(1+t)p_i^1}{e} \quad \text{export (taxed in country } j).$$

Here equivalence can no longer be obtained by adjustments only in either p_i^j or in e . If all p_i^1 were to change by $\frac{1}{1+t}$, then S would have to change which would change all Y_i^j and X_i^j, or e increase by $(1+t)$. Equally changing p_i^j by $(1+t)$, would require a change in S^j (D^2).

The impure VAT can be modeled directly using a fixed coefficient technology $\beta_{a_i}^j$ which represents the use of good a in the production of good i in country j.

In this case, the zero profit conditions for good i in country j become

$$p_i^j = wl_i^j + (r_i^j - \delta_i^j)k_i^j + \sum_e \beta_{a_i}^j p_a^j$$

where δ_i^j is depreciation rate on capital in j in sector i. r_i^j is depreciation rate of return on capital in sector i in j and $r = r_i^j - \delta_i^j$ is the common net of depreciation rate of return on capital across sectors in country i (capital is assumed immobile across countries).

Taxes on value-added of consumption type with full input credit yield zero profit conditions

$$\hat{p}_i^j = (1+t)(wl_i^j + (r_i^j - \delta_i^j)k_i^j) + \sum_e \beta_{a_i}^j p_a^j.$$

If we treat the lack of input credits on capital pure purchases as equivalent to allowing no deduction for depreciation from the gross return on capital, taxes on value-added of the income type with full input credit yield

$$\hat{p}_i^j = (1+t)wl_i^j + (r_i^j(1+t) - \delta_i^j)k_i^j + \sum_e \beta_{a_i}^j p_a^j$$

which allows income and consumption type VATs to be compared. If the income type VAT results in a smaller value of S it will typically be welfare preferred.

Export rebates at rates which differ from statutory rates used for taxed on input and apply to the total value of product rather than just value-added used directly can then be incorporated. In this case, under a destination-based VAT the cross country arbitrage conditions become

$$\hat{p}_i^j = e(1+t)p_i^h \quad \text{import (not taxed)}$$

$$\hat{p}_i^h = \frac{(1+t-r)p_i^j}{e} \quad \text{export (only partially taxed in country } j\text{)}$$

where r refers to the export rebate rate as in the Chinese structure described earlier. In this case given that the rebates apply to the value of all production, the zero profit conditions for exporting sectors become

$$\hat{p}_i^j = (1+t-r)(wl_i^j + (r_i^j - \delta_i^j)k_i^j) + \sum_e \beta_{a_i}^j p_a^j.$$

The issue then becomes the impacts of these impurities in the VAT system on trade patterns, S and hence on welfare. As emphasized in the introduction, we put all of VATs structure connected to non-trade effects (such as labor/leisure distortions) on one side and only evaluate trade effects.

5. Model-Based Analyses of the Experience with China's VAT Reform

5.1. *Data and parameterization*

Our VAT model of China with monetary non-neutralities incorporates two countries and three traded goods (agriculture and energy, manufactures, and other sectors). We construct a model compatible benchmark equilibrium data set for calibration (see Dawkins, Srinivasan and Whalley, 2001). Due to the multi-country character of the data set, ensuring model consistency of data is a problem in building the benchmark data. For simplicity, we use GTAP 5 version data for the sectoral gross output, intermediate inputs, import and export for China and the rest of the world. Applied export rebate rates are from Development Research Centre, State Council, China. Value-added tax rates are from Taxation Administration of China (See Table 3).

We use a Leontief technology to present total output; and Cobb-Douglas production with constant returns to scale as value-added function in the two countries. On the demand side, we use CES composites and initially set substitution elasticities to equal to 2 in both countries. We use this as the central case although the literature provides different estimates of this key elasticity. Many of the estimates of domestic and import good substitution are around 2 or greater than 2 (See Betina, 2003). Table 4 reports parameter values in production and preferences generated

Table 3. Commodity, Rate of VAT and Export Rebate Rate Used in the Model Simulation.

Commodity classification	Rate of VAT	Export rebate rate[1]
1. Agriculture	13%	0%
2. Energy product[2]	17%	6.31%
3. Textile	17%	6.31%
4. Other light manufacturing	17%	6.31%
5. Manufacture intermediate	17%	6.31%
6. Motor vehicle	17%	6.31%
7. Other transportation equipment	17%	6.31%
8. Electronic equipment	17%	6.31%
9. Other manufacturing goods	17%	6.31%
10. Service	3%	0%

[1]The rebate rate in this column are sourced from GTAP, see Zhi Wang (2003).
[2]Actually crude oil is levied at 17% for VAT.

Table 4. Parameters for the Model Generated by Calibration and Used in Numerical Simulation.

Shares in Cobb-Douglas Production Functions[3]

	China			Rest of the world		
	Share of capital	Share of labor	Share of intermediates	Share of capital	Share of labor	Share of intermediates
1. Agriculture	0.1241	0.5289	0.3470	0.2794	0.3280	0.3927
2. Energy product	0.3954	0.1947	0.4099	0.3631	0.2322	0.4047
3. Textile	0.2873	0.2258	0.4869	0.2171	0.3257	0.4572
4. Other light manufacturing	0.3090	0.2428	0.4481	0.2440	0.3106	0.4454
5. Intermediate manufacturing	0.3640	0.1635	0.4724	0.2383	0.3430	0.4187
6. Motor vehicle	0.4014	0.1338	0.4648	0.1680	0.3570	0.4750
7. Other transportation equipment	0.2922	0.1716	0.5362	0.1561	0.4221	0.4218
8. Electronic equipment	0.2277	0.1121	0.6602	0.1903	0.3241	0.4856
9. Other manufacturing goods	0.3095	0.1979	0.4926	0.1792	0.3639	0.4569
10. Service	0.3557	0.2795	0.3647	0.3010	0.4156	0.2834

by calibration, as well as shares of intermediate imports in China's imports that are used in counterfactual analysis.

Our benchmark case is a VAT with the impurities we analyze present. We then simulate counterfactuals. One is taxes on value-added of the consumption type and full export rebating (scenario 1); another is only VAT on value-added on consumption base (scenario 2); and a third is with full rebating of export taxes at state setting rate. We are also able to analyze cases where there is a substitute change in exchange rates and export rebates.

The rates of export rebates are clearly important. Statutory rates according to Chinese Law are listed in Table 3. Using the rate directly in our simulation procedure potentially overestimates the effect of export rebates on export and import for a number reasons. One is that the rates

[3]Original data used in calibration for production functions are from the GTAP version-5 database. We aggregate skilled and un-skilled labor and generate a labor endowment for China and the rest of the world. Land and sector specific resources are not taken into account in production.

listed in Table 3 are just for selected goods that belong to our model commodity classification rather than all the goods that are classified into these groups of commodities. Secondly, according to statistical data from China official documents, export rebates divided by the exports yield an average actual rebate rate across all the goods of around 5%. However, given a lack of information on export rebate by good, even though actual export rebate rates differ from the legal rates, to implement a full rebate simulation we simply use the rebate rates according to the law as our base case.

Our model calibrated parameters are reported in Tables 4 and 5. They show share pareameters in production, and in consumption.

5.2. *Simulation results*

We have used our calibrated model to simulate change in tax arrangements on China's trade flows welfare. We firstly consider to compare eliminate China's export rebate and appreciations of the RMB by 5% with a fixed money stock in both China and the rest of the world. Then we keep export rebate incorporate into our model, but shift income-based VAT to consumption basis. Finally, we calibrate impacts of joint

Table 5. Parameters for the Model Generated by Calibration and Used in Numerical Simulation.

Share parameters for imports and domestic goods in nested CES utility functions				
	China		Rest of the world	
	Imports demand	Domestic produced demand	Imports demand	Domestic produced demand
1. Agriculture	0.19	0.81	0.06	0.94
2. Energy product	0.25	0.75	0.08	0.92
3. Textile	0.35	0.65	0.21	0.79
4. Other light manufacturing	0.24	0.76	0.19	0.81
5. Manufacture intermediate	0.31	0.69	0.08	0.92
6. Motor vehicle	0.29	0.71	0.03	0.97
7. Other transportation equipment	0.41	0.59	0.08	0.92
8. Electronic equipment	0.54	0.46	0.14	0.86
9. Other manufacturing goods	0.35	0.65	0.13	0.87
10. Service	0.15	0.85	0.03	0.97

Table 6. Impacts of Elimination Export Rebate and Appreciation RMB on Welfare, Import and Export of China.

	Elimination export rebate		RMB revaluation 5%	
	% change in export	% change in import	% change in export	% change in import
1. Agriculture	0.00	0.00	−9.57	10.99
2. Energy product	−11.64	0.87	−9.62	11.28
3. Textile	−11.83	8.13	−9.89	17.58
4. Other light manufacturing	−11.69	9.19	−9.63	18.38
5. Manufacture intermediate	−11.65	1.19	−9.64	11.56
6. Motor vehicle	−11.64	0.50	−9.56	10.96
7. Other transportation equipment	−11.67	3.82	−9.65	13.81
8. Electronic equipment	−12.07	16.92	−10.07	25.16
9. Other manufacturing goods	−11.70	2.31	−9.85	12.55
10. Service	−11.64	0.34	−9.54	10.83
% change in EV	1.45		2.15	

elimination of export rebate and using consumption basis VAT on trade and welfare.

Results are presented in Tables 6 and 7. Table 6 shows that with elimination of the export rebate, all sectors in China increase their imports in quantity terms range from 0–16.9%, in which the biggest changes happen in textile, other light industries and electronic equipments. All the sectors decrease their exports, at the average of 11%. However, decreasing export causes increase in the final use in domestically-produced goods and thus welfare increases by 1.45%. To compare the alternatives between currency revaluation and tax arrangements, we then let China's RMB revalue by 5%, and find that the two instruments can be substituted.

We then turn to compare income-basis VAT and consumption-basis VAT. Table 7 shows if we tax imports rather than exports, imports decrease sharply around 20%. Exports changes very little compared to the imports. Welfare in this case decreases by 2.3%.

Finally, in Table 8 we calibrate the opposite case to China's currently impure VAT, which is the case of no export rebate with consumption-basis VAT. We find both exports and imports of China decrease substantially, with export decrease at around 11% and imports decrease at around 20%. Welfare thus loses 0.9%.

Table 7. Impacts of Moving to Consumption VAT and Joint Case of Elimination Export Rebates and Consumption VAT on Trade Flows and Welfare.

	Move to full export rebates		Move to Consumption tax arrangement		Move to both	
	% change in export	% change in import	% change in export	% change in import	% change in export	% change in import
1. Agriculture	32.12	−1.46	0.09	−20.63	32.24	−21.80
2. Energy product	28.28	−2.11	0.23	−23.47	28.58	−25.09
3. Textile	28.95	−19.90	0.66	−24.38	29.63	−39.51
4. Other light manufacturing	28.46	−22.38	0.16	−24.14	28.63	−41.14
5. Manufacture intermediate	28.31	−2.89	0.30	−23.35	28.68	−25.58
6. Motor vehicle	28.26	−1.22	0.09	−23.04	28.38	−23.99
7. Other transportation equipment	28.40	−9.30	0.27	−23.75	28.72	−30.86
8. Electronic equipment	29.80	−41.77	0.69	−24.19	30.32	−55.98
9. Other manufacturing goods	28.50	−5.61	0.80	−23.92	29.48	−28.22
10. Service	28.26	−0.84	0.02	−24.05	28.28	−24.69
% change in EV	−7.37		−2.30			−9.69

Table 8. Sensitivity of Elasticity Parameters in Demand.

	Varying the elasticity of substitution between domestic and foreign products only in China				
	0.5	0.75	1.0[4]	1.5	2.0
% change in imports					
Full export rebates	−10.42	−10.42	−10.42	−10.42	−10.42
Impure export rebates	0.00	0.00	0.00	0.00	0.00
Zero export rebates	10.88	10.88	10.88	10.88	10.88
% change in exports					
Full export rebates	29.01	29.01	29.01	29.01	29.01
Impure export rebates	0.00	0.00	0.00	0.00	0.00
Zero export rebates	4.13	4.13	4.13	4.13	4.13

[4]Because we use a CES form in the code, we use 0.999 rather than 1 here in execution.

References

Brean, D. J. S. (1998). Taxation in Modern China, New York: Routledge.

Buiter, W. H. (2003). "Deflation: Prevention and Cure", NBER Working Paper 9623.

Chao, C., E. Yu and W. Yu (2006). "China's Import Duty Drawback and VAT Rebate Policies: A General Equilibrium Analysis", *China Economic Review*, 17(4).

Chen, C., C. Mai and H. Yu (2006). "The Effect of Export Tax Rebates on Export Performance: Theory and Evidence from China", *China Economic Review*, 17(2): 226–235.

Cui, Z. (2003). "China's Export Tax Rebate Policy", *China: An International Journal* (September 2003): 339–349.

Dawkins, C., T. N. Srinivasan, and J. Whalley (2001). "Calibration," in (J. J. Heckman and E. E. Leamer, eds.) Handbook of Econometrics: Volume 5, Elsevier Science.

Ebrill, L. P., M. Keen, J. Bodin, and V. Summers (2001). "The Modern VAT", International Monetary Fund.

Eckaus, R. S. (2006). "China's Exports, Subsidies to State-Owned Enterprises and the WTO", *China Economic Review*, 17(1): 1–13.

Krugman, P. R. (1980). "International Trade Effects of Value-Added Taxation," NBER Working Paper No. 3163.

Lockwood, B., D. de Meza and G. D. Myles (1994a). "When Are Origin and Destination Tax Regimes Equivalent?", *International Tax and Public Finance*, 1: 5–24.

Lockwood, B., D. de Meza, and G. D. Myles (1994b), "The Equivalence Between Destination and Non-Reciprocal Restricted Origin Tax Regimes", *Scandinavian Journal of Economics*, 96: 311–328.

National Bureau of Statistics, PRC, "Chinese Statistical Yearbook", Available at http://www.stats.gov.cn.

Whalley, J. (1979). "Uniform Domestic Tax Rates, Trade Distortions and Economic Integration", *Journal of Public Economics*, 11: 213–221.

Willenbockel, D. (2006). "Structural Effects of a Real Exchange Rate Revaluation in China: A CGE Assessment", MPRA Paper No. 920, Available at http://mpra.ub.uni-muenchen.de/ 920/.

Yu, E., C. Chao and Z. Wang (2003). "Export Tax Rebates and Real Exchange Rate Devaluation: China's Experience in Recent Asia Financial Crisis — A Computable General Equilibrium Analysis", Available at http://www.gtap.agecon.purdue.edu/resources/download/1459.pdf.

Part IV

China in the World

CHINA'S GROWING ECONOMIC ACTIVITY IN AFRICA*

Hany Besada
Centre for International Governance Innovation (CIGI)

Yang Wang
University of Western Ontario

John Whalley
University of Western Ontario, NBER and Centre for International Governance Innovation (CIGI)

China's growing economic presence in Africa is the subject of great curiosity and even concern, particularly in Western media and policymaking settings What has driven this phenomena, what objectives does it reflect, and where is it headed? The focus of this curiosity is primarily Sub-Saharan Africa, where the majority of this activity is concentrated. Here we suggest that repeated claims that suggest China's dominant position with regard to Africa's foreign trade and investment flows is largely unfounded and exaggerated. For now the influence continues to be marginal relative to both current investment and trade flows involving Africa, and even smaller when it comes to China's investment outflows and overall trade. However, if present trends continue, China's investment and trade flows could surpass Africa's principal donor communities (World Bank and the IMF) and its principal trading partners (OECD) over the coming years. Trade between China and Africa is expanding at rates in the order of 30% per year, while FDI inflows to Africa from China are growing at similar rates. The African Development Bank now has its annual meetings not in Africa, but in Shanghai. The elevation of mean growth rates in Sub-Saharan Africa from around 4.5% to 6–6.5% in the last two years can in part be linked to the growing Chinese presence on the continent. Chinese enterprises are centrally involved in Africa in extractive industries, textiles and apparel, infrastructure, finance, and services. Seemingly, everywhere one looks in Africa, one now finds growing Chinese activity. This chapter attempts to document this phenomenon and explore the factors which underlie it.

*This chapter has been prepared with support from the Centre for International Governance Innovation (CIGI) Waterloo as part of CIGI'S Africa project. We are grateful to Andy Cooper, Weimin Zhou and Yao Li for discussions and assistance.

1. Introduction

Trade between China and continental Africa (exports and imports summed) rose from $10.6 billion to $73.3 billion between 2000 and 2007,[1] growing at rates in the order of 30% per year. Trade between Sub-Saharan Africa and China increased over the same years from $7 billion to $59 billion,[2] growing at 30% per year. China has become the third largest African trading partner,[3] behind the US and EU. FDI inflows to Africa from China are now growing at similar rates. China's FDI outward stock in Africa increased to $2.56 billion in 2006 from $49.2 million in 1990 and FDI outflows from China to Africa reached $520 million in 2006 up from $1.5 million in 1991.[4] In 2006, China accounted for 8.64% of total of Africa's exports and 9.59% of its imports,[5] and 1.4% of the continent's FDI inflows. The value of Chinese Official Development Assistance (ODA) to Africa was $2.3 billion in 2006,[6] or 8.4% of total ODA to Africa.

China now accounts for around 9% of Africa's oil and gas exports,[7] and comparable amounts of Africa's other key mineral exports (copper, gold, platinum, manganese, and etc). At the margin, China appears to be an increasingly substantial engine of growth in Africa, and this is for an economy which (at official exchange rates) may still have GDP per capita of only US$1500 per year, in contrast to the US$30,000 range for most OECD states.

In this chapter, we first document the size and rate of change of this growing presence, primarily focusing on trade and finance.[8] We

[1]MOFCOM Statistics & http://www.atimes.com/atimes/China/IL13Ad01.html & http://www.info.gov.hk/gia/general/200707/17/P200707170123.htm&http://en.wikipedia.org/wiki/Sino-African_relations & http://www.afdb.org/portal/page?_pageid=293,174339&_dad=portal&_schema=PORTAL&press_item=19012282&press_lang=us & http://www.info.gov.za/speeches/2007/07051515451001.htm.

[2]MOFCOM Statistics.

[3]http://www.iht.com/articles/2007/02/09/news/trip.php.

[4]2006 Statistical Bulletin of China's Outward Foreign Direct Investment & UNCTAD/UNDP, Asian Foreign Direct Investment in Africa: Towards a New Era of Cooperation among Developing Nations, New York, March 2007.

[5]MOFCOM Statistics & UNCTAD Handbook of statistics 2006–07. http://www.unctad.org/Templates/webflyer.asp?docid=8612&intItemID=1397&lang=1&mode=toc & based on our calculations.

[6]http://www.imf.org/external/pubs/ft/wp/2007/wp07211.pdf.

[7]EU and the US account for 36% and 33% respectively of Africa's oil and gas exports. http://www.dfid.gov.uk/pubs/files/china-factsheet-chinese.pdf, November 2007.

[8]Broadman, Harry (2007). "Africa's Silk Road: China and India's New Economic Frontier. Washington DC: The World Bank.

draw on secondary sources, including the recent IMF Direction of Trade Statistics 2006 Yearbook, 2006/2007 OECD & AfDB's African Economic Outlook report, UNCTAD Handbook of Statistics 2006–2007, and the 2007 UNCTAD's Asian Foreign Direct Investment in Africa report and others to provide a macro sub-continental picture, but also evaluate its concentration by type (resources, construction, etc.) and by country. We also discuss its rate of change, and projections of its growth. Inevitably, given that these developments are so recent, we are forced to use incomplete and often anecdotal information in putting the overall picture together.

We argue that what lies behind these developments involves a number of factors. Clearly China's size and rapid GDP growth are central, and to some degree these developments in Africa simply reflect a rapidly growing Chinese engagement globally rather than just in Africa. Chinese enterprises are now active in Latin Africa and in Europe, particularly in Ireland, Bulgaria and Romania. Some inside and outside China, and somewhat tongue-in-cheek, have suggested that growing Chinese presence in all these regions reflects Mao's military strategy in the interwar years in China of surrounding the towns (the OECD in global development terms) by expanding the villages (Africa, Latin America, and the fringes of Europe).

But we also argue that there are other factors which come into play in the African case. One is clearly China's concern to achieve more security of supply for resources (and especially oil and gas), rather than relying on global markets. Another is the search for new usage of large foreign exchange reserves, and the sense in China of potential political opposition in North America (but also in Europe) to proposed reserve financed buyouts, for example the Union Oil Company of California (UNOCAL) in the US three years ago. The strong commitment at the upper echelons of government in China to speed the growth and development of countries now poorer than China is also important. The approach is to set on one side human rights and governance concerns which have restrained OECD flows in the past and directly use commercial arrangements to fuel growth and development in Africa; in effect, filling the partial void now left in Africa by the OECD. The recent extensive spread of elected governments in Africa and infrastructure improvements further fuels these factors.

Responses to new adjustment resisting trade measures in the OECD against China in textiles and apparel as the Multi-Fiber arrangement (MFA) has been terminated as well, although the initial reaction of Chinese investors to MFA removal was to repatriate quota hopping foreign investment in China. Only subsequently as new measures have been applied to China, has barrier circumventing investment in this sector returned (see Dayaratna-Banda and Whalley, 2007). But clearly if these OECD adjustment resisting measures spread to other product areas (such as autos and electronics), the effect on Chinese FDI flows to Africa could be even larger. Also entering from anecdotal accounts are responses by Chinese enterprises to attempts in China by government agencies to limit corrupt practices by developing new activities in what are seen by such enterprises as lax accounting standard countries. Thus, multiple factors driving the recent growth of Chinese presence in Africa each seem to play a role.

The impact of these developments on Africa has been both significant and positive. Growth rates have been elevated, and with positive impacts on poverty alleviation. Given China's present and projected expansion in Africa over the coming future impacts will be even more pronounced. There are issues involving the delivery of this assistance (including links to corrupt practices), but mainly these flows provide large and largely untied development finance for Africa (in contrast to present conditional OECD flows) which impacts directly and positively on living standards and poverty alleviation across the continent. And if this presence continues to grow, China may eventually prove to be the new African growth engine that the OECD has hesitated to become. Implications follow for OECD policy toward Africa, and we briefly mention other non-OECD country activity in Africa, including India and Brazil. Africa may thus be but a small part of a rapidly changing global economic structure in which China is centrally involved, but for Africa this will likely prove to be highly significant.

This chapter is organized as follows: Section 3 summarizes China-Africa trade and China's investment in Africa. Section 4 discusses the broad orientation of China's policy in Africa and sets out data on China's aid to the continent and its effects on its economy. A more detailed analysis of China–Africa activity in energy and mineral resources is outlined in Section 5. Textile and apparel trade is discussed in Section 6. Some concluding remarks, including discussion of potential links to corrupt practices in China, are set out in Section 7.

2. Sino–Africa Trade and Investment Flows

China–Africa trade has increased sharply since 2000 when a formal China–Africa Cooperation Forum was initiated.[14] As Fig. 1 indicates, China's

[14]The China–Africa Forum on Cooperation was launched in October 2000 aimed to address globalization and enhance cooperation between China and African countries for bilateral social and economic development. "China–Africa Cooperation

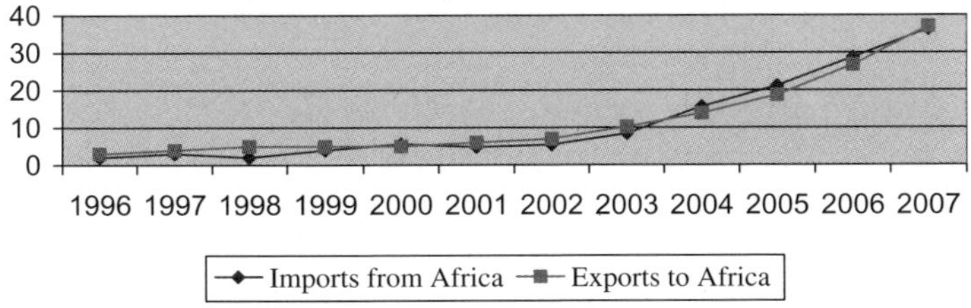

Fig. 1. China's trade with Africa ($bn).
Source: MOFCOM & http://www.tralac.org/pdf/20070220_TheAfrican_TradingRelationship_with_China.pdf.

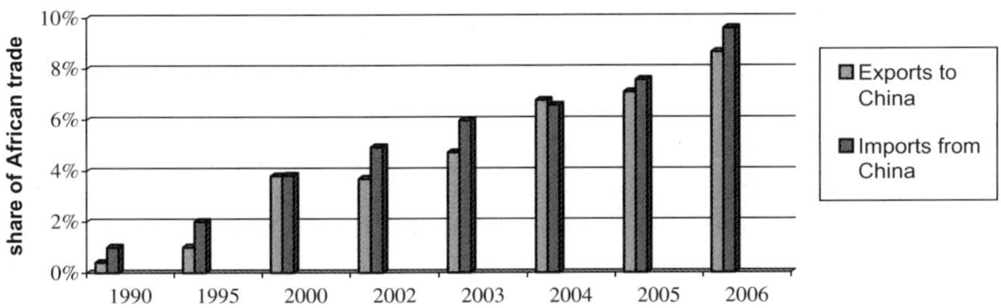

Fig. 2. Africa's trade with China.
Source: UNCTAD Handbook of statistics 2006–07, MOFCOM Statistics, Direction of Trade Statistics Yearbook 2006, IMF & http://www.imf.org/external/pubs/ft/wp/2007/wp07211.pdf & Broadman, Harry (2007) "Africa's Silk Road: China and India's New Economic Frontier. Washington DC: The World Bank.

bilateral trade with Africa grew from $10.6 billion in 2000 to $18 billion in 2003, $30 billion in 2004, $40 billion in 2005, $55 billion in 2006, and $73 billion in 2007. About two-thirds of all African exports to China are oil and related products.[15] This trade is expected to grow to $100 billion by 2010. Figure 2 shows the rapidly growing share of China's trade that Africa represents. China is now the continent's third most-important export market, behind the EU and the United States.[16] In 2005, for the first time, China became the largest individual country exporter for Sub-Saharan Africa with a market share of 7.7% and $13.4 billion in exports.[17]

Forum: Past, Present and Future," (2003) *www.china.org.cn*, December 11, http://www.china.org.cn/english/features/China-Africa/82189.htm.
[15]Shinn, David H. (2007) "Africa, China, the United States, and Oil," May 8, http://forums.csis.org/africa/?p=34.
[16]http://en.wikipedia.org/wiki/Sino-African_relations.
[17]http://www.agoa.gov/resources/US-African%20Trade%20Profile%202007%20-%20Final.pdf.

By 2010, the projections are for China to be Africa's leading trading partner overall.

In a large part, this growth reflects trade in energy and mineral products, but it also provides some insights into China's trade policies. In an effort to promote trade with the continent, China removed tariffs on 196 imports from 28 least developed Africa countries in 2005. While by the end of 2006, duty-free imports from Africa were put at $350 million, covering sesame, copper products, sheepskins, cacao and other products. In July, 2007, China expanded the coverage of African exports exempt from tariffs to 454 items. These included agricultural products, textiles and garments, wooden furniture, light industrial products, and mechanical and electric products. Currently, most African exports now receive duty-free access to China's market. These policy initiatives have also helped expand African exports to China.

Table 1 reports China's aid flows to Africa and Table 2 reflects China's top ten African trading partners. Mineral resources has been an especially important part of the growing trade. There is only limited African–China trade in intermediate goods, apart from those used in textiles and agro

Table 1. China's Aid and FDI Flows to Africa.

	$bn	Growth rates
(1) Chinese aid to Africa in 2006	2.3[9]	Not available
(2) Total aid to Africa in 2006 (including debt relief)	28[10]	23% from 2005 figures[11]
(1) 8.4% of (2)		
(3) Chinese FDI into Africa	0.52	Increase 30% compared to $0.4 bn 2005
(4) Total FDI into Africa	36[12]	Increase 24% compared to $29 bn in 2005[13]
(3) as % of (4) 1.4%		

Source: http://www.imf.org/external/pubs/ft/wp/2007/wp07211.pdf, http://www.oecd.org/document/17/0,2340,en_2649_33721_38341265_1_1_1_1,00.html & http://xyf.mofcom.gov.cn/aarticle/ckqita/200711/20071105225691.html.

[9] http://www.imf.org/external/pubs/ft/wp/2007/wp07211.pdf.
[10] http://www.oecd.org/document/17/0,2340,en_2649_33721_38341265_1_1_1_1,00.html.
[11] http://www.oecd.org/document/17/0,2340,en_2649_33721_38341265_1_1_1_1,00.html.
[12] http://xyf.mofcom.gov.cn/aarticle/ckqita/200711/20071105225691.html.
[13] http://www.unctad.org/Templates/webflyer.asp?docid=6733&intItemID=3642&lang=1.

Table 2. China's Top Ten African Trading Partners between 2004 and 2007 (US $).

	Years	China's exports	Annual China export growth rate (%)	China's imports	Annual China import growth rate (%)
Africa (Total)	2007	37.03 bn	38.7	36.28 bn	26.1
	2006	26.69 bn	42.9	28.77 bn	36.4
	2005	18.68 bn	35.3	21.1 bn	34.6
	2004	13.82 bn	35.7	15.64 bn	87.2
South Africa	2007	7.43 bn	28.8	6.61 bn	61.6
	2006	5.77 bn	50.7	4.09 bn	18.9
	2005	3.83 bn	29.6	3.44 bn	16.4
	2004	2.95 bn	45.5	2.96 bn	60.9
Angola	2007	1.23 bn	37.6	12.89 bn	17.9
	2006	894 m	140.3	10.93 bn	66.1
	2005	372 m	92.7	6.58 bn	39.5
	2004	194 m	32.7	4.72 bn	113.8
Sudan	2007	1.48 bn	5.0	4.13 bn	112.9
	2006	1.41 bn	9.3	1.94 bn	−25.7
	2005	1.29 bn	58.5	2.61 bn	53.3
	2004	815 m	70.5	1.71 bn	18.3
Nigeria	2007	3.79 bn	33.0	537 m	93.2
	2006	2.85 bn	23.9	278 m	−47.2
	2005	2.30 bn	34.0	527 m	13.8
	2004	1.72 bn	−3.7	463 m	546.4
Congo (Rep)	2007	419 m	73.9	2.83 bn	1.4
	2006	241 m	67.4	2.79 bn	22.4
	2005	144 m	55.5	2.28 bn	45.2
	2004	93 m	55.3	1.57 bn	92.6
Egypt	2007	4.36 bn	46.3	240 m	10.6
	2006	2.98 bn	54.4	217 m	2.8
	2005	1.93 bn	39.3	211 m	12.3
	2004	1.39 bn	48.3	187 m	23.0
Algeria	2007	2.69 bn	37.9	1.14 bn	697.2
	2006	1.95 bn	38.3	143 m	−60.7
	2005	1.41 bn	43.3	364 m	40.4
	2004	980 m	51.8	259 m	161.1
Morocco	2007	2.16 bn	37.6	422 m	17.5
	2006	1.57 bn	29.8	359 m	29.6
	2005	1.21 bn	27.9	277 m	29.6
	2004	943 m	35.6	214 m	33.0
Equatorial Guinea	2007	93 m	126.8	1.70 bn	−33.1
	2006	41 m	115.8	2.54 bn	76.4
	2005	19 m	85.7	1.44 bn	44.3
	2004	10 m	100.6	996 m	142.0

(Continued)

Table 2. (*Continued*)

	Years	China's exports	Annual China export growth rate (%)	China's imports	Annual China import growth rate (%)
Libya	2007	859 m	22.0	1.55 bn	−8.3
	2006	704 m	95.6	1.69 bn	79.4
	2005	360 m	41.4	942 m	126.0
	2004	255 m	45.9	417 m	917.8

Sources: Chinese Ministry of Commerce Statistics: 2004 China Trade Statistics, 2005 China Trade Statistics, 2006 China Trade Statistics and 2007 China Trade Statistics, http://www.mofcom.gov.cn.

business, and for now seemingly little incorporation of Sub-Saharan Africa into China coordinated global value chains.

For Sub-Saharan Africa, the share of Africa's total exports to China in five key commodities (oil, iron ore, logs, diamonds and cotton) increased to more than 80% in 2005, up from less than 50% in 1995. Available studies[18] suggest that between 1998 and 2003 China may have accounted for most of the increase in global demand for basic minerals and metals: 99% for nickel, 96% for steel, 76% for aluminum and 100% for copper. Indeed the continent's exports to China increased more than 50% per annum as China's demand for raw materials and oil increased sharply during this period. Similar growth rates apply for the period after 2003. As Table 2 also shows resource trade from Angola, Sudan, Algeria, Congo (Rep), Equatorial Guinea and South Africa accounts for the most part of China's imports from Africa. China's imports of manufactured products from Sub-Saharan Africa are also growing, but are geographically concentrated in Nigeria, South Africa, Morocco, Algeria and Egypt.[19]

Meanwhile, for seven Sub-Saharan African countries, China has become their largest trading partner in terms of total imports. Sudan, which in recent years has expanded energy trade with China, has the largest import share with China accounting for more that 14% of its total imports. This is followed by Tanzania and Ghana with 9.1%, Nigeria with 7.1%, Kenya and Ethiopia with 6.4% and Uganda with 5.1%.[20] The majority of these imports are manufactures.

[18]Lennon, J. (2004). *Overview of Chinese Commodities*, London: Macquarie Research Metals and Mining.

[19]Sandrey, R. (2006). "The African Trading Relationship with China." Cape Town: *Trade Law Centre for Southern Africa*.

This rapid import growth is linked to recent stronger African growth performance. African Development Bank and IMF data both show that African economic growth rate reached 5.7% in 2006[21] and 6.2% in 2007[22], and is expected to reach 8% in 2008[23] This faster African growth reflects strong demand for oil and mineral resources outside of Africa.

But more FDI flowing into Africa and stronger agricultural performance have also contributed to this growth. Having received $2.2 billion worth of FDI from all sources during the 1980s, Africa currently attracts approximately 36 billion dollars worth of FDI inflows.[24] FDI inflows to Africa from China, as Fig. 3 reports, were only $520 million in 2006, a small part of this total, but FDI into Africa from China has still dramatically increased during the years since 2003.

Table 3 reports data on the stock of China's FDI in Africa as of 2005 and compares the situation to 1990 to reflect the rapid growth. These Chinese FDI activities are seemingly different from those which are sourced from North America or the EU. FDI from the developed world is delivered by privately-owned enterprises focusing on profits over a specified period of

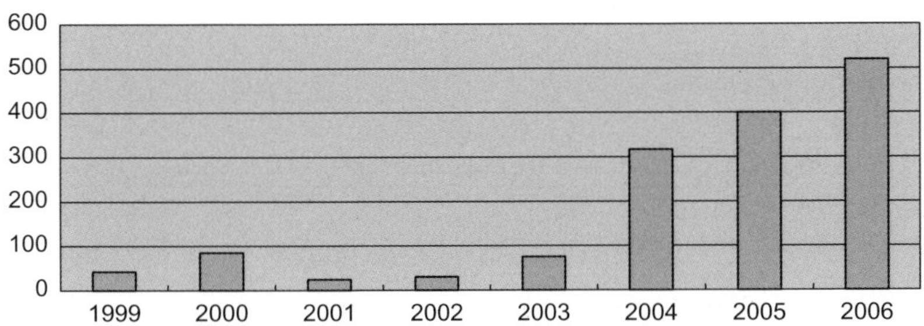

Fig. 3. China's FDI outflows to Africa, 1999–2006 ($ million).
Source: MOFCOM & UNCTAD (2007), Asian Foreign Direct Investment in Africa: Towards a New Era of Cooperation among Developing Countries, UNCTAD/ITE/IIA/2001/1, http://www.unctad.org/Templates/webflyer.asp?intDocItemID=13286&docid=8120&intItemID=1397&lang=1&mode=press & Broadman, H. (2007) "Africa's Silk Road: China and India's New Economic Frontier." Washington DC: The World Bank.

[20] Jenkins, R. C. Edwards (2005). The Effect of China and India's growth and Trade Liberalization on Poverty in Africa, Department of International Development, DCP 70, London: DFID.
[21] http://xyf.mofcom.gov.cn/aarticle/ckqita/200801/ 20080105360302.html.
[22] http://xyf.mofcom.gov.cn/ aarticle/xgxz/200803/20080305440906.html.
[23] http://xyf.mofcom.gov.cn/aarticle/ckqita/200802/20080205387517.html.
[24] "China and the promising Africa," (2007). *People's Daily Online*, May 18, http://english.people.com.cn/200705/18/eng20070518_375880.html & http://xyf.mofcom.gov.cn/aarticle/ckqita/200711/20071105225691.html.

Table 3. FDI Stock in Africa Originating from China (Millions of Dollars).

Region/country	1990	2005
Africa	49.2	1595.3
North Africa	3.4	618.4
Algeria	0.4	171.2
Egypt	1.8	39.8
Libya	1.0	33.1
Morocco	0.2	20.6
Sudan		351.5
Tunisia		2.2
Other Africa	45.9	976.9
Angola		8.8
Botswana		18.1
Cameroon	0.5	7.9
Cape Verde		0.6
Central African Republic	1.2	2.0
Chad	0.1	2.7
Congo		13.3
DRC		25.1
Cote d'Ivoire	0.6	29.1
Equatorial Guinea		16.6
Ethiopia		29.8
Gabon	2.9	35.4
Gambia	0.5	1.2
Ghana		7.3
Guinea		44.2
Kenya	0.5	58.3
Liberia		15.9
Madagascar	1.7	49.9
Mali	0.0	13.3
Mauritania		2.4
Mauritius	6.3	26.8
Mozambique	0.1	14.7
Namibia		2.4
Niger	0.1	20.4
Nigeria	6.7	94.1
Rwanda	2.9	4.7
Senegal	0.2	2.4
Seychelles		4.2
Sierra Leone	1.1	18.4
South Africa		112.3
Togo	0.2	4.8
Uganda		5.0
Tanzania	1.7	62.0
Zambia	3.2	160.3
Zimbabwe	2.5	41.6

Source: 2006 World Investment Report, UNCTAD.

time, and involves minimal risk. China's FDI on the sub-continent is more heavily undertaken by either partially or wholly state-owned enterprises. These have the objective of not simply making short-term profits, but also forming long-lasting relationships with communities and governments. They are assisted in part by access to low-cost capital seemingly financed by low-interest foreign exchange loans drawn for China's reserves. Due to China's increasing demands for resources to fuel high economic growth, a number of investments in Africa are linked to securing strategic reserves of mineral resources for Chinese industries.

This FDI surge (admittedly from a small base) is in part a response to the Chinese government's strategic call of "go out".[25] Chinese investors have established joint-ventures with local investors across the continent in a number of sectors, particularly in oil, agriculture, agribusiness, textile and light manufacturing sectors. Chinese FDI in agriculture has been strongly supported by African governments given its contributions to food security securing food needs. For the most part, these investments have helped raise GDP growth across Africa. Chinese investments have also provided a mechanism for assisting Chinese business to circumvent trade restrictions in the OECD against direct textile and apparel exports from China. These have helped to build local capacity, transfer technology and raise export levels for several African states. In Zimbabwe, for instance, for which tobacco has been among its top exports, Chinese investors have helped Zimbabwe process tobacco into cigarettes and export these as finished value-added products. Chinese investors and a local company have also formed joint ventures to establish a large cement factory in Gweru to meet national demand.[26]

These Chinese investments could be found in a wide variety of sectors, including so-called "fragile states" and projects that western investors have seemingly deemed too risky. In Mozambique, for example, Chinese companies have recently invested in a large new shopping center and an industrial warehouse in the capital, Maputo. They have also financed a Soya processing plant, reportedly worth $10 million and in a facility processing

---

[25] The strategic call of "go out" was launched in October 2000. Zhang, J. (2007). "Review on China FDI strategic system under the strategic call of 'go out'," April 2007, International Trade, http://www.itrade.org.cn/article.php?autoid=87&colum=%E4%B8%AD%E5%9B%BD%E7%BB%8F%E8%B4%B8.

[26] "Zimbabwe Eager to Strengthen Economic Ties with China," (2006). *People's Daily online*, September 28, http://english.peopledaily.com.cn/200609/28/eng20060928_307027.html.

prawns worth an estimated $12 million.[27] In Zambia, China has invested nearly $160 million in the mining sector.[28] In the Democratic Republic of the Congo (DRC), a country plagued by civil conflicts and political instability, China has investments in cobalt and copper. In Sierra Leone, another country emerging from a devastating civil war, China is now developing a luxury hotel and making other investments — going where others would seemingly fear to tread. In Uganda, a Chinese pharmaceutical firm is producing a new anti-malaria drug, and bidding on contracts to supply treated bed nets.[29]

Outside of the oil sector, the most significant investments by Chinese firms have been in infrastructural projects. For example, Chinese firms have been actively involved in the reconstruction of roads around Mozambique, where approximately two-thirds of the country's 600 km of roads have been reconstructed by Chinese multinationals. On the border between Mozambique and Tanzania, Chinese firms have also won a tender to rebuild a large bridge carrying cross border trade between the two countries. They have also recently won tenders to repair water treatment plants in Beira and Quelimane reportedly worth $15 million and in Maputo worth more than $30 million.[30] In Zimbabwe, China is investing in minerals, roads and farming.

Chinese enterprises have also bought a 70% stake in the Zimbabwe's only electricity generation facilities at Hwange and Kariba,[31] and stakes in the national railway. In Zambia, Chinese investors are working on a $600 million hydroelectric plant at Kafue Gorge.[32] In Angola, 30% of a $2 billion soft loan offered by China has gone to finance the building of railroads, schools, roads, hospitals and bridges.[33] In the DRC, China has begun work

[27] www.uk.cn/uploadfiles/2006428172021581.doc.

[28] Leggett, Karby (2005). "Staking a Claim — China Flexes Economic Muscle Throughout Burgeoning Africa," *Ethiopia Tecola Hagos*, http://www.tecolahagos.com/staking_claim.htm.

[29] Lyman, Princeton (2005). "China's Rising Role in Africa," presented to the US–China Commission on July 21, 2005, http://www.cfr.org/publication/8436/.

[30] http://www.fanrpan.org/newsflash.php?archive=2.

[31] http://allafrica.com/stories/200506200960.html.

[32] Joshua Eisenman, Jushua and Jushua Kurlantzick (2006) "China's Africa Strategy," *Current History*, May 2006, pp. 219–224, http://www.afpc.org/china-africa.shtml.

[33] Thompson, Drew (2005). "China's Emerging Interests in Africa: Opportunities and Challenges for Africa and the United States," *African Renaissance*, 2(4) (July/August 2005), at *http://www.csis.org/media/csis/press/0508_china_african_interests.pdf* (September 19, 2005).

on roads to facilitate mineral exports, and has evaluated potential future power projects as well.[34]

This growth of Chinese FDI (and primarily in resources, construction and infrastructure) reflects a Chinese decision at high level to contribute to South–South cooperation through mutually beneficial commercial relationships with the African continent. But at the same time, it also reflects commercial decisions made by individual Chinese enterprises. One claim supporting this is that Chinese enterprises have been successful in delivering comparable infrastructure projects at prices between 25% and 50% less than those other foreign investors charge.[35]

Anecdotal evidence also suggests a combination of factors that have allowed Chinese enterprises to both outbid and outperform Western counterparts across the continent in their investment activity. These include the use of cheaper Chinese materials; ample supply of Chinese labor which is often even less expensive than local labor and willing to live in isolated communities; access to subsidies provided by the Chinese Government to invest overseas and cheaper capital than local investors; as well as less pressure by the Chinese Government for state-owned companies to adhere to strict environmental and labor standards.

Especially important in the growing FDI picture are infrastructure projects and development initiatives by Chinese state-owned companies across the continent, even in countries without abundant mineral resources. Some have been directly aid-funded infrastructure projects assisting Africa governments. For example, in Guinea Bissau, China paid for the tiles and marbles of the parliamentary buildings. In East Africa, China provided financial support for, and assisted with the construction of new foreign ministry buildings and stadiums in both Djibouti and Uganda. All of these reflect the commitment by China to development and poverty alleviation programs in the continent.

While it is worth emphasizing that FDI from China is still small relative to total flows into Africa, its growth is rapid. Importantly, this recent growth in Chinese presence in Africa coexists with relatively stagnant OECD inflows despite government attempts to promote it. For instance, the US has, in recent years, initiated a plan "promoting African economic growth and opportunity partnership" aimed at encouraging American companies

[34]Lyman, Princeton (2005). "China's Rising Role in Africa," presented to the US–China Commission on July 21, 2005, http://www.cfr.org/publication/8436/.
[35]www.ids.ac.uk/ids/global/AsianDriverpdfs/DFIDAgendaPaper06.pdf.

to enter African markets.[36] But the aggregate impact has been small. European countries such as France have traditionally regarded Africa as their market due to colonial legacies and linguistic as well as cultural factors. In 2006, the European Union accounted for 32% of all Sub-Saharan exports, and its investment in Africa accounted for 36.6% of total investments on the continent.[37] Data for the US were 29.6% and 37% respectively.[38] Western states have maintained close relationships with Africa through language, information linkage and personnel exchanges, which assist in trade and finance and give Western countries substantial advantages. In comparison, Chinese enterprises have had to face disadvantages in language and culture differences. China's ability to rapidly expand its share of African trade and finance is thus all the more remarkable.

China's red carpet treatment for 50 of Africa's Heads of State in November, 2006, which formally commemorated five decades of Sino–African relations, bears testimony to the continent's current economic importance as seen from Beijing. High-profile state visits by top Chinese officials, including the Chinese President Hu Jintao and Chinese Premier Wen Jiabao to dozens of African states in recent months underscore its perceived importance. These visits occurred shortly after pledges to increase China's aid to Africa from $2.3 billion in 2006 to $10 billion by 2009[39] (in comparison, US aid to Africa is to reach $9 billion by 2010,[40] and EU aid to Africa to more than $20 billion depending on the next EU budget,[41] and to further expand China's trade and Foreign Direct Investment (FDI) with the continent.

---

[36] http://bic.cass.cn/English/InfoShow/Article_Show_Conference_Show.asp?ID = 364 & Title = Africa%20Beyond%202000 & strNavigation =Home-%3EForum&BigClassID=4& SmallClassID=11.

[37] http://web.worldbank.org/WBSITE/EXTERNAL/NEWS/0,,contentMDK:21052520 ~pagePK:64257043~piPK:437376~theSitePK:4607,00.html & 2007 World Investment Report, UNCTAD http://www.unctad.org/en/docs/wir2007p1_en.pdf.

[38] http://web.worldbank.org/WBSITE/EXTERNAL/NEWS/0,,contentMDK:21052520 ~pagePK:64257043~piPK:437376~theSitePK:4607,00.html & http://italy.usembassy.gov/pdf/other/RL31772.pdf.

[39] http://www.csmonitor.com/2007/0202/p06s01-woaf.html.

[40] Fletcher, Michael (2006). "Bush Has Quietly Tripled Aid to Africa," *Washington Post*, December 31, http://www.washingtonpost.com/wp-dyn/content/article/2006/12/30/AR2006123000941.html.

[41] Kroeger, Alix (2005). "EU Boosts Aid to Africa by $10 bn," *BBC News*, October 12, http://news.bbc.co.uk/2/hi/europe/4335954.stm.

3. The Objectives Behind China's Africa Policy

A starting point in understanding what is behind the growth in China's involvement in Africa is the central Chinese precept that business should not be mixed with politics. China's growing presence in Africa thus largely reflects commercial rather than other political considerations. To underscore the point, Chinese officials have repeatedly argued that attempts by other countries to link positions on democracy and human rights to economic integration violate the rights of sovereign countries. This position is reflected by comments of China's deputy foreign minister, Zhou Wenzhong: "Business is business. We try to separate politics from business.... You [the West] have tried to impose a market economy and multiparty democracy on these countries which are not ready for it. We are also against embargoes, which you have tried to use against us."[42]

The contrast is a seemingly Western policy of linking aid to African recipients to Western values or specific development models for African countries. In the process, Western governments have often set meeting political indicators in areas such as democracy, freedom, openness, transparency, and human rights as criteria for aid.[43] In contrast, China has promoted what it calls the "Beijing consensus"[44] in Africa by providing unconditional aid to African countries. This reflects an underlying Chinese position of not interfering in other countries' internal affairs and respecting country rights to choose the road of development that best suits them. In its financial dealings with Africa, either through aid or FDI, China thus does not typically use links to policy to impose its own value system or development model on African states.

[42]French, Howard (2004). "China in Africa: All Trade and No Political Baggage," *New York Times,* August 8, 2004.

[43]Zhang, Chun (2006). "'Neocolonialism' Label cannot be Pinned on China," Shanghai Research Center for International Issues, November 2002, http://www.sinofile.net/saiweng/sip_blog.nsf/d6plinks/YZHI-6VB8J3.

[44]The "Beijing Consensus" was brought forward spontaneously by international opinions against the background of China's fast economic development since the reform and opening up and considerable raise in people's living standard, while "Washington Consensus" was put forward deliberately and systematically. Participants of the "Washington Consensus" reached their consensus on the basis of actual acceptance of Neo-liberalism. "The 'Washington Consensus' and 'Beijing Consensus'," *People's Daily Online*, June 18, 2005, http://english.peopledaily.com.cn/200506/18/eng20050618_190947.html.

With Western aid increasingly tied to human rights and Western notions of economic reform, Africa has welcomed China's unconditional aid approach. Thus, when the Angolan government hesitated over accepting an IMF loan linked to transparency in its oil revenue accounting, the Chinese Export-Import Bank offered an interest-free loan with no such accounting required.[45] China also similarly funded infrastructure projects such as railroad, schools, roads, hospitals and bridges as well as, lay a fiber-optic network in Angola. In these cases, the wider Chinese interest was perceived to lie in developing country to country relationships in anticipation that resource project approvals would follow. One could claim that narrower self interest still prevailed, but it remains the case that such aid was untied; it promoted development, and had not been forthcoming from much wealthier OECD countries.

Equally, when the UN Security Council proposed sanctions against Sudan because of the Darfur situation, Beijing insisted on their position set out above, namely "the internal situation in the Sudan is an internal affair, and China is not in a position to impose upon Khartoum."[46] China then provided assistance in other ways. To help Sudan develop its oil industry, PetroChina invested $2.7 billion in Sudan, built a 1506 km oil pipeline, a crude processing plant with an annual capacity of 2.5 m tons, and several gas stations.[47] This not only changed Sudan from an oil importing to an oil exporting country, but also ensured Sudan had an integrated oil industry structure covering exploration, production, refining and transport for sales. In addition, China subsequently invested over $20 million to help the Sudan build other facilities, including schools and hospitals.[48] This unconditional investment and aid has flowed quickly into Sudan since China adopted a policy of non-involvement in Sudan's domestic affairs. But China's principle of not interfering in other countries' internal affairs through conditional aid or FDI has not restrained China from pursuing humanitarian concerns in Africa. For example, in 2004, China contributed 1,500 peacekeepers to UN missions across Africa, such as in Liberia.

---

[45] Lombard, Louisa (2006). "Africa's China Card", April 2006, http://www.foreignpolicy.com/story/cms.php?story_id=3419.

[46] French, "China in Africa: All Trade, with No Political Baggage," p. A12.

[47] Zhang, Chun (2006). "'Neocolonialism' Label cannot be pinned on China," Shanghai Research Center for International Issues, November 2002, http://www.sinofile.net/saiweng/sip_blog.nsf/d6plinks/YZHI-6VB8J3.

[48] He, WenPing (2006), "Partners in Development," *Beijing Review*, Vol. 44, http://www.bjreview.cn/EN/06-44-e/sp-1.htm.

Along with growing Chinese trade and foreign direct investment in Africa, Chinese aid to Africa has also growth correspondingly. China began to provide official development assistance and debt relief since the mid-1950s. From 1956 to May 2006, it contributed a total of $5.7 billion[49] for more than 800 aid projects.[50] Meanwhile, the value of Chinese aid in Africa reportedly reached $2.3 billion in 2006. More recently, China has aimed to keep to its long-standing commitments made to the continent from the early 1990s on, by providing financial assistance and facilitating the forgiveness of loans. More recently, the third summit of the Forum on China–Africa Co-operation, held from 3 to 5 November, 2006, took a number of steps in this direction. China pledged to double its 2006 aid flows to Africa by 2009. China also cancelled all debt stemming from Chinese interest-free government loans that matured at the end of 2005, estimated at approximately $1.4 billion, for the 31 highly indebted and least developed countries (LDCs) on the continent which had diplomatic relations with Beijing.

China also provided $3 billion in preferential loans and $2 billion in preferential buyer's credit to African states, and offered zero-tariff treatment for various exports to China from 30 of the least developed African countries. In order to further promote China's FDI in Africa and bilateral trade, a China–Africa development fund of $5 billion was set up by the Chinese government to encourage Chinese companies to invest in Africa and provide support to them. In the meantime China further opened its market to Africa, increasing from 190 to over 440 the number of export items to Beijing receiving zero-tariff treatment from the African LDCs.[51]

There has also been further assistance beyond direct financial flows. In Liberia, as well as in Mozambique[52], China has signed a memo, canceling all debts owing to it by these states — which jointly amounted to more than $35 million.[53] In Liberia's case, Beijing specially introduced a tariff exemption policy for all imports from Liberia.

[49] This stock figure may not be consistent with aid flows discussed throughout this paper.
[50] He, Wenping (2006). "China–Africa Relations Moving into an Era of Rapid Development," in: Africa Institute of South Africa, Inside AISA, October/December, pp. 3–6.
[51] Chee, Yoke Ling (2006). "China: Doubles Aid and Investment to Africa," *Third World Network*, November 5, http://www.twnside.org.sg/title2/finance/twninfofinance010.htm.
[52] http://www.poptel.org.uk/mozambique-news/newsletter/aim335.html#story7.
[53] http://www.csmonitor.com/2007/0209/p01s04-woaf.htm.

Another element in this picture is China's participation in the African Development Bank. China joined both the African Development Bank Group's (AfDB)[54] and the African Development Fund in 1985. Currently, China has 24,230 shares, or a 1.117% stake in the AfDB. Since joining, China has donated $314 million to the African Development Fund, supporting infrastructure construction, and poverty alleviation as well as educational projects in Africa. To further develop cooperation between China and the AfDB, Beijing signed a $2 million technical cooperation agreement in 1996. This agreement provides subsidies for Chinese experts who work on projects and bring advanced technology to Africa. So far, the Chinese government has paid $900,000 to support 14 projects in eight African countries.[55]

Chinese development assistance has also taken a variety of forms in Africa. Engineering, medical and agricultural teams have provided technical support to African states since the 1960s, although this accelerated by the late 1980s. China trained over 14,600 people in different fields for Africa.[56] In both Liberia and the Central African Republic, China has directly provided funding for training programs to strengthen the capacity of the civil service in these countries. In areas of small-scale agricultural production and hydro-irrigation, China has supported training programs that have involved thousands of African farmers across the continent.[57] In Djibouti, Ethiopia and elsewhere in the Horn of Africa, Beijing has in recent years supplied modern telecommunication equipment, along with training programs designed to help local entrepreneurs maintain their equipment.[58] During the 2006 Beijing Summit, China pledged to train 15,000 African professionals, send 100 senior agricultural experts to Africa, and set up ten special agricultural technology demonstration centers across the continent by 2009. Additionally, the number of Chinese government scholarships to

---

[54]The African Development Bank Group's (AfDB) is the main development finance institution in Africa and was established in 1964. It has 77 members, 53 from Africa and 24 outside the continent. The bank's priorities include the reduction of poverty, improving the living conditions of African populations and resource mobilization for the economic and social progress of its regional member countries.

[55]Zhang, Lu (2007). "Gathering to boost Sino–African ties," *China Daily*, May 14, http://www.china.org.cn/english/features/adb/210662.htm.

[56]Zhang, Chun (2006). "'Neocolonialism' Label cannot be Pinned on China," Shanghai Research Center for International Issues, November 2002, http://www.sinofile.net/saiweng/sip_blog.nsf/d6plinks/YZHI-6VB8J3.

[57]http://panafricannews.blogspot.com/2006_10_01 _archive.html.

[58]http://www.bjreview.com.cn/expert/txt/2006-12/15/content_50879.htm.

African students is planned to double from 2,000 per year in 2006 to 4,000 per year by 2009.[59]

China's aid has also financed building schools and clinics treating patients suffering from HIV/AIDS. China has thus far sent medical teams to 43 African countries, amounting to more than 16,000 person/visits, and helped treat 240 million patients,[60] including 180 million cases of HIV/AIDS.[61] Today more than 900 Chinese doctors work in Africa.[62] Furthermore, during November 2006's Beijing Summit, China's leadership announced the dispatching of more than 300 volunteers to Africa, RMB300 million for artemisinin (an anti-malaria drug) and 30 malaria prevention and treatment centers, and pledged to build more than 100 schools and 30 hospitals across the continent by 2009.[63]

At the same time, China's success in securing mineral rights in Africa has gone hand in hand with support for a wide range of construction projects and financial assistance. In Sudan, for instance, Beijing used its technical expertise and links to other government-owned companies to help the country's oil industry become a major export earner. It also invested some $2 billion in the country's Merowe hydropower dam, due to open in 2008, which is expected to provide for all of the country's energy needs for the next two decades.[64] China's Sino Hydro Corporation has helped Ghana build a 400 megawatt hydroelectric dam worth $600 million in the north of the country.[65] Beijing also helped build a $300 million dam project for Ethiopia.[66] In Rwanda, Chinese companies have paved more than 80% of

---

[59] Chee, Yoke Ling (2006). "China: Doubles Aid and Investment to Africa," *Third World Network*, November 5, http://www.twnside.org.sg/title2/finance/twninfofinance010.htm.

[60] Zhang, Chun (2006). "'Neocolonialism' Label cannot be Pinned on China," Shanghai Research Center for International Issues, November 2002, http://www.sinofile.net/saiweng/sip_blog.nsf/d6plinks/YZHI-6VB8J3.

[61] Thompson, Drew (2005). "China's Soft Power in Africa: From the 'Beijing Consensus' to Health Diplomacy," Jamestown Foundation *China Brief*, 5(21) October 13.

[62] Lyman, Princeton (2005). "China's Rising Role in Africa," presented to the US–China Commission on July 21, 2005, http://www.cfr.org/publication/8436/.

[63] Chee, Yoke Ling (2006). "China: Doubles aid and investment to Africa," *Third World Network*, November 5, http://www.twnside.org.sg/title2/finance/twninfofinance010.htm.

[64] http://www.jamestown.org/terrorism/news/uploads/cb_007_007a.pdf.

[65] "Africa: Western Leaders Monitor China–Africa Summit" (2007), www.allAfrica.com, May 17, http://allafrica.com/stories/200705161110.html.

[66] Joshua Eisenman, Jushua and Jushua Kurlantzick (2006). "China's Africa Strategy," Current History, May 2006, pp. 219–224, http://www.afpc.org/china-africa.shtml.

the main roads.[67] In late 2006, China agreed a $2 billion credit line to help fund infrastructure projects in Equatorial Guinea.[68]

Debt forgiveness and aid from China have also contributed to infrastructure development in African countries, which in turn has been key for political stability. Particularly important have been China's programs in education and health in Africa, which are recognized as central to African growth, and have improved local living standards. These infrastructure improvements have also helped African countries secure other loans and investment opportunities, contributing to further development. "South-South cooperation" has thus been centrally embodied in China's aid activity in Africa, which in turn has been welcomed by a large number of African governments.

4. Resources and China's Involvement in Africa

A key factor underlying China's recent rapid expansion in Africa is Beijing's desire to gain secure access to supplies of oil, gas and key minerals. The Chinese leadership has always emphasized that China's continued high growth will require a growing supply of raw materials, especially oil. The country's growing energy demands, coupled with relatively stagnant coal output[69] and falling domestic crude oil production,[70] prompted the country to look overseas for stable sources of mineral resources since the early 1990s. In 1993, a turning point for China came when it changed from a net exporter to a net importer of oil.

By late 2004 China had become the world's second largest oil user consuming 5.46 million barrels a day (bbl/d) (see Fig. 4), more than Japan's 5.43 million bbl/d, and placing it behind only the US at 19.7 million bbl/d.[71] Currently, China's oil consumption is put at 7 million barrels a

[67] Leggett, Karby (2005). "Staking a Claim China Flexes Economic Muscle Throughout Burgeoning Africa," Ethiopia Tecola Hagos, http://www.tecolahagos.com/staking_claim.htm.
[68] Country Profiles Foreign and Commonwealth Office, UK http://www.fco.gov.uk/servlet/Front?pagename=OpenMarket/Xcelerate/ShowPage&c=Page&cid=1007029394365&a=KCountryProfile&aid=1019672564304.
[69] http://www.rice.edu/energy/publications/docs/AsianEnergySecurity_MainStudy.pdf.
[70] http://www.pnl.gov/aisu/pubs/engenvup.pdf.
[71] US Department of Energy, Energy Information Agency: Country Analysis Brief: China, September 15, 2005, and Downs, Erica: "The Chinese Energy Security Debate", China Quarterly, No. 1777, March 2004, pp. 21–41.

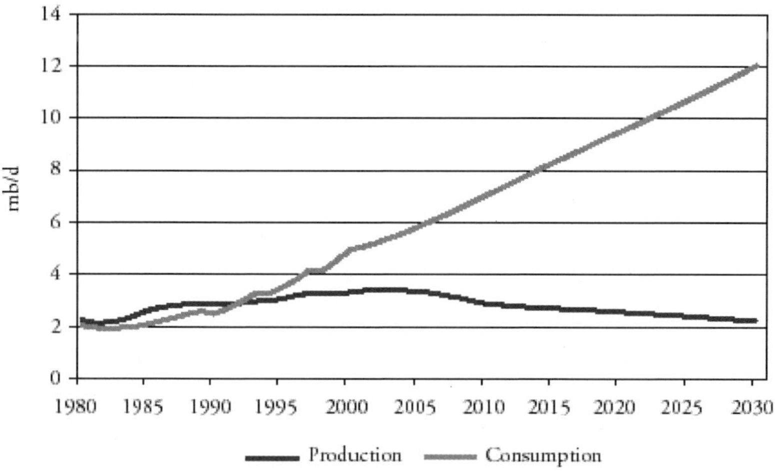

Fig. 4. China's growing gap between oil demand and domestic production (mb/d). *Source*: *International energy agency*, 2002, p. 53.

day while the US consumes about 20 million barrels.[72] China's oil and gas imports are projected to increase to 60% of its total oil and gas demand by 2020 from the current level of 33%,[73] while its oil consumption is expected to increase by 10% per annum.[74] Approximately 40% of the increase in global oil demand between 2000 and 2004 and 2002 to 2006 is attributed to China's rapid demand.[75] China's oil imports from Asia's oil producing states are not sufficient to meet either its current or projected energy demands and Chinese officials seemingly believe there are limits to Middle East oil and gas production, especially given its current primary allocation to Europe and the US.

As a late entrant to the global oil market, Africa represents perhaps the last major source of oil reserves which is not primarily managed by major Western energy companies, and hence available for Chinese corporations to invest in and ultimately partly control. Libya's 39 billion barrels of

[72]Shinn, David H. (2007). "Africa, China, the United States, and Oil," May 8, http://forums.csis.org/africa/?p=34.

[73]Goodman, Peter (2004). "China Invests Heavily in Sudan's Oil Industry" *The Washington Post*, December 23.

[74]Blair, David (2005). "Oil-Hungry China Takes Sudan under Its Wing," *The Telegraph*, April 23.

[75]www.palgrave-journals.com/development/journal/v50/n3/full/1100407a.html.

oil reserves and Nigeria's 36 billion barrels are twice the size of China's proven reserves. Africa has only 9% of the world's proven petroleum reserves compared to almost 62% for the Middle East. IHS Energy, an oil and gas consulting firm, believes that Africa will provide 30% of the world's growth in hydrocarbon production by 2010. A US Department of Energy study projected that African oil production would rise 91% between 2002 and 2025. African oil tends to be high quality and low in sulfur, making it particularly desirable to refiners. Africa currently supplies almost one third of China's oil imports.[76]

In recent years, Chinese state-owned enterprises have not only invested heavily in foreign oil reserves and but have also used Chinese construction and engineering to assist African oil producing exporters such as Nigeria, Zimbabwe, Angola, Sudan, Gabon and Algeria in further developing their oil, gas and other mineral resources. In 2005, China imported more than 38 million tons of crude oil from Africa, about one-third of China's oil imports,[77] and this reflects major investments in oil and gas projects in countries such as Nigeria, Sudan, Gabon and Angola.

Table 4 indicates that oil, minerals and other natural resources account for the major part of Africa's exports to China. Currently, all exports of Angola to China are oil. Exports of Sudan, Nigeria and Congo (DRC) are also all largely oil. The huge reserves of minerals in DRC imply that its

Table 4. Resource Exports to China in 2005 in (Percentage of Total Trade).

	Crude oil	Metals	Wood	Cotton
Angola	100			
Sudan	98.8			
Nigeria	88.9			
Congo	85.9			
Gabon	54.8		42.3	
DRC		99.6		
Ghana		59.8		
South Africa		45.6		
Cameroon			39.7	
Tanzania			23.4	53.8

Source: OECD Development Center, 2006.

[76]Shinn, David H. (2007). "Africa, China, the United States, and Oil," Center for Strategic and International Studies (CSIS) Africa Policy Forum, May 8.
[77]York, Geoffrey, 'China, Africa Forging Closer Ties.' *Globe and Mail*, November 10, 2006.

exports are mainly metals. Gabon, Cameroon and Tanzania are abundant in timber which is imported by China. Agricultural products, such as cotton, also play an important role in Tanzania's exports to China. In 2006, oil and gas accounted for 62% of Africa's exports to China, followed by non-petroleum minerals and metals with 13%. China's high demand for oil, minerals and other natural resources is thus motivating active engagement in investment in these sectors and strengthening economic cooperation with Africa.

By country, the following situations apply:

4.1. *Nigeria*

As a member of OPEC, Nigeria is the largest oil producer in Africa and the eleventh-largest producer in the world. Nigeria is a major oil supplier to both Western Europe and the US, producing roughly 2.5 million barrels per day. Nigeria's proven oil reserves are approximately 35.2 billion barrels, and there are plans by the Nigerian government to expand this to 40 billion barrels by 2010. In July 2005, PetroChina finalized a deal reported to be worth $800 million with the Nigerian National Petroleum Corporation to purchase approximately 30,000 barrels of oil per day for five years.[78] In January, 2006, the Chinese state-owned China National Offshore Oil Corporation (CNOOC) acquired a 45% stake in a Nigerian offshore oil and gas field reported to be worth more than $2.27 billion. The company subsequently promised to additionally invest up to $2.25 billion in field development.[79] In addition, China has won a license to operate four of Nigeria's oil blocs as part of wider package involving a commitment to build a hydro power station. China is currently reported to be considering $7 billion in investments in Nigeria, covering a wide variety of sectors.[80]

4.2. *Angola*

Angola is the second-largest oil producer in sub-Saharan Africa after Nigeria with oil production expected to reach 2 million barrels per day by 2008.

[78] "China, Nigeria Sign Oil Supply Pact" (2005). *Xinhua News Agency*, July 9.
[79] "Linebaugh, Kate and Shai Oster (2006). "CNOOC Pays $2.27 Billion for Nigerian Oil Gas Stake," *The Wall Street Journal*, January 10.
[80] Onyebuchi Ezigbo (2005). "Nigeria–China Sign $800 million Crude Oil Sale Agreement," *This Day* (*Lagos*), July 11, on the web at http://allafrica.com/stories/printable/200507111391.html. Dianna Games (2005). "Chinese the New Imperialists in Africa, *Business Day Johannesburg*, February 21, Available at http://allafrica.com/stories/printable/200502210104.html.

Angola also has major offshore sources of gas. China has invested heavily in Angola given relative political stability.[81] In March, 2004, China granted Angola a $2 billion soft loan as part of a longer term aid package in exchange for a contract to supply 10,000 barrels of crude oil per day.[82] Under the agreement, the proceeds of the loan will be heavily invested in infrastructure construction, with 70% of funds earmarked for Chinese companies and the remaining 30% going to local subcontractors, including funds for Chinese companies to build railroads, schools, roads, hospitals, bridges, and offices; lay a fiber-optic network; and train Angolan telecommunications workers.[83] According to the World Bank, Angola accounted for half of China's oil imports from Africa in 2005, and exported 25% of its oil production to China.[84]

4.3. *Sudan*

Sudan has proven reserves of some 563 million barrels of oil. Since 1999, Chinese enterprises have invested more than $3 billion in pipeline construction and in refineries.[85] The China National Petroleum Corporation (CNPC) entered Sudan in 1996 and now is the single largest shareholder in a major project with a 40% share[86] of $1.7 billion in the Greater Nile Petroleum Operating Company, which is Sudan's largest petroleum company and controls Sudan's oil fields. CNPC's operation, which also discovered additional oil in Sudan, produced 500,000 barrels per

[81] Shinn, David H. (2007). "Africa, China, the United States, and Oil," Center for Strategic and International Studies (CSIS) Africa Policy Forum, May 8.

[82] Lee, Don (2004). "China Barrels Ahead in Oil Market," *The Los Angles Times*, November 14, 2004, at http://energybulletin.net/3159.html (September 19, 2005).

[83] Thompson, Drew (2005). "China's Emerging Interests in Africa: Opportunities and Challenges for Africa and the United States," *African Renaissance*, 2(4) (July/August 2005), at *http://www.csis.org/media/csis/press/0508_china_african_interests.pdf* (September 19, 2005).

[84] Broadman, Harry G. (2006). *Africa's Silk Road: China and India's New Economic Frontier* http://web.worldbank.org/WBSITE/EXTERNAL/COUNTRIES/AFRICAEXT/0,,contentMDK:21056305 ~ pagePK:146736 ~ piPK:146830 ~ theSitePK:258644,00.html.

[85] Brookes, Peter and Ji Hye Shin (2006). "China's Influence in Africa: Implications for the United States," *Backgrounder #1916*, February 22, at http://www.heritage.org/research/asiaandthepacific/bg1916.cfm.

[86] The other partners in the joint venture of the Greater Nile Petroleum Operating Company include Talisman Energy of Canada, the Sudanese Government and Petronas of Malaysia. Goodman, Peter (2004). 'China Invests Heavily in Sudan's Oil Industry' *The Washington Post*, December 23.

day in 2006 and was expected to reach 750,000 barrels per day in 2007.[87] In addition, China has recently signed new partnership agreements to extract oil from the Melut Basin and Darfur.[88] China now takes 64% of Sudan's oil exports, which are approximately 7% of China's total oil imports.[89]

4.4. *Zambia*

China is now the world's largest consumer of copper, followed by the United States.[90] Zambia–CRC hold the largest copper deposit in the world. In 2004, proven copper reserves in the southern African states were put at 2 billion tons. In 2005, the China Non-Ferrous Metals Corporation in Africa (NFCA) invested $160 million[91] in the Chambishi Copper Mine, one of Zambia's largest copper mines, and holds an 85% stake.[92] Besides copper, Zambia's mineral resources spans a range of metals, particularly gold, gemstones, a variety of industrial minerals and potential energy resources — uranium, coal and hydrocarbons. Chinese companies have also invested in coal and gemstone mining. China has also begun to invest in copper and cobalt mines in the neighboring DRC.

4.5. *Zimbabwe*

Zimbabwe is blessed with abundant gold reserves and is home to the world's second-largest platinum mines. Zimbabwe together with South Africa constitutes China's major source of platinum and iron ore.[93] In addition, China is Zimbabwe's largest importer of tobacco, one of the country's major exports China has made large investments in Zimbabwe's tobacco

[87]Shinn, David H. (2007). "Africa, China, the United States, and Oil," Center for Strategic and International Studies (CSIS) Africa Policy Forum, May 8.
[88]http://www.cfr.org/content/publications/attachments/Africa_Task_Force_Web.pdf.
[89]Blair, David (2005). "Oil-Hungry China Takes Sudan under Its Wing," *The Telegraph*, April 23.
[90]"China Scoops Up Minerals, Infrastructure Contracts," *SouthScan* (*London*), June 30, 2005. Posted to the web July 6, 2005, http://allafrica.com/stories/printable/200507060674.html.
[91]Leggett, Karby (2005). "Staking a Claim China Flexes Economic Muscle Throughout Burgeoning Africa," *Ethiopia Tecola Hagos*, http://www.tecolahagos.com/staking_claim.htm.
[92]Zhang, Xiaoyu (2005). "A Promising Market for Resources Development in Zambia," Vol.11, 2005, *International Economic Cooperation*.
[93]Brookes, Peter and Ji Hye Shin (2006). "China's Influence in Africa: Implications for the United States," *Backgrounder #1916*, February 22, at http://www.heritage.org/research/asiaandthepacific/bg1916.cfm.

production and processing, and the agriculture industry. In September, 2006, China announced a $200 million capital injection in Zimbabwe's farming, manufacturing and mining.[94] The largest deal announced was the $1.3 billion agreement in 2006 with China Machine-Building International Corporation to mine coal and build thermal-power generators in Zimbabwe aimed to reduce the country's electricity shortage.[95]

4.6. *Gabon*

Gabon has proven oil reserves of roughly 2.5 billion barrels. The China National Petrochemical Corporation (SINOPEC) plans to explore both onshore and offshore in Gabon.[96] A Chinese consortium also recently signed a $3 billion iron ore deal in Gabon, which includes extending a railway and building a bulk commodities and container port.[97]

4.7. *South Africa*

South Africa has large reserves of several minerals, including diamonds. Mineral products are the major exports from South Africa to China, accounting for 65.3% of South Africa's exports to China in 2005. In 2006, China imported $1.47 billion worth of mineral products and $1.19 billion worth of diamonds, with growth rates of 41.3% and 24% from 2005.[98]

4.8. *Liberia and West Africa*

China and Liberia have signed a preliminary deal to allow China's second-largest state oil and gas firm, Sinopec Group, to explore for oil and gas in the West African state.[99] In addition, a small West African country,

[94] "Zimbabwe eager to strengthen economic ties with China," (2006). *People's Daily online*, September 28, http://english.peopledaily.com.cn/200609/28/eng20060928_307027.html.

[95] "China Undates," (2006). *Mines and Communities*, June 16, http://www.minesandcommunities.org/Action/press1109.htm.

[96] Brookes, Peter and Ji Hye Shin (2006). "China's Influence in Africa: Implications for the United States," Backgrounder #1916, February 22, at http://www.heritage.org/research/asiaandthepacific/bg1916.cfm.

[97] "Africa: Western Leaders Monitor China–Africa Summit" (2007). The Nation (Nairobi), May 17, http://allafrica.com/stories/200705161110.html.

[98] "China–South African Supplement: Open to Trade," (2007). Beijing Review.

[99] "Africa: Western Leaders Monitor China–Africa Summit" (2007). The Nation (Nairobi), May 17, http://allafrica.com/stories/200705161110. html.

Equatorial Guinea, has proven oil reserves estimated at 1.28 billion barrels. Although Equatorial Guinea has attracted less investment from China in oil sector than Angola and Sudan, it is still an important supplier of crude. Since 1999, Equatorial Guinea has been China's third largest African supplier. In 2006, its oil exports to China exceeded $2.5 billion.[100] Chinese companies are expected to bid for oil blocs in the 2007 licensing round.[101] Chinese companies also run a major timber operation in this country.[102] The Republic of Congo, Sub-Saharan Africa's fifth largest oil producer, also has 1.5 billion barrels in proven reserves. They may become potential oil exporters and Chinese investment has also begun here. China has also begun to invest in cobalt and copper mines in the Republic of Congo.

China's emphasis on securing reliable sources of minerals in Africa for its own economy is also reflected in its approach to vertical integration and ownership of oil production facilities through to transportation tankers. As a means of securing oil for Chinese consumers below international market prices, instead of buying rights for future exploration and development, Chinese enterprises have concentrated on purchasing equity shares in established oil fields. With a vision of turning themselves into global players in the energy market, Chinese oil companies in Africa, such as the China National Petroleum Corporation, have sought to secure equity positions which will enhance their ability to learn industrial practices, minimize risks and allow for technology transfer. This strategic judgment thus also partly explains China's long-term vision with regard to its engagement with Africa. Chinese enterprises thus have plans to be involved with the development of oil reserves in Africa for the long haul.

While China's position in oil in Africa is growing, it is nonetheless worth emphasizing that Western companies remain the largest consumers of Africa's oil and related products. Currently, over 18% of US crude oil imports are sourced from Africa,[103] and by 2015 this is projected to jump

[100]Shinn, David H. (2007). "Africa, China, the United States, and Oil," Center for Strategic and International Studies (CSIS) Africa Policy Forum, May 8.

[101]Country Profiles Foreign and Commonwealth Office, UK, http://www.fco.gov.uk/servlet/Front?pagename=OpenMarket/Xcelerate/ShowPage&c=Page&cid=1007029394365&a=KCountryProfile&aid=1019672564304.

[102]Leggett, Karby (2005). "Staking a Claim China Flexes Economic Muscle Throughout Burgeoning Africa," Ethiopia Tecola Hagos, http://www.tecolahagos.com/staking_claim.htm.

[103]Cohen, Ariel and Rafal Alasa, (2007). "Africa's Oil and Gas Sector: Implications for US Policy," *Backgrounder* #2052, July 13, http://www.heritage.org/Research/Africa/bg2052.cfm.

to 25%.[104] Of US oil imports from Africa, Nigeria accounts for 47%, and Algeria and Angola provide 19% each.[105] In 2003 alone, US companies invested $10 billion in African oil.[106] The American oil company Chevron Texaco invested over $5 billion during 1998–2003 in its African projects,[107] and planned to spend another $20 billion in Africa over the following five years.[108] It owns a 40% stake in the joint venture Chevron Nigeria Limited (CNL) with NNPC which is the second largest oil producer in Nigeria and produces approximately 400,000 barrels per day.[109] Another American oil company Exxon-Mobil laid a $3.7 billion 670-mile oil pipeline from Chad to the Atlantic coast in Cameroon,[110] and also holds 40% shares of Mobil Producing Nigeria Unlimited with a yield of around 900,000 barrels per day.[111] Exxon alone invested nearly US$10 billion in three deep-sea oil exploitation projects in Angola in 2000[112] The French oil company Total, one of the top four oil companies in the world, plans to invest $10 billion in Nigeria and $5 billion in Angola during the next five years for oil exploration.[113] British/Dutch Shell owns 55% of the 30 billion barrels of oil reserves in Nigeria (since 2002), and 40% of the 2.2 million barrels of daily output in Nigeria.[114] In comparison, China's oil explorations and operations in Africa remain small. Currently, China's oil

[104]National Intelligence Council, "External Relations and Africa," discussion paper, March 16, 2004, www.dni.gov/nic/PDF_GIF_2020_Support/2004_03_16_papers/external_relations.pdf. (May 10, 2007).
[105]US Department of Energy, Energy Information Administration, "US Imports by Country of Origin," April 19, 2007, http:// tonto.eia.doe.gov/dnav/pet/pet_move_impcus_a2_nus_ep00_im0_ mbblpd_a.htm (April 19, 2007).
[106]Zhang, Chun (2006). "'Neocolonialism' Label cannot be Pinned on China," Shanghai Research Center for International Issues, November 2002, http://www.sinofile.net/saiweng/sip_blog.nsf/d6plinks/YZHI-6VB8J3.
[107]"Africa: Oil Firms Plan Large African Investments," October 27, 2003, http://allafrica.com/stories/200310271010.html.
[108]Swindells, Steve (2004). "Chevron to Invest $20 Billion in African Oil, Natural Gas," The Oil Daily, September 30, http://goliath.ecnext.com/coms2/gi_0199-893254/Chevron-to-Invest-20-Billion.html.
[109]http://en.wikipedia.org/wiki/Petroleum_in_Nigeria.
[110]Silverstein, Ken (2003). "Pipeline's Profits May Bypass Africans," *Los Angeles Times,* June 17, http://www.commondreams.org/ headlines03/0617-06.htm.
[111]http://en.wikipedia.org/wiki/Petroleum_in_Nigeria.
[112]"US Targets Oil in Africa," (2005). *People's Daily Online*, August 2005, http://english.peopledaily.com.cn/200508/05/eng20050805_200508.html.
[113]Zhang, Chun (2006). "'Neocolonialism' Label cannot be Pinned on China," Shanghai Research Center for International Issues, November 2002, http://www.sinofile.net/saiweng/sip_blog.nsf/d6plinks/YZHI-6VB8J3.
[114]http://en.wikipedia.org/wiki/Petroleum_in_Nigeria.

imports from Africa are less than one third of US oil imports from the continent.[115]

While Sino–African oil trade is developing rapidly due to the Chinese focus on partnering in infrastructure development, it is often viewed by Africans as more mutually beneficial than trade with OECD countries. For instance, at the end of 2003, PetroChina had invested $2.7 billion in Sudan, built 1,506 km in oil pipeline, a crude processing plant with an annual capacity of 2.5 m tons, and several gas stations. This ensured that Sudan has a complete oil industry system from exploration, production, refining and transport to sales. In addition, China invested over $20 million to help the Sudan build other facilities including schools and hospitals. In comparison, Western companies have explored for oil for over 50 years in Nigeria. However, the country continues to import gasoline, and it does not have its own oil production and processing system. Western oil companies are also believed to pay less attention to infrastructure investment. China's energy policy in Africa is thus seen, for now, by both parties as being more fully implemented in ways which yield mutual benefits.

5. Textile and Apparel Investments

A further element in the growth of China's trade and investment in Africa has been the continued cooperation with African states in circumventing new trade restrictions specifically targeted against China following the removal of the Multi-Fiber Arrangement (MFA) in 2005. The situation is complex since immediately following the termination of the MFA, some of the quota-hopping foreign investment, induced to enter Africa to avoid trade restrictions on apparel imports in the OECD from China, was induced to return to China. It has been the subsequent new restrictions against China (see Dayaratna-Banda and Whalley, 2007) under China's WTO accession terms that have induced new investment flows.

The Multi-Fiber Arrangement (MFA) was originally set up by the European Union (EU), Canada and the US in 1974 to protect their clothing and textile industries from more efficient producers in Asia by capping the amount any country could export to them. Under successive MFAs, country and product coverage expanded as more developing-country

[115] Zhang, Chun (2006). "'Neocolonialism' Label cannot be Pinned on China," Shanghai Research Center for International Issues, November 2002, http://www.sinofile.net/saiweng/sip_blog.nsf/d6plinks/YZHI-6VB8J3.

exporters became involved and more categories of textiles and clothing were progressively added to the agreements. China's exports of clothing and textiles to OECD countries were highly restricted by MFA quotas before the removal of the MFA at the end of 2004. During the MFA implementation period, quota utilization rates in OECD countries for Chinese imports for the MFA category were extremely high, and some of them were nearly 100%.

One of the further effects of the MFA has been its generation of quota-hopping foreign investment (Whalley, 2006). In order to circumvent trade restrictions under the MFA, some Chinese clothing and textile firms moved production away from their newly quota-restrained homes to temporarily unconstrained countries. One of the areas especially suitable for quota-hopping foreign investment was Sub-Saharan Africa.

Africa's textile and apparel sector also benefited from the US Africa Growth and Opportunity Act (AGOA) in May, 2000 that allowed textile exports of 38 eligible African countries with tariff and quota exemptions if they meet certain rules. Those included a restriction that the product's raw materials originate either in the exporting country or in the US. But African countries categorized as least developed[116] were exempt from this additional requirement. Their products are allowed duty-free access into the US market under the condition that the final assembly of the textile products takes place in the exporting country, no matter where the yarn spinning, fabric weaving or knitting occurs. This opening in the US clothing market created a ready market for AGOA countries.

These advantages for those African textile-exporting countries of less constrained quotas and preferential market access into the EU and the US attracted investments from many Chinese companies. By way of example, textiles and clothing became Lesotho's economic mainstay, which at one point employed 56,000 workers — accounting for virtually every manufacturing job in the country. Between 1999 and 2001, US imports from Kenya, Lesotho, Madagascar, Mauritius and South Africa increased by 66%. From 2001 to 2004, the average increase of Lesotho exports to the US was over 85%. In 2003, Africa exported \$1.2 billion of clothing and textiles to the US, a 50% increase from the previous year. The market share of sub-Saharan Africa in the US textiles market increased between

[116] A least developed country is a country with per capita incomes of \$1,500 or less in 1998.

2002 and 2004. China has been credited with promoting Africa exports in both textiles and clothing in this process.

The MFA termination in January, 2005 brought sharp product specific increases in China's exports to the US and the EU in the initial 4-month period (January–April 2005). While the aggregate exports of clothing and textiles surged substantially to both the US and the EU in this period, the largest percentage and absolute surges came from China. And these increases were accompanied by the fall in the market share of non-Asian suppliers, including Sub-Saharan Africa. During the first quarter of 2005, textile and apparel exports from Africa to the US fell to \$270 million from \$370 million during the same period the year before, and the market share of Sub-Saharan Africa in the US textiles market dropped in the year of 2005.

6. Other Considerations and Concluding Remarks

China's remarkable growth and its growing presence in Africa is the focus of this paper and we attempt to document its content, coverage and speed of change. China's trade and investment with Africa are growing rapidly and China is now a significant marginal source of stimulus to Africa. Claims abound that a significant portion of the increase in Africa's growth rate in recent years is reflective of an enlarged Chinese presence.[117] Africa has clearly gained, and most likely significantly from this interaction. And somewhat paradoxically, China with GDP per capita of perhaps US\$1,800 (rather than the OECD with incomes per capita of around US\$30,000) is now a major source of new developmental finance in Africa.

There are, however, other considerations involved with this growing presence not discussed above. One is the claim that despite all the benefits, China's growing presence is also co-mingled with responses to attempts to discipline corrupt practices at home and this amount to exported corruption. Stories of Chinese enterprises approaching African governments offering reserve financed low interest loan infrastructure projects on conditions that contracts are awarded to specified Chinese enterprises tend to underscore such concerns, and emphasize the incentive to conduct business lax accounting standard jurisdictions in Africa. Another is claims by local unions of low wage employment of local workers on the continent by Chinese enterprises, and even displacement of local labor by

[117] http://www.american.com/archive/2006/november/chinas-new-scramble-for-africa.

arriving Chinese labor. Both arguments have been used to suggest negative consequences follow for Africa from a growing Chinese presence.

In the bigger picture, however, such claims have to be seen alongside the large benefits flowing to Africa from China's involvement. Whether or not corruption at home motivates some amount of FDI, Africa seems to benefit. Meanwhile, labor adjustments from Chinese FDI appear to be small, especially given the large FDI in oil and resources. The bottom line would seem to be that large trade and investment benefits have already accrued to Africa from China's growing presences, and more seem poised to follow. China in Africa is thus seemingly a highly positive story for Africa and also offers an even more promising future for the continent.

References

Africa Programme (2003). *Opening a Sino–US Dialogue on Africa*, Washington DC: CSIS.

Blair, D. (2005). 'Oil-Hungry China Takes Sudan under Its Wing,' *The Telegraph*, April 23, 2005.

Broadman, H. (2007). "Africa's Silk Road: China and India's New Economic Frontier." Washington DC: The World Bank.

China Brief, Jamestown Foundation, 7(7) (April 5, 2007).

China Daily (2005). '3/21 China's Economy to Grow 8% Annually from 2006 to 2010.'

'China, Nigeria Sign Oil Supply Pact' (2005). *Xinhua News Agency*, 9 July.

Dayaratna-Banda, O. G. and J. Whalley (2007). "After the MFA, the CCAs (China Containment Agreements)," *Asia Trade Review*, 3(1): 27–54.

Direction of Trade Statistics Yearbook (2006). IMF.

Lee, D. (2004). 'China Barrels Ahead in Oil Market,' *The Los Angeles Times*, November 14, 2004.

Downs, E. (2004). "The Chinese Energy Security Debate", *China Quarterly*, no. 1777, March: 21–41.

French, H. (2004). 'China in Africa — All Trade, with No Political Baggage,' *The New York Times*, August 8.

Goodman, P. (2004). 'China Invests Heavily in Sudan's Oil Industry' *The Washington Post*, December 23.

He, W. (2006). "China–Africa Relations Moving into an Era of Rapid Development," in: Africa Institute of South Africa, *Inside AISA*, October/December, 3–6.

IMF Direction of Trade Statistics (2005).

Jenkins, R. C. E. (2005). The Effect of China and India's growth and Trade Liberalization on Poverty in Africa, Department of International Development, DCP 70, London: DFID.

Lennon, J. (2004). *Overview of Chinese Commodities*, London: Macquarie Research Metals and Mining.

Linebaugh, K. and S. Oster (2006). 'CNOOC Pays $2.27 Billion for Nigerian Oil Gas Stake,' *The Wall Street Journal*, January 10.

McLaughlin, A. (2005). "A Rising China Counters US Clout in Africa," *The Christian Science Monitor*, March 30.

MOFCOM Statistics.

OECD Development Center (2006).

Sandrey, R. (2006). "The African Trading Relationship with China." Cape Town: *Trade Law Centre for Southern Africa.*

'The Host with the Most' (2007). *The Economist*, May 19–25.

UNCTAD Handbook of Statistics 2006–07.

UNCTAD/UNDP, Asian Foreign Direct Investment in Africa: Towards a New Era of Cooperation among Developing Nations, New York, March 2007.

UNCTAD, World Investment Report 2007: Transnational Corporations, Extractive Industries and Development.

US Department of Energy, Energy Information Agency (2005). Country Analysis Brief: China.

Whalley, J. (2006). "The Post-MFA Performance of Developing Asia," NBER working paper No.12178.

World Bank (2004). Patterns of Africa–Asia Trade and Investment, Potential for Ownership and Partnership, Africa Region Private Sector Group, Washington: World Bank. Vol. 2.

York, G. (2006). 'China, Africa Forging Closer Ties.' *Globe and Mail*, 10 November.

Chen, Y. (2005). "A Research on Economic Globalization and its Influences to Overseas Chinese Economy", *World Regional Studies*, 12(3) September.

Websites

http://allafrica.com/stories/200506200960.html

http://bic.cass.cn/English/InfoShow/Arcitle_Show_Conference_Show.asp?ID=364&Title=Africa%20Beyond%202000&strNavigation=Home%3EForum&BigClassID=4&SmallClassID=11

http://www.atimes.com/atimes/China/IL13Ad01.html

http://en.wikipedia.org/wiki/Sino-African_relations

http://en.wikipedia.org/wiki/Foreign_exchange_reserves

http://panafricannews.blogspot.com/2006_10_01_archive.html

http://web.worldbank.org/WBSITE/EXTERNAL/NEWS/0,, contentMDK:21052520~pagePK:64257043~piPK:437376~theSitePK: 4607,00.html

http://www.american.com/archive/2006/november/chinas-new-scramble-for-africa

http://www.bloomberg.com, November 3, 2006

http://www.bjreview.com.cn/expert/txt/2006-12/15/content_50879.htm

http://www.cfr.org/content/publications/attachments/Africa_Task_Force_Web.pdf

http://www.csmonitor.com/2007/0202/p06s01-woaf.html

http://www.csmonitor.com/2007/0209/p01s04-woaf.htm

http://www.evancarmichael.com/African-Accounts/1667/IIC-Other-Debt-Creating-Financial-Flows-TRADE-AND-CAPITAL-FLOWS-BETWEEN-CHINA-AND-AFRICA.html

http://www.fanrpan.org/newsflash.php?archive=2

http://www.ids.ac.uk/ids/global/AsianDriverpdfs/DFIDAgendaPaper06.pdf

http://www.iht.com/bin/print?id=4881100

http://www.imf.org/external/pubs/ft/wp/2007/wp07211.pdf

http://www.oecd.org/document/17/0,2340,en_2649_33721_38341265_1_1_1_1,00.html

http://www.jamestown.org/terrorism/news/uploads/cb_007_007a.pdf

http://www.mofcom.gov.cn

www.palgrave-journals.com/development/journal/v50/n3/full/1100407a.html

http://www.pnl.gov/aisu/pubs/engenvup.pdf

http://www.poptel.org.uk/mozambique-news/newsletter/aim335.html#story7

http://www.rice.edu/energy/publications/docs/AsianEnergySecurity_MainStudy.pdf

http://www.tralac.org/pdf/20070220_TheAfrican_TradingRelationship_with_China.pdf

http://www.uk.cn/uploadfiles/2006428172021581.doc

http://www.unctadxi.org/templates/Pages_1006.aspx

THE POST MFA PERFORMANCE OF DEVELOPING ASIA*

John Whalley
University of Western Ontario; CIGI and NBER

This paper assesses the impact thus far that the termination of trade restrictions under the Multi Fibre Arrangement (MFA), which up to the end of 2004 applied to exports of clothing and textiles in key OECD markets, has had on Asian suppliers. The speculation prior to MFA termination had been that large increases of Chinese exports would ensue, and at the expense of other Asian suppliers. Using data from US, EU, China and other sources, the picture that emerges is only small impacts on aggregate US and EU imports of clothing and textiles, and equally only small impacts on aggregate China's exports of clothing and textiles. There are, however, large changes in the country pattern of trade, and also within more narrowly defined product categories. There are large increases in shipments from China to both the US and the EU, and for the US proportionally more so in textiles than in clothing. But the US accounts for only 20% of China's exports of clothing and textiles, and exports to Japan (comparable in size to the US) hardly change, and to Hong Kong fall sharply. There are also large price falls for shipments to the US and to certain EU countries (Germany). The shares of other Asian suppliers in US markets generally hold up well, with the largest falls occurring in preferentially treated non Asian suppliers such as Mexico. In EU markets, with the exception of India, all non Chinese Asian suppliers experience falls in their market share.

1. Introduction and Summary

January 2005 saw the termination of the global system of trade restraints on exports of textiles and clothing that had operated first under the original GATT from 1974, and later under the WTO from 1994. This system, known as the Multi Fibre Agreement (MFA), was of particular significance to the Asian economies and its prospective demise had prompted much

*This paper has been prepared as a background paper for the Asian Development Outlook 2006 to be published by the Asian Development Book. I am grateful to Ted James and Lea Sumulong both for comments and help in data tabulation and synthesis, and to Frank Harringan for comments.

speculation prior to January 2005 of what the possible effects could be. These economies had seen large increases of exports of textiles and clothing prior to the removal of the MFA, and especially of clothing, as they had moved up the ladder of industrialization from largely agricultural to modern manufacturing and service based economies over a thirty to forty year period.

Typically, the first major export good in the early high growth experiences in Asia had been clothing since it involved relatively simple labour intensive production methods and small amounts of capital equipment. Early in Asian growth Japan in 1930s and 50's, and subsequently Korea, Taiwan and Hong Kong in 1960's and 1970's, all saw sharp increases in exports of clothing as they grew. In the Korean case, clothing exports grew rapidly from the early 1960's to account for over 50% of exports, with this share then progressively falling back as exports of steel, electronics, chemicals and other products grew later and production of manufactures moved away from clothing. The textile and clothing sectors were thus critical for these economies in providing an intitial platform for growth of manufacturing value added, employment and trade beyond their immediate contribution to GDP.

Later it was the lower wage Asian economies of China, India, Indonesia, Cambodia, Bangladesh, Pakistan, Nepal and others who experienced rapid trade growth in clothing.[1] The larger and more diversified of these economies (China, India and Indonesia) had the larger share of this trade and this is still the case today. But the smaller and lower wage exporters (Cambodia, Bangladesh, Pakistan and Nepal) continue to expand production and like Korea earlier also now have well over 50% of their total exports in the clothing sector (over 80% for Cambodia and Nepal).

Evaluating the impacts of removal of the MFA system of trade restraints on the suppliers from developing Asia is the task set for this piece, and any analysis needs to take into account both their complexity and changing circumstances over time. MFA trade restraints reflected mutually agreed bilateral (country to country) limits on growth rates of exports on a product by product basis which were renegotiated every five years after 1974. The larger export markets under restraint were those of the United States and

[1] See also the discussion of the relative competitiveness of different supplying countries and their wage costs in USITC (2004). Table 3.1 (p. 3–7) provides data on hourly compensation separately for textile and clothing industries for 2002 for these Asian suppliers (with the exception of Nepal and Cambodia).

the European Union, but others including Canada were similarly restrained. But when the Uruguay Round of Global Trade Negotiations was concluded in 1994, and which also lead to the creation of the World Trade Organization (WTO) in the same year, a commitment was entered into by both importing and exporting countries to progressively phase out the MFA system of restraints over ten years. This was to be completed by the end of 2004, but most of the adjustments involved were delayed until the end of the ten-year implementation process.

Also when the resulting Agreement on Textile and Clothing (ATC) was negotiated in 1994 China was outside the WTO/GATT and still had a long road to travel to become a WTO member (accomplished in December 2001, seven years after the ATC was agreed). Expectations among larger Asian suppliers such as India, Indonesia, Pakistan, Bangladesh and others were initially high for the post MFA period, but had to be revised once China's accession to the WTO was at hand. In addition, other trade restraints not included in the MFA system (such as tariff and anti dumping duties) remained in place; and key importers such as the US and EU had entered into preferential arrangements with regional suppliers as part of regional trade agreements, quite separate from the MFA. This included Mexico for the US and Turkey for the EU, both of whom had seen sharp growth in exports under these arrangements.

A further effect of the MFA had been its generation of quota hopping foreign investment; moving production away from newly constrained to temporarily unconstrained countries and inefficiently proliferating clothing industries in more countries than would have been the case in the absence of the MFA. It was believed that MFA elimination would be a major negative for the more marginal infrastructure and distance constrained suppliers (such as Nepal) that this process had spawned as global production became more concentrated in a smaller number of core supplying countries.

Prior to January 2005, there had also been much speculation as to what the impacts of MFA termination would be on the dynamic and more rapidly growing Asian exporters, and especially of clothing. Much of this focused on China as the largest shipper, and India as the second largest; but also included Pakistan, Philippines, Korea, Hong Kong, Indonesia, Bangladesh, Sri Lanka, Nepal, Cambodia, Vietnam and others. It was widely believed that production in and exports from Asia would grow significantly post MFA, but that production in and exports from China would increase even more rapidly, since China was believed the most efficient Asian supplier of clothing items. MFA abolition was also seen as a further positive for

Asian suppliers in that it would significantly weaken the effects of the trade preferences extended by the US and EU, mainly in the 1990's, to non-Asian suppliers including Mexico (by the US) and Turkey (by the EU) under regional trade agreements. The import shares of these preferential suppliers had been growing significantly prior to MFA removal.

Asian exporters, as a broadly defined group, were expected to gain market share in the US and the EU both from MFA abolition and with it the weakening of preferences to non Asian suppliers, but individual country effects were anticipated to vary. These impacts were thought likely to reflect a series of country specific factors. One was the relative importance of the quota constrained US and EU markets for individual countries. China, for instance, was shipping more clothing to Japan which was already free of restraint than to the US and the EU, but this feature was special to China who accounted for around 80% of Japan's imports. Other countries, such as India, shipped more heavily to the US and the EU and so quota removal would impact a larger fraction of exports.

Special country situations also entered. Bangladesh was already free of restraint in EU markets prior to MFA abolition and was thought likely to lose EU market share to newly quota free imports from elsewhere. Vietnam remained under restraint post MFA as a non-WTO member. Where countries stood in their industrialization process was yet another factor. Cambodia, for instance, was a rapidly growing supplier but at an early stage of industrialization. Their growth rate was thought probably to fall a little under MFA elimination but likely be little affected. In contrast, the Philippines as a long standing MFA participant with established MFA quota and higher cost structure was thought likely to see acceleration in the relative decline they had experienced over the 3–4 year prior to January 2005. Some countries, including Bangladesh and Pakistan, benefited from GSP tariffs and the weakening of these preferences was a further factor. Impacts on fibre producers (cotton exporters such as Pakistan and others) also entered.

Over 12 months on from January 2005 China's textile and clothing exports have increased, as expected,[2] but only at a modest rate of 7% for clothing (see Table 5). Also aggregate imports of textiles and clothing by both the US and the EU have increased at modest rates (6% for US clothing imports). But there have been sharp increases in China's exports to the US

[2]Also see the recent discussion of the impacts of MFA removal in James (2005).

and the EU; 56% for US clothing imports from China. The increases are several hundreds of percent in some categories of clothing, and export prices for Chinese clothing sold in these markets have fallen sharply. These have been accompanied by sharp falls in Chinese exports to Hong Kong, and close to flat exports to Japan (which are of roughly equalize to China's exports to the US). Increases in China's exports to the US and the EU occur most dramatically in the few months immediately following MFA abolition, and in part reflect expectations by Chinese shippers of subsequent pressure from the US and the EU for new export restraints, which were introduced in the form of bilaterally negotiated restraint agreements in the summer and fall of 2005. There is thus substantial volatility in monthly Chinese trade data following the removal of the MFA. Data for the month of October 2005, for instance, show Chinese clothing exports falling by 18% from month earlier figures, while data for January 2006 show large increases in exports in some key product categories.

Exports from Asian suppliers other than China to the US (India, Pakistan, Bangladesh, Indonesia, Vietnam and Cambodia) have held up reasonably well to the termination of the MFA and most have increased, although at more modest rates than has been true for China.[3] The Philippines, whose industry was already in relative decline, and Sri Lanka has witnessed declines in exports along with suppliers with remote locations and weak infrastructure (Nepal). All non-Chinese Asian suppliers except India experience falls in their market share in the EU. There are clear negative effects on consumer prices in previous quota constrained OECD markets (the US and the EU), and employment in clothing in OECD countries continues to fall (it was also falling prior to 2005).

Several factors seem to account for this overall picture of country impact. One is that new restraints on China introduced in 2005 in US and EU markets (after the MFA was terminated) have mitigated the effects of quota abolition on further Chinese increases in exports. Suppliers outside of China also seem to have been successful in exploiting niches in apparel export items (knitwear for Bangladesh, carpets for Pakistan) and this has made their exports correspondingly less vulnerable to competition from other suppliers. Furthermore, China is now emerging as a slightly higher cost source of supply in some clothing categories compared to lower wage countries elsewhere such as Vietnam, Cambodia and Pakistan.

---

[3]This is similar to the conclusion reached by James (2005).

These initial indications of impact of MFA removal naturally lead to discussion of what are some possible medium to longer term scenarios' for the Asian economies for their clothing and textile exports which might follow the initial period analyzed here. The central element in such scenarios seems to be a continuing growth of both clothing production in and exports from Asia as higher cost OECD production and inter OECD trade (which has had the protection of MFA quotas) is displaced by substantially lower cost Asia supply. This process is seen as likely to be accelerated by a weakening of the effects of preferences for non Asian suppliers (Mexico (US), Turkey (EU)) as MFA quotas disappear.

The country composition within Asia of these growing exports remains uncertain, but extreme gravitation to China and India as the two large low cost suppliers with economies of scale would seem unlikely. If China and India follow their current high growth trajectories for several years (or decades), they will likely follow growth profiles similar to Korea and Taiwan from the 1960s to today of initially high export shares in clothing which progressively decline as wages rise and other higher technology exports come on stream. If other Asian low-wage suppliers (Vietnam, Cambodia) grow at lower rates than China and India they will have an increasing cost advantage relative to China, and their export shares will likely increase more rapidly. And if the infrastructure weak and geographically more remote suppliers, such as Nepal, see further reductions in export shares, the prospect is for a smaller number of Asia's suppliers to dominate clothing exports and each with sharply higher exports than today.

2. Asian Development and Textiles and Clothing Trade

To assess the potential effects on Asian supplying countries of the termination of the MFA, it is helpful to also have background on both the global industry and its links to Asian growth performance.[4] The global textile and clothing industry reflects a supply chain involving production of raw fibres through to final stage retailing which spans both countries and different stages of processing. In this, three broad types of raw fibres (cotton, wool and synthetics), along with more niche fibres such as silk, provide the raw input for the industry. There are then a series of distinct production processes which involve first preparing the fibres for spinning, then spinning

[4]Also see the discussion of the global industrial and trade structure in textiles and clothing in both Nordas (2004), and USITC (2004).

the fibres, processing these into fabrics, and finally cutting and making fabrics into finished items (which include both clothing and textile products for the home). Distribution of final product proceeds through middle men and/or larger retailers with integrated purchasing units who deal directly with producers of finished items. Other elements of the production process, such as dyeing and finishing, also partly determine the final product quality and price.

The growth of a globally based textile and clothing industry in Asia began four decades ago when Hong Kong, Taiwan, and Korea first became large exporters of low cost clothing. In the early 1980's, these three suppliers accounted for around 30% of world clothing exports. But by 2000, their share had fallen to around 8%, and a new generation of low cost suppliers had emerged; lead by China, India, Pakistan, Indonesia, Philippines and Thailand. Today, China is the largest exporter of clothing in Asia, followed by India.

To place global trade in textiles and clothing today in context, textiles and clothing are around 7% of world exports, with clothing accounting for around 57% of the total (ILO (2005)). On the import side, the US, Japan and the EU provide the largest markets, with Canada, Australia and Norway providing smaller markets. By the end of 2004 only the US, the EU and Canada maintained MFA quotas and these were of uneven country coverage (importantly the EU excluded Bangladesh from quota restraint). The precise commodity classification and coding used in each country for MFA quotas varied, but a small number of key MFA categories comprised most trade in clothing. Shirts, pants, blouses and coats accounted for nearly 50% of US clothing imports in 2004.

The textile and clothing industries in the various Asian countries differ significantly from one another, and also from other related product areas such as footwear where production and retailing tend to be integrated and occur more frequently within the same global firm. Early stages of textile and clothing industry activity are relatively capital-intensive and involve significant machinery and typically occur in consolidated large firms. It is the stage of cutting and making fabrics into finished items which is highly labour-intensive and which low wage Asian suppliers have been able to enter so successfully over the last four decades. In most countries, the number of firms involved is larger than at earlier stages, and many of the firms involved are small or medium-sized.

The structure of the textile and clothing industry also varies significantly by country. China tends to import fabrics and concentrate on cutting and finishing, while India imports relatively little fabric. China's clothing industry, through large inward FDI, is heavily integrated into global distribution systems and has direct involvement of OECD retailers. India's industry, in contrast, has less direct involvement with retailers. As Tewari (2005) argues, the competitive edge of Chinese suppliers involves much more than low wage costs. China's producers are integrated into the marketing, distribution, and supply management networks of locally-based Hong Kong, Taiwanese, and Korean manufactures who have long experience of industrial markets and the need for timely high quality delivery of product.

It has been ever-growing imports in the OECD, and primary from Asia that, have been the source for substantial pressures over the years to slow the adjustment of impacted domestic industry. OECD production of both fabrics and clothing has been highly regionally concentrated and had relatively low wage and higher average age employees, making redeployment of labour displaced by imports more difficult than has been the case for other industries. Both employment and output of industries in the OECD competing with Asian suppliers has declined consistently over the last three decades, although these adjustments have been substantially slowed by trade restraints.

These restraints had their origins in a 1962 short-term (one year) agreement between the US and a small number of Asian suppliers of cotton textiles to restrain export growth to provide domestic industry a breathing space for adjustments to occur. But this initial agreement, after renewal, then grew into a series of longer term (five yearly) agreements covering ever more exporters and products and was in turn, to lead to a wider MFA in the then GATT in 1974 which covered most major OECD importers as well as the US (and importantly, the EU). The MFA itself then underwent a series of five-year renewals and extensions which also progressively involved more countries and products. And from the mid 1980's on, these arrangements became further complicated with a growing series of preferential arrangements negotiated by the large importers (the US and the EU) with key supplying countries.

These latter agreements have typically covered much more than just textile and clothing exports, but they have contained special preferential arrangements in textiles and clothing exempting specific countries from MFA quotas (or weakening their application). In the last ten years these have lead to a large growth in supply from preferential suppliers outside of Asia. Mexico under its NAFTA preference today accounts for nearly

15% of US clothing imports (second only to China), and Turkey under its partnership agreement with the EU accounts for 10% of EU imports. The removal of the MFA weakens these margins of preference, which now will only apply to non MFA trade restraints such as tariffs.

The potential global impacts of MFA abolition have been the subject of a number of quantitative model based analyses which are summarized in a recent survey paper by Walkenhorst (2005), who reviews 27 assessments of potential impact drawn from 14 different studies. In these, estimates of global benefits of MFA removal range from 0.02%–1.49% of world GDP. Some studies show MFA removal accounting for up to 2/3 of the total global benefits from the WTO Uruguay Round; others put these gains more modestly at 5% of the total. Some show developing countries as the major beneficiaries of MFA removal; others show developing countries as losing in aggregate. Walkenhorst attributes this wide variation in model based results to different modeling assumptions, parameter values, use of base year, and other model features. But the theme which emerges in all model results is that substantial welfare benefits have been expected to accrue to the large importing countries (the US and EU), the initiators of the MFA system of restraints, and with accompanying significant increases in imports. These model results thus emphasize the sectoral interest driving OECD policy (the concern being to slow adjustment costs) more so than overall national interest.

3. The Asian Trade Response Post MFA

Data on complete bilateral global trade flows (by product and by pair of countries) for the months immediately following the termination of the MFA are not yet available. What is available are individual country data for certain importing and exporting countries. Much of the existing literature on the effects of MFA trade restrictions draws on US data from the Office of Textiles and Apparel. Such analyses are usually only supplemented by data on the EU, but can be deceptive for certain countries where non US/ non EU markets are important for exports. For China, for instance, Japan currently represents a larger export market than either the US or the EU (see Emerging Textiles (2005)) and the Japanese market was not under restraint from MFA quotas. But China also accounts for around 80% of Japan's imports of clothing, and post MFA shipments to Japan will likely increase little. China's shipments to Hong Kong are also substantial. For other exporters, the EU and the US are the dominant export market and analysis based on data from EU and US sources is more indicative of overall trends.

Aggregate data on trade flows of textiles and clothing over the period following MFA abolition are also difficult to interpret for a number of reasons. One is that the trade response varies substantially across MFA product categories. Another is that the period following MFA abolition is characterized by sharp product specific export increases from China to the US and the EU in the months immediately after the 2005 abolition, while in subsequent months embargoes applied to certain products and trade in some commodities between some countries effectively ceased (in the summer of 2005 in certain products). Precisely which month's data is used to assess the impacts of MFA abolition can thus make a large difference. For instance, a recent and widely cited ILO (2005) study on the impacts of MFA abolition only used data for the four-month period January–April 2005. Now more recent data for more months is available which is used here. Another problem is conflicting data from exporting and importing countries. Chinese government data on China's clothing exports, for instance, differ from US government import data.

Tables 1 and 2 report US import data in total and by country of source for 2002, 2003, 2004 and 2005 both in value and volume terms and for the two separate categories of clothing and textiles (Table 1 for clothing, Table 2 for textiles).[5] These data are most recent available.[6] They show that US imports of clothing grew post MFA at an annual rate of 6% in value terms and 10% in volume terms, while imports of textiles grew at an annual rate 1% in value terms and 3% in volume terms. While these growth rates for clothing in both value and volume terms exceed 2004, they are below those for 2003 for clothing in value terms. Growth rates for US textiles imports in both volume and value terms are sharply below those for 2004. This thus suggests a small aggregate effect on US imports of clothing and textile imports in the immediate post MFA period.

[5]This builds on and further develops data previously reported in James (2005).

[6]However, preliminary US data for the month of January 2006 and reported in Emerging Textiles.com (6 February 2006) show how quickly things can change. Emerging Textiles report that increases in January US apparel and textiles imports are as high as several thousand percent for women's cotton knit blouses and cotton shirts, 132% in women's cotton coat, 339% in other cotton coats, 128% in nightwear, and 507% for men's wool suits. They also report "astonishing" growth in several textile categories. Some of these import increases reflect shipments which were held up in 2005 that could now enter without being charged to the 2006 quota under the bilateral US–China restraint agreement.

Table 1. US Import Values of Clothing by Supplier by Year.

	Value (US$ mn)				Change (%)			Market Share (%)			
	2002	2003	2004	2005	2003/02	2004/03	2005/04	2002	2003	2004	2005
Asia-Pacific Suppliers											
People's Republic of	5,593.70	7,257.59	8,927.86	15,144.10	29.75	23.01	69.63	9.82	11.87	13.78	22.04
China	3,877.24	3,701.79	3,848.98	3,510.57	(4.53)	3.98	(8.79)	6.81	6.05	5.94	5.11
Hong Kong, China											
India	1,901.47	2,001.54	2,217.10	2,976.17	5.26	10.77	34.24	3.34	3.27	3.42	4.33
Indonesia	2,041.50	2,157.96	2,402.83	2,875.31	5.70	11.35	19.66	3.58	3.53	3.71	4.18
Viet Nam	895.07	2,374.55	2,562.46	2,724.65	165.29	7.91	6.33	1.57	3.88	3.96	3.97
Bangladesh	1,883.15	1,848.07	1,977.56	2,371.68	(1.86)	7.01	19.93	3.31	3.02	3.05	3.45
Philippines	1,815.11	1,853.42	1,785.56	1,830.40	2.11	(3.66)	2.51	3.19	3.03	2.76	2.66
Thailand	1,718.53	1,711.62	1,799.37	1,807.79	(0.40)	5.13	0.47	3.02	2.80	2.78	2.63
Cambodia	1,042.45	1,239.65	1,428.99	1,712.84	18.92	15.27	19.86	1.83	2.03	2.21	2.49
Sri Lanka	1,413.17	1,435.79	1,549.39	1,650.22	1.60	7.91	6.51	2.48	2.35	2.39	2.40
Pakistan	878.30	1,015.45	1,137.67	1,258.79	15.62	12.04	10.65	1.54	1.66	1.76	1.83
Macau, China	1,146.42	1,281.98	1,436.39	1,198.17	11.82	12.04	(16.58)	2.01	2.10	2.22	1.74
Republic of Korea	2,061.95	1,806.07	1,808.82	1,154.62	(12.41)	0.15	(36.17)	3.62	2.95	2.79	1.68
Taipei, China	1,576.22	1,611.11	1,548.92	1,134.43	2.21	(3.86)	(26.76)	2.77	2.63	2.39	1.65
Malaysia	720.07	685.72	711.99	677.85	(4.77)	3.83	(4.79)	1.26	1.12	1.10	0.99
Brunei Darussalam	195.17	205.48	215.16	167.09	5.28	4.71	(22.34)	0.34	0.34	0.33	0.24
Mongolia	155.84	176.88	227.03	134.41	13.50	28.36	(40.80)	0.27	0.29	0.35	0.20
Nepal	107.87	129.45	97.98	61.15	20.00	(24.31)	(37.59)	0.19	0.21	0.15	0.09
Turkmenistan	32.66	46.67	44.56	35.48	42.92	(4.52)	(20.39)	0.06	0.08	0.07	0.05
Fiji Islands	74.23	79.55	85.77	19.06	7.17	7.82	(77.78)	0.13	0.13	0.13	0.03
Uzbekistan	17.98	25.07	9.82	15.97	39.40	(60.82)	62.54	0.03	0.04	0.02	0.02

(*Continued*)

Table 1. (*Continued*)

	Value (US$ mn)				Change (%)			Market Share (%)			
	2002	2003	2004	2005	2003/02	2004/03	2005/04	2002	2003	2004	2005
Maldives	110.56	93.73	81.05	4.72	(15.22)	(13.52)	(94.18)	0.19	0.15	0.13	0.01
Kyrgyz Republic	3.19	9.62	6.63	3.73	201.83	(31.14)	(43.67)	0.01	0.02	0.01	0.01
Kazakhstan	3.48	16.89	13.42	3.35	385.72	(20.53)	(75.07)	0.01	0.03	0.02	0.00
Armenia	9.47	7.31	7.18	1.36	(22.74)	(1.89)	(81.10)	0.02	0.01	0.01	0.00
Tajikistan	0.06	6.91	3.13	0.02	12,212.64	(54.78)	(99.45)	0.00	0.01	0.00	0.00
Sub-total Asia-Pacific	**29,274.86**	**32,779.88**	**35,935.63**	**42,473.94**	**11.97**	**9.63**	**18.19**	**51.39**	**53.60**	**55.48**	**61.81**
DMC Suppliers											
excluding PRC	23,681.16	25,522.29	27,007.76	27,329.84	7.77	5.82	1.19	41.57	41.73	41.70	39.77
Preferential Suppliers											
CAFTA	9,092.51	9,181.50	9,509.46	9,104.10	0.98	3.57	(4.26)	15.96	15.01	14.68	13.25
Mexico	7,424.20	6,903.74	6,684.84	6,078.36	(7.01)	(3.17)	(9.07)	13.03	11.29	10.32	8.85
Sub-Sahara	1,097.55	1,510.85	1,757.48	1,464.44	37.66	16.32	(16.67)	1.93	2.47	2.71	2.13
Andean (ATPA)	750.96	1,051.31	1,323.04	1,429.22	40.00	25.85	8.03	1.32	1.72	2.04	2.08
Canada	1,610.11	1,568.62	1,504.41	1,273.40	(2.58)	(4.09)	(15.36)	2.83	2.56	2.32	1.85
Jordan	384.21	582.08	956.16	1,082.52	51.50	64.27	13.22	0.67	0.95	1.48	1.58
CBI	378.60	429.51	442.69	490.91	13.45	3.07	10.89	0.66	0.70	0.68	0.71
Egypt	347.86	381.77	422.29	444.29	9.75	10.61	5.21	0.61	0.62	0.65	0.65
Israel	416.24	396.30	336.20	288.55	(4.79)	(15.17)	(14.17)	0.73	0.65	0.52	0.42
Singapore	286.23	269.71	242.49	156.89	(5.77)	(10.09)	(35.30)	0.50	0.44	0.37	0.23
Bahrain	178.17	163.68	155.87	117.43	(8.13)	(4.78)	(24.66)	0.31	0.27	0.24	0.17
Australia	237.50	202.27	209.29	113.13	(14.84)	3.47	(45.95)	0.42	0.33	0.32	0.16
Morocco	75.25	75.63	74.30	55.89	0.51	(1.76)	(24.78)	0.13	0.12	0.11	0.08
Tunisia	34.89	33.69	44.01	52.84	(3.43)	30.61	20.08	0.06	0.06	0.07	0.08

(*Continued*)

Table 1. (*Continued*)

	Value (US$ mn)				Change (%)			Market Share (%)			
	2002	2003	2004	2005	2003/02	2004/03	2005/04	2002	2003	2004	2005
Chile	10.26	10.80	24.01	23.42	5.27	122.37	(2.47)	0.02	0.02	0.04	0.03
Federated States of Micronesia	14.35	13.49	10.55	0.96	(6.00)	(21.80)	(90.85)	0.03	0.02	0.02	0.00
Sub-total Preferential Suppliers	**22,338.88**	**22,774.96**	**23,697.08**	**22,176.36**	**1.95**	**4.05**	**(6.42)**	**39.22**	**37.24**	**36.59**	**32.27**
Non-Preferential Suppliers											
EU15	1,997.88	2,059.89	2,067.58	1,925.80	3.10	0.37	(6.86)	3.51	3.37	3.19	2.80
Turkey	1,189.70	1,257.31	1,168.60	943.77	5.68	(7.06)	(19.24)	2.09	2.06	1.80	1.37
Japan	170.98	221.48	289.94	86.51	29.54	30.91	(70.16)	0.30	0.36	0.45	0.13
World	**56,962.95**	**61,162.08**	**64,767.67**	**68,714.52**	**7.37**	**5.90**	**6.09**	**100.00**	**100.00**	**100.00**	**100.00**

Note: Sum of non-preferential and preferential suppliers does not add up to world total because some minor suppliers are not included; numbers may not sum precisely due to rounding. CBI excludes CAFTA member countries.
Source: US Department of Commerce, OTEXA office.

Table 1. US Import Volumes of Clothing by Supplier by Year.

	Volume (mn sqm)							Market Share (%)			
	2002	2003	2004	2005	2003/02	2004/03	2005/04	2002	2003	2004	2005
Asia-Pacific Suppliers											
People's Republic of	1,564.96	2,289.85	2,972.52	5,885.40	46.32	29.81	97.99	9.07	12.14	14.90	26.74
China	927.72	913.03	941.68	1,124.65	(1.58)	3.14	19.43	5.38	4.84	4.72	5.11
Bangladesh											
Indonesia	594.64	617.98	703.40	823.40	3.93	13.82	17.06	3.45	3.28	3.53	3.74
Viet Nam	315.38	739.18	777.05	801.51	134.38	5.12	3.15	1.83	3.92	3.89	3.64
India	508.70	532.07	609.34	790.20	4.59	14.52	29.68	2.95	2.82	3.05	3.59
Cambodia	439.86	527.68	634.68	709.99	19.97	20.28	11.87	2.55	2.80	3.18	3.23
Hong Kong, China	821.26	785.44	738.96	596.62	(4.36)	(5.92)	(19.26)	4.76	4.16	3.70	2.71
Pakistan	382.06	443.63	519.28	577.75	16.12	17.05	11.26	2.21	2.35	2.60	2.62
Thailand	490.26	496.14	533.10	536.74	1.20	7.45	0.68	2.84	2.63	2.67	2.44
Philippines	550.53	545.57	513.57	518.73	(0.90)	(5.87)	1.00	3.19	2.89	2.57	2.36
Sri Lanka	393.89	395.02	415.05	453.75	0.29	5.07	9.33	2.28	2.09	2.08	2.06
Taipei,China	575.76	590.78	571.98	391.48	2.61	(3.18)	(31.56)	3.34	3.13	2.87	1.78
Republic of Korea	649.95	575.58	624.40	360.42	(11.44)	8.48	(42.28)	3.77	3.05	3.13	1.64
Macau, China	318.92	375.77	447.11	291.82	17.83	18.98	(34.73)	1.85	1.99	2.24	1.33
Malaysia	192.57	191.29	210.58	211.34	(0.67)	10.09	0.36	1.12	1.01	1.06	0.96
Mongolia	52.97	54.85	61.49	39.64	3.55	12.11	(35.54)	0.31	0.29	0.31	0.18
Brunei Darussalam	37.35	43.67	49.10	37.65	16.93	12.42	(23.32)	0.22	0.23	0.25	0.17
Turkmenistan	15.55	22.53	21.83	20.41	44.87	(3.08)	(6.51)	0.09	0.12	0.11	0.09

(Continued)

Table 1. (*Continued*)

	Volume (mn sqm)							Market Share (%)			
	2002	2003	2004	2005	2003/02	2004/03	2005/04	2002	2003	2004	2005
Nepal	37.91	39.24	34.82	19.20	3.51	(11.27)	(44.85)	0.22	0.21	0.17	0.09
Uzbekistan	12.45	13.32	6.16	7.78	7.05	(53.75)	26.29	0.07	0.07	0.03	0.04
Fiji Islands	20.21	17.63	21.28	4.15	(12.79)	20.73	(80.48)	0.12	0.09	0.11	0.02
Kyrgyz Republic	2.40	5.74	4.82	3.18	139.36	(16.04)	(33.92)	0.01	0.03	0.02	0.01
Maldives	38.69	40.37	37.90	2.37	4.35	(6.13)	(93.74)	0.22	0.21	0.19	0.01
Kazakhstan	4.04	11.17	14.67	1.23	176.62	31.32	(91.59)	0.02	0.06	0.07	0.01
Armenia	3.65	2.75	3.35	1.05	(24.85)	22.08	(68.66)	0.02	0.01	0.02	0.00
Tajikistan	0.04	4.89	2.75	0.01	12,491.19	(43.73)	(99.75)	0.00	0.03	0.01	0.00
Sub-total Asia-Pacific	**8,951.72**	**10,275.18**	**11,470.90**	**14,210.49**	**14.78**	**11.64**	**23.88**	**51.88**	**54.47**	**57.50**	**64.55**
DMC Suppliers											
excluding PRC	7,386.75	7,985.33	8,498.38	8,325.09	8.10	6.42	(2.04)	42.81	42.33	42.60	37.82
Preferential Suppliers											
CAFTA	3,494.42	3,685.16	3,790.83	3,787.31	5.46	2.87	(0.09)	20.25	19.54	19.00	17.20
Mexico	2,157.20	1,977.28	1,896.21	1,703.43	(8.34)	(4.10)	(10.17)	12.50	10.48	9.50	7.74
Sub-Sahara	277.23	398.79	440.30	376.76	43.85	10.41	(14.43)	1.61	2.11	2.21	1.71
Jordan	87.68	135.65	227.37	260.93	54.71	67.62	14.76	0.51	0.72	1.14	1.19
CBI	219.48	235.14	228.23	254.68	7.14	(2.94)	11.59	1.27	1.25	1.14	1.16
Andean (ATPA)	152.85	205.14	252.74	238.17	34.21	23.21	(5.77)	0.89	1.09	1.27	1.08
Canada	291.66	262.08	244.55	189.63	(10.14)	(6.69)	(22.46)	1.69	1.39	1.23	0.86
Egypt	128.28	138.55	156.03	164.69	8.01	12.62	5.55	0.74	0.73	0.78	0.75
Israel	118.87	119.45	102.82	80.32	0.49	(13.92)	(21.89)	0.69	0.63	0.52	0.36
Singapore	66.78	57.76	46.73	28.77	(13.51)	(19.10)	(38.42)	0.39	0.31	0.23	0.13
Bahrain	37.41	31.94	30.41	22.28	(14.61)	(4.79)	(26.74)	0.22	0.17	0.15	0.10

(*Continued*)

Table 1. (*Continued*)

	Volume (mn sqm)							Market Share (%)			
	2002	2003	2004	2005	2003/02	2004/03	2005/04	2002	2003	2004	2005
Australia	34.55	33.18	32.78	17.30	(3.98)	(1.19)	(47.24)	0.20	0.18	0.16	0.08
Morocco	17.45	15.92	13.77	6.69	(8.75)	(13.49)	(51.41)	0.10	0.08	0.07	0.03
Tunisia	8.04	4.93	4.83	4.93	(38.71)	(2.04)	2.04	0.05	0.03	0.02	0.02
Chile	1.25	0.78	2.42	2.44	(37.30)	208.35	1.04	0.01	0.00	0.01	0.01
Federated States of Micronesia	5.97	5.57	4.71	0.53	(6.78)	(15.47)	(88.84)	0.03	0.03	0.02	0.00
Sub-total Preferential Suppliers	**7,099.10**	**7,307.31**	**7,474.75**	**7,138.86**	**2.93**	**2.29**	**(4.49)**	**41.14**	**38.74**	**37.47**	**32.43**
Non-Preferential Suppliers											
Turkey	346.88	373.93	307.40	239.34	7.80	(17.79)	(22.14)	2.01	1.98	1.54	1.09
EU15	153.01	153.57	137.82	116.79	0.36	(10.26)	(15.26)	0.89	0.81	0.69	0.53
Japan	26.74	34.60	40.47	7.68	29.37	16.97	(81.02)	0.15	0.18	0.20	0.03
World	**17,255.66**	**18,863.75**	**19,951.00**	**22,012.99**	**9.32**	**5.76**	**10.34**	**100.00**	**100.00**	**100.00**	**100.00**

Notes: Sum of non-preferential and preferential suppliers does not add up to world total because some minor suppliers are not included; numbers may not sum precisely due to rounding. CBI excludes CAFTA member countries.
Source: US Department of Commerce, OTEXA office.

Table 2. US Import Value of Textiles by Supplier by Year.

	Value (US$ mn)				Change (%)			Market Share (%)			
	2002	2003	2004	2005	2003/02	2004/03	2005/04	2002	2003	2004	2005
Asia-Pacific Suppliers											
People's Republic of	410.94	467.32	575.68	896.96	13.72	23.19	55.81	6.04	6.96	7.90	12.07
China	671.56	627.84	666.35	665.48	(6.51)	6.13	(0.13)	9.88	9.35	9.15	8.95
Republic of Korea											
Taipei,China	474.82	425.37	432.39	415.13	(10.41)	1.65	(3.99)	6.98	6.33	5.93	5.58
Pakistan	427.89	416.36	509.15	411.33	(2.69)	22.29	(19.21)	6.29	6.20	6.99	5.53
India	131.68	140.81	150.52	183.57	6.93	6.89	21.96	1.94	2.10	2.07	2.47
Indonesia	124.20	113.62	133.96	138.80	(8.52)	17.90	3.61	1.83	1.69	1.84	1.87
Thailand	160.87	128.09	129.07	123.07	(20.38)	0.77	(4.64)	2.37	1.91	1.77	1.66
Malaysia	47.44	46.57	45.34	35.09	(1.85)	(2.64)	(22.61)	0.70	0.69	0.62	0.47
Hong Kong, China	110.63	58.00	50.65	34.29	(47.57)	(12.68)	(32.30)	1.63	0.86	0.70	0.46
Philippines	48.99	65.77	57.72	17.55	34.26	(12.24)	(69.59)	0.72	0.98	0.79	0.24
Viet Nam	4.52	13.68	16.89	14.75	202.43	23.53	(12.67)	0.07	0.20	0.23	0.20
Sri Lanka	34.13	20.91	12.97	7.66	(38.74)	(37.95)	(40.99)	0.50	0.31	0.18	0.10
Uzbekistan	24.90	17.49	13.72	4.25	(29.76)	(21.58)	(69.04)	0.37	0.26	0.19	0.06
Cambodia	5.81	2.76	2.52	1.68	(52.52)	(8.47)	(33.22)	0.09	0.04	0.03	0.02
Bangladesh	2.38	2.71	3.26	1.13	13.75	20.43	(65.45)	0.04	0.04	0.04	0.02
Turkmenistan	2.40	2.24	1.79	1.00	(6.50)	(20.08)	(44.47)	0.04	0.03	0.02	0.01
Tajikistan	0.86	0.22	2.97	0.70	(74.14)	1,238.34	(76.50)	0.01	0.00	0.04	0.01
Nepal	0.03	0.11	0.10	0.18	277.32	(9.14)	84.59	0.00	0.00	0.00	0.00
Macau, China	0.62	0.00	0.01	0.02	(99.42)	171.95	105.50	0.01	0.00	0.00	0.00
Mongolia	0.10	0.00	0.01	0.02	(96.99)	158.90	134.41	0.00	0.00	0.00	0.00
Fiji Islands	0.02	0.00	0.01	0.00	(75.25)	192.53	(83.09)	0.00	0.00	0.00	0.00
Brunei Darussalam	–	0.00	–	–		(100.00)		–	0.00	–	–
Kazakhstan	0.03	0.10	0.04	–	281.23	(62.83)	(100.00)	0.00	0.00	0.00	–
Kyrgyz Republic	–	0.02	–	–		(100.00)		–	0.00	–	–
Armenia	–	0.00	–	–		(100.00)		–	0.00	–	–
Sub-total Asia-Pacific	**2,684.82**	**2,550.00**	**2,805.14**	**2,952.65**	**(5.02)**	**10.01**	**5.26**	**39.49**	**37.96**	**38.50**	**39.72**
DMC Suppliers											
excluding PRC	2,273.88	2,082.68	2,229.46	2,055.69	(8.41)	7.05	(7.79)	33.45	31.00	30.60	27.65

(Continued)

Table 2. (*Continued*)

	Value (US$ mn)				Change (%)			Market Share (%)			
	2002	2003	2004	2005	2003/02	2004/03	2005/04	2002	2003	2004	2005
Preferential Suppliers											
Canada	1,197.79	1,200.42	1,205.52	1,209.35	0.22	0.42	0.32	17.62	17.87	16.55	16.27
Mexico	643.69	604.78	654.56	674.71	(6.04)	8.23	3.08	9.47	9.00	8.98	9.08
Israel	120.95	137.37	155.39	153.88	13.57	13.12	(0.97)	1.78	2.04	2.13	2.07
Andean (ATPA)	23.35	28.32	31.97	42.63	21.26	12.91	33.33	0.34	0.42	0.44	0.57
Egypt	36.72	42.55	30.00	26.25	15.87	(29.49)	(12.48)	0.54	0.63	0.41	0.35
Australia	22.79	19.58	20.57	21.89	(14.08)	5.05	6.44	0.34	0.29	0.28	0.29
CAFTA	14.14	14.11	19.24	15.52	(0.15)	36.35	(19.34)	0.21	0.21	0.26	0.21
Sub-Sahara	14.86	16.16	18.69	14.62	8.70	15.69	(21.79)	0.22	0.24	0.26	0.20
Bahrain	23.21	14.50	8.20	9.39	(37.53)	(43.45)	14.46	0.34	0.22	0.11	0.13
Chile	0.88	1.02	3.09	5.01	15.83	202.54	62.21	0.01	0.02	0.04	0.07
Morocco	0.27	0.42	0.58	3.46	55.26	38.34	497.12	0.00	0.01	0.01	0.05
Singapore	0.37	0.89	0.73	0.80	137.48	(18.04)	10.30	0.01	0.01	0.01	0.01
CBI	1.08	1.32	1.13	0.78	22.70	(14.62)	(30.95)	0.02	0.02	0.02	0.01
Tunisia	0.45	0.98	1.31	0.26	116.58	32.99	(80.23)	0.01	0.01	0.02	0.00
Jordan	–	0.06	0.02	0.00		(59.67)	(89.40)	–	0.00	0.00	0.00
Sub-total Preferential Suppliers	**2,100.56**	**2,082.48**	**2,150.99**	**2,178.55**	**(0.86)**	**3.29**	**1.28**	**30.90**	**31.00**	**29.52**	**29.31**
Non-Preferential Suppliers											
EU15	1,331.96	1,403.03	1,536.96	1,477.97	5.34	9.55	(3.84)	19.59	20.89	21.10	19.88
Japan	281.22	292.88	341.22	333.10	4.15	16.50	(2.38)	4.14	4.36	4.68	4.48
Turkey	180.15	156.89	208.40	237.47	(12.91)	32.83	13.95	2.65	2.34	2.86	3.19
World	**6,798.57**	**6,717.85**	**7,285.68**	**7,433.35**	**(1.19)**	**8.45**	**2.03**	**100.00**	**100.00**	**100.00**	**100.00**

Note: Sum of non-preferential and preferential suppliers does not add up to world total because some minor suppliers are not included; numbers may not sum precisely due to rounding. CBI excludes CAFTA member countries.
Source: US Department of Commerce, OTEXA office.

Table 2. (*Continued*)

	Volume (mn sqm)				Change (%)			Market Share (%)			
	2002	2003	2004	2005	2003/02	2004/03	2005/04	2002	2003	2004	2005
Asia-Pacific Suppliers											
People's Republic of	644.22	747.68	968.41	1,769.41	16.06	29.52	82.71	5.45	6.35	7.59	13.45
China	1,006.12	1,161.23	1,403.69	1,485.84	15.42	20.88	5.85	8.51	9.87	11.00	11.30
Republic of Korea											
Pakistan	993.46	868.42	1,024.66	917.26	(12.59)	17.99	(10.48)	8.40	7.38	8.03	6.97
Taipei,China	638.04	544.17	567.43	574.25	(14.71)	4.27	1.20	5.39	4.62	4.45	4.37
India	193.39	186.89	213.70	383.15	(3.36)	14.35	79.30	1.63	1.59	1.67	2.91
Indonesia	348.39	287.57	334.67	357.22	(17.46)	16.38	6.74	2.95	2.44	2.62	2.72
Thailand	416.31	335.92	325.13	301.63	(19.31)	(3.21)	(7.23)	3.52	2.85	2.55	2.29
Malaysia	127.06	141.41	144.47	107.55	11.30	2.16	(25.55)	1.07	1.20	1.13	0.82
Hong Kong, China	97.45	50.48	62.64	69.35	(48.20)	24.10	10.71	0.82	0.43	0.49	0.53
Viet Nam	13.67	38.83	48.05	51.94	184.10	23.73	8.11	0.12	0.33	0.38	0.39
Philippines	113.10	133.42	108.29	42.68	17.97	(18.83)	(60.59)	0.96	1.13	0.85	0.32
Sri Lanka	59.39	46.24	27.69	16.63	(22.14)	(40.12)	(39.93)	0.50	0.39	0.22	0.13
Uzbekistan	63.65	46.46	30.91	13.02	(27.01)	(33.46)	(57.87)	0.54	0.39	0.24	0.10
Bangladesh	7.54	9.09	8.92	3.23	20.68	(1.89)	(63.85)	0.06	0.08	0.07	0.02
Cambodia	11.76	6.40	6.26	2.67	(45.56)	(2.23)	(57.39)	0.10	0.05	0.05	0.02
Turkmenistan	6.70	8.73	4.34	2.35	30.27	(50.30)	(45.77)	0.06	0.07	0.03	0.02
Tajikistan	0.60	0.16	2.34	0.52	(73.79)	1,379.25	(77.67)	0.01	0.00	0.02	0.00
Nepal	0.01	0.01	0.02	0.15	67.40	100.90	559.01	0.00	0.00	0.00	0.00
Macau, China	2.21	0.01	0.03	0.01	(99.33)	89.59	(57.28)	0.02	0.00	0.00	0.00

(*Continued*)

Table 2. (*Continued*)

	Volume (mn sqm)				Change (%)			Market Share (%)			
	2002	2003	2004	2005	2003/02	2004/03	2005/04	2002	2003	2004	2005
Mongolia	0.04	0.00	0.00	0.00	(99.67)	(41.85)	6,343.94	0.00	0.00	0.00	0.00
Fiji Islands	0.02	0.00	0.01	0.00	(89.08)	616.36	(88.08)	0.00	0.00	0.00	0.00
Brunei Darussalam	–	0.00	–	–		(100.00)		–	0.00	–	–
Kazakhstan	0.09	0.12	0.16	–	25.89	34.45	(100.00)	0.00	0.00	0.00	–
Kyrgyz Republic	–	0.02	–	–		(100.00)		–	0.00	–	–
Armenia	–	0.00	–	–		(100.00)		–	0.00	–	–
Sub-total Asia-Pacific	**4,743.21**	**4,613.27**	**5,281.82**	**6,098.88**	**(2.74)**	**14.49**	**15.47**	**40.10**	**39.19**	**41.38**	**46.37**
DMC Suppliers											
excluding PRC	4,098.98	3,865.58	4,313.40	4,329.46	(5.69)	11.58	0.37	34.65	32.84	33.79	32.92
Preferential Suppliers											
Canada	2,712.03	2,745.99	2,747.88	2,590.72	1.25	0.07	(5.72)	22.93	23.33	21.53	19.70
Mexico	1,136.28	1,087.77	1,227.75	1,154.88	(4.27)	12.87	(5.93)	9.61	9.24	9.62	8.78
Israel	375.28	455.92	500.33	473.31	21.49	9.74	(5.40)	3.17	3.87	3.92	3.60
Egypt	99.84	121.79	75.20	68.47	21.98	(38.25)	(8.96)	0.84	1.03	0.59	0.52
CAFTA	46.94	53.74	67.03	44.94	14.49	24.71	(32.95)	0.40	0.46	0.53	0.34
Australia	52.59	30.95	28.93	33.48	(41.15)	(6.51)	15.70	0.44	0.26	0.23	0.25
Andean (ATPA)	16.55	16.02	20.31	26.98	(3.16)	26.74	32.84	0.14	0.14	0.16	0.21
Bahrain	63.42	35.27	18.33	21.55	(44.38)	(48.05)	17.60	0.54	0.30	0.14	0.16
Sub-Sahara	22.84	14.59	17.47	10.96	(36.12)	19.68	(37.25)	0.19	0.12	0.14	0.08
Chile	0.88	1.13	2.86	3.17	27.80	153.16	10.79	0.01	0.01	0.02	0.02
Singapore	0.12	0.76	1.24	2.12	512.72	63.02	71.04	0.00	0.01	0.01	0.02
Morocco	0.10	0.34	0.47	1.25	250.24	35.90	167.54	0.00	0.00	0.00	0.01
CBI	1.32	1.87	2.04	1.10	41.50	8.68	(45.99)	0.01	0.02	0.02	0.01
Tunisia	0.17	0.34	0.59	0.13	99.47	70.58	(77.97)	0.00	0.00	0.00	0.00
Jordan	–	0.13	0.05	0.00		(62.19)	(98.92)	–	0.00	0.00	0.00

(*Continued*)

Table 2. (*Continued*)

	Volume (mn sqm)				Change (%)			Market Share (%)			
	2002	2003	2004	2005	2003/02	2004/03	2005/04	2002	2003	2004	2005
Sub-total Preferential Suppliers	**4,528.38**	**4,566.64**	**4,710.45**	**4,433.06**	**0.84**	**3.15**	**(5.89)**	**38.28**	**38.80**	**36.90**	**33.71**
Non-Preferential Suppliers											
EU15	1,598.76	1,599.83	1,649.72	1,553.44	0.07	3.12	(5.84)	13.52	13.59	12.92	11.81
Turkey	319.29	274.58	304.87	282.47	(14.00)	11.03	(7.35)	2.70	2.33	2.39	2.15
Japan	232.63	228.25	286.53	266.57	(1.88)	25.53	(6.96)	1.97	1.94	2.24	2.03
World	**11,828.46**	**11,770.16**	**12,764.81**	**13,151.88**	**(0.49)**	**8.45**	**3.03**	**100.00**	**100.00**	**100.00**	**100.00**

Note: Sum of non-preferential and preferential suppliers does not add up to world total because some minor suppliers are not included; numbers may not sum precisely due to rounding. CBI excludes CAFTA member countries.
Source: US Department of Commerce, OTEXA office.

But beneath this aggregate picture there is a substantial amount of change by supplying country. Table 1 shows the changing percentage composition of US clothing imports by supplying country. China's value share increases by 8.2% points (from 13.8% to 22%), with China, Hong Kong, and Macao in combination (with transshipment though the latter two) increasing their value share by slightly less, 6.9% points. Volume shares for China increase considerably more, by 11.8%, and China, Hong Kong, and Macao by 9.9%. The larger volume than value share increases reflect price falls for China's exports to US markets as quota restraints are eliminated. These increases in US market shares for China reflect not only the removal of MFA restraints and production increases in the larger and more efficient supplying country, but also the general increase in Chinese exports across the board which occurred in 2005 in a wider range of products than textiles and clothing.

Shares of non Chinese suppliers (also reported in Table 1) show increases in both value and volume for India, Bangladesh, Indonesia and Cambodia (value share increase only) steady value shares for Sri Lanka, Vietnam, Pakistan and falls in value shares for Korea, Philippines, and Taiwan. A striking feature of Table 1 is that no share of any non Asian supplier increases. Value shares for Mexico, CAFTA (Honduras, Guatemala), CBI countries (Dominican Republic), and Turkey all fall. The Asian value share of US imports of textiles and clothing increases from 55.3% to 61.7%, but this is less than the increase in China's share. The fall in the share of the non Asian suppliers exceeds the fall in share of non Chinese Asian suppliers.

These data thus suggest that an increased share of the US market for clothing (in value terms) has accrued to China in the post MFA period, but this has occured more at the expense of non Asian suppliers (and especially Mexico) than at the expense of Asian suppliers. The larger change in share for non Asian suppliers also occurs relative to a smaller initial base than is true for Asian suppliers.

The picture in textiles in Table 2 is different from that in clothing. The share of China in US imports shows a much larger proportional increase (and especially in volume terms) while the shares of all Asian suppliers shows smaller increases in proportional terms than is the case for clothing. The fall in the share of non-Asian suppliers is smaller in proportional terms. This suggests larger inter-country substitution effects between China and other Asian suppliers for textile exports than for clothing.

Tables 3 and 4 report more detail on growth rates of US imports of textiles and clothing combined in both value and volume terms and for

Table 3. Growth Rates of the Value of US Imports of Textiles and Clothing, by Category, by Supplying Country* (% Change in 2005 relative to 2004).

Product Category	World	Bangladesh	Cambodia	China	India	Indonesia	Nepal	Pakistan	Philippines	Sri Lanka	Thailand	Vietnam
Clothing												
Cotton Clothing	10.4	37.2	18.9	182.9	47.1	54.0	−45.4	13.6	15.6	19.6	17.3	3.1
MMF Clothing	1.6	−4.6	21.3	72.8	13.2	−2.5	−91.2	−20.0	−17.2	−8.5	−9.9	6.3
Cotton/MMF Baby Wear	1.5	7.2	43.7	8.2	8.5	−15.7	40.3	−10.7	3.6	−9.7	−9.1	41.9
Wool Clothing	4.2	−20.3	−5.9	232.8	8.7	30.3	−15.4	1400.0	−13.0	−43.9	−47.5	32.5
Silk and Vegetable Fibre Clothing	−9.5	−59.6	273.7	−9.0	0.7	31.7	−31.4	45.7	72.0	−26.7	56.3	34.5
Textile Products												
Cotton Textiles	−17.2	−77.3	313.7	1.5	3.7	−29.8		−23.0	−57.9	11.4	0.3	−83.7
MMF Textiles	7.9		−49.5	65.6	85.4	35.8		−16.3	−76.3	−40.2	−5.9	−9.1
Blended Textiles	6.0			94.8	10.9	−5.0		−10.4	−53.7		−11.2	102.2

Note: Calculations by W. James based on data from US OTEXA.

Table 4. Growth Rates of the Volume of US Imports of Textiles and Clothing, by Category, by Supplying Country* (% Change in 2005 relative to 2004).

Product Category	World	Bangladesh	Cambodia	China	India	Indonesia	Nepal	Pakistan	Philippines	Sri Lanka	Thailand	Vietnam
Clothing												
Cotton Clothing	14.7	36.5	5.9	214.6	46.1	53.9	−40.4	16.3	15.1	22.5	18.5	6.6
MMF Clothing	7.7	−1.5	20.6	140.3	−0.3	−2.5	−79.5	−14.5	−15.5	−5.6	−11.1	−2.9
Cotton/MMF Baby Wear	1.3	10.2	42.8	5.2	15.4	−15.7	37.8	−8.5	12.9	−0.3	−11.8	45.4
Wool Clothing	7.8	8.0	−44.5	301.3	−1.7	30.3	−11.7	600.0	−19.3	−44.0	−56.8	23.1
Silk and Vegetable Fibre Clothing	−10.8	−60.2	138.8	−8.3	−9.7	−31.7	8.1	86.9	−40.9	−40.0	49.1	52.6
Textile Products												
Cotton Textiles	−10.8	−69.9	228.7	17.5	29.1	−29.8		−11.1	−51.1	10.7	9.0	−82.8
MMF Textiles	14.0		−68.1	163.1	376.6	35.8		−14.7	−65.1	−43.9	−1.4	4.4
Blended Textiles	2.7			102.9	25.2	−5.0		−3.2	−49.5		−28.4	140.3

Note: Calculations by W. James based on data from US OTEXA.

various products by country categories for 2005 relative to 2004. These show substantial variation across product categories for each country, and large increases in several categories for China; more so in volume than in value terms. Countries with falls in value and volume shares, such as Philippines and Thailand, show negative growth rates for more categories than for countries with expanding shares such as Cambodia.

Table 5 presents import data for the EU combined across clothing and textiles for 2003, 2004, and 2005 (data for 11 months projected onto a 12-month basis). For the EU, the growth rate of imports for 2005 is 6.1%, above that for 2004 (4.8%) and even more so compared to the period 2000–2003 (3.4% over three years). This thus suggests more impact of MFA

Table 5. EU Imports of Textiles and Clothing, Total and By Country, 2000, 2003, 2004 and 2005[7].

	2000	2003	2004	2005
Value of Imports Bill Euro	69.5	66.7	69.9	74.2
Import Share by Supplying Country (%)				
Asia				
China	17.5	21.4	23.0	30.7
India	7.1	6.8	6.8	7.5
Bangladesh	4.2	4.9	5.6	5.0
Pakistan	3.1	3.4	3.6	3.0
Hong Kong	5.1	3.3	3.0	2.2
Indonesia	3.9	2.8	2.6	2.2
S. Korea	3.1	2.2	1.9	1.4
Thailand	2.2	1.9	1.9	1.6
Sri Lanka	1.4	1.2	1.3	1.1
Taiwan	2.0	1.3	1.1	0.8
Vietnam	1.3	0.9	1.1	1.1
Cambodia	0.4	0.6	0.7	0.6
Macao	1.0	0.7	0.6	0.4
Philippines	0.6	0.5	0.5	0.3
Nepal	0.2	0.1	0.1	0.1
Total Asia	53.4	52.2	53.8	57.9
Non Asia				
Turkey	12.1	15.2	15.2	14.7
Romania	4.4	6.3	6.1	5.5
Tunisia	4.3	4.5	4.1	3.6
Morocco	3.9	3.9	3.7	3.2
Bulogna	1.3	1.7	1.8	1.7
Total Non-Asia	26.1	31.6	30.8	28.7

[7]These data relate only to the first 11 months of 2005, and the total imports for the year have been projected onto a 12-month basis.

abolition on EU imports, but the import growth rate remains at levels comparable to the US.[8]

The EU value share of imports from China increases by 7.7% points in 2005, a slightly larger increase in proportional penetration of EU markets by China post MFA than for US. As Table 5 indicates, the import share from China had been growing in the EU prior to MFA removal, with a 5.5% share increase between 2000 and 2004. The removal of the MFA thus accelerates an existing trend.

The impact on both Asian and non Asian suppliers to the EU differs from that of the US case. Only for India is there an increases in market share in 2004. In all other cases shares either fall or hold steady. In some cases, such as Bangladesh, the contrast to the US situation is pronounced with an increase in US market share accompanied by a fall in EU market share. This case reflects the feature that Bangladesh shipped to the EU free of restraint under the MFA.

The total share of Asian suppliers to the EU market increases from 53.8% to 57.9%, an increase of 4.1% points and as with the US less than the increase in China's share. In contrast to the US case, the shares all non Asian suppliers fall, and significantly so for Romania, Tunisia and Morocco, but the aggregate impact on non Asian suppliers is smaller than in the US case. The broad picture is thus similar to that for the US of a reduction in import share for both non Chinese Asian suppliers and non Asian suppliers to the EU accompanying the increased market share of China.

The increase in import share in both the EU and US markets for China reflects not only the abolition of MFA quotas. It also reflects an across the board increase in Chinese exports to the US and the EU during this period. As Table 6 reports, China's growth rates of exports of all commodities were 35% in both 2003 and 2004, and between 2003 and 2004 exports of textiles and clothing to the US grew at 22.1%, below the average growth rate of Chinese exports, while data for 2005 show a growth rate of 67.6%. The growth rate of EU textiles and clothing imports from China for 2004–2005 data is 39.7%. Table 6 therefore suggests a significant incremental effect of MFA abolition on China's share of imports by the US and the EU, but the general across the board increase in China's exports also accounts for a significant fraction of China's increased share in US and EU markets in 2005.

[8]Francois and Spinanger (2005) also present an evaluation of textile and clothing trade policies in the EU post MFA.

Table 6. China's Growth Rates of Textile and Clothing Exports Compared to China's Overall Trade Growth.

Annual Growth Rates of China's Textile and Apparel Exports (Value Terms)		
	To the US	To the EU
2002–2003	23.1%	
2003–2004	22.1%	
2004–2005	67.6%	39.7%
Annual Growth Rates of the Value of China's Exports of All Commodities		
2000	11%	
2001	7%	
2002	22%	
2003	35%	
2004	35%	

Sources: WTO (2005), US Dept of Commerce, Census Bureau, Foreign Trade Division, and Tables 1, 3 and 5.

Table 7. China's Clothing Exports By Region and Broad Product Type Post MFA Abolition.

	China's Exports Jan–Sept 2005 in $bill	% Change	% Change in unit prices
A. Total clothing Exports			
Total	43.4	6.7	14.5
Japan	9.4	4.5	2.7
US	7.6	189.0	−24.6
Hong Kong	4.0	−43.7	15.2
EU	8.5	79.4	0.7
Of which Germany	1.9	157.8	−21.6
B. Knit Ware Exports			
Japan	4.2	6.9	4.4
US	2.9	388.3	−42.9
Hong Kong	1.9	−48.1	9.4
Germany	0.7	258.3	−22.7
C. Women's Clothing Exports			
Japan	5.2	−0.1	3.5
US	4.7	120.4	−8.3
Hong Kong	2.1	−31.4	8.4
Germany	1.3	79.0	−0.6

Source: Emerging Textile.com; Ctri.gov.ca.

Table 7 provides data from Chinese sources on changes in China's overall exports of clothing to all markets for the period January–September 2005. These data show a modest 6.7% increase in total Chinese exports, accompanied by a 189% increase in exports to the US (larger than in US data) and a 79% increase in exports to EU (and 158% increase to Germany). Exports to Japan (which in 2005 exceeded those to the US) rise only 4.5%

Table 8. Examples of Products Showing Large Positive and Negative Changes in US Imports from China (% Import Change Oct. 2004–Oct. 2005).

Categories of US Imports from China	% Change in imports Oct 2004-Oct 2005 by category
Blue Denim Fabric	754.5
Cotton Shirts	1416.4
Cotton Sweaters	1476.9
Cotton Nightwear	939.5
Wool Knit Shirts/Blouses	2738.6
Wool Sweaters (Women and Girls)	641.5
Synthetic Fibre Skirts	418.9
Silk Sweaters	−60.7
Silk Nightwear	−40.8

and exports to Hong Kong fall by 43%. There are also sharp falls in unit values for exports to the US and Germany (but not for the EU). More extreme versions of this pattern also occur in data for knit ware exports and women's clothing. These data thus emphasize the point that the post MFA increase in China's exports of textiles and clothing is concentrated on US and EU markets, and most heavily the US. These large import increases are also accompanied by sharp price falls as quota restraints are eliminated. However, China is unusual among Asian suppliers in having a more significant share of exports of textiles and clothing going to non US–non EU markets.

Finally, Table 8 shows some of the sharp variations across product categories in trade changes between the US and China following the removal of the MFA. In this table, trade in product categories is reported for a sample of MFA code lines which report both large positive and negative changes in imports. Some categories show increases of over 1000% in US imports from China. Other products, in contrast, show trade falls of over 40%. Sub aggregate data thus show considerable variation around the broad trends discussed above.

4. Country Impacts of MFA Abolition

Because the circumstances of each Asian supplier differ, to gauge the impact of MFA abolition on individual countries the special situation of each needs to be taken into account. Some have come under separate restraint (such as China), some are not WTO members (Vietnam) and had special arrangements in place prior to MFA abolition and can be restrained by WTO members in the post MFA regime, some had special preferential arrangements for trade in products covered by the MFA (Bangladesh), some had rapidly expanding domestic industries (Cambodia), in other cases the sector was in relative decline (Philippines) prior to the termination of the MFA. Here the situation in each country is briefly summarized.

4.1. *China*

China's exports to US and EU markets perform differently across various product categories. China's exports to US markets increase by 214% in 2005 for cotton clothing products, 140% for clothing using man made fibre, and 301% for wool clothing. Cotton baby ware exports to the US, however, only increase by 5%. Exports to the EU of T-shirts increase in 2005 by 108%, sweaters and pullovers increase by 187%, while exports of women's suits fall by 34%.

The ILO report (2005) discusses Chinese data on textile exports between January and April 2005 in more detail and compares them to data for the same period in the prior years, as well as providing similar analysis for the EU. They argue that growth rates of trade decline month by month over this period because exporters anticipated that quotas would be abolished and postponed shipments from the final quarters of 2004 to the first quarter of 2005. This was in part because the carry over flexibility provisions that were part of the MFA did not apply for the last year of the MFA. Also the anticipation that transitional safeguards might be invoked by the US and EU against China under China's WTO accession provisions prompted accelerated shipments in early 2005.

The ILO report (2005) also suggests that competition among China's exporters has been a factor in trade performance immediately upon MFA termination. They report, by way of example, that the quota utilization rate in the EU for Chinese imports for the MFA category covering parkas and anoraks was nearly 100% in contrast to only 20% for Korea. They suggest that extremely high quota utilization rates for China prompted an initial post MFA surge as constrained domestic suppliers began to compete in foreign markets, a phenomenon missing for countries with low utilization rates.

They also note that China is not only a major exporter of textiles and clothing prior to MFA abolition but also a major importer of fibres

(3rd world wide), principally of wool, and cotton and also of equipment for textile and clothing production. They also suggest that wage rates had been rising in the sector prior to MFA abolition, while hours worked had been falling which would also affect post MFA performance.

4.2. *India*

Growth rates of India's exports to the US for 2005 also vary among product categories, but not to the same extent as for China. Cotton clothing exports to the US increase by 44%, wool clothing exports fall slightly by 2%, baby ware exports increase by 15%. ILO (2005) data for early 2005 show an increase in India's textile exports between January and March 2005 alongside a fall in exports of clothing and ready made garments.

During the first two months of 2005 data from the US Office of Textiles and Apparel (quoted by both Ghosh and Ray (2005)) and ILO (2005) allow a comparison between Indian and Chinese imports and show sharply higher market shares in the US for both India and China for men's cotton shirts (4.9% from Jan–Feb 2004 increasing to 7.4% for India, and 1.7% increasing to 5.7% for China), alongside other market share data changes where China sharply outperforms India.

In cotton fibre dresses, for instance, China's share increased to 18.2% from 10.8% while India's share was flat at 13.7% from 13.6% in 2004. In men's cotton trousers, China's share increased sharply from 1.5% to 12.2%, while India's share was flat at 2.2%. In women's cotton trousers, India's share fell to 1.4% from 1.8% while China's share increased sharply to 13.3% from 1.9%.

India differs from China in both having much smaller imports of fabrics and equipment, and also has significant shipments to non MFA quota restrained countries, but these are to different markets from China. Bharat Textile (2005) report, for instance, that the United Arab Emirates accounted for 7% of India's textile exports and 10% of clothing exports in 2003–2004.

4.3. *Pakistan*

Pakistan is a case where the positive effects of the removal of MFA restraints were offset by other factors, and overall Pakistan's share of US and EU markets falls little. Pakistan, like other non-Chinese Asian suppliers exhibits less volatility in import shares in the US for individual product categories than is the case for China. ILO (2005) report increases in textile and clothing exports for the first four months of 2005, but also report that a 13.4% EU antidumping duty on bed wear and the reintroduction of a 12% tariff on textile exports restrained export growth.

4.4. *Indonesia*

Indonesia represents a case where their post MFA import share of clothing in US markets rises but in the EU their share falls. Exports of cotton clothing to the US increase by 54%, wool clothing by 30%, while silk and baby ware both fall.

The increase in share in the US is consistent with the initial enthusiasm found in Indonesia in the first three-month period after MFA elimination for export prospects. The Trade/Investment Reports series from the US Embassy in Jakarta (2005) reports on a meeting of garment and textile manufacturers, academics and Indonesian government officials held in April 2005 which concluded that as of April Indonesia's textile and garment sector was holding up well, and American and European mid-end garment buyers were continuing to place orders in Indonesia. There were reports of orders being stepped up by importers in the US and the EU as a hedge against safeguards against China. Indonesia's mid-high end textiles (especially synthetics) were reported as remaining competitive. One US buyer at the meeting claimed that Indonesian garment producers dominated other suppliers (including China) for price, quality, compliance and service.

4.5. *Bangladesh*

The impact of MFA removal on Bangladesh's export performance in textiles and clothing is discussed in Khondker *et al.* (2005). They also report data for the first four-month period after MFA elimination, along with preliminary data for May of 2005. Their data show clothing exports by Bangladesh from the first four-month period after January 2005 that were lower, but an export increase in May 2005 resulted in an export growth rate of 8.7% over the same 2004 period. They highlight the rapid growth of knitwear products in the EU and US markets (also stressed by Leiema (2005)). Although sales to the US are small, exports to the EU by Bangladesh are large. An issue in US markets for Bangladesh was lack of GSP treatment since the domestic content of exports is low. Rules of origin in the EU market were also a factor in determining GSP treatment.

4.6. *Cambodia*

Cambodia is a case where strong growth rates of exports before MFA abolition continued after MFA removal. ILO (2005) report that clothing exports account for 80% of export earnings in Cambodia, with two-thirds going to the US and one-third to the EU. The value of these exports had increased sharply from US $ 26 million in 1995 to US $ 1.9 billion in 2004 reflecting low cost production in Cambodia and steadily improving quality accounting for this growth. This growth momentum has remained in 2005 despite MFA elimination.

4.7. *Vietnam*

Vietnam clothing exports to the US remain flat in the post MFA period. Cotton clothing exports to the US increased by 15%, wool clothing exports increased by 23%, while silk products increased by 9%. A major factor underlying restrained export growth is that Vietnam is not yet a WTO member and US quotas remain in place against Vietnam under the 2001 Bilateral Trade Agreement (BTA) with the US. Vietnamese exports increased rapidly under this agreement from $47 million of US clothing imports from Vietnam in 2000 to $2.4 billion in 2003. But the growth rate of US imports of clothing from Vietnam fell from 65% in 2003 to 6% in 2004 and 6% in 2005.

Although the EU eliminated its quotas against Vietnam under an earlier bilateral agreement, exports remained subject to a 14% tariff and special incentives for imports from Tsunami affected countries affected Vietnamese exports to the EU in the post MFA adjustment period. Despite these developments Vietnam's share in EU market has been stable.

4.8. *Philippines*

For the Philippines, there has been a significant reduction in import shares of both textiles and clothing after MFA removal. Wool clothing exports to the US decline by 19% in 2005, and silk product exports decline by 40% and in both the US and EU markets. The Philippines is a case of an early MFA entrant with large amounts of quota acquired from its exports in the early years of the MFA (1970–2000) suffering reduced exports shares as the MFA is terminated. Philippine exports of clothing had already fallen from $3 billion in 2000 to $2.9 billion in 2001, and to $2.6–2.7 billion between 2002 and 2004 as other lower cost suppliers began to increase exports. Philippine exports were thus already under pressure from lower cost suppliers, and the removal of the MFA seems only to have served to accelerate this trend.

4.9. *Nepal*

Nepal is a case where import shares in the US and EU markets fall significantly post MFA somewhat reflecting several dire predictions made for the effects to follow MFA elimination. Cotton based clothing exports to the US fall by 45%, and wool clothing exports by 15%. With geographical remoteness, poor infrastructure, and quota-driven outsourcing from India, Nepal had been seen as a country likely to see significant negative impacts from MFA removal. Saakha (2005) suggested that post MFA only 20% of production units in Nepal's clothing industry would remain open in the longer run.

5. Impacts on Employment and Wage Rates

The elimination of the MFA in January 2005 was also widely anticipated to have significant employment effects. Employment in the US, the EU and other importers which had been steadily falling for some years under ever growing import pressures was thought likely to continue to decline (especially for clothing), and at a faster rate after MFA removal. Employment was though likely to rise in export expanding countries (especially China), but fall in other Asian countries losing market share to China.

These potential employment losses were viewed with great apprehension in the lower income countries, including Cambodia, Nepal and Vietnam, since textiles and clothing constituted a large portion of manufacturing (and urban) employment. For these countries, at early stages of labour-intensive manufactured production, clothing represents the dominant employment opportunity in urban areas for many workers. In addition, in many countries the majority of workers in the clothing industry are female (90% in Cambodia), and alternative opportunities for employment for these workers are even more restricted, and the potential pressure on female wage rates was also thought likely to be large.

Table 9 reports employment data for the US and the EU spanning both the period prior to the abolition of the MFA and the months following its removal. They show an ongoing process of adjustment in both textiles and clothing that prior to the termination of the MFA was strong and

Table 9. US and EU Employment in Textiles and Clothing Post MFA US.

1995	2000	Jun04	Dec04	Jan05	Feb04	Mar05	Apr05	May05	June05
Employment in Clothing (thousands)									
814	497	285.9	271.9	269.3	267.2	262.8	262.2	258.5	256
Employment in Textiles (thousands)									
688	595	417.8	411.2	409.6	408.0	406.6	403.2	403.7	401.4

EU*

1995	2000	2002	% decline Mar 04–Mar 05	
			EU15	EU25
Employment in Clothing (thousands)				
1032	856	766	9.8%	11%
Employment in Textiles (thousands)				
1122	939	913	2.5%	3%

*Data for France, Germany, Italy, Portugal, Span and the UK.
Sources: ILO (2005); Nordas (2004).

progressive, and considerably more so in clothing than in textiles. Between 1995 and the end of 2004 employment in the US clothing industry fell by nearly 60%; while falls in the EU were somewhat smaller. Table 9 also shows a monthly time trend for post MFA employment in both textiles and clothing industries which approximately mirrors the pre MFA removal period. Employment in both the US and the EU continue to fall and in both textile and clothing, and at about the same rate as prior to the removal of the MFA. No acceleration of adjustment due to MFA removal appears discernable in either case.

There is only limited data available thus far on the employment impacts of MFA removal on textile and clothing industries in Asian exporting countries. In China, where the textile and clothing industry directly employs around nine million workers (around 22% of formal employment in manufacturing) and another 80 million workers are indirectly dependent on the textile and clothing industry (ILO (2005)) the abolition of the MFA and the resulting increase in exports was thought likely to generate increased employment. However, around 80% of production of textile and clothing in China is still for the domestic market, and export increases are concentrated on trade with the EU and US, with the overall trade increase smaller. According to the ILO (2005) the trade restrictions imposed by the US in late May 2005 affected $2 billion of exports and 140,000 jobs, and so trade effects on employment should be more clearly discernable when better data becomes available.

Elsewhere, Khondker *et al.* (2005) report on a UNDP survey covering 35 firms producing ready-made garments in 4 areas in Bangladesh. None of the firms report a reduction in employment after MFA abolition, and 19 of the 35 firms hired more workers after MFA abolition. They claim no reports of factory closures in Bangladesh following MFA removal. The textile and clothing sector is central to the Bangladesh economy accounting for 75% of export earnings, and after agriculture is the largest employer; 80% of employees are female.

The Philippines represents a case of reduced employment post MFA, but as noted earlier this trend was in place prior to MFA abolition. ILO (2005) reports that textile and clothing employment was around 700,000 in 2002 and had declined to 215,000 by 2004. They also report that between January and May 2005 28 establishments reduced production, and 12 permanently closed, but these numbers were smaller than for 2004.

In Cambodia, in contrast, these had been significant increases in employment prior to MFA abolition as Cambodia's exports of textile and clothing products grew. The ILO (2005) report that over 270,000 workers are employed in over 200 clothing factories and around 90% are female. In 2005 16 new large plants were scheduled to begin production.[9]

In India, growth in both clothing and textile exports to both the US and the EU provides a positive post MFA employment picture. Vietnam shows a small reduction in employment with declining trade share, and Pakistan a significant increase with the stronger trade performance.

6. Other Considerations and Concluding Remarks

Besides the immediate short term impacts of MFA removal on trade flows and employment, there are also a number of other broader considerations to be factored in when evaluating the possible impacts of MFA abolition on the Asian economies in the medium to longer term.

One issue involves the welfare impacts on Asian countries of removing MFA quota restrictions as against the impacts on trade, since while these restrictions lower export volumes they also have the effect of raising prices. It is possible therefore that the export growth of Asian shippers post MFA may be accompanied by welfare losses for Asian countries due to accompanying price falls. These price effects were evaluated by Trela and Whalley (1990) in their general equilibrium evaluation of the effects of MFA

[9] Also see the discussion of the Cambodia situation in Spinager (2005).

restrictions on developing countries, who concluded that the net effect on developing countries remained positive since volume increases in exports more that compensated for price falls.[10] The sharp falls in prices of Chinese exports in the US and the EU markets in the data above, however, suggest that this issue may merit further investigation. Pure price effects and quality downgrading as quotas terminate are comingled.

Another issue relates to additional indirect effects on Asian suppliers associated with removal of the MFA quota regime, and how these are to be taken into account when evaluating the effects of MFA removal on Asian shippers. One of these is the impact of removal of internal quota allocation schemes in Asian countries, especially for clothing exports. Trela and Whalley (1995) pointed out that these schemes typically involve yearly reallocation of most quota to established firms and effectively either prevent or discourage the entry of new dynamic (and smaller) firms into exporting activities. Trela and Whalley provide some general equilibrium calculations that suggest which these quota allocation schemes can have a more detrimental effect on exporting countries than the MFA quota themselves. To the extent this is the case, the removal of these internal effects for exporters could provide a larger source of gain for Asian exporters than the more direct trade impacts of the removal of the MFA quotas.

Yet, another issue relates to developments on the tariff front. In addition to MFA quota restriction, clothing has been subject to relatively high tariffs in both US and EU markets (and higher in the US than the EU). MFA abolition does not directly affect these tariff levels, but the WTO Doha Round negotiations may have a significant impact on Asia exporters if formula based multilateral tariff liberalization occurs at the end of the Round. At the time of writing, a formula based negotiated reduction seemed the likely outcome, which would benefit significantly Asian clothing suppliers.

Finally come the effects of MFA removal on the medium term growth performance of the Asian economies. The earlier discussion in this paper is largely of the impacts on trade, but rapidly increasing exports of labour intensive clothing also characterize the first stages of industrialization and rapid growth for lower income developing economies. In establishing growth

[10] Although see Krishna and Tan (1999) who argue that some of the returns from quota under the MFA (quota rents) accrued to concentrated retailers and middle men. Under MFA abolition these effects would be mitigated, and the suggested impacts on developing countries changed.

rate quotas for exports, the MFA put in place a regime where new entrants to clothing exports had to slowly cumulate sufficient quota to allow export growth to occur. As MFA quotas disappear, the prospect is for more rapid growth by the lower wage countries in the region and a compression in the time needed to grow income per capita rapidly. In the medium term this may yield larger impacts on the lower wage Asian suppliers, but data to confirm these trends will have to await the outcome.

References

BharatTextile.com (2005). Indian Textile Exports: Post MFA Scenarios, December 9, 2005.

Emerging Textiles.com (2005). China's Apparel Exports Began Declining in September, December 7, 2005.

Francois, J. and D. Spinanger (2005). Post-ATC Textile and Clothing Trade Policies in the EU: Eyes Wide Shut, Centre for Economic Policy Research, London and Tinbergen Institute, Rotterdam (Francois) and Kiel Institute for World Economics, Kiel, (Spinanger), December.

Ghosh, S. K and S Ray (2005). Gainers and Losers, Post MFA. The Hindu Business Line, May 20, 2005.

Hati, A. S. Khanal, J. Larsen, P. Smart, R. Sona and I. Ianni (2005). The Expiration of the Multi Fibre Arrangement: An Analysis of the Consequences for South Asia, Mimeo, Latollette School of Public Affairs, University of Wisconsin-Madison.

Hiyashi, M. (2002). Trade in Textiles and Clothing: Priority Issues for Women in the Post ATC, UNGAD mimeo.

ILO (2005). Promoting Fair Globalization in textiles and Clothing in a Post-MFA Environment, International Labour Office, ILO, Geneva.

James, W. E. (2005). Outlook for Asian Textile and Clothing Trade in the Post Quota Era, Textile Outlook International, November–December 2005, pp. 150–181.

Khondker, B. H. A. Razzaque and M. Ahmed (2005). Exports, Employment and Working Conditions in the Post MFA RMG Industry, Mimeo paper prepared for International Labour Office.

Krishna, K and Tan (1994). *Rags and Riches.* University of Michigan Press.

Lezema, M. (2005). Speech to Bangladesh Knitwear Sourcing Trade Show, New York, November 15, 2005.

Nadvi, K and J. Thorburn (2004). Challenges to Vietnamese Firms in the World Garment and Textile Value Chain, and the Implications for Alleviating Poverty. *Journal of the Asia-Pacific Economy*, 9(2): 249–267.

Nordas, H. (2004). The Global Textile and Clothing Industry Post the Agreement on Textiles and Clothing, WTO Discussion Paper, No. 5.

OECD (2005). Summary of Studies and Reports on the Impact of Textile Quota Elimination, OECD (mimeo).

Spinanger, D. (2005). Cambodia after Quotas: Will the Garment Industry Be Gone With the Wind?. Bangkok, World Bank, April.

Sceakha, K. S. (2005). We still Haven't Given up Hope, Nepal News.com, January, 2005.

Tewari, M. (2005). The Role of Price and Cost Competitiveness in Apparel Exports, Post MFA: A Review, Indian Council for International Economic Relations, New Delhi, Working Paper, No. 173, November 2005.

Trade/Investment Reports of US Embassy Indonesia (2005). Indonesia Government Sector Post Multi Fibre Agreement.

USITC (2004). Textiles and Apparel: Assessment of the Competitiveness of Certain Foreign Suppliers to the US Market, US International Trade Commission, Publication 3671, January 2004.

Walbenhorst, P. (2005). Quantitative Assessment of Textiles Trade Liberalization: A Survey, *Journal of Economic Integration*, 20(1): 139–157.

World Bank (2004). Managing the Transition to a Responsible Global Textiles and Garment Industry, MFA Forum, World Bank.

WTO (2005). World Trade Report 2005, World Trade Organization, Geneva.

Part V

Chinese Enterprises and Labour Mobility

A NUMERICAL SIMULATION ANALYSIS OF (HUKOU) LABOUR MOBILITY RESTRICTIONS IN CHINA*

John Whalley[a,b,c,†] and Shunming Zhang[d]
[a] *University of Western Ontario, Canada*
[b] *National Bureau of Economic Research, Inc. (NBER, Cambridge), United States*
[c] *Center for Economic Studies — Institute for Economic Research (CES-ifo, Munich), Germany*
[d] *Xiamen University, China*

We use numerical simulation methods to analyze the Hukou system of permanent registration in China which many believe has supported growing relative inequality over the last 20 years by restraining labour migration both between the countryside and urban areas and between regions and cities. Our aim is to inject economic modelling into the debate on sources of inequality in China which thus far has been largely statistical. We first use a model with homogeneous labour in which wage inequality across various geographical divides in China is supported solely by quantity-based migration restrictions (urban–rural areas, rich–poor regions, eastern-central and western (non-coastal) zones, eastern and central-western development zones, eastern–central–western zones, more-disaggregated six regional classifications, and an all-31 provincial classification). We calibrate this model to base case data and when we remove migration restrictions all wage and most income inequality disappears. Results from this model structure points to a significant role for Hukou restrictions in supporting inequality in China. We then present a further model extension in which urban house price rises retard rural–urban migration. The impacts of removing Hukou restrictions on migration are smaller, but are still significant. Finally, we modify the model to capture labour productivity differences across regions, calibrating the modified model to estimates of both national and regional Gini coefficients. Removal of migration barriers is again inequality improving but less so.

*We thank Jim Davies, Stephen McGurk, Randy Spence and Terry Sicular and seminar group at the University of Western Ontario for their comments. We are grateful for support under IDRC-MIMAP programme. We also acknowledge helpful comments from a seminar group MIMAP meeting in Manila (February 2003).
†Corresponding author. Department of Economics, University of Western Ontario, London, Ontario, Canada N6A 5C2. jwhalley@uwo.ca (J. Whalley).

1. Introduction

The statistical literature on inequality in China (Bramall and Jones, 1993; Chen, 1996; Hare and West, 1999; Jalan and Ravallion, 1998; Kanbur and Zhang, 1999; Lyons, 1991; Rozelle, 1994; Tsui, 1991, 1993, 1996, 1998a,b) is widely interpreted as pointing to growing national relative inequality in recent years. According to received wisdom based on some of this literature, the national Gini coefficient from China on income inequality has increased to over 0.4 from 0.3 over the last 15 years or so. This change coexists with more slowly growing inequality within the urban and rural segments of the economy (as measured by Gini coefficients), and also within coastal zones and inland segments of the economy. A sharp increase in the income/capita gap across these divides is usually taken to account for increased national relative inequality. Absolute poverty as measured by head count ratios and other measures consistently falls in Chinese data reflecting strong GDP growth in recent years.

A number of attempts have been made to account for this inequality change profile using statistical techniques as in the literature listed above. Econometric literature including Zhao (1999) and Shi, Sicular, and Zhao (2002) focuses mainly on the determinants of migration decisions, and not on the size of the efficiency gains involved nor impacts on wage rates in a consistent micro-based structure model. Our aim here is to use numerical simulation methods to provide fresh insights on these dimensions of the issue.

We focus on the system of Hukou in China, or registered permanent residence, which is location specific. Not having Hukou in urban areas means that migrants receive no education or health benefits and cannot purchase housing, since title to it cannot be registered by them. Effectively, Hukou operates as a barrier to urban/rural migration in China and supports large regional wage differentials which labour markets do not compete away. We ask how much inequality there would have been in China without the Hukou system.

Our starting point is the literature on the global consequences of immigration restrictions (see Hamilton and Whalley, 1984). In this literature, differences in both wage rates and GDP/capita across countries are assumed to be supported by immigration restrictions in a world with country specific factor inputs and downward sloping marginal product of labour schedules for otherwise potentially mobile labour. Parameters for an assumed underlying technology are calibrated so as to be consistent with observed data on wage differentials, labour shares of income, and GDP and population by country, and counterfactuals are performed to analyze the impacts of immigration barrier removal. Assumptions that there is homogenous labour across countries or that there are efficiency differences across countries are used as alternatives in these exercises.

Here we make calculations for China as to what the impacts of removing internal (Hukou) barriers to regional labour mobility on inequality could be using data on both aggregate and regional GDP/capita using similar methods. In so doing we elaborate on the earlier methodology used to analyze global migration restrictions by using a simple basic model which we sequentially modify in further model elaborations. We first ignore inequality within regions and treat labour as homogenous both across regions and across individuals. In this model wage rates across regions are equalized when migration restrictions are moved. With region-specific fixed factors, regional differences in GDP/capita do not disappear with barrier removal although they fall sharply and national inequality is much reduced. Significant efficiency gains also accrue from barrier removal in this model. We also discuss the implications of relaxing the assumption of region specific immobile capital for results.

We then introduce region specific house price effects and capture their dampening impacts on migration. This is motivated by the desire to also capture the impacts of increases in urban house prices and housing rents in China on urban–rural mobility over ten years. We develop a two-good general equilibrium model with goods and housing, in which location specific housing stocks support differing urban and rural house prices. In equilibrium migration equalizes the real value of wage rates and we incorporate differences in house prices across regions through region specific true cost of living indices. Removing Hukou restrictions in this model again generates labour flows into urban areas which are now smaller, and significant redistribution occurs between urban dwellers whose house prices rise and rural dwellers whose house prices fall.

Finally, we extend the basic model by also assuming a distribution of labour productivities (or efficiency types) within each region and calibrate an extended model to both regional and national estimates of Gini coefficients before barrier removal, and also regional and national data on GDP/capita. Here, to simplify things, we assume that when mobility occurs across regions a representative segment or slice of the distribution of productivities moves and adds result to the distribution within the receiving region proportional to that distribution. We again remove migration barriers and calculate national inequality in the absence of Hukou restrictions. Significant efficiency impacts again occur but reductions in national inequality are smaller.

While findings from these exercises are data and parameter sensitive, they nonetheless jointly point to significiant impacts from Hukou system in supporting growing overall relative inequality in China, and significant efficiency gains from its removal. They also show how economic modelling as well as statistical techniques can be used to analyze inequality change.

2. Analysis of Hukou Restriction Removal Using A Basic Model

The objective of our chapter is to assess how inequality in China might behave if not for the Hukou system of permanent registration acting as set of restrictions on labour mobility. We calibrate models of inter-regional labour mobility in China to base case data in the presence of Hukou restrictions and eliminate these restrictions. We then use the model-generated counterfactural equilibria to assess how many people might migrate, and what the economy-wide efficiency gains might be. In a later model extension we calibrate both on national and regional Gini coefficients and calculate how these change when individuals differ with regions.

We first use a simple model in which each region produces a single good Y according to a region-specific production function in which labour enters as a homogeneous factor input which is mobile across all regions. We first assume region-specific fixed factors (rents) which yield decreasing returns to scale and so in the fully mobile labour case even if wage rates are equalized across regions, GDP per capita across regions will not be.

In this simplest version labour is the only factor of production which is mobile across regions and capital is a fixed factor immobile across regions. We later relax this assumption and consider mobile capital as well as labour. In this simplest model form the regional production function is

$$Y_s = f_s(L_s), \quad s = 1, \ldots, S \tag{1}$$

where Y_s is production in region s, L_s is labour used in region $s, f_s' > 0$ and $f_s'' < 0$. We assume that $\sum_s L_s = L$ (full employment), and labour market clearing across regions determines the common wage $W = W_s$ ($s = 1, \ldots, S$), where there are no barriers to labour mobility. Labour receives its marginal product in all regions in this case and

$$W = f_s'(L_s), \quad s = 1, \ldots, S. \tag{2}$$

If there are barriers to mobility of labour across regions, then the inter-regional labour allocation no longer corresponds to that supporting a market clearing wage. Suppose this allocation is given as L_s^0 $(s = 1, \ldots, S)$ such that $\sum_s L_s^0 = L$, then the marginal products of labour across regions will differ and wage rates W_s $(s = 1, \ldots, S)$ will also differ, i.e. $f_s'(L_s^0)$ differs across s. Removing inter-regional barriers to labour mobility in this case implies an efficiency gain for the economy if marginal products of labour are equalized across regions.

Figure 1 illustrates the case of a 2-region urban–rural economy. Here, initial migration restrictions support wage rate differences across regions while the common wage $W = W_{\mathrm{U}} = W_{\mathrm{R}}$ applies when migration restrictions are removed. Income per capita across the two regions still differs with no migration restrictions as region-specific rents differ. Income inequality is much reduced but not eliminated in this case as wage converges across regions. An efficiency gain accrues, as shown, to the whole economy.

If we assume a diminishing marginal product production function in each region of the form

$$Y_s = A_s L_s^{\alpha_s}, \quad s = 1, \ldots, S \tag{3}$$

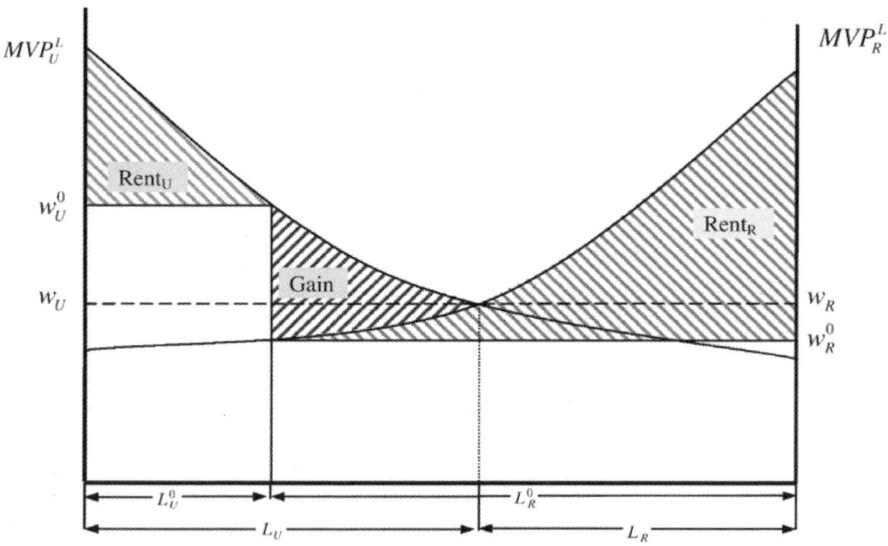

Fig. 1. Gains from eliminating labour mobility restrictions in a 2-region model.

then with decreasing marginal productivity of labour the regional wage W_s is given as

$$W_s = \frac{\partial Y_s}{\partial L_s} = \alpha_s A_s L_s^{\alpha_s - 1}, \quad s = 1, \ldots, S \tag{4}$$

and regional rents, R_s, are[1]

$$R_s = Y_s - W_s L_s, \quad s = 1, \ldots, S. \tag{5}$$

Income in region s, I_s, is given by

$$I_s = Y_s, \quad s = 1, \ldots, S. \tag{6}$$

and, assuming equal proportional shares in rents within the region, income per worker in each region, J_s, is given by the average product of labour $J_s = \frac{I_s}{L_s} = \frac{Y_s}{L_s}, s = 1, \ldots, S$.

In equilibrium

$$\sum_s L_s = L \tag{7}$$

where L is the national endowment of labour.

Typically, the size of the work force and population by region will differ. If the total national population is N, and the population in region s is N_s, then $N = \sum_s N_s$, and the average income in each region $s, \bar{I}_s$, is given by

$$\bar{I}_s = \frac{I_s}{N_s} = \frac{Y_s}{N_s} = \frac{R_s}{N_s} + \frac{W_s L_s}{N_s}, \quad s = 1, \ldots, S. \tag{8}$$

National income $I = \sum_s I_s = \sum_s Y_s$, and national average income, $\bar{I}$, is

$$\bar{I} = \frac{I}{N} = \frac{\sum_s I_s}{\sum_s N_s} = \frac{\sum_s Y_s}{\sum_s N_s}. \tag{9}$$

The average wage per individual in region s is

$$\bar{W}_s = \frac{W_s L_s}{N_s}, \quad s = 1, \ldots, S \tag{10}$$

in which case $\bar{I}_s = \frac{R_s}{N_s} + \bar{W}_s$.

[1]We assume here that labour migrates only in response to its regional wage, not also its proportional share in rents. The model can be recast in this form and different numerical results will apply.

We can extend this model to cases where capital is mobile across regions. In the extreme case where all capital is mobile, specialization equilibria can easily occur under elimination of Hukou labour mobility restrictions in which there is no production in some regions. Given that in reality capital refers both to regionally immobile land, and other capital such as equipment and machinery that is mobile in the intermediate term, we use a model extension in which there is both regionally fixed (specific) capital and regionally mobile capital. If we model capital in region s as part fixed and part mobile, then the product production function in each region is of the form

$$Y_s = A_s K_s^{\beta_s} L_s^{\alpha_s}, \quad s = 1, \ldots, S \tag{11}$$

where K_s refers to mobile capital used in region s. Specific factors, including immobile capital, are represented by A_s, and $\beta_s + a_s < 1$. In this case, the return of mobile capital will be the same in all regions and equal the marginal value product of capital in the region. This return B is given as

$$B = \frac{\partial Y_s}{\partial K_s} = \beta_s A_s K_s^{\beta_s - 1} L_s^{\alpha_s}, \quad s = 1, \ldots, S \tag{12}$$

and in equilibrium the market in mobile capital will clear, $\sum_{s=1}^{S} K_s = K$, where K is the economy wide endowment of mobile capital.

If there are no barriers to labour mobility, the common wage rate W is

$$W_s = \frac{\partial Y_s}{\partial L_s} = \alpha_s A_s K_s^{\beta_s} L_s^{\alpha_s - 1}, \quad s = 1, \ldots, S \tag{13}$$

and labour market clearing again determines the wage. As before, if there are barriers to mobility then the inter-regional labour allocation no longer corresponds to that supporting a market clearing wage. Removing inter-regional barriers to labour again implies an efficiency for the economy as marginal products of labour are equalized across regions, but the size of the gain will differ from the fully capital immobile case. In calibrating such a model we set the total return to both mobile and immobile capital equal to the same total return across the capital under an assumption of fully fixed capital. We then vary the assumed portions of mobile and immobile capital in repeated calculations to explore sensitivity of model results.

If we assume $S = 2$ we can group China in a number of ways which mirror regional classifications of data from Chinese Statistical Yearbooks. There are: *urban* and *rural*; *rich* and *poor*, *eastern coastal* and *central and western* (non-coastal) zones; *eastern and central* and *western development* zones. If $S = 3$, we group by *eastern*, *central* and *western* zones. We also consider a 6 region case of Northern China, Northeastern China, Eastern China, Central and Southern China, Southwestern China, and Northwestern China. There are 31 provinces, centrally administered municipalities and autonomous regions in China in total[2] and we also explore a 31-region variant of the model that captures all of these. Differences in results across these cases reflect the degree and form of regional disaggregation used in alternative empirical applications of the model.

The models set out above with the two different treatments of capital mobility can be used numerically to assess the distributional impacts of removing Hukou migration restrictions by first calibrating observed wage GDP/capita differences across the various two region divides set out above for China and then recomputing a counterfactual equilibrium with removal of restrictions. To do this we use a benchmark data set for a given initial year in the presence of Hukou restrictions on labour mobility, and assess the implications of removing mobility restrictions given the observed initial differences in GDP/capita and wage inequality. In the capital immobile case, if Y_s, L_s, and W_s are observed and given by data, we can use the model in calibration mode and solve the system of $2S$ Eqs. (3) and (4) for the $2S$ unknowns A_s and α_s. We can then compute a counterfactual equilibrium for this simple model in which $W = W_s$ $(s = 1, \ldots, S)$ and labour mobility restrictions are eliminated. Comparing the original data to the solution generated as the counterfactual model equilibrium then yields as an evaluation of the impacts of Hukou on both national and regional income inequality in this simple case. A similar approach can be used in more detailed multi-region calculations and with mobility of a portion of capital where the rate of return across regions is equalized and there is full employment of capital.

In Table 1 we reported the 2001 base year data used in calibration for the 2, 3, and 6 regions. These are GDP/capita by region, where rate differentials across regions work force and population by region. We assume the ratio of the work force to the population in any region is fixed and when a worker moves between regions, a corresponding multiple of the population also moves. Data for the full 31-regions version is

[2]We treat all the provinces, centrally administered municipalities and autonomous regions in China as separate and distinct entitles (provinces) in more detailed regional reported later.

Table 1. Data Used to Calibrate 2, 3 and 6 Region Formulations of Chinese Inter-Regional Labour Mobility Model for Alternative Regional Grouping (All data for 2001[a]).

	Regional classification[b] used in model variants					
	Urban–rural	Rich–poor	EC–CW	EC–WD	E–C–W	6 regions[c]
GDP per capita by region						NC 9.22246
(10^3 RMB)	U 12.38835	R 13.29862	EC 12.08961	EC 9.77881	E 12.08961	NEC 9.93508
						EC 11.03664
					C 6.36075	CSC 7.78470
						SWC 4.71466
	R 6.05665	P 5.79754	CW 5.79994	WD 5.03428	W 4.94210	NWC 5.43888
Wage rate by region						NC 9.61953
(10^3 RMB)	U 16.63805	R 11.30238	EC 10.40758	EC 9.24304	E 10.40758	NEC 8.55412
						EC 9.82212
					C 7.28020	CSC 8.01942
						SWC 6.04259
	R 5.73975	P 6.71116	CW 6.77753	WD 5.99797	W 6.03203	NWC 6.00533
Work force by region						NC 68.458
(10^6 individuals)	U 142.236	R 218.465	EC 264.782	EC 447.666	E 264.782	NEC 45.216
						EC 187.020
					C 218.451	CSC 182.539
						SWC 105.539
	R 482.291	P 412.062	CW 365.745	WD 182.861	W 147.294	NWC 41.755

(Continued)

Table 1. (*Continued*)

	Regional classification[b] used in model variants					
	Urban–rural	Rich–poor	EC–CW	EC–WD	E–C–W	6 regions[c]
Population by region						NC 147.35
(10^6 individuals)	U 472.20	R 442.38	EC 527.10	EC 903.36	E 527.10	NEC 106.96
						EC 365.77
					C 447.91	CSC 354.39
						SWC 200.86
	R 795.63	P 825.45	CW 740.73	WD 364.47	W 292.82	NWC 91.96

[a]All data are from the Chinese Statistical Yearbook (2002).
[b]The regional classifications are presented in more details in footnote 3 (page 7).
[c]NC, NEC, EC, CSC, SWC, and NWC denote Northern China (5 provinces), Northern China (3 provinces), Eastern China (7 provinces), Central and Southern China (6 provinces), Southwestern China (5 provinces), and Northwestern China (5 provinces), respectively.

available on request. Using these data as an input, through calibration we determine the model parameters A_s and a_s, as well as regional outputs Y_s^0, rents R_s^0, and other variables $I_s^0, \bar{I}_s^0, I^0, \bar{I}^0, J_s^0, J^0$, and $\bar{W}_s^0$. We assess the impacts of eliminating Hukou restrictions on all endogenous model variable $Y_s, L_s, W_s, R_s, I_s, \bar{I}_s, I, \bar{I}, J_s, J, \bar{W}_s$, and solve the model in counterfactual model for the case where wage rates are equalized across regions and thus determine the migration impacts on work force and population by region.

For the construction of the base year data we have used when calibrating alternative versions of the model we first rank provinces from rich to poor (on an income (GDP)/capita basis), taking the top ten provinces (approximately 35% of the population) as the rich group. The remaining provinces make up the poor group. We next group provinces into two eastern coastal and central and southern (non-coastal) provincial groupings, and two eastern and central and western development zones. We also divide the 31 provinces into three zones and six regions. We finally consider all Chinese provinces in a 31-region version of the model.[3] Since data on Chinese GDP/capita (average income) and wage differentials are only readily available on a provincial basis, we use data for all 31 provinces, centrally administered municipalities, and autonomous regions to group

[3]There are 31 provinces, centrally administered municipalities and autonomous regions in Chinese mainland. The 31 provinces, centrally administered municipalities and autonomous regions ranked from rich to poor by GDP per capita are Shanghai, Beijing, Tianjin, Zhengjiang, Guangdong, Jiangsu, Fujian, Liaoning, Shanong, Heilongjiang, Hebei, Xinjiang, Hubei, Jilin, Hainan, Inner mongolia, Hunan, Quinghai, Henan, Chongqing, Shanxi, Ningxia, Tibet, Anhui, Jiangxi, Sichuan, Shaanxi, Guangxa, Yunnan, Gansu, Guizhou. The first 10 provinces are grouped as rich. The 21 provinces which follow are group as poor. Mainland China is divided into 6 regions as follows; Northern China includes 5 provinces: Beijing, Tianjin, Hebei, Shanxi, Inner Mongolia; Northwestern China includes 3 provinces: Liaoning, Jilin, Heilongjiang; Eastern China in includes 7 provinces: Shanghai; Jiangsu, Zhejiang, Anhui, Fujian, Jingxi, Shandong; Central and Southern China includes 6 provinces: Henan, Hubei, Hunan, Guangdong, Guangxi, Hainan; Southwestern China includes 5 provinces: Chongqing, Sichuan, Guizhou, Yunnan, Tibet; Northwestern China inludes 5 provinces: Shaanxi, Gansu, Qinghai, Ningxia, Xinjiang. The Eastern Coastal zone includes 12 provinces: Beijing, Tianjin, Hebei, Liaoning, Shanghai, Jiangsu, Zhejiang, Fujian, Shandong, Guangdong, Guangxi, Hainan. The Central zone includes 9 provinces: Shanxi, inner Mongolia, Jilin, Heiongjiang, Anhui, Jiangxi, Henan, Hubei, Hunan. The Western zone includes 10 provinces: Chongqing, Sichuan, Guizhou, Yunnan, Tibet, Shiaanxi, Gansu, Qinghai, Ningxia, Xinjiang. The Western Development zone includes 12 provinces as Inner Mongolia, Guangxi, and western zone, In Tables 2 and 3 and in the discussion that follows, EC–CW zones denote Eastern Coastal zone–Central and Western zones, EC–WD zones denote Eastern and Central zone–Western Development zone, E–C–W zones denote Eastern zone–Central zone–Western zone.

regions in China in various ways. We consider seven different regional divides grouping data on population, output, work force, and wage rate for each.

Table 2 reports results for numerical simulations showing the impacts of Hukou elimination in model variants using alternative Chinese regional divides for the regional specific fixed capital case. The changes reported imply that for the urban–rural 2-region case the per capita income differential falls from 2:1 to 7:10, while in case two (rich–poor) it falls from over 7:3 to 4:3. In the urban–rural case, approximately 48% of the work force and 45% of the population move from rural to urban areas after Hukou removal. Around 17% of the population remains in rural areas. They become richer, their average income (GDP per capita) being 1.42 times higher than that in urban areas. Total output increase by about 13%, and GDP per capita and income per worker both increase. In rich–poor cases, there are smaller migration effects after Hukou removal (approximately 25% of the work force and the population move), and total output increases only by about 3.2%. In the other 2-region cases (EC–CW and EC–WD) there are smaller migration effects from Hukou removal, while total output and GDP per capita and income per worker again increase. These smaller effects occur because there is an urban–rural divide within each region, and the main migration effect is urban–rural rather than geographical. In the 3-region E–C–W case there are large migration effects out of Central–Western and Eastern zones after Hukou removal. Total output increases by about 3.0%. In the 6-region case, migration effects between regions are small, and total output increases by about 1.7%.

The picture that emerges from Table 2 is that Hukou registration is a significant policy impediment preventing the achievement of a more equal distribution of incomes and wages in China. The number of people who would migrate across regions after its removal in the first four cases is 600 million people (1/2 of the population of China). Unlike the international migration case where Hamilton and Whalley (1984) found very large efficiency effects due to larger initial wage dispersion, the efficiency effects gains are more modest but still significant. The gain is 13% of national output in the first case, and considerably smaller at 1.7–32% in the other three geographical divide cases. In each case wage differentials across regional divides are eliminated with the removal of Hukou restrictions, and average incomes across regions are more closely equalized. The differences that remain average are due to differences in rents across regions.

Table 2. Impacts of Hukou Elimination in Alternative Regional Divides in Fixed Capital Version of Inter-Regional Labour Mobility Model for China (Changes Relative to Base Case Data for 2001).

	Urban–rural	Rich–poor	EC–CW	EC–WD	E–C–W	6 regions
Change in value of output (10^6 RMB)	U 3682.041	R 1812.917	EC 1243.425	EC 884.753	E 1242.262	NC 209.063
	R −2087.854	P −1170.085	CW −1003.264	WD −701.386	C −412.046	NEC 21.482
					W −565.689	EC 627.506
						CSC −91.040
						SWC −450.122
						NWC −137.214
	N 1414.187	N 342.831	N 240.161	N 183.267	N 324.537	N 179.574
Change in average income per capita (10^3 RMB)	U −3.49215	R −4.88382	EC −2.55705	EC −0.98651	E −2.54224	NC −1.27485
	R 6.55073	P1.33713	CW 1.02269	WD 1.94103	C 0.82027	NEC −1.30699
					W 1.79173	EC −1.72180
						CSC 0.26247
						SWC 1.75336
						NWC 2.06898
	Nl.11544	N0.27041	N0.18943	N0.14455	N0.20865	N0.1464
Change in income per worker (10^3 RMB)	U −18.72939	R −7.30444	EC −5.02016	EC −2.02573	E −5.01631	NC −2.80248
	R 5.22525	P 2.63985	CW 2.52885	WD 3.84133	C 1.71637	NEC −0.80406
					W 3.59331	EC −3.42974
						CSC 0.45684
						SWC 0.29488
						NWC 4.50013
	N2.24287	N0.54372	N0.38089	N0.29066	N 0.41955	N0.28480

(*Continued*)

Table 2. (*Continued*)

	Urban–rural	Rich–poor	EC–CW	EC–WD	E–C–W	6 regions
Change in wage rate (10^3 RMB)	U −7.89761 R 1.00169	R −2.56094 P 2.03028	EC −1.66614 CW 1.96391	EC −0.50160 WD 2.74347	E −1.66614 C 1.46124 W 2.70943	NC −0.87809 NEC 0.18732 EC −1.08268 CSC 0.72202 SWC 2.69885 NWC 2.73611
Change in work force by region (migration millions of individuals)	U 302.81913 R −302.81913	R 158.40700 P −158.40700	EC 135.07144 CW −135.07144	EC 101.17314 WD −101.17314	E 134.93051 C −53.32496 W −81.60556	NC 23.51675 NEC 2.54381 EC 69.89272 CSC −11.18622 SWC −65.03726 NWC −19.72979
Change in population by region (migration millions of individuals)	U 579.01525 R −579.01525	R 318.69952 P −318.69952	EC 271.82831 CW −271.82831	EC 201.97491 WD −201.97491	E 270.46951 C −108.54383 W −161.92568	NC 49.94098 NEC 5.63122 EC 134.97694 CSC −22.88965 SWC −124.04133 NWC −43.61816

Table 3. National Gain and Migration Under Hukou Elimination for More Detailed Regional Groupings in the Model.

	2 region EC–CW model	2 region EC–WD model	2 region E–C–W model	6 regions model	31 provinces model
National gain from removal of Hukou restrictions as % of GDP	2.25110	1.71781	3.04198	1.68320	6.92509
Work force migration (million)	135.07144	101.17314	134.93051	134.93051	175.60454

Table 3 reports a more detailed 31-region calculation using the model. Compared to the small dimensional geographical divides results showing gain of 1.7 to 3% of GDP, an increase in output of around 7% results, and differentials in both GDP/capita and income per worker across regions are sharply narrowed. The direction of migration is from poor to rich provinces, that is, from Henan, Guizhou, Sichuan, Anhui, Guangxi, Yunnan, Shaanxi, Gansu, Hunan, Chongqing, Jiangxi, Hebei, Shanxi, to Guangdong, Shanghai, Beijing, Zhejiang, Jiangsu, Fujian, Tianjin. The overall picture conveyed by these results is that removal of Hukou registration plays a more major role in reducing relative income inequality in China in a more disaggregated model calculation.

Table 4 reports results both for versions of the model incorporating differing degree of capital mobility. As explained above, fully capital mobility is not consumed since in this case specialization equilibrium can occur in the model. As the portion of capital assumed mobile increase from 0 (same as Table 3) to 75%, the national gain increases and more labour moves between regions. Within 75% of capital mobile the gain rises to 24% GDP; some 70% larger the fixed capital case. These results occur because as labour leaves rural areas Hukou restrictions are removed, this raises the marginal product of capital in the receiving region and capital also moves. This in turn raises further the marginal product of labour in receiving region and more labour moves. Factor flows between regions in this model are thus complementary to one another, even though factors are substitutes in production. These results as a set thus indicate that estimates of gains from elimination of Hukou restrictions while sensitive to assumptions on capital mobility still remain large, and that elimination of Hukou restrictions will have a significant and positive effect on national inequality.

Table 4. Impacts of Hukou Elimination with Partial Capital Mobility Between Regions in 2-Region (Urban-Rural Divide) Model.

Portion of capital in each region assumed mobile	National gain from removal of Hukou restriction as % of GDP	Urban–rural change work force migration (millions)
0.00	13.25557	302.81913
0.25	15.13038	343.56609
0.30	15.63167	353.91916
0.35	16.19088	365.14706
0.40	16.81720	377.28546
0.45	17.52169	390.33198
0.50	18.31692	404.21656
0.55	19.21732	418.75242
0.60	20.23816	433.53891
0.65	21.39473	448.03190
0.70	22.69865	461.17796
0.75	24.15291	471.76949

3. Extending the Model to Capture House Price Effects on Migration Across Regions

A key feature of the urban–rural divide in modern day China missing in the model variants discussed above is large differences in housing (apartment) prices between the larger cities and village communities. Apartments in Beijing routinely sell for US $100,000, and with average annual household incomes of around US $2000 in Beijing area, even at 5% the imputed income on apartments owned outright can be larger than annual cash income. Thus, households who received apartments at low (or zero) prices in urban areas in the late 1980's or the early 1990's have a large advantage over rural dwellers who might wish to move to the cities following a removal of Hukou restrictions. In this case the effect of added inward migration will be to drive up urban house prices further and this house price effect will act to dampen additional migration. Less migration following Hukou elimination appears in models incorporating house price effects in contrast to models which do not incorporate them; but working with them involves the use of a more complex analytical structure.

We have modified the basic capital immobile model set out in Section 2 to also incorporate house price effects stemming from additional urban–rural migration. We consider the 2-region urban–rural divide. We capture impacts of urban house prices on urban–rural mobility decisions by using a general equilibrium model with goods and housing separately identified, and with housing prices in urban and rural differing reflecting market segmentation due to location. In this case, removing Hukou restrictions generates labour flows from rural to urban areas, but when these are included increases in urban house prices retard additional migration. Labour flows under Hukou removal are smaller and significant further redistribution occurs between urban dwellers whose house prices rise and rural dwellers whose house prices fall. Efficiency gains from Hukou removal will tend to be smaller in models with house price effects since the number of migrants will be smaller.

We can present this model variant more formally as follows. We once again denote L_s as the labour in region s before Hukou removal. The regional production functions are again

$$Y_s = A_s L_s^{\alpha_s}, \quad s = U, R \tag{14}$$

and the regional wage rates W_s, are given as

$$W_s = P_{\mathrm{G}} \frac{\partial Y_s}{\partial L_s} = P_G \alpha_s A_s L_s^{\alpha_s - 1}, \quad s = U, R \tag{15}$$

where P_{G} is the goods price, and regional rents, R_s, are

$$R_s = P_{\mathrm{G}} Y_s - W_s L_s, \quad s = U, R. \tag{16}$$

Income in region s is I_s

$$I_S = P_{\mathrm{G}} Y_S, \quad s = U, R. \tag{17}$$

National income $I = \sum_s I_s$. Full employment of labour in this model again implies that

$$\sum_s L_s = L \tag{18}$$

where L is the national endowment of labour.

We assume that there is continuum of individuals who vary in terms of their preferences toward goods and housing and who are uniformly distributed over a unidimensional interval $[t_{\mathrm{R}}, t_{\mathrm{U}}]$ for a parameter t. t is a Cobb–Douglas preference function parameter varying across all individuals. $\hat{t}$ is the critical value of the preference parameter such that urban individuals all have $\hat{t}$ values above $\hat{t}$ and lie on the interval $[\hat{t}, t_{\mathrm{U}}]$ and rural individuals all have t values below $\hat{t}$ and lie on the interval index $[t_{\mathrm{R}}, \hat{t}]$. The continuum of individuals $[t_{\mathrm{R}}, t_{\mathrm{U}}]$ are assumed to differ in preference shares parameters for Cobb–Douglas preferences defined as

$$V_t(G,H) = G^{1-t}H^t, \quad t \in [t_{\mathrm{R}}, t_{\mathrm{U}}] \tag{19}$$

where G is consumption of goods, and H is consumption of housing.

We assume for simplicity that all individuals in urban and rural areas have endowments of housing E_{U} and E_{R} that are similar in structure, but differ in size. Their incomes are

$$\begin{aligned} I_t^{\mathrm{U}} &= R_{\mathrm{U}}X_t^{\mathrm{U}} + W_{\mathrm{U}}L_{\mathrm{U}}X_t^{\mathrm{U}} + P_{\mathrm{U}}E_{\mathrm{U}}X_t^{\mathrm{U}} \\ &= (P_{\mathrm{G}}Y_{\mathrm{U}} + P_{\mathrm{U}}E_{\mathrm{U}})X_t^{\mathrm{U}}, \quad t \in [\hat{t}, t_{\mathrm{U}}] \end{aligned} \tag{20}$$

$$\begin{aligned} I_t^{\mathrm{R}} &= R_{\mathrm{R}}X_t^{\mathrm{R}} + W_{\mathrm{R}}L_{\mathrm{U}}X_t^{\mathrm{R}} + P_{\mathrm{R}}E_{\mathrm{R}}X_t^{\mathrm{R}} \\ &= (P_{\mathrm{G}}Y_{\mathrm{R}} + P_{\mathrm{R}}E_{\mathrm{R}})X_t^{\mathrm{R}}, \quad t \in [t_{\mathrm{R}}, \hat{t}] \end{aligned} \tag{21}$$

where X^{U} and X^{R} are uniform distribution random variable on $[\hat{t}, t_{\mathrm{U}}]$ and $[t_{\mathrm{R}}, \hat{t}]$.

Utility maximization subject to a budget constraint in each case implies

$$G_t^{\mathrm{U}} = \frac{1-t}{P_{\mathrm{G}}}I_t^{\mathrm{U}} \quad \text{and} \quad H_t^{\mathrm{U}} = \frac{t}{P_{\mathrm{U}}}I_t^{\mathrm{U}}, \quad t \in [\hat{t}, t_{\mathrm{U}}] \tag{22}$$

$$G_t^{\mathrm{R}} = \frac{1-t}{P_{\mathrm{G}}}I_t^{\mathrm{R}} \quad \text{and} \quad H_t^{\mathrm{R}} = \frac{t}{P_{\mathrm{R}}}I_t^{\mathrm{R}}, \quad t \in [t_{\mathrm{R}}, \hat{t}]. \tag{23}$$

A general equilibrium in this model involves an equilibrium value $\hat{t}$, and the division of the population into urban and rural components is endogenously determined. Before Hukou removal an equilibrium is characterized by wage rates W_s, a goods price P_{G}, urban and rural house prices P_{U} and P_{R} such that the following conditions hold.

[1] (Good Market Clearing) $Y_{\mathrm{U}} + Y_{\mathrm{R}} = \int_{\hat{t}}^{t_{\mathrm{U}}} G_t^{\mathrm{U}}\mathrm{d}t + \int_{t_{\mathrm{R}}}^{\hat{t}} \mathrm{G}_t^{\mathrm{R}}\mathrm{d}t$;

[2] (House Market Clearing) $\int_{\hat{t}}^{t_{\mathrm{U}}} H_t^{\mathrm{U}}\mathrm{d}t = E_{\mathrm{U}}$ and $\int_{t_{\mathrm{R}}}^{\hat{t}} H_t^{\mathrm{R}}\mathrm{d}t = E_{\mathrm{R}}$;

[3] (Labour Market Clearing) $L_{\mathrm{U}} + L_{\mathrm{R}} = L$.

If we consider the case of Hukou removal, under the assumption that all individuals have identical amounts of labour in urban and rural areas, then labour is allocated by region such that

$$L_{\mathrm{U}} = \frac{t_{\mathrm{U}} - \hat{t}}{t_{\mathrm{U}} - t_{\mathrm{R}}}L \quad \text{and} \quad L_{\mathrm{R}} = \frac{\hat{t} - t_{\mathrm{R}}}{t_{\mathrm{U}} - t_{\mathrm{R}}}L. \tag{24}$$

After Hukou removal we need to add a migration equilibrium condition involving a money metric measure of the relative valuation of a unit of income across the two regions $\frac{\mathrm{TCL}(U,\hat{t})}{\mathrm{TCL}(R,\hat{t})}$, where TCL refers to the true cost of living index. This term reflects the different price levels across the two regions due to different housing prices. As TCL indices enter when making migration decisions, individuals take into account not only wage rate differences across regions, but also the different cost of housing.

To construct this metric we use the indirect utility functions

$$V_t(I_t^{\mathrm{U}}) = \left\{\frac{1-t}{P_{\mathrm{G}}}\right\}^{1-t}\left\{\frac{t}{P_{\mathrm{U}}}\right\}^{t} I_t^{\mathrm{U}}, \quad t \in [\hat{t}, t_{\mathrm{U}}] \tag{25}$$

$$V_t(I_t^{\mathrm{R}}) = \left\{\frac{1-t}{P_{\mathrm{G}}}\right\}^{1-t}\left\{\frac{t}{P_{\mathrm{R}}}\right\}^{t} I_t^{\mathrm{R}}, \quad t \in [t_{\mathrm{R}}, \hat{t}] \tag{26}$$

for which the TCL indices are

$$\mathrm{TCL}(U,t) = \left[\left\{\frac{1-t}{P_{\mathrm{G}}}\right\}^{1-t}\left\{\frac{t}{P_{\mathrm{U}}}\right\}^{t}\right]^{-1}, \quad t \in [\hat{t}, t_{\mathrm{U}}] \tag{27}$$

$$\mathrm{TCL}(R,t) = \left[\left\{\frac{1-t}{P_{\mathrm{G}}}\right\}^{1-t}\left\{\frac{t}{P_{\mathrm{R}}}\right\}^{t}\right]^{-1}, \quad t \in [t_{\mathrm{R}}, \hat{t}]. \tag{28}$$

The equilibrium condition that migration must satisfy changes from the model with house price effects is

$$\frac{W_{\mathrm{U}}}{W_{\mathrm{R}}} = \frac{\mathrm{TCL}(U,\hat{t})}{\mathrm{TCL}(R,\hat{t})} = \left[\frac{P_{\mathrm{U}}}{P_{\mathrm{R}}}\right]^{\hat{t}}. \tag{29}$$

A general equilibrium after Hukou removal is thus given by the critical value of the share parameter $\hat{t}$, wage rates W_s, goods price P_{G}, and urban and rural house prices P_{U} and P_{R} such that the following conditions hold.

[1] (Good Market Clearing) $Y_{\mathrm{U}} + Y_{\mathrm{R}} = \int_{\hat{t}}^{t_U} G_t^{\mathrm{U}}\mathrm{d}t + \int_{t_R}^{\hat{t}} G_t^{\mathrm{R}}\mathrm{d}t$;

[2] (House Market Clearing) $\int_{\hat{t}}^{t_U} H_t^{\mathrm{U}}\mathrm{d}t = E_{\mathrm{U}}$ and $\int_{t_{\mathrm{R}}}^{\hat{t}} H_t^{\mathrm{R}}\mathrm{d}t = E_{\mathrm{R}}$;

[3] (Labour Market Clearing) $L_{\mathrm{U}} + L_{\mathrm{R}} = L$;

[4] (Migration Condition) $\frac{W_{\mathrm{U}}}{W_{\mathrm{R}}} = \left[\frac{P_{\mathrm{U}}}{P_{\mathrm{R}}}\right]^{\hat{t}}$.

The general equilibrium condition [2] can be written as

$$\begin{aligned}E_{\mathrm{U}} &= \int_{\hat{t}}^{t_U} H_t^{\mathrm{U}}\mathrm{d}t = \int_{\hat{t}}^{t_U} \frac{t}{P_{\mathrm{U}}} I_t^{\mathrm{U}}\mathrm{d}t = \int_{\hat{t}}^{t_U} \frac{t}{P_{\mathrm{U}}}(P_{\mathrm{G}}Y_{\mathrm{U}} + P_{\mathrm{U}}E_{\mathrm{U}})X_t^{\mathrm{U}}\mathrm{d}t \\ &= \frac{P_{\mathrm{G}}Y_{\mathrm{U}} + P_{\mathrm{U}}Y_{\mathrm{U}}}{P_{\mathrm{U}}} \int_{\hat{t}}^{t_U} tX_t^{\mathrm{U}}\mathrm{d}tP_{\mathrm{U}}E_{\mathrm{U}} \\ &= \frac{1}{2}(t_{\mathrm{U}} + \hat{t})(P_{\mathrm{G}}Y_{\mathrm{U}} + P_{\mathrm{U}}E_{\mathrm{U}}) \quad \text{and} \quad P_{\mathrm{U}}E_{\mathrm{U}} \\ &= \frac{\frac{1}{2}(t_{\mathrm{U}} + \hat{t})}{1 - \frac{1}{2}(t_{\mathrm{U}} + \hat{t})} P_{\mathrm{G}}Y_{\mathrm{U}} \end{aligned} \tag{30}$$

and

$$\begin{aligned}E_{\mathrm{R}} &= \int_{t_R}^{\hat{t}} H_t^{\mathrm{R}}\mathrm{d}t = \int_{t_R}^{\hat{t}} \frac{t}{P_{\mathrm{R}}} I_t^{\mathrm{R}}\mathrm{d}t = \int_{t_R}^{\hat{t}} \frac{t}{P_{\mathrm{R}}}(P_{\mathrm{G}}Y_{\mathrm{R}} + P_{\mathrm{R}}E_{\mathrm{R}})X_t^{\mathrm{R}}\mathrm{d}t \\ &= \frac{P_{\mathrm{G}}Y_{\mathrm{R}} + P_{\mathrm{R}}E_{\mathrm{R}}}{P_{\mathrm{R}}} \int_{t_R}^{\hat{t}} tX_t^{\mathrm{R}}\mathrm{d}tP_{\mathrm{R}}E_{\mathrm{R}} = \frac{1}{2}(\hat{t} + t_{\mathrm{R}})(P_{\mathrm{G}}Y_{\mathrm{R}} + P_{\mathrm{R}}E_{\mathrm{R}}) \text{ and}\end{aligned}$$

$$P_{\mathrm{R}}E_{\mathrm{R}} = \frac{\frac{1}{2}(\hat{t} + t_{\mathrm{R}})}{1 - \frac{1}{2}(\hat{t} + t_{\mathrm{R}})} P_{\mathrm{G}}Y_{\mathrm{U}}. \tag{31}$$

The general equilibrium condition [1] holds from Equations (30) and (31).

We use this model to explore the dampening effect of house price rises on migration by comparing the induced migration from Hukou elimination across the model variants. One of these captures house price effects, and the second does not. The latter model is structurally the same as the basic model in the preceding section, but is calibrated to different data which removes housing expenditures from GDP (and hence is smaller than GDP data used in the previous section) to make the data used in the with and without house price effect models comparable.

To implement these two models we again calibrate to base case data for 2001 and consider Hukou removal. From Chinese Statistical Yearbook (2002) urban and rural non-housing GDP in 2001 are 5849.777 million RMB and 4818.849 million RMB. If we assume the shares of housing/apartments in GDP in urban and rural areas to be 22.5% and 18.50%,[4] then the

[4]See the discussion in Wang and Zuo (1999) which supports estimates of this size for the mid-1990's appealing to survey evidence from various sources.

base case value of endowments of housing are 1316.200 and 891.487. The consumption value of non-housing goods in the urban and rural areas is 4533.577 (=5849.777 – 1316.200) and 3927.362 (=4818.849 – 891.487). Urban and rural labour are 148.236 and 482.291, and wage rates are 16.638 and 5.740. Rents are 2067.219 (=4533.577 – 16.638 × 148.236) and 1159.132 (=3927.362 – 5.740 × 482.291).

For the model which ignores housing price effects, we use the same as in Section 2 to analyze the effects of Hukou removal, but only focus on the non-housing portion of the economy which is smaller. Through calibration we compute the scale and share parameters in production as $A_{\mathrm{U}} = 298.8121$ and $A_{\mathrm{R}} = 50.4371$, $\alpha_{\mathrm{U}} = 0.5440$ and $\alpha_{\mathrm{R}} = 0.7049$. Equilibrium outcomes after Hukou removal are output: $Y_{\mathrm{U}} = 9116.090$ and $Y_{\mathrm{R}} = 1251.721$, work force: $L_{\mathrm{U}} = 535.296$ and $L_{\mathrm{R}} = 95.231$, common wage rate: $W_{\mathrm{U}} = W_{\mathrm{R}} = 9.265$. Labour migration under Hukou removal is $535.296 - 148.236 = 482.291 - 95.231 = 387.060$.

To evaluate the impacts of Hukou removal in the presence of house price effects, we use the model above and compare model results without and with house price effects. We assume equilibrium prices in the base case are $P_{\mathrm{G}} = 1$, $P_{\mathrm{U}} = 1$ $P_{\mathrm{R}} = 1$. $Y_{\mathrm{U}} = 4533.577$ and $Y_{\mathrm{R}} = 3927.362$, $E_{\mathrm{U}} = 1316.200$ and $E_{\mathrm{R}} = 891.487$, $L_{\mathrm{U}} = 148.236$ and $L_{\mathrm{R}} = 482.291$, $W_{\mathrm{U}} = 16.638$ and $W_{\mathrm{R}} = 5.740$, $R_{\mathrm{U}} = 2067.219$ and $R_{\mathrm{R}} = 1159.132$, $I_{\mathrm{U}} = 4533.577$ and $I_{\mathrm{R}} = 3927.362$. Calibration yields the scale and share parameters as $A_{\mathrm{U}} = 298.8121$ and $A_{\mathrm{R}} = 50.4371$, $\alpha_{\mathrm{U}} = 0.5440$ and $\alpha_{\mathrm{R}} = 0.7049$.

In this case if we assume $t_{\mathrm{U}} = 0.2344$ and $t_{\mathrm{R}} = 0.1544$, this implies a value of $\hat{t} = 0.2156$, which is consistent with the proportion of the population in urban and rural areas in base case data and given by $\frac{t_{\mathrm{U}}-\hat{t}}{t_{\mathrm{U}}-t_{\mathrm{R}}}$ and $\frac{\hat{t}-t_{\mathrm{R}}}{t_{\mathrm{U}}-t_{\mathrm{R}}}$. This implies $\int_{\hat{t}}^{t_U} I_t^{t_{\mathrm{U}}}\mathrm{d}t = 5849.777$ and $\int_{t_R}^{\hat{t}} I_t^{t_{\mathrm{R}}}\mathrm{d}t = 4818.49$. Then $\int_{\hat{t}}^{t_U} G_t^{\mathrm{U}}\mathrm{d}t = 4533.577$ and $\int_{\hat{t}}^{t_U} H_t^{\mathrm{U}}\mathrm{d}t = 1316.200$, $\int_{t_R}^{\hat{t}} G_t^{\mathrm{R}}\mathrm{d}t = 3927.362$ and $\int_{t_R}^{\hat{t}} H_t^{\mathrm{R}}\mathrm{d}t = 891.487$.

To analyze Hukou removal in this case, in the base case $t_{\mathrm{U}} = 0.2344$ and $t_{\mathrm{R}} = 0.1544$, this implies a new equilibrium value of $\hat{t} = 0.1760$. The equilibrium prices are $P_{\mathrm{G}} = 1.000$, $P_{\mathrm{U}} = 1.647$ and $P_{\mathrm{R}} = 0.419$. Other variables are $Y_{\mathrm{U}} = 8394.802$ and $Y_{\mathrm{R}} = 1887.051$, $L_{\mathrm{U}} = 460.035$ and $L_{\mathrm{R}} = 170.492$, $W_{\mathrm{U}} = 9.927$ and $W_{\mathrm{R}} = 7.802$, $R_{\mathrm{U}} = 3827.859$ and $R_{\mathrm{R}} = 556.949$, $I_{\mathrm{U}} = 8394.802$ and $I_{\mathrm{R}} = 1887.051$, $\int_{\hat{t}}^{t_U} I_t^{\mathrm{U}}\mathrm{d}t = 10{,}562.420$ and $\int_{t_R}^{\hat{t}} I_t^{\mathrm{R}}\mathrm{d}t = 2260.536$. Under Hukou elimination $\int_{\hat{t}}^{t_U} G_t^{\mathrm{U}}\mathrm{d}t = 8394.802$ and $\int_{\hat{t}}^{t_U} H_t^{\mathrm{U}}\mathrm{d}t = 2167.617$, $\int_{t_R}^{\hat{t}} G_t^{\mathrm{R}}\mathrm{d}t = 1887.051$ and $\int_{t_R}^{\hat{t}} H_t^{\mathrm{R}}\mathrm{d}t = 373.485$. Labour migration under Hukou removal in this case is =460.035−148.236 = 482.291 − 170.492 = 311.799 and efficiency gain from elimination of Hukou restrictions is = 12,822.955 − 10,668.626 = 2154.329. Rising house prices thus serve to dampen migration relative to the 387.05 value from the comparable no house price rise model. The size of efficiency gains is also reduced.

4. A Model With a Distribution of Productivities Within Regions

The model set out above can be elaborated on to also incorporate within region efficiency (or productivity) differences across individuals and hence inequality within regions both before and after the elimination of Hukou. This also allows us to calibrate the model not only to wage differentials across regions, but also to urban and rural Gini coefficients. With these features present, wage differentials across individuals will not disappear with elimination of Hukou restrictions as in the basic model presented above. We limit our discussion of this case to the model from where capital is fully immobile across regions.

Table 5 estimates of urban, rural and national household income Gini coefficients from Chang (2002) which show how income inequality has changed China over the 20 or so years. This is representative of data claimed to show the growing income divide in China (but see the earlier footnote 1 on the implications of alternative data for recent years). At national level there is consistent worsening of national inequality which is seemingly always more unequal than regional inequality (as measured by the Gini coefficient). In our base case data we use Gini coefficients for urbane–rural, rich–poor, EC–CW, EC–WD. E–C–W, and NC–NEC–EC CSC–CSC–SWC NWC for 2001 reported in Chinese People Daily (November 4th, 2003 and March 30th, 2004) which are close to Chang's (2002) estimates. These are displayed later in Table 6.

To incorporate efficiency differences across individuals within regions into the model we use a functional form for the distribution of incomes within regions which through calibration implies a distribution of the efficiencies of labour across individuals within region. This approach allows us to specify initial differences in efficiencies across individuals in specific regions of economy so as to also calibrate a modified version of the simple model to within region inequality as measured by Gini coefficients for each region, as well as to national Gini inequality measure of income inequality. In this model variant removing labour mobility restrictions once again

Table 5. Regional and National Gini Coefficient for Household Income in China from 1978 to 2000.

Year	Urban areas	Rural areas	National
1978	0.160	0.212	
1979	0.160	0.241	
1980	0.150	0.241	0.330
1981	0.150	0.232	
1982	0.150	0.246	
1983	0.160	0.244	
1984	0.190	0.227	0.300
1985	0.190	0.304	
1986	0.200	0.305	
1987	0.230	0.303	
1988	0.230	0.310	
1989	0.230	0.310	
1990	0.240	0.307	
1991	0.250	0.313	
1992	0.270	0.329	
1993	0.300	0.321	
1994	0.280	0.342	0.400
1995	0.280	0.323	0.415
1996	0.290	0.329	0.424
1997	0.300	0.337	0.425
1998	0.295	0.336	0.456
1999			0.457
2000	0.320		0.458

Source: Chang (2002).

equalizes wage rates per efficiency unit labour across regions, but with differing endowments of efficiency units of labour across individuals wage rate inequality will remain both across individuals and across regions when Hukou restrictions are removed. An elimination of Hukou restrictions will be equalizing, but compete equality of wage rates across individuals within regions will not be achieved as efficiency differences remain.

We assume that when mobility of labour occurs across regions, labour moves in the form of a representative portion or slice of the distribution of productivities. This departs the leaving region, and adding itself proportionally to the distribution of productivities in the receiving region. This is a treatment that simplifies the analysis, and leaves the within region distribution of productivities unchanged in both migrating and receiving regions as mobility occurs. The regional income distribution changes however, because of the presence of region specific rents.

The model we use for this case can be formally stated as follows. The same Eqs. (3) (4) (5) (6) and (7) characterize the production side of the model, but there are now also distributions of income within regions which reflect differences in the efficiency of labour within regions. Denoting N_s as the number of people in region s, and L_s as labour in efficiency units in region $s(N_s \neq L_s)$, we have average regional incomes $\bar{I}_s$, national income I, average national income $\bar{I}$, and the average region wage $\bar{W}_s$ as in Eqs. (8) (9) and (10) above.

The functional form for the income distribution within each region s can take many forms. We assume the non-linear form

$$I_s^n = C_s + D_s n + E_s n^{\delta s}, \quad n = 1, \ldots, N_s, \quad s = 1, \ldots, S. \tag{32}$$

where n is an index $1, \ldots, N_s$ across the individual N_s in regions ranked from poor to rich, and C_s, D_s, E_s and δ_s are parameters of the distribution functions. This provides sufficient free parameters to calibrate the model to both regional and national Gini coeffiecients through a generated distributed of efficiencies. We could alternatively use a functional form from the class used in distributional literature such as a Pareto distribution, although the implied distribution of efficiencies would not be Pareto. If a simple linear form were used there would not be sufficient free parameters for calibration.

Using Equation (32), we calibrate the model to satisfy $2S+1$ conditions reflecting total income and Gini coefficient constraints and in addition use the same calibration conditions for the simple model above. Since

$$I_s = \sum_{n=1}^{N_s} I_s^n = \sum_{n=1}^{N_s} [C_s + D_s n + E_s n^{\delta_s}], \quad s = 1, \ldots, S, \tag{33}$$

$$\begin{aligned} G_s &= \frac{1}{2N_s^2 \bar{I}_s} \sum_{n=1}^{N_s} \sum_{n'=1}^{N_s} \left| I_s^n - I_s^{n'} \right| \\ &= 1 - \frac{1}{N_s^2 \bar{I}_s} \sum_{n=1}^{N_s} \sum_{n'=1}^{N_s} \min \left\{ I_s^n, I_s^{n'} \right\}, \quad s = 1, \ldots, S \end{aligned} \tag{34}$$

where G_s is the region s Gini coefficient in incomes.[5]

[5]See Sen (1973).

The national Gini coefficient, g, is given by

$$G = \frac{1}{2N^2\bar{I}}\left\{\sum_{s=1}^{S}\sum_{n=1}^{N_s}\sum_{n'=1}^{N_s}\left|I_s^n - I_s^{n'}\right| + 2\sum_{s\neq s'}\sum_{n=1}^{N_s}\sum_{n'=1}^{N_s'}\left|I_s^n - I_{s'}^{n'}\right|\right\}$$

$$= 1 - \frac{1}{N^2\bar{I}}\left\{\sum_{s=1}^{S}\sum_{n=1}^{N_s}\sum_{n'=1}^{N_s}\min\{I_s^n - I_s^{n'}\}\right.$$

$$\left. + 2\sum_{s\neq s'}\sum_{n=1}^{N_s}\sum_{n'=1}^{N_s'}\min\{I_s^n - I_{s'}^{n'}\}\right\}. \quad (35)$$

One difficulty in implementing this model variant is that initial data on regional and national Gini coefficients and estimates of regional and national GDP/capita can be mutually inconsistent. Where this occur, we have adopted a procedure of accepting data on regional and national GDP/capita, and accepting one or more of the Gini coefficient estimates for 2001 and setting remaining Gini coefficients at bounds implied by mutual consistency requirements. In the main, these are close to the available literature estimates, but do depart from these slightly. No other procedure short of modifying other portions of input data seem to suggest itself.

For the urban–rural case above where $S = 2$, $I_{\mathrm{U}} = 5849.777$, $I_{\mathrm{R}} = 4818.847$ and $I = 10668.626$ from Section 2. If the three Gini coefficients (drawing on Chang, 2002) are set as $G_{\mathrm{U}} = 0.3200$, $G_{\mathrm{R}} = 0.3500$ and $G = 0.4600$, and these are used as inputs into calibration. This allows us to calibrate the model for $8(=4 \times 2)$ unknown distribution function parameters: C_s, D_s, E_s, and δ_s for $s = U, R$. If we then remove Hukou restrictions and compute a new model solution the three computed Gini coefficients reported on Table 5 are $G_{\mathrm{U}} = 0.3572$, $G_{\mathrm{R}} = 0.3687$ and $G = 0.3705$. Compared to the case of the simple model, the impact on inequality of Hukou removal is smaller, but it is still significant and especially so for national inequality.

For the rich–poor case above S also equals 2, and $I_{\mathrm{R}} = 5883.043$ and $I_{\mathrm{P}} = 4785.583$, $I = 10668.626$ (from Section 2). Drawing on Liu, Yao, and Zhang (2001) we set the three Gini coefficients to be $g_{\mathrm{R}} = 0.4094$, $g_{\mathrm{P}} = 0.2030$, and $g = 0.4600$. We again calibrate the model and compute the $8(= 4 \times 2)$ unknown parameters: C_s, D_s, E_s and δ_s for $s =$ R, P, and remove Hukou restrictions computing a new model solution. The three Gini coefficients in this solution are $G_{\mathrm{R}} = 0.4236$, $G_{\mathrm{P}} = 0.1692$, and $G = 0.3739$.

Impacts on inequality in this case are smaller compared to the simple model but still significant. Impacts on the three Gini coefficients differ from the urban–rural case because the initial dispersion in Gini coefficients is larger. For the eastern coastal–central and western case again $S = 2$, $I_{\mathrm{EC}} = 6372.436$, $I_{\mathrm{CW}} = 4296.190$ and $I = 10{,}668.626$ from Section 2. Appealing again to Liu, Yao, and Zhang (2001) we now set the three Gini coefficients as $G_{\mathrm{EC}} = 0.4119$, $G_{\mathrm{CW}} = 0.2040$ and $G = 0.4600$. Using these, we can again calibrate the model and remove Hukou restrictions. The three new Gini coefficients $G_{\mathrm{EC}} = 0.3979$, $G_{\mathrm{CW}} = 0.1123$, and $G = 0.3470$. For the eastern central–western development 2-region case, $G_{\mathrm{EC}} = 0.4186$, $G_{\mathrm{WD}} = 0.1600$ and $G = 0.4600$. Removing Hukou restrictions gives the three Gini coefficients $G_{\mathrm{EC}} = 0.2244$, $G_{\mathrm{WD}} = 0.1813$, and $G = 0.2291$.

We have consolidated these results into a single table (Table 6) which reports base case and counterfactual Gini coefficients for this extended model applied to four alternative regional divides (urban–rural, rich–poor, and eastern coastal–central and western provinces). We also report summary statistics of both regional and national inequality based on the Theil measure (see Theil, 1967) since this is a decomposable measure. Impacts of Hukou removal on inequality as represented by the Gini coefficients are significant. Using both Gini coefficients and Theil measures, national inequality is reduced, but inequality can either worsen or improve at a regional level. In departing region, inequality typically improves due to the equal distribution of rents. It can however change the other way due to wage change which affects the relative size of wage income and rents. Impacts on inequality are reduced relative to the simple model set out above since the dispersion of rents. Impacts on inequality are reduced relative to the simple model set out above since the dispersion in efficiencies across individuals implies that some inequality in wage rates remains after Hukou removal.

We also report Theil measures for within and between region before and after Hukou removal. The national Theil measure is

$$T = \frac{1}{N}\sum_{n=1}^{N}\frac{I_n}{\bar{I}}\log\frac{I_n}{\bar{I}} \tag{36}$$

where T_s is the Theil measure in region s. It can also be written in additive form across measures for each region

$$T = \sum_{s=1}^{S} T_s \frac{N_s\,\bar{I}_s}{N\,\bar{I}} + \sum_{s=1}^{S}\frac{N_s\,\bar{I}_s}{N\,\bar{I}}\log\frac{I_s}{\bar{I}}. \tag{37}$$

The two terms in the right hand side of Equation (37) are within and between Theil measures.

Table 6. Effects of Hukou Elimination on Regional and National Gini Coefficients and Theil Measures of Inequality Using A Model with Distribution of Efficiencies within Regions.

Regional divide in model variant and data in column headings				
Urban–rural	Rich–poor	EC–CW	EC–WD	E–C–W
1 Regional and national Gini coefficients				
Gini coefficients before Hukou removal				
$G_{\mathrm{U}} = 0.3200$	$G_{\mathrm{R}} = 0.4094$	$G_{\mathrm{EC}} = 0.4119$	$G_{\mathrm{EC}} = 0.4186$	$G_{\mathrm{E}} = 0.4226$
$G_{\mathrm{R}} = 0.3500$	$G_{\mathrm{P}} = 0.2030$	$G_{\mathrm{CW}} = 0.2040$	$G_{\mathrm{WD}} = 0.1600$	$G_{\mathrm{C}} = 0.1440$
				$G_{\mathrm{W}} = 0.1600$
$G = 0.4600$	$G = 0.4600$	$G = 0.4600$	$G = 0.4600$	$G = 0.4600$
Gini coefficients after Hukou removal				
$G_{\mathrm{U}} = 0.357188$	$G_{\mathrm{R}} = 0.423638$	$G_{\mathrm{EC}} = 0.397921$	$G_{\mathrm{EC}} = 0.224439$	$G_{\mathrm{E}} = 0.254828$
$G_{\mathrm{R}} = 0.368747$	$G_{\mathrm{P}} = 0.169154$	$G_{\mathrm{CW}} = 0.112343$	$G_{\mathrm{WD}} = 0.181277$	$G_{\mathrm{C}} = 0.189328$
				$G_{\mathrm{W}} = 0.113556$
$G = 0.370538$	$G = 0.373878$	$G = 0.347042$	$G = 0.229139$	$G = 0.259639$

(Continued)

Table 6. (*Continued*)

Regional divide in model variant and data in column headings				
Urban–rural	Rich–poor	EC–CW	EC–WD	E–C–W
2 Theil measures of inequality				
Theil measures before Hukou removal				
$T_{\mathrm{U}} = 0.171850$	$T_{\mathrm{R}} = 0.291932$	$T_{\mathrm{EC}} = 0.285837$	$T_{\mathrm{EC}} = 0.173458$	$T_{\mathrm{E}} = 0.122389$
$T_{\mathrm{R}} = 0.203112$	$T_{\mathrm{P}} = 0.0788384$	$T_{\mathrm{CW}} = 0.102791$	$T_{\mathrm{WD}} = -0.118314$	$T_{\mathrm{C}} = -0.075694$
				$T_{\mathrm{W}} = -0.070750$
$T^{\mathrm{l}}_{\mathrm{w}} = 0.185971$	$T_{\mathrm{w}} = 0.1961614$	$T_{\mathrm{w}} = 0.212126$	$T_{\mathrm{w}} = 0.123277$	$T_{\mathrm{w}} = 0.043293$
$T^{\mathrm{l}}_{\mathrm{b}} = 0.064300$	$T_{\mathrm{b}} = 0.084295$	$T_{\mathrm{b}} = 0.065886$	$T_{\mathrm{b}} = 0.035041$	$T_{\mathrm{b}} = 0.069722$
$T = 0.250270$	$T = 0.280437$	$T = 0.278010$	$T = 0.158318$	$T = 0.113015$
Theil measures after Hukou removal				
$T_{\mathrm{U}} = 0.224532$	$T_{\mathrm{R}} = 0.315792$	$T_{\mathrm{EC}} = 0.256137$	$T_{\mathrm{EC}} = 0.096899$	$T_{\mathrm{E}} = 0.136043$
$T_{\mathrm{R}} = 0.234890$	$T_{\mathrm{R}} = 0.063729$	$T_{\mathrm{CW}} = 0.025677$	$T_{\mathrm{WD}} = 0.077606$	$T_{\mathrm{C}} = 0.083320$
				$T_{\mathrm{W}} = 0.025021$
$T^{\mathrm{l}}_{\mathrm{w}} = 0.226873$	$T_{\mathrm{w}} = 0.233030$	$T_{\mathrm{w}} = 0.186570$	$T_{\mathrm{w}} = 0.094884$	$T_{\mathrm{w}} = 0.115340$
$T^{\mathrm{l}}_{\mathrm{b}} = 0.009734$	$T_{\mathrm{b}} = 0.010959$	$T_{\mathrm{b}} = 0.010367$	$T_{\mathrm{b}} = 0.002850$	$T_{\mathrm{b}} = 0.010194$
$T = 0.236607$	$T = 0.243990$	$T = 0.196937$	$T = 0.097735$	$T = 0.125534$

T_{w} refers to the Theil measure for within region inequality, T_{b} to between region inequality.

The majority of inequality is within region inequality, and this increases as Hukou restrictions are removed. Across region inequality falls sharply reducing national inequality. This is made clear by the decomposition results reported in Table 6.

5. Conclusions and Remarks

This chapter presents numerical simulation results on the impacts of the Hukou system of permanent registration on income inequality and labour migration in China. Our aim is to use numerical modelling to help assess the contribution of various policy and other factors in China in either contributing to or retarding inequality in China. We use three model variants to develop results. The base model is taken from Hamillon and Whalley (1984), who evaluated the impacts of cross country immigration restrictions on global inequality, and we examine four 2-region cases, a 3-region case, a 6-region case, and 31-province case in which alternative groupings and divisions in Chinese data are used. A second house model captures the effects of higher urban house prices in retarding rural labour movement in to urban areas. A final extension allows for productivity differences across individuals within each region in the model and explores income inequality impacts for five model cases.

All model results point towards a significant role for the Hukou system in preventing movement of labour which moves the Chinese economy towards a more equal distribution of income. There effects are smaller in the second two-model variants than in the first. We see all models as a simplification from a more complex reality, and so we do not aim to provide firm point estimates of impact. But the themes of results seem clear, and in addition we offer a simulation approach which can also be used for the analysis of mobility restrictions in other economies in ways different from existing econometric literature which focus on the determinants of mobility more than impacts on overall equality and efficiency.

References

Bramall, C. and Jones, M. E. (1993). Rural Income Inequality in China Since 1978, *Journal of Peasant Studies*, 21: 41–70.

Chang, G. H. (2002). The Cause and Cure of China's Widening Income Disparity. Department of Economics, University of Toledo. http://unr.edu/homepage/elliottp/cer134chang.pdf.

Chen, J. (1996). Regional Income Inequality and Economic Growth in China, *Journal of Comparative Economics*, 22: 141–164.

China State Statistics Bureau (2002). China Statistical Yearbook. China Statistical Press, Beijing.

Hamilton, B. and J. Whalley (1984). Efficiency and Distributional Implications of Global Restrictions on Labour Mobility, *Journal of Development Economics*, 14: 61–75.

Hare, Denise, West and A. Loraine (1999). Spatial Patterns in China's Rural Industrial Growth and Prospects for Alleviation of Regional Income Inequality, *Journal of Comparative Economics*, 27: 475–497.

Jalan, Jyotsna, Ravallion and Martin (1998). Transient Poverty in Post-reform Rural China, 1952–1985, *Journal of Comparative Economics*, 26: 338–357.

Kanbur, Ravi, Zhang and Xiaobo (1999). Which Regional Inequality? The Evolution of Rural–Urban and Inland–Coastal Inequality in China from 1983 to 1995, *Journal of Comparative Economics*, 27: 686–701.

Liu, Aying, Yao, Shujie, Zhang and Zongyi (2001). Convergence of China's Regional Income: 1952–97, *Chinese Economic Review*, 12: 243–358.

Lyons and Thomas P. (1991). Interprovincial Disparities in China: Output and Consumption, 1952–1987, *Economic Development and Cultural Change*, 39: 471–506.

Rozelle and Scott (1994). Rural Industrialization and Increasing Inequality: Emerging Patterns in China's Reforming Economy, *Journal of Comparative Economics*, 19: 362–391.

Sen and Amartya (1973). On Economic Inequality. Oxford University Press.

Shi, Xinzheng, Sicular, Terry, Zhao and Yaohui (2002). Analyzing Urban–Rural Income Inequality in China. Paper Presented at the International Symposium on Equality and Social Justice in Transitional China, Beijing, July 11–12.

Theil (1967). Economics and Information Theory. North-Holland, Amsterdam.

Tsui and Kai-yeun (1991). China's Regional Inequality, 1952–1985, *Journal of Comparative Economics*, 15: 1–21.

Tsui and Kai-yuen (1993). Decomposition of China's Regional Inequalities, *Journal of Comparative Economics*, 17: 600–627.

Tsui and Kai-yuen (1996). Economic Reform and Interprovincial Inequality in China, *Journal of Development Economics*, 50: 353–368.

Tsui and Kai-yuen (1998a). Factor Decomposition of Chinese Rural Income Inequality: New Methodology, Empirical Findings, and Policy Implications, *Journal of Comparative Economics*, 26: 502–528.

Tsui and Kai-yuen (1998b). Trends and Inequalities of Rural Welfare in China: Evidence from Rural Households in Guangdong and Sichuan, *Journal of Comparative Economics*, 26: 783–804.

Wang, Feng, Zuo and Xuejin (1999). Inside China's Cities: Institutional Barriers and Opportunities for Urban Migrants, *American Economic Review: AEA Papers and Proceedings*, 89(2): 276–280.

Zhao and Yaohui (1999). Leaving the Countryside: Rural-to-Urban Migration Decisions in China, *American Economic Review*, 890: 281–286.

CHINESE EXPERIENCE WITH GLOBAL 3G STANDARD-SETTING*

John Whalley
University of Western Ontario, NBER and CIGI

Weimin Zhou
University of Western Ontario, CIGI and
Shanghai Jiaotong University (SJTU)

Xiaopeng An
China Center for Information Industry Development

China's growth strategy as set out in the 11th 5-Year plan in 2005 called for the upgrading of product quality, the development of an innovation society, and reduced reliance on foreign intellectual property with high license fees. Consistent with this policy, China has been involved in recent years with the development of a Chinese standard in third-generation (3G) mobile phone technology, both in negotiating the standard and seeing it through to commercialization. Most recently the allocation of licenses has been announced. In this standards-setting experience, a group of Chinese enterprises, with government support, joined forces to pursue this opportunity. This report documents Chinese standard-setting efforts from proposal submission to ITU to the current large-scale trial network deployment in China and overseas trial network operations in South Korea. We discuss the underlying objectives for this initiative, evaluate its effectiveness, and assess its broader implications for Chinese development policy.

We both document and evaluate the China's experience with 3G international standards, both in terms of initial international negotiation of the standard in the ITU in 2000, and also its subsequent commercialization. This is the first case of a developing country both originating and successfully negotiating a telecommunications standard and this experience raises issues for China's future development strategy based on product and process upgrading in manufacturing. We argue that while precedent setting from an international negotiating point of view, the experience has thus far is

*We are grateful to The Center for International Governance Innovation (CIGI) for support of this work, and to Yao Li, Xin Xian, Shunming Zhang, Yuezhou Cai, Yan Dong, and Huifang Tian for comments. The first author also acknowledges the support of the Liebnitz Foundation, Germany, under their "*Reinventing Europe*" programme.

unproven commercially. But the lessons learned will benefit future related efforts in follow-on technologies if similar Chinese efforts are made.

The issues that have come with the commercialization of the Chinese TD-SCDMA standard have involved competition from parallel and emerging technologies such as WCDMA, CDMA2000 and WiMAX, financing, technology development and finding qualified labor. These are all beyond the process involved in the initial international standard negotiation. The lessons from this experience would seem to be that negotiating a standard in international bodies is one thing; seeing it through to profitable commercialization is another. Commercialization is thus far largely in the Chinese market, but if the reduction in foreign license fees is large enough this can financially justify the effort.

1. Introduction

China's growth strategy as set out in the 11th 5-Year plan in 2005 called for the upgrading of product quality, the development of an innovation society, and reduced reliance on foreign intellectual property with high license fees. This policy is reflected in Chinese efforts in global standard-setting for the third-generation (3G) of a wireless telecommunications standard. China successfully negotiated the adoption of its own standard (TD-SCDMA) in the International Telecommunications Union in 2000, and Chinese enterprises have been engaged in its commercial development since. Most recently, the allocation of licenses has been announced. Here we both document and evaluate this experience.

In the history of wireless technology development, only the EU, the United States, Japan and, more recently, South Korea have participated in standards-setting activities. This is the first time that a non-OECD/developing country has participated in this firm-concentrated and highly R&D-intensive area of activity. The Chinese third-generation wireless standard (3G) is named TD-SCDMA (Time Division–Synchronous Code Division Multiple Access), and since its initial submission as a response to a call for proposal by the International Telecommunications Union (ITU) in 1997 it has received substantial support from the Chinese government in both negotiation and commercialization. More recently, after eight years of development, TD-SCDMA has moved on from a concept to a fledging industry. A large-scale trial network covering ten Chinese cities is now under way and 28 more cities are planned to be covered. In overseas markets, a trial network is in service in South Korea and a commercial network has been put into use in Italy.

China's stated motives for entering this highly firm-concentrated and R&D-intensive area are to reduce the high license fees to foreign IPR holders, but also to put in place the basis for future standards development.

Taking a broader view, this standard-setting initiative is part of a growth strategy of creating an "innovative economy" covering education, R&D, and mega projects delineated in an important state directive *The Guidelines on National Medium- and Long-term Program for Science and Technology Development 2006–2020.*

For China, the main challenge posed by this standard-setting experience has come in finding successful commercialization. The appropriate commercialization strategy for the government to follow is unclear from literature. The TD-SCDMA standard has yet to receive wide deployment in either domestic or overseas markets. It has also been hard to follow other countries' experience due to difference in technology capacity, market position and other factors.

Another challenge has been the emergence of an alternative system which claims to be an advance on all the current major wireless systems including TD-SCDMA — the IP-based WiMAX system which has higher data rate transmission and lower costs with wider coverage per base station. A problem, therefore, is that even if the commercialization succeeds, it may soon be overtaken by WiMAX. Critics of WiMAX argue that it is poor in mobility which is supposedly an important feature of wireless mobile system. Nevertheless, WiMAX has already been deployed by Sprint and Clearwire in the US, and SK in Korea.

Thus challenges remain for China in further commercialization and market deployment of the TD-SCDMA standard. But China's commitment to its deployment, especially in the domestic market, is unwavering. They claim that the trial TD-SCDMA network covering ten cities is currently the largest network in the world, and with learning-by-doing the technology is expected to improve further and has the potential to overtake the other two standards which are currently more advanced in technological maturity. In May, 2008, the Chinese government carried out the restructuring of telecommunications operators[1] which was widely thought to precede the final issuance of repeatedly postponed 3G licenses. Recently the

[1]On May, 2008, the Ministry of Industry and Information Technology, the National Development and Reform Commission and the Ministry of Finance, PRC, jointly issued a statement of "Notification of Furthering Telecommunications Industry Reform" and announced a restructuring plan for the country's telecom operators. According to the restructuring plan, the existing six Chinese operators will be changed into the pattern of "3+1", with China Unicom's CDMA business incorporated into China Telecom to form a new China Telecom company, China Unicom's GSM network included into China Netcom to form a new China Unicom, China Tietong incorporated into China Mobile to form a new China Mobile company, and China Satcom remaining unchanged.

Minister for Industry and Information Technology has announced how the third-generation (3G) mobile telecom licenses will be issued to Chinese operators at the beginning of 2009.[2]

In the sections that follow, we document Chinese participation both in the global 3G standards negotiation and the subsequent commercialization of China's homegrown standard. This is followed by a brief exploration of its future given the competitive emergence of an alternative technology WiMAX. We then evaluate the likely success of this initiative in both the short and long term, stressing the challenges in commercialization beyond the negotiation of the standard.

2. Chinese 3G Global Standards Negotiation

We first discuss the successful negotiation of the Chinese 3G standard in the International Telecommunications Union (ITU) in 2000, the first such standard negotiated by a developing country. The 3G negotiation was different from the standard-setting experience in the first and second generations of wireless standards where nation or regional entities (i.e. the European Union) played a dominant role. The third generation was initiated and harmonized by ITU, a UN agency.[3]

The ITU follows a voting policy on its decisions of equal weight per country (i.e. each member country has one vote). In recent decades the ITU has shifted from an emphasis on spectrum allocation to one on standards-setting which is reflected in increased amounts of money spent on the ITU — over a quarter of a billion US dollars in 2003–2004 (Ryan, 2005).

Ryan (2005) argues that the ITU's legal authority in the international telecommunications area has been diluted by regional and sovereign

---

[2]See page 25 for details.

[3]As Ryan (2005) notes, the ITU was established in 1865 as an European organization from the outset. For more than 50 years, European powers controlled the ITU (originally called the International Telegraph Union), and its voting system favoured the largest European countries. After its involvement in World War II, the United States began to take a more active interest in participating in international telecommunications standardization efforts through the United Nations. However, the United States still viewed the ITU as a hindrance to the management of radio communications (through what it viewed as the ITU's imposition of state-imposed policies versus its own laissez-faire policies and ideals). The United States only appointed temporary ambassadors to attend ITU radio conferences. In the 1980s, however, the ITU began to loosen its policies, which had favoured PTTs and similar government organizations. Although US participation in the ITU is still tentative, the level of US involvement has continued to gain momentum ever since.

interests to the point that it mostly plays a voluntary consensus-seeking function. The ITU lacks legal structure (it does not have a permanent charter), and it is possible for it to dissolve at any point if member countries no longer perceive value in the consensus-building approach that it offers. Thus the ITU must achieve consensus in standards negotiation; its standards must be found to be useful, and, in spite of its long standing existence, it must constantly demonstrate its value to its members to survive.

The acceptance of the TD-SCDMA standard as one of the major 3G global standards by the ITU in 2000 was a great success for China. It is the only one successfully negotiated by a developing country in ITU.[4]

The process leading to this outcome began in April, 1997, when the ITU called for proposals for new Radio Transmission Technology (RTT) for IMT-2000 (the dubbed 3G standard) from around the world. Specifications for evaluation were also provided. This call reflected new emerging technology beyond the existing 2G standards adopted in wireless industry and the perceived need to codify and move forward with an agreed infrastructure standard.

At the start, China only formed an evaluation team headed by Shumin Cao[5] and registered it with the ITU. But this facilitated China gaining knowledge of global standard setting mechanisms (e.g. In October, Shumin Cao attended an ETSI[6] conference with other Chinese representatives, the first time that Chinese representatives attended such an event).

Later in 1998 the Ministry of Post and Telecommunications (MPT, the precursor of the now Ministry of Industry and Information Technology, MIIT) and the Ministry of Science and Technology (MOST) jointly held a conference and solicited suggestions for a Chinese 3G candidate proposal.

---

[4]Suttmeier *et al.* (2006) note that "during the tenth five-year period (2001–2005), MOST (Ministry of Science and Technology) sponsored a series of "megaprojects" in conjunction with its "863" High-Technology Program. Among the megaprojects was a major initiative on standards titled "Key Technical Standards Project," which included R&D support for WAPI, AVS, 3G telephony, optical networks, IP technologies, and other standards that have gained prominence. Reportedly, some 29 standards have resulted from this work, of which 13 have been submitted to ISO, IEC, or ITU for consideration". So far, only TD-SCDMA has been accepted by the international Standard Setting Organizations.

[5]Shumin Cao was head of the China 3G evaluation team; Chair of Working Group 5 of Task Group 8/1 of ITU; also head of the first Chinese telecommunications standardization organization — China Wireless Telecommunication Standard (CWTS) — which was established in April, 1999, and joined 3GPP in 1999.

[6]ETSI stands for The European Telecommunications Standards Institute, a standard-setting organization of EU.

During the conference, Xu Guanghan, a senior consultant of Telecom Science and Technology Research Institute, made a presentation on the SCDMA standard and put forward the framework of TD-SCDMA. Among all the proposals, TD-SCDMA was selected to be the sole proposal of Chinese candidate for IMT-2000.

Intensive work on drafting the standard followed. On 29th, June 1998 — the last day set by the ITU for the submission of International Mobile Telecommunication 2000 (IMT-2000) standards — the China Academy of Telecom Technology (CATT), representing China as an ITU member, submitted the proposal to Geneva which was signed by the Minister and two Vice-Ministers of the Ministry of Information Industry (MII). At the deadline for proposal submissions, the ITU had received 16 proposals from North America, Europe, Japan and China. Except for the TD-SCDMA proposal, all of the other proposals were from developed countries — the United States, European Union, Japan and South Korea.

During the period of proposal evaluation that followed, a Chinese evaluation team played an active role in promoting TD-SCDMA. Suttmeier *et al.* (2006) cite an unpublished Chinese standard strategy paper in 2004 which argued that the Chinese government recognized that special measures were necessary to enhance China's effective participation in international standard-setting bodies. These included the development of expert teams who had the language ability, better knowledge of how international standardization bodies operate, and technical expertise to effectively represent China in these forums.

The IMT-2000 conference initially had the objective of consolidating all the submitted CDMA-based proposals into a single standard, and the submitted TDD proposals into another standard. This objective changed, however, as work progressed. Its final recommendation (ITU 2000a) was for five different radio interfaces to be adopted for terrestrial IMT-2000 services: The first was equivalent to the Euro-Japanese Wideband CDMA solution, the second was the US. CDMA2000 solution, the third was the Euro–China TDMA/CDMA hybrid (TD-SCDMA), the fourth was the evolution of D-AMPS and GSM to EDGE,[7] and the fifth was ETSI's DECT.[8] The first three of these were effectively 3G standards.

[7]EDGE (Enhanced Data rates for GSM Evolution) is an extension on top of 2G standards — GSM and D-AMPS. Though recognized as part of ITU's 3G definition, EDGE is most frequently referred to as 2.75G. Its potential for further upgrading is limited compared to the first three.

[8]DECT or Digital Enhanced Cordless Telecommunications (formerly Digital European Cordless Telephone) is an ETSI standard for digital portable phones (cordless home

China had pursued other similar special measures in other standard-setting efforts such as WAPI, but had not succeeded in gaining acceptance of their standards by international Standard-Setting Organizations (SSOs). One of the elements explaining TD-SCDMA's success was Siemens' support for TD-SCDMA as a joint partner of this technology[9] and China's maneuvering in the negotiation as a third standard to be adopted alongside the EU-backed and USA-backed standards. However, whether the TD-SCDMA negotiation success represents an isolated event or whether it reflects a negotiating strategy that can also be used in the future is still unclear.

After a third Generation Partnership Project (3GPP) standardization body was established in 1998, 3GPP took on the task of detailed drafting of standards,[10] ITU shifted towards setting global frameworks for requirements, spectrum allocations, interworking, and other matters. On 16th March, 2001, at the 11th plenary session of the 3GPP, all technical specifications of the TD-SCDMA standard were accepted by 3GPP and were included in 3GPP's Release 4.[11] Though it was claimed by Chinese press to be a breakthrough indicating that TD-SCDMA had been accepted not only by the ITU but also by an industry alliance of operators and vendors, its concrete impact awaited its commercialization.

3. TD-SCDMA Commercialization

The commercialization of the Chinese 3G standard has proved to be challenging. The issues with commercializing the Chinese TD-SCDMA standard have been competition from parallel standards and new emerging technologies such as WCDMA, CDMA2000 and WiMAX financing, technology development, and finding qualified labor. These all which

telephones), commonly used for domestic or corporate purposes. DECT can also be used for wireless broadband data transfers. DECT is recognized by the ITU as fulfilling the IMT-2000 requirements and thus qualifies as a 3G system.

[9]In order to promote a uniform standard WCDMA in Europe, the Siemens proposed TD-CDMA was abandoned, which led Siemens to switch their support to the Chinese TD-SCDMA.

[10]3GPP is dominated by ETSI — an EU standards-setting organization — and only develops the 3G standards that are based on the UTRA related proposals. Therefore a sister project named Third Generation Partnership Project 2 (3GPP2) was established in January 1999 to facilitate the development of 3G standards for the cdma2000 related proposals.

[11]3GPP standards are structured as *Releases*, discussion of 3GPP thus frequently refers to the functionality in one release or another. Release 4 originally called the Release 2000 which added features including an all-IP Core Network.

go beyond the process involved in the initial international standard negotiation. But these issues were already becoming evident at the time negotiation was completed. At the time CATT (China Academy of Telecom Technology) submitted the Chinese proposal to ITU, China's leading telecommunications equipment manufacturers such as Huawei and ZTE were only producing SPC exchanges, and had little experience in producing other wireless telecommunications equipment. By comparison, the other two IMT-2000 standards adopted had already been worked on for over ten years and equipment was available.[12]

3.1. *Technology leading to TD-SCDMA*

TD-SCDMA derives from SCDMA, an indigenous wireless access technology, developed by Beijing Xinwei Telecom Technology Inc., a joint venture of CATT (China Academy of Telecom Technology) and Cwill (standing for Chinese Wireless Local Loop, founded by two Chinese working in the United States) founded in 1995. As a government agency, CATT has received RMB 15 million from the National Key Technologies R&D Program under the Ministry of Science and Technology (MOST) and RMB 10 million from the State Planning Committee (precedent of National Development and Reform Commission) for SCDMA development.[13] Cwill mainly provided technology. In 1998, SCDMA successfully passed a state-level pilot network test, which not only helped its subsequent deployment[14] but also won support from Chinese government for the technology embedded in the new standard–TD-SCDMA.

3.1.1. *Datang telecom/datang mobile and early commercialization activity*

The commercialization of the TD-SCDMA standard has centrally involved Datang Technology Co. Ltd., an enterprise associated with the Ministry

---

[12]The ITU had been developing IMT-2000 since 1985, previously termed Future Public Land Mobile Telephone System (FPLMTS). In ETSI, the European standardization body, UMTS standardization started in 1990 when a sub-technical committee SMG5 was established.

[13]See Nan Qiao, Yixuan Lu, TD-SCDMA Legend, http://www.cww.net.cn/zhuanti/td_scdma/default.html.

[14]The indigenous nature of SCDMA also helped in it gaining government support. For example, in January, 2004, MII released a Notice for Trial Deployment of Telecommunication Infrastructure in Selected Suburban Areas, in which it stipulated that SCDMA be the only suggested wireless access system. http://www.mii.gov.cn/art/2005/12/29/art_992_4083_1.html.

of Information Industry at that time. Originally, development of the standard was taken up by Xin Wei, a joint venture of Datang Telecom Technology Co., Ltd. and Cwill. But at the end of 1999, when TD-SCDMA became a possible standard likely to be accepted by the ITU and with commercialization on the agenda, a difference of opinion occurred between Datang and Xin Wei over the likelihood of successful commercialization. Finally the decision was taken to transfer TD-SCDMA development to Datang.

Datang had another ally in commercializing TD-SCDMA — Siemens, and the proposed standard was based on a combination of technologies from Datang and Siemens. Their cooperation started in 1998 and focused on the development of TSM, an interim format bridging from the earlier 2G standard GSM to TD-SCDMA. Between 1998 and 2003, Siemens invested US$ 70 million in TD-SCDMA development[15] and set up joint laboratories with Datang in Beijing, Munich, Berlin, Milan, Vienna and London. At one point, over 500 Siemens researchers were working in China. However, in view of the rapid development of rival technologies, Datang decided to move to a new LCR (Low Chip Rate) format which is in hindsight proved to be the right decision. However, this change was resisted by Siemens and led to the breakup of their partnership in 2003. Soon afterwards, on August 29th, 2003, Siemens and Huawei announced the creation of a new joint venture between them with a joint investment of US$ 100 million focusing on TD-SCDMA development in which Siemens owned 51% of the equity.

Datang also began a restructuring during the commercialization of TD-SCDMA. In 2002, to speed up commercialization, Datang Mobile was spun off from Datang Telecom Technology Co. specifically to focus on this task. Its research team is comprised of three parts, one was its mother company in Beijing, i.e. those who had been conducting TD-SCDMA development, another one was from Shanghai which had engaged in GSM development, the other one was from Xi'an which had been involved in WCDMA development. By the first half of 2003, the whole research team comprised 130 researchers.

Since its establishment, Datang Mobile has faced the challenge of shortage of financial resources for commercial development.[16] According

[15]Managing Director of Siemens' Mobile Network provided this data in a press conference, http://www.c-fol.net/news/content/12/20030901092516.html.

[16]A complex system like a wireless standard development requires substantial investment. GSM was mainly promoted by operators, and manufacturers only started

to 21st *Century Economy Report* (2007), the funds required by Datang Mobile for regular operations were approximately RMB 400 million (about US$ 50 million) annually. Their gap between expenditures and income was around RMB 200 million (US$ 25 million) each year, and so subsidies and policy loans to Datang Moible became an important source of funding. It also noted that in 2003, Datang Mobile got over RMB 200 million (about US$ 25 million) from MII and NDRC in form of special funds. After that, loans of RMB 200–300 million had been provided annually. Again in 2007, to facilitate equipment manufacturing, the China Development Bank provided a 15-year interest free loan of RMB 4.6 billion (about US$ 580 million) to Datang Mobile which took the form of a TD-SCDMA Olympic and Commercialization Network Engineering Construction project.[17]

In addition, Datang Mobile's shareholding company — Datang Telecom Technology Co. — also received financial support from various banks at later stages of TD-SCDMA commercialization. For example, in 2007, Datang Telecom Technology Co. received RMB 30 billion (about US$ 4 billion) from the China Development Bank of which the interest rate involved was about two-thirds of the commercial interest rate.[18]

3.1.2. *Spectrum allocation*

The commercialization of the TD-SCDMA standard has also been integrally involved with spectrum allocation. This has yet to be finalized as licenses are yet to be issued, but the decisions made in this area will influence the success of the commercialization.

At the beginning of TD-SCDMA commercialization, few operators or manufacturers except Datang were interested in this area. Even domestic wireless manufacturers, such as Huawei and ZET who had invested in WCDMA and CDMA2000, did not carry out any R&D on TD-SCDMA. To improve market confidence, MII released a 3G spectrum allocation plan on October 23rd, 2002, 155 MHz for TD-SCDMA (a core spectrum range

to invest in the development of GSM after ten operators promised to purchase their products. As a manufacturing company, Qualcomm gained wide support from the American government, operators and cooperated with South Korea in the rollout of the first CDMA network.

[17] See "4.6 Billion RMB of Interest-free Loan Finalized, Datang Mobile's Fund Demand 3 Billion RMB This Year", *21st Century Economy Report*, April 26, 2007, website: http://tech.sina.com.cn/t/2007-04-26/09181484475.shtml.

[18] *The Finance and Economy Times* (Cai Jing Shi Bao). See http://www.cww.net.cn/article/html/2007/6/297/66244.html.

of 55M [1880∼1920M, 2010∼2025M] plus an extra spectrum range of 100M [2300∼2400M]), 60MHz for WCDMA and 60MHz for CDMA2000 which are both in the core spectrum range assigned by ITU for IMT-2000.

Currently, TD-SCDMA technology only uses the core spectrum range of 55M. The extra 100MHz assigned is thought to be advantageous for the global deployment of TD-SCDMA because this range is not used by WCDMA and CDMA2000. This means that the TD-SCDMA standard can be a complementary extension network when operators face spectrum shortage. An outcome of the spectrum allocation favoring TD-SCDMA deployment in the future was that Siemens announced a follow-up investment of €50 million for the development of TD-SCDMA the following day of the 3G spectrum allocation announcement.[19]

Spectrum was assigned free to operators in China during the 1G and 2G deployment, but as a scarce resource, it had been allocated by auction in most of the OECD countries. In the 3G spectrum allocation, auction was again widely adopted in the EU, which contributed large revenue to the governments, especially in EU (see Table 1). However, in the countries where the 3G market did not develop as quickly as in the 2G era, auction license fees became a financial burden for operators. Some argued that there had been extensive overbidding and miscalculation of the licenses' value. Several firms handed back their 3G licenses or postponed the setting up of their 3G infrastructure, completely writing off the license fee in their accounts (Gruber, 2005). In the second half of 2006, the 3G market in Europe started to grow, and whether auction prices were reasonable or not from a long-term point of view is now an open question. For now, however, in light of the European experience the Chinese government would adopt spectrum auctions in the 3G deployment. This will facilitate commercialization of the TD-SCDMA standard, but at a cost to the Chinese government of revenues.

3.1.3. *TD-SCDMA industry alliance*

Another element in the commercialization of the TD-SCDMA standard has been the TD-SCDMA Industry Alliance. In view of the complexity and difficulties of TD-SCDMA commercialization, and also partly due to the breakdown in cooperation between Datang Mobile and Siemens, under the

[19]Nan Qiao, Yixuan Lu, "TD-SCDMA Legend" http://www.cww.net.cn/zhuanti/td_scdma/default.html.

Table 1. 3G Mobile Licensing in Selected Countries.

Country	No. of licenses	Mobile incumbents	Method	Date awarded	Total amount paid (US$ million)
Austria	6	4	Auction	November 2000	618
Belgium	4	3	Auction	March 2001	421.2
Denmark	4	3	Sealed bid auction	September 2001	472
Finland	4	3	Beauty contest	March 1999	Nominal
France	4	3	Beauty contest + fee	July 2001	553 each, plus 1% of revenue
Germany	6	4	Auction	August 2000	46,140
Greece	3	3	Hybrid	July 2001	414
Italy	5	4	Hybrid	October 2000	10,180
Netherlands	5	5	Auction	July 2000	500
Norway	4	2	Beauty contest + fee	November 2000	88
Spain	4	3	Beauty contest + fee	March 2000	480
Sweden	4	3	Beauty contest	December 2000	Nominal
Switzerland	4	2	Auction	December 2000	119.8
UK	5	4	Auction	April 2000	35,400

Sources: Johannes Bauer and Yu-Chieh Lin (2004).

call of three Chinese government agencies — MII, NDRC and MOST, an industry alliance for TD-SCDMA was established in October, 2002, with eight Chinese manufacturers as the initiators including the four leaders in Chinese telecommunications infrastructure equipment manufacturing industry (Datang Mobile, Huawei, ZTE and Potevio). In 2003, six more domestic companies joined. Four of them were chip developers who aimed to rapidly improve chip design and manufacturing capacity which had also been a weak link in the Chinese wireless industry chain.

The alliance also received public subsidies from the government. For example, in 2004, MII, NDRC and MOST jointly set up the *TD-SCDMA R&D and Industrialization Project* investing RMB 768 million (about US$ 100 million) to support the TD-SCDMA Industry Alliance.[20]

As in the case of other technologies such as WAPI (WLAN Authentication and Privacy Infrastructure), the TD-SCDMA alliance

[20]See http://it.sohu.com/20070703/n250884236.shtml.

intended to gain support from foreign companies by encouraging them to partner with Chinese domestic manufacturers. This was expected to speed up the development of TD-SCDMA, and also to facilitate the acceptance of TD-SCDMA products by the world market. In turn, foreign companies were also to gain profile in the Chinese market.

In the infrastructure equipment manufacturing sector, four partnering organizations involving Chinese companies and leading foreign firms have been established. They are Datang Mobile and Alcatel (Alcatel received 3% ownership of Datang Mobile for RMB 300 million, with additional RMB 100 million for R&D in antenna development), Huawei and Siemens (they created a joint venture called TD Tech Ltd. in which Siemens has 51% ownership), ZTE and Ericsson (they reached a strategic cooperative agreement), and Potevio and Nokia (they created a joint venture in October, 2005 in which Potevio has 51% ownership).

In the terminal sector, chip development has been a weak link for Chinese terminal manufacturing. To strengthen this link, three state enterprises — T3G, Commit and Datang — were established during 2002 and 2003. T3G was established by Philips (in 2006, Philips Semiconductors was spun off from Royal Philips and became NXP), Datang Mobile and Samsung in January, 2003. Motorola later joined as a new shareholder in 2005. Commit was established in 2002 by 17 leading domestic and foreign manufacturers, including Potevio, the CATT (China Academy of Telecom Technology), Texas Instruments (China), Nokia (China) Investment Co. Limited and LG Electronics, Inc. Commit later went bankrupt due to a shortage of funding in the first half of 2008.

Another related chip development company is Spectrum Communications, established by overseas Chinese Ping Wu in Silicon Valley in April, 2001. This company has grown rapidly over the past few years, and now has R&D centers and branch offices both in the US (Silicon Valley, San Diego) and in China (Shanghai, Beijing, Shenzhen). In 2003, it successfully developed the SC6600B, the world's first GSM/GPRS (2.5G) baseband chip with integrated multimedia and power management functions. A year later, it developed the SC8800A, the world's first single chip dual-mode TD-SCDMA/GSM baseband chip. After that, a series of upgraded chips were developed before February, 2007. Eight versions were released, the latest one being SC8800H, a single chip solution which supports HSDPA/TD-SCDMA/GSM/GPRS/EDGE. As stated on Spreadtrum's homepage, its products support a broad range of wireless communications standards, including GSM, GPRS, EDGE, TD-SCDMA, W-CDMA, HSDPA, HSUPA, as well as future standards of wireless communication. Its financial operations have also been successful. In June, 2007, it completed an initial public offering and listing on NASDAQ stock market exchange. In January, 2008, it acquired US-based RFIC design company — Quorum Systems, Inc. According to a Merrill Lynch report released in October, 2006, Spreadtrum had 10% of China GSM/GPRS market.[21] These developments implied both that access to the TD-SCDMA standard could grow through these chip developments and also that competitive technologies were also more widely available.

Recently, China Mobile joined this alliance in July, 2008, being the first operator member of this alliance. China Mobile is the best performing telecommunications operator in China, its participation is expected to have influential impact on the TD-SCDMA commercialization.

So far, leveraging Chinese government's support, the TD-SCDMA alliance has covered the whole industry chain including operating, manufacturing (e.g. chipset, platform software, handset, antenna, infrastructure equipment and testing instruments) and sales channeling. Currently, the alliance has 58 members, providing technologies over the whole industry chain of TD-SCDMA system which includes (Appendix A shows the first 40 members as of 2006).

3.1.4. *TD-SCDMA forum*

A further related element of the commercialization of TD-SCDMA has been the TD-SCDMA Forum. Similar to other promoting bodies of wireless systems such as GSM Association (GSMA) and CDMA Development Group (CDG),[22] TD-SCDMA Forum was established to promote the technology after it was approved by ITU as one of IMT-2000 standards. These organizations include both manufacturers and operators from all over the world and aim to provide a platform for all stakeholders to communicate and coordinate. Among the co-founders of the Forum were China Mobile, China Telecom, China Unicom, Datang, Huawei, Motorola, Nortel and Siemens. The Forum was accepted by the 3GPP (3rd Generation

[21] The other major competitors on China market are MTK (40%), TI (23%), ADI (10%), Philips (6%), Agere (4%), Inflieon (3%), in brackets are their market shares. See http://www.eefocus.com/html/06-12/120_1166415091.shtml.

[22] GSMA was committed to promoting GSM and WCDMA which are both dominantly sponsored by EU telecommunications standard-setting organization, ETSI. CDG was established to promote CDMA and the evolved 3G version, CDMA 2000.

Partnership Project) as its MRP (Market Representative Partner) in 2005. The Forum also signed partnership agreements with major international telecom organizations, such as GSMA and CDG. The Forum now has over 300 members from more than 30 countries, covering all sectors of the value chain, namely standardization agents, operators, vendors, content providers, financial and investment organizations and research institutions.

However, compared with the GSMA and CDG bodies, its global impact is still small. For example, the GSMA was founded in 1987 by 15 operators committed to the joint development of a cross border digital system for mobile communications. Now it is a global trade association representing more than 740 GSM mobile Operator Members across 219 countries and territories around the world. In addition, over 210 Associate Members (manufacturers and suppliers) support the Association's Initiatives as key partners (GSM Association Brochure 2008).

The CDMA Development Group (CDG), founded in December 1993, is an international consortium of companies who have joined together to speed the adoption and evolution of 3G CDMA wireless systems around the world. The CDG comprises of CDMA service providers and manufacturers, application developers and content providers. Currently it has 108 members, including 42 Cellular, PCS and WLL Operators Members, 14 Subscriber Unit Vendors, five Test Equipment Vendors, 17 Other Telecommunications Companies, 17 Network Equipment Vendors, nine Application Developers, three Reciprocal Members and one Affiliate Member (CDMA Development Group official website).

3.1.5. *Tests and national standard entitlement*

No other wireless standard has undergone as many tests as TD-SCDMA in its commercialization. To speed up the development and maturation of the TD-SCDMA standard, under the government support, manufacturers and operators have conducted a series of laboratory and fields tests.

These tests have helped uncover problems with the TD-SCDMA technology. For example, *China Daily* reported in mid-2005 that during the terminal laboratory test period, the result of a series of tests showed that the TD-SCDMA terminal performance was not satisfactory due to poor chip function, and interoperability was also not up to expectations. After further tests, in September 2005 MII released test results for TD-SCDMA, claiming that the Project has achieved remarkable breakthroughs proving the feasibility of an independent TD-SCDMA network deployment. With the initial success of the laboratory tests, on January 20th, 2006, TD-SCDMA was announced to be the national standard for China's wireless telecommunications industry. The other two standards were announced to be industry standards half a year later.

After the laboratory tests, more field tests were then carried out. In December 2005, an "Application Demo Network Experiment" was initiated aiming to test the field performance of TD-SCDMA terminals. Six Chinese operators participated in this test. In February 2006, a "TD-SCDMA Scale Network Technology Application Experiment" was initiated under the joint guidance of NDRC, MOST and MII to test the field performance of the TD-SCDMA application in the presence of large traffic load and intensive coverage. It covered Beijing, Shanghai, Qingdao, Xiamen and Baoding. China Telecom, Chine Netcom and China Mobile constructed test networks in Shanghai/Baoding, Beijing/Qingdao and Xiamen respectively. In mid-November, the tests reached a "user friendly" stage during which thousands of users were invited to test the network performance. Costs for these tests were fully covered by the Chinese government.

3.1.6. *TD-SCDMA Large-scale commercialization trial network*

A large-scale TD-SCDMA commercialization trial network deployment began with China Mobile's tender invitation in April, 2007. This covered eight cities. China Telecom and China Netcom also took their deployment to two other cities (see Appendix B).

China Mobile finalized its selection of infrastructure vendors for the rollout of its TD-SCDMA test network in eight cities under a tender amounting to RMB 26.7 billion. According to Ovum and Jean-Charles Doineau (2007), ZTE was to win about 45.5% of the tender. Ericsson, which is the OEM for ZTE's technology, were to be granted 1.2% of the total contract. Following ZTE, Datang was to win about 27.5% of the contract. Alcatel-Lucent, through its Alcatel Shanghai Bell subsidiary as a partner of Datang was to own a subset of this contract. Potevio was granted 2.7%. Finally TD Tech (a joint venture between Huawei and Seimens) won about 13.8% of the contract.[23] In sum, the major winners were those who had invested substantially in the R&D and subsequently gained better performance in the previous TD-SCDMA network tests.

[23]See http://www.telecomasia.net/article.php?id_article=4226.

Meanwhile, China Mobile began testing more than 20 types of TD-SCDMA-compliant handsets in eight cities in China. The result of the testing helped China Mobile come to the company's procurement decisions for later terminal tender. Units being tested include those from ZTE, Samsung Electronics and LG Electronics, which passed initial tests covering core technologies. In December, 2007, China Mobile announced its plan to purchase 30,000–40,000 TD-SCDMA-based 3G phones via public bidding to begin tests on the third-generation network. China Mobile finally purchased 60,000 TD-SCDMA mobile phones, more than its original plan. The tender winners were New Postcom[24] (21,000), Lenovo (10,500), Hisense (10,500), ZTE (9,000), Samsung (4,500) and LG (4,500). Spreadtrum became the chip supplier to New Postcom and Lenovo, MTK to Hisense and ZTE, T3G to Samsung. A second round of terminal tender followed right afterwards and was won by Huawei, Yulong, Huali and Panda. Spreadtrum, Datang and T3G were the main chip suppliers again.

Infrastructure network construction was largely finished by January, 2008. On April 1st, 2008, China Mobile initiated commercial service based on the TD-SCDMA trial network in eight cities. Voice traffic service charges are lower than current service and there are some subsidies to handset purchaser. Also the new feature of video phone service is added. The current trial network can accommodate 8 million customers, almost 95% of the current GPRS customers in China, the largest 3G network in the world. China Mobile CEO, Wang Jianzhou, clarified that the first round of investment totaled RMB 15 billion (over US$ 2 billion). China Netcom and China Unicom had also set up a TD-SCDMA network in another two cities which was taken over by China Mobile later.

According to ChinaTechNews.com released on August 21st, 2008,[25] the Ministry of Industry and Information Technology of China has announced its approval of China Mobile's nationwide commercial trial network based on TD-SCDMA technology. The approval notification says that network construction of TD-SCDMA should be accelerated and a specific plan should be made to ensure smooth progress of the construction. It requires

[24]New Postcom is a private telecommunications company established in 2005. Based on OEM contract, it has formed strategic partnership with Datang. In the tender of the wireless infrastructure equipment initiated by China Mobile, New Postcom won 5.61%. In this terminal tender, it won about 35%; as a new enterprise, this achievement is really impressive and surprising.

[25]http://www.chinatechnews.com/2008/08/21/7313-china-mobile-will-start-nationwide-td-scdma-commercial-trial-in-china/.

China Mobile to do careful research and produce a follow-up network development plan to promote the industrialization of TD-SCDMA. At the same time, the company should contact and communicate with the relevant equipment suppliers, terminal channel suppliers and users to jointly promote the growth of the TD-SCDMA industry chain. The approval also provides an overview of the frequency of the TD-SCDMA network, the number field and the development of terminals.

Recently, China Mobile announced that the coverage of the TD-SCDMA trial would expand by another 28 cities, totaling 38 cities which demonstrates higher data service demand in a survey conducted by China Mobile.[26] The second round network construction plan features the compatibility with 2G network (GSM) and shared core network which can be used in 2G (i.e. GSM), 3G (i.e. TD-SCDMA and its evolved versions such as HSDPA), and even TD-LTE (i.e. 4G version of TD-SCDMA).

Currently, the deployed network infrastructure has been upgraded to a high-speed downlink packet access (HSDPA) — an enhanced version. Datang Mobile is working toward an evolution of TD-SCDMA that will eventually incorporate LTE (Long-Term Evolution).[27]

3.1.7. *Overseas exploration*

Although the test network deployment is in China, a first overseas test network was also established in South Korea. In April, 2007, a TD-SCDMA trial network costing US$ 58 million entered service in South Korea. This network was jointly constructed by Datang, ZTE (base station) and Samsung (core network). SK Telecom also announced their intention of investing equivalent to around RMB 50 million in R&D for TD-SCDMA. This initial success in overseas market testing reflects previous cooperation between the two countries in telecommunication technology development. More importantly, it also implies further cooperation possibilities between the two. As South Korea is advanced in 3G applications, its cooperation will provide a good test environment for TD-SCDMA and subsequently the two parties can both make further progress.[28]

The first commercial TD-SCDMA network in Europe, an outcome of the cooperation between POTEVIO and Italian MYWAVE, was put into

[26] http://www.cww.net.cn/news/html/2008/8/28/2008828934332452.html.

[27] http://electronics.ihs.com/news/2008/abi-tdscdma-china.htm. Also for details about evolution of TD-SCDMA, please see the section.

[28] Some reports stated that small-scale TD-SCDMA test networks have also been constructed in France and Romania.

use on September 23rd, 2008.[29] In previous July, POTEVIO and MYWAVE jointly announced the construction of a TD-SCDMA trial network. On July 18th, 2008, the two companies signed a cooperating agreement and the construction began on September 1st, 2008. As the first commercial TD-SCDMA network in Europe, the net had been put into use on September 12th, providing R4 and HSDPA service. According to TD-SCDMA Industry Alliance, the two companies are carrying out negotiation for the next network construction. POTEVIO said it would offer the updated products for MYWAVE and further its cooperation with other foreign carriers to ship TD-SCDMA into Europe.

3.1.8. *Licensing*

Chinese 3G licensing has been postponed repeatedly due to uncertainty over the maturity of the new Chinese standard and potential industry restructuring to occur along with the licensing process. With the onset of the recent financial crisis in November 2008, the Chinese government announced an economic stimulus plan which included telecommunications investment. In this context, the Minister for Industry and Information Technology announced on December 12th, 2008, that third-generation (3G) mobile telecom licenses were to be issued to Chinese operators at the beginning of 2009. China Mobile will receive a license for TD-SCDMA, China Unicom and China Telecom will receive licenses for WCDMA and CDMA2000 respectively. To avoid duplication in the infrastructure investment, the Minister emphasized the necessity of agreement between the operators on infrastructure sharing before licensing.[30] In January 2009, the licensing was finally carried out.

4. Evaluation of China's 3G Experience

Evaluating the success of China's efforts at TD-SCDMA standards negotiation and subsequent commercialization and the lessons it offers

---

[29]TD-SCDMA Industry Alliance announced "POTEVIO Set up The First Commercial TD-SCDMA Network in Europe" <http://www.tdscdma-alliance.org/english/news/list.asp?id=4440>.

[30]See "China to Award 3G Licenses in Early 2009", *China Economic Review*, December 15, 2008. The move is expected to generate US$ 29.1 billion in investments from the three operators. According to telecom consultancy BDA China, the operators have already budgeted for US$ 43.4 billion in 3G-related capital expenditure, including projects completed this year or planned for completion over the next three years.

for similar further efforts is difficult since at this stage commercialization remains in progress. It seems fair to say that this process has been slower than at first thought, but it is still possible that major financial rewards will result. It is too early to tell. As we mention in our introduction, China's motives for engaging in this highly firm-concentrated and R&D-intensive area are to reduce license fees paid to foreign IPR holders; to set the basis for standards development; and more broadly, to integrate the standard setting initiatives into the state strategy of creating an "innovative economy." And even if for now commercialization is largely restricted to the Chinese market the first of these objectives will likely be met.

4.1. *License fee reduction*

It is still too early to assess the benefits of license fee reduction from TD-SCDMA. One can claim that even if restricted to the Chinese market, a 3G Chinese standard sharply reducing foreign royalties will pay for itself. But Kennedy (2006) claims that Chinese government has drafted two dozen industry and national standards in information technology (including TD-SCDMA), but the gains from these to China have been small. Chinese industry has not collected significant royalties from these standards, cross licensing of standards between Chinese and foreign companies has yet to occur, foreign firms have not turned over their intellectual property as a result of these standards, and products based upon these standards have met with only limited commercial success.

Not unusual for standard-setting initiatives, a well-defined licensing mechanism has not yet been established for TD-SCDMA. Some Standard-Setting Organizations (SSOs) require a member whose proprietary technology is included in the standard to license that technology to other members of the SSO either free of charge or on "fair, reasonable or non-discriminatory (FRND)" terms. But the definition of FRND is unclear. Some of the key companies involved have rejected the idea of licensing on FRND terms. For example, Qualcomm overtly only negotiates with other companies on a one-to-one basis. As an outcome of its aggressive IPR policy, Qualcomm has gained a substantial amount of revenue from licensing. Table 2 shows that Qualcomm's licensing and royalty fees account for approximately 30% of its total revenues and about twice its R&D expenses.

In the still short history of standard-setting competition in the wireless telecommunications industry since 1980s, a series of disputes have occurred between different standard sponsors and not unusually, political power is involved in the resolution. For example, during the development of GSM

Table 2. Qualcomm's Patent Revenue and Other Selected Financial Items (US$ million).

	2002	2003	2004	2005	2006	2007
Revenues	2920	3847	4880	5673	7526	8871
– Licensing and royalty fees	835	985	1366	1929	2750	3106
– Equipment and Services	2086	2862	3514	3744	4776	5765
Research and development	440	523	720	1011	1538	1829
Net income	360	827	1720	2143	2470	3303

Source: Qualcomm Co. annual reports.

standard, according to a Memorandum of Understanding (MoU) released in 1987 by a large group of European telecoms operators, GSM was to become an open, non-proprietary standard with open interface requiring IPR coordination.[31] But Motorola, as the owner of nearly 60 of the 130 patents involved in GSM at that time, refused to cooperate in cross-licensing. Instead it chose to engage in cross-licensing only with leading companies that also had valuable patent licenses to offer in return. EU PTTs then announced that no contract would be granted to those who refused to cooperate in cross-licensing (Gessler, 2002).

In the 1990s, a well-known example of cross-licensing is between Qualcomm, Ericsson and Nokia. Qualcomm stated it was willing to grant licenses for CDMA2000, but not for the other CDMA proposals unless some conditions were met. Ericsson stated that they were prepared to grant licenses to any standard, provided that all essential IPRs pertaining to the standards would be licensed reciprocally, i.e. no other company would refuse to license their IPR (Gessler, 2002).[32]

[31] Gessler (2002) stated that "The terms for IPR cooperation are less that clear than with wording like "low cost licensing" or "cross-licensing". But the practice in Europe at that time with state-owned national monopolies, telecoms R&D was tied to quasi-vertical integration so that not much was patented, and patents were freely licensed among (related) suppliers and component producers.

[32] Gessler (2002) also noted the political and diplomatic efforts involved in the dispute. He stated that "Qualcomm communicated their position to the US government, which resulted in actions from the United States such as in the TransAtlantic Business Dialogues (TABD). Qualcomm's contention was that the adoption of WCDMA as a global standard would create technical barriers to trade for US industry, and that Ericsson's IPR claims were part of such a strategy. Their lobbying with the US government resulted, among other things, in a letter from Secretary of State Madeleine Albright to the European Commission, in which US demands on free and fair trade were presented. The actions from the US government were in part also triggered by an early decision by the European Commission to require European countries to license IMT-2000 bands to an ETSI standard (WCDMA). This was interpreted as a violation of World

A more recent example is between Qualcomm and Nokia. The two companies had been at odds since April, 2007, when the previous licensing agreement between them expired. Nokia said it should pay a lower royalty rate than it had been because it controlled important technology with its own patents.

Settling such disputes has been very costly in terms of both money and time. In the case of Qualcomm vs. Ericsson, it took the two companies three years to settle the patent lawsuit finally. As part of the settlement, Ericsson gains access to San Diego-based Qualcomm's mobile phone technology and agrees to buy its mobile phone infrastructure division for an undisclosed amount of money.[33] The settlement between Qualcomm and Nokia was reached in July, 2008. Mark McKechnie, an industry analyst with American Technology Research, estimated that the settlement could mean as much as $400 million in royalties paid to Qualcomm next year based on a calculation of 2 percent royalty fee on the 100 million phones equipped with Qualcomm technology that it seemed likely to sell though a 5 percent royalty arrangement is more typical in the industry. Meanwhile, the resolution could also save Qualcomm as much as $200 million a year in legal bills.[34]

Similar licensing disputes may occur with the commercialization of Chinese TD-SCDMA. This so-called indigenous Chinese standard has a substantial portion of foreign patents[35] which increase the difficulty of licensing fees negotiation given the IPR policies adopted by some incumbent companies such as Qualcomm.

In the absence of an established licensing mechanism,[36] an option for Chinese manufacturers and others to cope with blocking patents (e.g. system for code division multi-access communication) is to pursue

---

Trade Organization (WTO) agreements, and interaction between the United States and Europe led to a reinterpretation of the agreements. As a result, the European Commission was careful to point out that it did not mandate the ETSI UMTS standards for all operators bidding for 3G licenses in Europe. Instead they left the licensing procedures up to the different member states of the EU, and recommended that no standards requirements be put on the licensees."

[33]See "Ericsson, Qualcomm Resolve Wireless Phone Dispute" http://findarticles.com/p/articles/mi_hb5553/is_/ai_n22392652.

[34]See "Qualcomm and Nokia Settle Patent Lawsuit", http://www.iht.com/articles/2008/07/24/technology/qualcomm.php.

[35]It is hard to estimate the number of patents in the TD-SCDMA. It varies widely in different reports, ranging from 7% to over 50% for China share in the total patents.

[36]One of the criteria of entering TD-SCDMA Industry Alliance is the sharing of IPRs which is not accepted by the incumbent wholly-owned foreign companies.

alternative technologies to replace the blocking one. Both South Korea and China are currently making efforts to develop OFDM (orthogonal frequency-division multiplexing), MIMO (multiple input and multiple output) and other technologies, hoping they can be used to avoid the blocking patent. The aim is to break Qualcomm's monopoly position in the CDMA-based standard competition era.

4.1.1. *Learning as the basis for future standards development*

The experience of developing TD-SCDMA, and its success or failure, will also help build up China's know-how in negotiation and commercialization of standardization in general, which, in turn, will benefit further standard-setting activities such as 4G. This has also been an objective of Chinese policy in this area.

It is not clear which strategy that China adopted secured the success in the negotiation in ITU. One view is that Chinese negotiators maneuvered by allying with the US and EU and leveraging its promising domestic market. This tactic might not be repeatable in the follow-on standard-setting negotiations, since concrete alliances need to be established based on joint technology cooperation and common commercial interests.

Also Chinese TD-SCDMA commercialization up to now remains unproven, although clearly lessons have been learned for future commercialization. One issue is the repeatedly postponed licensing which is sometimes attributed to the less than satisfactory testing performance of TD-SCDMA trial network to allow more time for the TD-SCDMA to improve its performance. This strategy of improving the success probability of a homegrown standard by facilitating its earlier deployment in the domestic market or naming it the national standard is a common practice in almost all of the countries involved in global standards setting. According to Gessler (2002)'s detailed description of the 2G and 3G standardization process in the United States and EU, it seems that though the United States claims to apply a "hands-off" approach in standards selection, the United States may have delayed the 2G licensing in order to give CDMA (which is sponsored mainly by an American company — Qualcomm) some time to improve its technical performance. In the 3G deployment, the European Commission overtly requires European countries to license IMT-2000 bands to an ETSI standard (WCDMA). Gandal, Salant and Waverman (2003) notes that "the reason for their favoring WCDMA is possibly due to the fact that it puts them on even footing with CDMA 2G equipment suppliers and operators whereas CDMA2000 would give the latter a competitive cost and time to market advantage".

The benefits of first deployment in the market are that, the first system deployed is expected to improve faster than the followers based on learning-by-doing (Arthur, 1989; Cowan, 1991; Bassanini and Dosi, 1998). Another benefit of first-mover strategy is gaining higher penetration in market expanding and leveraging network development[37] (Katz and Shapiro, 1985) especially if there is no compatibility between different standard-based networks. In the case of wireless systems competition, incompatibilities can be offset by interconnection agreements between different standard network operators (Gandal, Salant and Waverman, 2003; Laffont and Tirole, 2000), but telecommunications operators still have to agree on interconnection fees based on customer base size and network performance and can maneuver on the terms of acceptance or extension of agreements. In the case of the interconnection where network effects do not play an important role, a first mover advantage can reflect Stackelberg leader-follower competition (Stackelberg, 1934).

Another element of benefit from the prospective success of TD-SCDMA is its ability to produce applications programs specific to the TD-SCDMA system. The network effect deriving from complementary products also helps tilt the market in favor of TD-SCDMA. Currently mobile TV based on a Chinese indigenous application program called CMMD is applied to TD-SCDMA standard.[38] If more programs specific for TD-SCDMA could be developed TD-SCDMA could have a better chance to win the market.

An important factor affecting the operators' selection of standard is its potential of continual improvement where transmission data rate is the key performance indicator. All sponsors of the three main 3G standards (WCDMA, CDMA2000 and TD-SCDMA) have devoted themselves to continual evolution following the market deployment of their respective systems. The original transmission speed specified by ITU (i.e. 144 kbit/s for vehicular high speed; 384 kbit/s for medium speed; and 2048 kbit/s for indoor) is too low to realize multi-media data service function. More recent versions of the major standards[39] (including TD-SCDMA) can support up

[37]Network effects refer to the phenomenon whereby a service/good becomes more valuable as more people use it, thereby encouraging ever-increasing numbers of adopters.
[38]Another application applied to TD-SCDMA standard is video phone.
[39]The evolution version of WCDMA is HSDPA, HSUPA; CDMA2000 EV-DO, CDMA2000 EV-DV for CDMA2000; China also has developed its enhanced version of TD-SCDMA-HSDPA.

to 14 Mbit/s at which speed some multi-media application programs can be better applied.

In the longer term, all these three major 3G standards are moving towards LTE (Long Term Evolution) version, aiming to compete against an alternative wireless system which is developed from IP-based technology — WiMAX.[40] The evolution of TD-SCDMA to LTE version is supported not only by the current TD-SCDMA Industry Alliance but also, more important, by a key state R&D project named Future Technologies for Universal Radio Environment (FuTURE).[41]

The FuTURE project was initiated in 2001. Its main objective was to develop beyond 3G/4G systems. Meanwhile, it also aims to help TD-SCDMA smoothly evolve to a fourth generation technology. Liu *et al.* (2006) presented an evolution map from TD-SCDMA to future terrestrial universal radio environment (FuTURE) TDD in China. They suggest the evolution will occur in four phases: low chip rate (LCR), high-speed downlink/uplink packet access (HSxPA)/TD-SCDMA EV 1x, long-term evolution (LTE) TDD, and FuTURE beyond 3G TDD. Currently HSxPA has already been commercialized and used by TD-SCDMA. The evolution to LTE version is on the way as a pilot demonstration network, which claims to meet the ITU's IMT-Advanced (i.e. dubbed 4G) specifications (i.e. 100 Mbit/s for high mobility and 1 Gbit/s for low mobility), has already been successfully launched in Shanghai's Changning District at a cost of RMB 150 million (about US$ 19.2 million).[42]

---

[40]WiMAX has emerged as one of the leading standards designed to deliver both fixed and mobile wireless broadband, backed by a consortium led by Intel, Motorola and others. Currently, it is supported by the IEEE, the global computing body, and ITU. This system is based on TCP/IP — the technology that underpins the internet. Technically it is called IEEE 802.16 standard and designed to deliver IP data traffic at multiple megabits per second over a range of several kilometers. As its designed speed is much higher than that of the original version of the three dedicated network-based systems (i.e. WCDMA, CDMA2000 and TD-SCDMA), WiMAX sponsors claim it a 4G system. However, in order to facilitate the commercialization and earlier market deployment, it applied to ITU for a 3G standard status and gained the approval on October 19, 2007. At present, it is already being deployed by Sprint and Clearwire in the US and SK in Korea.

[41]It is a National High-Tech R&D Program labeled "863" FuTURE project. For details about China's Science and Technology system, please see Whalley and Zhou (2007).

[42]China claims that this pilot network is the world's first 4G mobile communications trial system. Before that in September, 2006, Samsung Electronics claimed at the annual Samsung 4G Forum in Jeju Island that it had developed the world's first demonstration of 4G mobile technology whose data rates have reached 100Mbps on a vehicle moving at up to 60 kms/hr, with cell-to-cell handover, and up to 1Gbps inside the exhibition area.

Another lesson from the TD-SCDMA development is how to find partners for technology development. The breakup of cooperation between Datang Mobile and Siemens as well as the bankruptcy of Commit demonstrate the difficulty of finding appropriate partners. Maybe a result of the difficulty in partnering with western MNCs is that during the execution of FuTURE project cooperation is more likely found to be with South Korean and Japanese companies based on their common interests in lowering licensing fees. For example, a memorandum was signed by four standard setting organizations from China, Japan and South Korea in 2002 which specifically identified 4G as a focus cooperation area.[43]

A further element of potential benefit from TD-SCDMA is its potential evolution over time as a lower cost standard, and the learning from this experience for other possible technologies. Kennedy (2006) discusses WAPI (Wired Authentication and Privacy Infrastructure) as a new national technical standards strategy that could lead to conflict with the international community over standard-setting. Other related initiatives include product tracking and remote identification (RFID), digital audio-video coding and decoding (AVS), the formats of audio-video disc players (EVD), and digital home networking and next-generation internet protocols. Standards-setting for the high-technology industry in China is clearly a complex matter. At the same time, China's standards strategy is part of the wider technology development strategy being followed.

4.1.2. *Standards as part of the national strategy of an "innovative economy"*

China's activity in international standards-setting has to be seen as part of China's wider development policy. This is based on ever deeper integration into the global economy, continual product quality upgrading to underpin export growth, and reduced reliance on expensive foreign IPR. In part the source of these policies lie with China's so-called "technology trap".

[43]On November 7, 2002, four standard organizations in China, Japan and Korea (namely, CCSA, ARIB, TTC and TTA) signed a MoU for mutual cooperation in the growth and development of the information and telecommunication industries of the three countries. They agreed to mutually exchange views and information on the status of the industries and to contribute to the works of standard organizations of regional and global levels through cooperation (ITU, 2003). In mid-2004, South Korea, Japan and China were reported to be collaborating on 4G technology.

According to Kennedy (2006), despite progress on a number of dimensions of technological development (including a manned space program), China is still dealing with problems which are seen as a frustrating indigenous technological progress. China's patenting activity is seen as disappointing and Chinese products rarely incorporate indigenous intellectual property. In turn, China's remarkable growth as a center of manufacturing and emergence as a significant exporter of high-technology goods still involves dependence on foreign technologies that has seemingly deepened following China's accession to the WTO.

China's determination to escape from a "technology trap" is best reflected in *The Guidelines on National Medium- and Long-term Program for Science and Technology Development 2006–2020* released in early 2006. Next generation of wireless broadband technology (e.g. 3G, beyond 3G/4G, etc.) is listed as one of the most important technology development projects — Mega Projects. In addition to the general targets of technology development such as patent accumulation and talent cultivation, 3G and other indigenous standards setting initiatives are expected to contribute to the establishment of vertically-integrated industry chains and support for enterprises instead of government research institutes is to play a dominant role in the indigenous innovation system.[44]

These strategies respond to China's widely recognized weaknesses in domestic science and technology development, including low enterprise R&D and government research institutes with limited connections to industry. Given the increasingly aggressive IPR strategy adopted by western countries, China is seen as needing to shift from a high degree of dependence on foreign technology to the development of indigenous technology.

Western scholars usually argue that these weaknesses are fundamentally attributed to China's weak IPRs regime (e.g. Kennedy, 2006). Though recently a small but growing number of papers have challenged the validity of current patent systems and advocate change (e.g. Farrell and Shapiro, 2008), the Chinese government seems to prefer to gradually strengthen the existing regime. The implementation of this involves other related areas such as antitrust law and venture capital market development.

A point of debate between indigenous standard support and new technology development is that with increasing returns due to network

[44]There is no official document release for 3G development strategy, but one for another indigenous Chinese standard RFID was released in 2006 titled *China RFID Technology Policy White Paper*. These two points were stated clearly in that official document.

effects or learning-by-doing, the market might adopt an inferior technology (Arthur, 1989; Cowan, 1991; Shy, 2001; David, 1985; etc.). Some counter arguments have been made. For example, Cowan (1991) emphasized that it was difficult to identify the best technology for those with uncertain merits. Bassanini and Dosi (1998) proposed that in a market with rapid technological change, no predictions can be made by simply looking at theoretical considerations alone. Thus with high uncertainty of outcomes in this industry, Chinese government support for TD-SCDMA should perhaps remain as cautious and gradual.[45]

Therefore, China's strategy for extensive government involvement in standards-setting and its commercialization, as in the case of TD-SCDMA, thus need to also be seen relative to these constraints and the broader objectives of development policy. But whether effective commercialization can be achieved at reasonable cost, and how easy further international negotiation will be remains unproven. At the end of the day TD-SCDMA may remain for a whole as largely a standard for the domestic Chinese market on which future development can build, and it can evolve into a 4G standard. The saving in foreign license fees may still justify the financial investment in the standard, and if this is so this approach may be the one used with future standards initiatives.

5. Concluding Remarks

In this chapter we discuss Chinese experience with both international negotiation of 3G standard (TD-SCDMA) and its subsequent commercialization. Our discussion is in the context of China's wider development strategy based on quality upgrading, and achieving an innovative economy. Standards-setting in telecom used to be an area reserved for developed countries. Chinese entry into this field has aroused great interests as well as doubts. In view of the highly intensive R&D investment required for standard development and deployment, together with the complicated negotiation in global standards competition, it seems to be ambitious for China to develop the TD-SCDMA initiative. And although Chinese efforts have resulted in some progress, it is still uncertain how successful the TD-SCDMA strategy will be and by how

[45]As a matter of fact, Chinese government support to TD-SCDMA during its commercialization has been cautious and gradual, which is partly reflected in the planned licensing covering three standards instead of one for TD-SCDMA.

much China can benefit. But even if its deployment is mainly in the Chinese market, the savings in foreign license fees may justify the effort.

This chpater first describes briefly the general wireless standardization process and the main Chinese and international organizations involved in 3G standards negotiation. It then provides background to Chinese major stakeholders in 3G standardization together with documentation of China's 3G experience of attempts to commercialize. This raises several issues concerning both the proposal process and commercialization as well as its prospective evolution to 4G and an alternative technology — WiMAX.

Due to the complex and evolving nature of wireless technology, it is hard to tell which standard will prove stronger in the long term. Wireless technology experts claim that each have their own advantages which can also be integrated together (Gessler, 2002). At later stages of 3G harmonization under ITU, the concept of family technology arose with multi-radio access technologies grouped together providing interconnection between them to ensure seamless roaming. The key blocking factor for technology integration is intellectual property. With learning by doing/using, China now has the possibility to take part in future market developments. But a lot of detail will determine success or failure of standard setting initiatives, such as R&D cooperation, financing mechanisms, IPR negotiation and others. The emergence of a WiMAX-based standard will likely have substantial impact on the value of the TD-SCDMA standard as well as other wireless technologies.

In conclusion, wireless standard competition is dynamic and hard to predict in outcome, and the technologies involved are extremely complex. What China has done in the 3G area may prove to be pragmatic and well-founded, but how much the intervention will cost in the long term and with what return is unclear. As the nature of high technology is high-risk and high-uncertainty, it is hard to predict whether this Chinese homegrown 3G standard will succeed or not, or how big a market share it can gain. However, even it fails to gain a significant international market share, the domestic market deployment may cover its R&D investment and infrastructure deployment. Its impact on national innovative capacity accumulation and international competitiveness can also still be substantial from a long-term point of view as long as China holds to its current development strategy.

Appendix A. TD-SCDMA Industry Alliance Members and Their Major Specialization.

Specialized areas	Company	Brief description
Chipset solution	T3G Technology Co. Ltd	State enterprise.
		Incorporated in January 2003.
		A joint venture of Philips, Datang Mobile, Samsung and Motorola. T3G's founding partners are Philips, Datang Mobile, Samsung, Motorola joined and became a new investor in January 2005.
	Commit Inc.	State enterprise.
		Established in February 2002.
		Investors consisting of 17 well-known enterprises such as China Potevio Corporation, China Academy of Telecommunications Technology (CATT), Texas Instruments (China), Nokia (China) Investment Co. Limited, LG Electronics, Inc., and Hyper Market International Limited and etc.
	China Academy of Telecommunications Technology/Datang Telecom Technology and Industry Group	State enterprise.
		Its subsidiary — China mobile, established in 2002 — is the major sponsor of TD-SCDMA. Partnering with Nortel, Alcatel, etc.
		Product coverage: chipset, terminal, base station, etc.
	Spreadtrum Communications	Established in 2001 by 17 overseas Chinese entrepreneurs, headquartered in Silicon Valley, with several branch offices in China.
	Chongqing Chongyou Information Technology Co., Ltd	State enterprise.
		Funded mainly by Chongqing Post and Telecom University, partly from government.

(*Continued*)

Appendix A. (*Continued*)

Specialized areas	Company	Brief description
	Comlent	TD-SCDMA RF IC chip, base band chip.
	RDA Microelectronics	Founded in 2004 in Shanghai with funding from the world's premier Private Equity Funds.
Software	Koretide Corporation	Established in June of 2000. 3G operating system.
	Bright Oceans Inter-Telecom Corporation	A public high-tech enterprise listed on the Shanghai Stock Exchange since 2000.
Handset	Hisense Group	Established in 1994.
	SHANGHAI DBTEL Industry Co. Ltd	Established in 1993, subsidiary of Taiwan DBTEL group.
	UTStarcom	Headquartered in the Silicon Valley in US with more than ten R&D centers in the US, China, India, Korea and Canada.
	Haier Mobile	
	China Electronics Corporation	State enterprise.
	Inventec Appliances (Shanghai) Co., Ltd.	A foreign-funded IT enterprise established in Shanghai as early as 1991.
	TCL Mobile Communication Co., Ltd	Set up in 1999.
	Legend (Beijing) Ltd.	
	Holley Group	A privately owned incorporation.
	Yulong	
	Ningbo BIRD Co., Ltd	A Chinese enterprise.
	Shanghai Simcom	The first research and development subsidiary company of SIM Technology Group, a listed company on the Hong Kong Stock Exchange.
	Longcheer Group	
Antenna	Zhongshan Tongyu	
	Xi'an Haitian Antenna Technologies Co., Ltd.	A high-tech stock enterprise.
	Andrew	Foreign company.
	MOBI	
Infrastructure Equipment	Huawei Technologies Ltd.	Partnering with Siemens Communications Group, TD Tech Ltd. was formally established on March 18, 2005, in Beijing.

(*Continued*)

Appendix A. (*Continued*)

Specialized areas	Company	Brief description
	ZTE Corporation	Founded in 1985, China's largest listed telecommunications manufacturer and wireless solutions provider.
	Potevio Corporation	State enterprise. Founded in 1980, originally called China Posts and Telecommunications Industry Corporation.
	Alcatel Shanghai Bell	The first foreign invested company with a share in China's telecommunications industry.
	Guangzhou New Postcom Equipment Co. Ltd.	
	FiberHome Technologies Group	Descendant of Wuhan Research Institute of Post and Telecommunications.
	Comba Telecom Systems	Comba listed on the Hong Kong Stock Exchange in 2003.
	ACE Achieve Group	A Chinese high-tech enterprise.
	Shenzhen CFC Network Technology Co., Ltd.	A Chinese high-tech enterprise.
	China Electronics Technology Group Corporation No 14 Institute	China Electronics Technology Group Corporation is a State Key Enterprise.
Testing Instruments	Beijing Zhong Chuang Telecom Test Co., Ltd. (ZCTT)	A Chinese high-tech enterprise, established in 1995 and went public in 2003.
	Hubei Zhongyou Technology Industry & Commerce Co., Ltd.	A Chinese high-tech enterprise.
	Beijing StarPoint Telecommunications Software Co., Ltd.	
	China Electronics Technology Group Corporation No 41 Institute	China Electronics Technology Group Corporation is a State Key Enterprise.

Notes: State Key Enterprises are directly under the leadership of the State-owned Assets Supervision and Administration Commission of the State Council (SASAC).
Sources: Yihui Lu (2007), Chinese Strategy for Developing Indigenous Standards based on the Commercialization Experience of Chinese Indigenous 3G standard, ITIS Industry Observation (in Chinese) and companies' websites.

Appendix B. 10 Cities' TD-SCDMA Infrastructure Network Construction.

		Main Suppliers					
Tenderee	City	ZTE	Datang Telecom	TD Tech	Potevio	New Postcom	Network construction progress
China Mobile	Beijing	✓					More than 2000 base stations. ZTE occupies all.
	Shanghai		✓			✓	More than 2000 base stations.
	Guangzhou		✓			✓	2116 base stations by November 2007, covering 1153 km^2.
	Shenzhen	✓		✓			About 2000 base stations.
	Tianjin	✓			✓		Completed by October 2007. ZTE and Potevio share the market.
	Shenyang	✓		✓			
	Qinhuangdao	✓			✓		Completed by August 2007. ZTE and Potevio share the market.
	Xiamen	✓		✓			About 150 base stations completed by September 2007, shared by ZTE and TD Tech.
China Telecom	Baoding		✓	✓			104 base stations in Stage 1; 100 base stations in Stage 2 (finished 92%). Tender for Stage 2: 0.82 billion RMB.
China Netcom	Qingdao	✓	✓				150 base stations in Stage 1; 300 base stations in Stage 2. Tender for Stage 2 is 0.8 billion RMB. ZTE and Datang ASB: 50% to 50%.

Source: Liu, Jing (2008) "TD-SCDMA in 10 Cities: Facing Network Test", *China Electronics News*. Available online at http://www.cena.com.cn/Article/tongxin/TDzhuanti/2008-03-14/20080314135803_6810.shtml.

References

Arthur, W. B. (1994). Increasing Returns and Path Dependence in the Economy. Ann Arbor: University of Michigan Press.

Arthur, W. B. (1989). Competing Technologies, Increasing Returns, and Lock-in by Historical Events, *Economic Journal*, 97: 642–65.

Bassanini, A. and G. Dosi (1998). Competing Technologies, International Diffusion and the Rate of Convergence to a Stable market structure, IIASA Interim Report # IR-98-012.

Bauer, J. and Y. C. Lin (2004). Transition Paths to Next-Generation Wireless Devices, Paper prepared for presentation at the 32nd Research Conference on Communication, Information and Internet Policy Arlington, VA, October 1–3, 2004.

Cowan, R. (1991). Tortoises and Hares: Choice Among Technologies of Unknown Merit, *Economic Journal*, 101: 801–814.

David, P. (1985). Clio and the Economics of QWERT, *The American Economic Review Papers and Proceedings*, 75(2): 332–337.

Farrell, J. and C. Shapiro (2008). How Strong Are Weak Patents? *American Economic Review*, 98(4): 1347–1369.

Gandal, N., D. Salant and L. Waverman (2003). Standards in Wireless Telephone Networks, *Telecommunications Policy*, 27: 325–332.

Gessler, F. (2002). The Development of Wireless Infrastructure Standards, PhD dissertation submitted to the Royal Institute of Technology, Industrial Economics and Management, Stockholm.

Katz, M. and C. Shapiro (1985). Network Externalities, Competition and Compatibility, American Economi Heinrich Freiherr von Stackelberg, 1934, Marktform und Gleichgewicht (Market Structure and Equilibrium), *Vienna. View*, 75(3): 424–440.

Kennedy, S. (2006). The Political Economy of Standards Coalitions: Explaining China's Involvement in Standards Wars. *Asia Policy*, 2: 41–62.

Laffont, J. J. and J. Tirole (2000). Competition in Telecommunications. Cambridge, Massachusettes: The MIT Press.

Liu, G., J. Zhang, P. Zhang, Y. Wang, X. Liu, and S. Li (2006). Evolution Map from TD-SCDMA to FuTURE B3G TDD, *Communications Magazine, IEEE*, 44(3): 54–61.

Qiao, N. and Y. Lu, TD-SCDMA Legend. Available at http://www.cww.net.cn/zhuanti/td_scdma/default.html.

Ryan, P. (2005). The Future of the ITU and its Standard-Setting Functions in Spectrum Management, Standards Edge: Future Generation (Sherrie Bolin, ed.) p. 341, Sheridan Books.

Shy, O. (2001). The Economics of Network Industries, Cambridge University Press.

Suttmeier, P., X. Yao and A. Tan (2006). Standards of Power? Technology, Institutions, and Politics in the Development of China's National Standards Strategy, NBR Special Report. National Bureau of Asian Research.

von Stackelberg, H. F. (1934). Marktform und Gleichgewicht (Market Structure and Equilibrium), Vienna.

Whalley, J. and W. Zhou (2007). Technology Upgrading and China's Growth Strategy to 2020, CIGI Working Paper No. 21.

Zhang, P. and L. Li (2003). Research and Demonstration on Beyond 3G Systems, The 14th IEEE 2003 International Symposium on Personal, lndoor and Mobile Radio Communication Proceedings, p. 1919.

STATE-OWNED ENTERPRISE BEHAVIOURAL RESPONSES TO TRADE REFORMS: SOME ANALYTICS AND NUMERICAL SIMULATION RESULTS USING CHINESE DATA

John Whalley* and Shunming Zhang†
University of Western Ontario, Canada
†*Xiamen University, China*

We note the absence of prior literature on analytical structures to be used for China and other economies with extensive SOEs when evaluating behavioural responses of SOEs to trade policy and other changes. This is despite both the large empirical literature discussing the productivity effects of Chinese SOE enterprise reform, and wider policy discussion of the potential impacts of various reform initiatives. We present two simple analytical formulations of SOE behaviour in response to trade policy change with the aim of investigating how traditional competitive models of enterprise behaviour can mislead when used in policy debate. One formulation centres on SOE managerial control. In this enterprise managers are politically appointed, expect any non-performing loans to be recapitalized by state banks and hence capital is centrally allocated by credit rationing. The managers are assured to maximize the size of the enterprise rather than profits since this yields maximal networking benefits to managers. This implies labour is priced at its average rather than its marginal product, and with a competitive non-manufacturing (agricultural) industry free trade is not optimal policy. The other assumes worker control of SOEs and that workers satisfice in their supply of effort to the enterprise given both fixed wage rates and enterprise employment and otherwise shirk or pursue second jobs. In this formulation the enterprise meets their budget constraint and covers costs. With leisure in the preferences of enterprise members, their leisure consumption

*Department of Economics, The University of Western Ontario (UWO); National Bureau of Economic Research, Inc. (NBER); Center for Economic Studies–Institute for Economic Research (CES-ifo, Munich) and The Centre for International Governance Innovation (CIGI, Waterloo). Address: Department of Economics, The University of Western Ontario, London Ontario N6A 5C2 Canada. Phone: (1 519) 661 - 3509. Fax: (1 519) 661 - 3666. jwhalley@uwo.ca.

†Department of Finance, Xiamen University (XMU). Address: Department of Finance, School of Economics, Xiamen University, Xiamen Fujian 361005, P.R.China. Phone: (86 592) 218 - 6165. Fax: (86 592) 218 - 6165. szhang@xmu.edu.cn.

will be implied by the satisfying behaviour of the enterprise and will be non-optimal. In both model variants, implications for trade policy are different from those of a standard competitive model, and computations using models calibrated to 2003 Chinese data suggest the differences can be large.

1. Introduction

It seems widely agreed in the literature both that the institutional structure of China's economy remains significantly different from that of the OECD economies, and that to analyze policy issues in China using simple western style neoclassical models based on household utility and firm profit maximizing behaviour can be potentially misleading. Nowhere is this more the case than in the trade policy area where simple competitive structures are now widely used to analyze a range of Chinese trade policy issues including the implications of WTO accession and China's regional trade agreements (see Ianchovichina and Martin, 2004). This is despite China's industrial sector continuing to heavily feature state- or communally-owned enterprises (national, provincial, municipal government, publicly funded research institutes, and other). Previous literature on Chinese SOEs has been mainly econometric; assessing performance, profitability and labour hiring (examples are Bigsten, Liu, and Zhang, 2002; Cull and Xu, 2003; Liu, 2002). None to our knowledge has been analytic.

Here we present two different analytical structures which we use to analyze the behavioural response of communally-owned enterprises in China to trade policy changes using numerical simulation methods. The ways that we model behavioural responses imply departures from Pareto optimality relative to competitive structures, and so free trade is not best policy if no changes are made to enterprise structure. Since our analysis also applies to other economies with SOEs, we also emphasize the analytical gap in existing literature so far as model based analyses of the behavioural response of SOEs to such policy changes, as trade liberalization is concerned. In the first of these, we assume that enterprises are managed by political appointees and that the state banking system will receive funds from the central bank to cover any non-performing loans through a recapitalization. Capital is thus centrally allocated via credit rationing, and with (effectively) no servicing costs of debt the cost of capital to management is zero. Enterprises are assumed to be entirely under managerial control, and we assume management hires labour in a competitive labour market paying the going wage. If politically appointed enterprise managers are motivated by the returns they receive from networking both with other managers and more broadly within the political structure, they will seek to maximize the size of the enterprise subject to the constraint of covering labour costs rather than profits, since larger size confers more personal network benefits on management. This, in turn, means that enterprises hire labour up to the point that the wage they pay equals the average rather than the marginal value product of labour. Typically, too much labour will be hired (relative to a Pareto optimal outcome) in free trade and a tariff will worsen things. While a simplified analytical treatment, the key for our purposes is that in such an economy with state-owned enterprises in the industrial sector and competitive enterprises elsewhere (in agriculture), labour is misallocated by freely functioning product and labour markets, and free trade need not to be the best policy.

We first show this for a case where the manufacturing sector has a single SOE and the economy is a price taker (removing monopoly power for the SOE), and then extend this to a more complex case where SOEs and competitive firms co-exist within the same sector. We use data for China for 2003 to calibrate both models. We are also able to make calculations of the cost to China of free trade in such a world and assess the welfare implications of Chinese trade policy changes in the SOE models relative to a comparable competitive model.

We then present a second formulation of SOE behaviour in which we assume that the workforce, rather than management, collectively determines output. If the enterprise budget construct is not met the enterprise will close and workers will lose their jobs. We assume that both employment and wage guarantees apply for workers, who engage in satisficing behaviour in terms of their supply of effort in meeting the enterprise budget constraint. Once enough effort is expended to generate output to meet this constraint, labour shirks or engages in moonlighting (second jobs). Capital is again assumed to be centrally allocated at no cost to the enterprise. Here the analytical point is that from the enterprise budget constraint, the effort level of workers is determined. This implies that if preferences for workers are defined over both goods and leisure, the marginal utility of leisure will not equal the marginal productivity of additional effort in SOE production. Again, a departure from Pareto optimality occurs relative to a traditional competitive structure. We also apply this formulation to 2003 Chinese data showing that free trade is again not the best policy, and also extend the model to the case where both private firms and an SOE produce manufactuing output.

Both of these formulations are only crude abstractions from the more complex and diverse world of communally-owned production units which characterize the contemporary Chinese economy. Attempts to combine these two formulations face the difficulty that only one objective function for the enterprise can easily be accommodated. Also, state-owned enterprise reform in China has proceeded in recent years in ways that imply that neither of these two simple formulations is entirely satisfactory. But given the seeming absence of prior analytical literature on the behavioural response of SOEs to trade policy change, and the implication we stress that in both model variants free trade is no longer best policy, we believe that our analyses are of wider interest given that numerical results from competitive models are now extensively cited in trade policy debute in China.

Many other potential formalizations of SOEs can probably be constructed, and we do not claim that ours are in any way definitive. However, the ones we present are simple and transparent and lead to different policy implications from the traditional competitive case. These formulations thus provide an initial base for further work, rather than definitive analyses of how Chinese SOEs actually respond to policy change in practice. Numerical simulation work on economies such as China needs to take into account more specificity of economic structure than currently appears in the literature, since simple application of conventional neoclassical models to Chinese policy reform (such as trade liberalization) can mislead.

2. The State-Owned Enterprise Sector in China

The state-owned enterprise sector in China, while declining somewhat in significance in recent years, is large, pervasive and embodies complex and interlocking forms of ownership and corporate control. Bill Gates at a recent World Economic Forum Conference in Davos (Gates, 2005) suggested that China has created a new form of capitalism with heightened dynamism, meritocratic management, and superior labour force organization. However, we tend to view China as perhaps closer to a new form of socialism or communism rather than a new form of capitalism. In this new form, central direction through planning has been removed but production units in the urban manufacturing sector remain largely communal with many diverse organizational forms in their ownership and management structure.[1]

[1]See Broadman (2001).

Competition between communally-owned units both can be and typically is aggressive, but many of these entities make losses, and the banking system has been used until recently as the mechanism for recapitalizing loss making SOEs and servicing large non-performing loans.[2] Most of these enterprises also involve politically appointed management who, in turn, seem to operate so as to maximize enterprise size for personal network (Guanxi) benefits rather than for profits. Also, individual economic behaviour in China is much more heavily reflective of group (family, village, town, county, district, province, country) interest over individual interest than is true of OECD economies.

However measured, collectively owned and controlled enterprises in China's industrial sector is substantial, even through the precise mix of public and private ownership is hard to ascertain because of the complexity of organizational form. An example of this complexity is provided by Lenovo, who recently received substantial media attention for their buy out of IBM's PC Business. Lenovo is a quoted company listed on the Hong Kong and New York exchanges which has grown quickly since its establishment in 1984. However, 43% of Lenovo's stock (a controlling interest) is held by Legend Holdings who in turn are under the control of the Chinese Academy of Natural Sciences through a 65% holding. Thus, Lenovo is effectively a communally-controlled entity even through seemingly widely discussed in the media as a private company.

Fan and Wang (2004) and Tan, Wang and Zhang (2005) (both quoted by Liu (2005)) estimate that of 1,134 listed companies in China in 2001, 61.4% are under local government control, 12.6% are under central government control, 3.4% are collectivelly controlled, and 12.8% are privately controlled, with 5.2% unaccounted for. The privately controlled component is up from 3% in 1993, but still represents a significant minority of publically listed companies. Data on ownership forms for both listed and non-listed enterprises are reported in a variety of forms in the China Statistical Yearbooks, and are also quoted by Broadman (2001). In his data, in 1999 SOEs and collective enterprises accounted for 63% of gross value-added of all enterprises and SOEs and collective enterprises accounted for 70% of 1999 industrial sector employment.

This communally-owned and managed structure while complex in its detail is clearly central to any evaluation of trade policy changes in China

[2]See Bonin and Huang (2002) who suggest that perhaps 60% of loans to the banking sector are non-performing, in contract to official estimates in the 25% range.

since the behavioural response of production units of this form will differ from that of competitive private firms as typically modelled in current numerical analyses of Chinese trade policy changes. Previous numerical modelling literature on China either adopts simple competitive assumptions as in Ianchovichina and Martin (2004), or variants of monopolistically competitive models. Modelling capturing explicit representations of SOEs behaviour is absent. As we note above, analytical literature on SOE behaviour seems not to be available and this is the gap we attempt to partially fill.

3. Models Capturing the Behavioural Response by Chinese SOEs to Trade Policy Change

Any analytical structure used to represent the behavioural response of SOEs in China to policy or other shocks (such as prices changes) will inevitably only provide an abstraction from a more complex reality. The point emphasized here is that the behavioural response of such enterprises to policy change is likely to depart from that of the competitive privately-owned firm which provides the center piece of Western neo-classical economic analysis, and analytical frameworks for the analysis of SOE behaviour are not well developed in literature.

Here we consider two alternative formulations of SOE behavioural response to trade policy change. In the first, SOEs are assumed to be under managerial control with managers politically appointed. We assume that capital is effectively centrally allocated by rationed credit via the banking system, and that all losses from non-performing loans made to state-owned enterprises are covered through a recapitalization mechanism via the state-owned banking system. As such, capital is effectively free to management but access to it is constrained via credit rationing. We then assume that enterprise managers seek to maximize personal gain from networking and political connections (Guanxi). A simple representation of this is to assume that enterprise managers seek to maximize enterprise size rather than profits. The implication is that if managers hire labour in a competitive labour market (a strong and simplifying assumption in the Chinese case) and pay labour its going wage, they will hire labour up to the point that the product price equals the average value product of labour, rather than the marginal value product as in the competitive case.

In such a world, free trade will typically not be the best policy since there is a departure from the conditions for Pareto efficiency. Average product pricing of labour by SOEs will typically imply that the SOE sector is too large relative to Pareto efficiency, and protection of this sector via trade barriers can be Pareto improving. With a more complex formulation capturing co-existence of SOEs and private firms in the manufacturing sector, if private firms provide marginal production conditions for Pareto efficiency will be satisfied at the margin but inframarginal production will be inefficiently provided by SOEs that are individually too large.

Our second formulation, in contrast, assumes that the work force rather than management collectively controls the enterprise. Workers in SOEs are assumed to have job and wage guarantees (the so-called Iron Rice Bowl system), and collectively determine output in response to product prices set on world markets (plus or minus ad valorem trade interventions). Capital is again assumed centrally allocated by credit rationing, and to be at zero cost to the enterprise with losses again covered via recapitalization through the banking system. In this case, workers collectively engage in satisficing behaviour, supplying effort to produce enough output to meet their enterprise budget constraint, but otherwise engage in shirking or moonlighting (taking second jobs). Here, with the firm budget constraint effectively determining output a fall in a product price (such as with the removal of protection) will increase output rather than reduce it as in the competitive case. Moreover, effort levels of workers are determined from the enterprise production function and the enterprise budget constraint due to the satisfycing bahaviour of workers. This implies that if leisure enters preferences for these workers the marginal valuation of leisure (reduced effort) will not equal the marginal value of extra effort in production in SOEs. Again, a departure from Pareto optimality not present in a competitive model will occur and free trade again will not provide best policy.

Our purpose in using these two simple formulations is to highlight both the differences in behaviour relative to the conventional competitive firm case and the relative lack of analytical literature in this area on which to draw in assessing behavioural response in China to trade policy change given the large presence of SOEs. Also, the implication is that in the absence of enterprise reform, free trade will typically not provide the appropriate trade policy stance.

3.1. *Managerial control models*

We consider two version of models incorporating SOE managerial enterprise control: a simple model in which we assume there is only a single state-owned enterprise in the manufacturing sector and a more complex variant in which both SOEs and competitive firms co-exist in the manufacturing sector. In both cases, we assume there are two sectors in the economy, an agricultural sector with private competitive enterprises and a manufacturing sector with either only a single SOE or a single SOEs along with a series of atomistic competitive firms.

We consider a small open economy case with two goods (agriculture and manufacturing) both consumption and produced. The world prices for the two goods (agriculture and manufacturing) are P_A^0 and P_M^0. Domestic prices are then given by world prices plus (or minus) the effect of ad valorem border measures (either import tariffs or export subsidies), i.e.

$$P_A = (1 + r_A)P_A^0 \quad \text{and} \quad P_M = (1 + r_M)P_M^0 \tag{1}$$

where P_A and P_M are domestic prices of the agricultural and manufacturing products, and r_A and r_M are agricultural and manufacturing import tariffs or export subsidies ($r_A > 0$ and $r_M > 0$ indicate tariffs, and $r_A < 0$ and $r_M < 0$ indicate export subsidies).

In the agricultural sector we assume a decreasing returns to scale production function

$$Y_A = \phi_A L_A^{\alpha_A} \tag{2}$$

where Y_A is agricultural output, L_A is labour used in agriculture, ϕ_A is a units term (scalar parameter), and $\alpha_A < 1$ is the production exponent. We assume that in this sector labour is paid its marginal product, i.e. the wage rate is

$$W_A = P_A \frac{\partial Y_A}{\partial L_A} = P_A \phi_A \alpha_A L_A^{\alpha_A - 1} \tag{3}$$

and agricultural rent is $R_A = P_A Y_A - W_A L_A$.

In the manufacturing sector the production function is

$$Y_M = \phi_M L_M^{\alpha M} \tag{4}$$

where Y_M is manufacturing output, L_M is labour used in manufacturing, ϕ_M is a units term (scalar parameter), and $\alpha_M < 1$ is the production exponent.

The use of capital by the enterprise is captured simply in the fixed factor implied in the decreasing returns production function. Capital is assumed to be allocating via centralized credit allocation through the banking system, but recipients of loans (and hence capital) expect that any servicing costs of the loan will be covered by central recapitalization of the banking system, and they can allow the loans to remain as non-performing. We assume managers of the enterprise are politically appointed and are concerned with the size of their personal network rather than profits. Thus networking benefits are assumed to be collinear the size of the enterprise they manage. Thus, in this simple model with a single SOE, labour is paid its average value product since managers maximize enterprise size measured by output Y subject to the enterprise budget constraint.

Since capital is effectively unpriced, this implies that

$$P_M Y_M = W_M L_M + R_M \tag{5}$$

where R_M is the (given) surplus to be transfered to the state by the SOE. This, in turn, implies that labour receives its average value product plus its share of required surplus rather than its marginal product. This implies that conditions for Pareto efficiency are violated, and as a result in such a model free trade will typically not be best policy.

On the demand side of the model, domestic consumption of agricultural and manufacturing output reflect utility maximizing behaviour by a single representative household, which for convenience we assume to be of Cobb-Douglas form, i.e.

$$U = X_A^{\theta_A} X_M^{\theta_M}, \quad \theta_A + \theta_M = 1 \tag{6}$$

where X_A and X_M are consumption of agricultural and manufacturing, and θ_A and θ_M are Cobb-Douglas exponents.

Household income is given by

$$I = P_A Y_A + P_M Y_M + r_A P_A^0 Z_A + r_M P_M^0 Z_M + P_A^0 Z_A^0 + P_M^0 Z_M \tag{7}$$

where $Z_A = X_A - Y_A$ and $Z_M = X_M - Y_M$ are the net trade in each product (positive indicating imports and negative indicating exports) and we assume any surplus accruing to the state is recycled to consumers as lumpsum transfers.

The household budget constraint implies that

$$I = P_A X_A + P_M X_M. \tag{8}$$

From the household budget constraint there will be balanced trade in equilibrium. If preferences are Cobb-Douglas, domestic consumption of the two goods is given by

$$X_A = \frac{\theta_A I}{P_A} \quad \text{and} \quad X_M = \frac{\theta_M I}{P_M}. \tag{9}$$

Equilibrium conditions for this structure are that then there is full employment of labour

$$L_A + L_M = L \tag{10}$$

and wage rates are equalized across the two sectors

$$W_A = W_M. \tag{11}$$

In a more complex version of this model we assume that there both SOEs and private firms operate in the manufacturing sector. Labour is assumed mobile between agriculture and manufacturing and private firms will provide the marginal source of supply of output, but SOEs will hire labour up to the point that the wage paid equals the enterprise average value product. We thus assume both an SOE and competitive firms now operate in the manufacturing sector, and designate domestic prices for each to allow for trade interventions to be firm specific. We again consider two sectors, agriculture with private competitive enterprises and manufacturing, now with both SOEs and private groups. For simplicity we consider only one SOE.

We again set the world prices as P_A^0, P_S^0 and P_P^0. Domestic prices are again assumed to be given by world prices plus (or minus) the effect of ad vlorem border measures (either import tariffs or export subsidies), i.e.

$$P_A = (1+r_A)P_A^0 \quad \text{and} \quad P_S = (1+r_S)P_S^0 \quad \text{and} \quad P_P = (1+r_P)P_P^0 \tag{12}$$

where P_A, P_S and P_P are domestic prices of the agricultural and manufacturing SOEs and private groups product, r_A, r_S and r_P are agricultural and manufacturing import tariffs and export subsidies ($r_A > 0$, $r_S > 0$ and $r_P > 0$ indicate import tariffs, and $r_A < 0$, $r_S < 0$ and $r_P < 0$ indicate export subsidies).

In the agriculture sector the production function, wage rates, and agricultural rents are the same as in the simple model, see (2) and (3).

In the manufacturing sector the production function for both SOEs and the private firms is

$$Y_m = \phi_m L_m^{\alpha_m} \quad \text{for } m = S, P \tag{13}$$

where Y_m is manufacturing output, L_m is labour used in manufacturing, ϕ_m is a units term (scalar parameter), and $\alpha_m < 1$ is the production exponent. Capital is thus treated as a fixed factor in the private firms.

In the SOE, labour is paid its average value product plus its share of any required surplus and capital is unpriced, and so

$$P_S Y_S = W_S L_S + R_S \tag{14}$$

where R_S is the (given) surplus paid to the government by the SOEs.

For the private firms in the manufacturing sector we assume that labour is paid its marginal product, i.e. the wage rate is

$$W_P = P_P \frac{\partial Y_P}{\partial L_P} = \alpha_P P_P \phi_P L_P^{\alpha_p - 1} \tag{15}$$

and rent is $R_P = P_P Y_P - W_P L_P$.

Domestic consumption of agricultural and manufacturing output again reflects utility maximizing behaviour, which for convenience we assume to be Cobb-Douglas, i.e.

$$U = X_A^{\theta_A} X_S^{\theta_S} X_P^{\theta_P}, \quad \theta_A + \theta_S + \theta_P = 1 \tag{16}$$

where X_A and X_m are consumption of agricultural and manufacturing products, and θ_A and θ_m are Cobb-Douglas exponents for $m = S, P$.

Income is now given by

$$\begin{aligned} I = {} & P_A Y_A + P_S Y_S + P_P Y_P + r_A P_A^0 Z_A + r_S P_S^0 Z_S \\ & + r_P P_P^0 Z_P + P_A^0 Z_A^0 + P_S^0 Z_S^0 + P_P^0 Z_P^0 \end{aligned} \tag{17}$$

where $Z_A = X_A - Y_A$, $Z_S = X_S - Y_S$ and $Z_P = X_P - Y_P$ are net trades (positive indicates imports and negative indicates exports) in each product. The household budget constraint is

$$I = P_A X_A + P_S X_S + P_P X_P \tag{18}$$

and domestic consumption of the three goods are given by

$$X_A = \frac{\theta_A I}{P_A} \quad \text{and} \quad X_S = \frac{\theta_S I}{P_S} \quad \text{and} \quad X_P = \frac{\theta_P I}{P_P}. \tag{19}$$

The equilibrium conditions are again that there is full employment of labour

$$L_A + L_S + L_P = L \tag{20}$$

and wage rates are equalized across the two sectors

$$W_A = W_S = W_P. \tag{21}$$

Since labour in the SOE group of firms in the manufacturing sector receives its average value product plus its share of any transferred surplus, rather than its marginal product, an equilibrium will again not satisfy conditions for Pareto optimality and free trade again need not be best policy. But now the departure from Pareto optimality involving marginal supply to the market is absent, and the allocation issue is between SOEs and private firms within manafacturing, with the SOEs too large relative to Pareto optimality.

3.2. *Worker control models*

We next consider two versions of models incorporating worker control rather than managerial control of SOEs. In the basic worker control model SOE behaviour reflects joint decision making on output by the members of each enterprise. We assume both the membership of the enterprise and the enterprise wage rate are fixed and that enterprise members must jointly meet the enterprise budget constraint. If they fail to cover costs by selling output, the enterprise is bankrupt and workers lose their jobs. Enterprise members thus collectively satisfice and meet the enterprise budget constraint by setting an effort level which yields the required output. They then either shirk or expend additional effort on second jobs. In the simple version of this model we consider only a single state-owned enterprise in the manufacturing sector and two sectors; agriculture with private competitive enterprises and manufacturing with only a single SOE. As with the managerial control model, we then consider an extension with both SOEs and private firms in manufacturing.

For this model domestic prices are again given from world prices by (1). In the agricultural sector the production function is as described in the simple managerial control model (see (2) and (3)). In the simple version of the model with only SOEs in manufacturing, the labour input in the agriculture sector is assumed fixed, so output is always same. In SOEs, the labour input available in terms of the number of manufacturing employees is also fixed, but their effort level is endogenous and hence output is endogenous. In the more complex model with mobile labour in the private sector which spend both manufacturing and agriculture, labour used in agriculture may vary.

For the manufacturing SOE sector we write the production function as

$$Y_M = \phi_M[\lambda L_M]^{\alpha_M} \tag{22}$$

where λ denotes the endogenously determined level of effort and L_M is the membership size of the enterprise. λ is effectively determined by the enterprise budget constraint since workers supply effort which satisfies the enterprise budget constraint. These activities are modelled simply as resulting in leisure consumption for SOE members and are represented by the term $(1-\lambda)L_M$. This budget constraint for the SOE in the manufacturing sector can be written as

$$P_M Y_M = W_M L_M + R_M \tag{23}$$

where R_M is again the required surplus of the enterprise transferred to the state.

On the demand side of the model, domestic consumption of agricultural and manufacturing product again reflect utility maximizing behaviour, but the model involves separately specifying the demand side behaviour of workers employed in the agricultural sector and in the SOE in manufacturing.

Income of workers employed in agricultural and manufacturing workers are

$$I_A = P_A Y_A + {}_{\gamma A}[r_A P_A^0 Z_A + T_M P_M^0 Z_M + P_A^0 Z_A^0 + P_M^0 Z_M^0] \tag{24}$$

$$I_M = P_M Y_M + {}_{\gamma M}[r_A P_A^0 Z_A + r_M P_M^0 Z_M + P_A^0 Z_A^0 + P_M^0 Z_M^0] \tag{25}$$

where γ_A and γ_M refer to the shares of the tariff revenue distributed by government to workers in agricultural and manufacturing sectors with $\gamma_A + \gamma_M = 1$. Z_A and Z_M are again the net trades in each product (positive indicates imports and negative exports).

Preferences for workers in the agricultural sector are defined only over agricultural and manufacturing goods, and leisure does not appear. We use this simplifying treatment since a departure from Pareto optimality involving leisure consumption would only occur in the manufacturing sector we were to specify leisure consumption by both types of agents. These preferences are Cobb-Douglas

$$U_A = X_{AA}^{\theta_{AA}} X_{AM}^{\theta_{AM}}, \quad \theta_{AA} + \theta_{AM} = 1. \tag{26}$$

The household budget constraint is

$$P_A X_{AA} + P_M X_{AM} = I_A. \tag{27}$$

Consumption of the two agricultural and manufacturing workers is

$$X_{AA} = \frac{\theta_{AA} I_A}{P_A} \quad \text{and} \quad X_{AM} = \frac{\theta_{AM} I_A}{P_M}. \tag{28}$$

For the consumers receiving income from working in the manufacturing sector SOE, their utility is now defined over 3 goods, consumption of agricultural and manufacturing goods and leisure, given by $(1-\lambda)L_M$. In the Cobb-Douglas case this is

$$U_M = X_{MA}^{\theta_{MA}} X_{MM}^{\theta_{MM}} [(1-\lambda)L_M]^{\theta'_{MM}}, \quad \theta_{MA} + \theta_{MM} + \theta'_{MM} = 1. \tag{29}$$

The household budget constraint is

$$P_A X_{MA} + P_M X_{MM} = I_M. \tag{30}$$

Consumption of the two agricultural and manufacturing goods by manufacturing workers is

$$X_{MA} = \frac{\theta_{MA}}{\theta_{MA} + \theta_{MM}} \frac{I_M}{P_A} \quad \text{and} \quad X_{MM} = \frac{\theta_{MM}}{\theta_{MA} + \theta_{MM}} \frac{I_M}{P_M}. \tag{31}$$

The net trades are

$$Z_A = X_{AA} + X_{MA} - Y_A \quad \text{and} \quad Z_M = X_{AM} + X_{MM} - Y_M. \tag{32}$$

With this formulation, the marginal utility of leisure will not necessarily equal the marginal value of additional effort in production, since the requirement is that the enterprise members meet their budget constraint or face loss of their jobs. This means that satisficing bahaviour (in the sense of Simon) occurs at enterprise level and determines leisure consumption of enterprise workers. Thus

$$\lambda \phi_M [\lambda L_M]^{\alpha_M - 1} \neq \theta'_{MM} X_A^{\theta_A} X_M^{\theta_M} [(1-\lambda)L_M]^{\theta'_{MM} - 1} \tag{33}$$

and this provides an additional departure from Pareto Optimality besides those conventionally associated with trade interventions (such as a tariff at the border) in a competitive model and will imply consumption of leisure inconsistent with Pareto optimality. Production will also be affected by a tariff and a changed value of λ. The additional distortion of leisure consumption relative to Pareto optimality implies that free trade again need not be the best policy since in free trade (33) will apply. A trade intervention will affect consumption and production, but may also improve matters in terms of the leisure distortion.

A equilibrium for this model is characterized by an equilibrium value of λ, and the wage rate. Given λ, the output of the SOE, and both household budget constraints are then determined. Agricultural output is determined by domestic prices and the agricultural production function given L_A Consumption by each household type can be determined and international trade is given by the difference between production and consumption of each good. Trade balance follows directly from the budget constraint. λ can be changed by trade policy interventions since domestic prices will change. If reduction in a tariff lowers domestic prices and raises output of manufacturing from the budget constraint (23), this is opposite to the behaviour in a traditional competitive model in which a lowered tariff reduces output in the protected sector. Because of the satisficing behaviour of enterprise members in terms of effort supply, the marginal utility of leisure will not necessarily equal the marginal value of extra effort in manufacturing production. The marginal valuation of leisure by workers in manufacturing on the one hand and the additional potential output from increased effort on the other will not be the same. This is a departure from Pareto optimality on the consumption and product sides which exists along with conventional distortions of trade. Free trade again need no longer be best policy because of the presence of the additional leisure distortion.

In a more complex form of the worker control model, we can again consider two sectors, agriculture but with both private competitive enterprises and private firms in manufacturing. Domestic prices are again given from world prices by (12). The agricultural sector is the same.

For the manufacturing SOE, the production function is again

$$Y_S = \phi_S[\lambda L_S]^{\alpha_S} \tag{34}$$

where λ denotes the endogenously determined level of effort, and L_S is the membership of enterprises. Labour is paid its average value product and its share of any required surplus and capital is unpriced, hence (14) holds.

For the private sector in manufacturing the production functions is

$$Y_P = \phi_P L_P^{\alpha_P} \tag{35}$$

and labour is paid its marginal product, i.e. the wage rate is given by (15).

Income of workers employed in agricultural and manufacturing workers are

$$I_A = P_AY_A + \gamma_A\big[r_AP_A^0Z_A + r_SP_S^0Z_S + r_PP_P^0Z_P + P_A^0Z_A^0 + P_S^0Z_S^0 + P_P^0Z_P^0\big] \quad (36)$$

$$I_S = P_SY_S + \gamma_S\big[r_AP_A^0Z_A + r_SP_S^0Z_S + r_PP_P^0Z_P + P_A^0Z_A^0 + P_S^0Z_S^0 + P_P^0Z_P^0\big] \quad (37)$$

$$I_A = P_PY_P + \gamma_P\big[r_AP_A^0Z_A + r_SP_S^0Z_S + r_PP_P^0Z_P + P_A^0Z_A^0 + P_S^0Z_S^0 + P_P^0Z_P^0\big] \quad (38)$$

where γ_A, γ_S and γ_P refer to the shares of the tariff revenue distributed by government to workers in agricultural and manufacturing sectors with $\gamma_A + \gamma_S + \gamma_P = 1$. Z_A, Z_S and Z_P are again the net trades in each product (positive indicates imports and negative exports).

Preferences for workers in the agricultural sector are defined only over agricultural and manufacturing goods, and leisure does not appear. We use this simplifying treatment since a departure from Pareto optimality involving leisure consumption would only occur in the manufacturing sector we were to specify leisure consumption by both types of agents. These preferences are Cobb-Douglas

$$U_A = X_{AA}^{\theta_{AA}}X_{AS}^{\theta_{AS}}X_{AP}^{\theta_{AP}}, \quad \theta_{AA} + \theta_{AS} + \theta_{AP} = 1. \quad (39)$$

The household budget constraint is

$$P_AX_{AA} + P_SX_{AS} + P_PX_{AP} = I_A. \quad (40)$$

Consumption of the two agricultural and manufacturing workers is given by

$$X_{AA} = \frac{\theta_{AA}I_A}{P_A} \quad \text{and} \quad X_{AS} = \frac{\theta_{AS}I_A}{P_S} \quad \text{and} \quad X_{AP} = \frac{\theta_{AP}I_A}{P_P}. \quad (41)$$

For the consumers receiving income from working in the manufacturing SOEs sector, their utility is now defined over three goods, consumption of agricultural and manufacturing goods and leisure, given by $(1-\lambda)L_S$. In the Cobb-Douglas case this is

$$U_S = X_{SA}^{\theta_{SA}}X_{SS}^{\theta_{SS}}[(1-\lambda)L_S]^{\theta'_{SS}}X_{SP}^{\theta_{SP}}, \quad \theta_{SA} + \theta_{SS} + \theta'_{SS} + \theta_{SP} = 1. \quad (42)$$

The household budget constraint is

$$P_A X_{SA} + P_S X_{SS} + P_P X_{SP} = I_S. \tag{43}$$

Consumption of the three agricultural and manufacturing goods by manufacturing workers is

$$X_{SA} = \frac{\theta_{SA}}{\theta_{SA} + \theta_{SS} + \theta_{SP}} \frac{I_S}{P_A} \quad \text{and} \quad X_{SS} = \frac{\theta_{SS}}{\theta_{SA} + \theta_{SS} + \theta_{SP}} \frac{I_S}{P_S} \quad \text{and}$$

$$X_{SP} = \frac{\theta_{SP}}{\theta_{SA} + \theta_{SS} + \theta_{SP}} \frac{I_S}{P_P}. \tag{44}$$

For the consumers receiving income from working in the manufacturing private firms sector, their utility is now defined over three goods. In the Cobb-Douglas case this is

$$U_P = X_{PA}^{\theta_{PA}} X_{PS}^{\theta_{PS}} X_{PP}^{\theta_{PP}}, \quad \theta_{PA} + \theta_{PS} + \theta_{PP} = 1. \tag{45}$$

The household budget constraint is

$$P_A X_{PA} + P_S X_{PS} + P_P X_{PP} = I_P. \tag{46}$$

Consumption of the three agricultural and manufacturing goods by manufacturing workers is

$$X_{PA} = \frac{IP}{P_A} \quad \text{and} \quad X_{PS} = \frac{IP}{P_S} \quad \text{and} \quad X_{PP} = \frac{I_P}{P_P}. \tag{47}$$

The net trades are

$$Z_A = X_{AA} + X_{MA} - Y_A \quad \text{and} \quad Z_M = X_{AM} + X_{MM} - Y_M. \tag{48}$$

We can extend our treatment of the demand side of the economy by specifying preferences for workers in both private firms and in the agricultural sector defined only manufacturing and agricultural goods. The demand side structure is thus similar to that of the simple model.

The extended model departs from the simple model in having an endogenously determined wage $W_A = W_P$ such that labour markets in the private manufacturing and agricaulture sector in combination clear, i.e.

$$L_A + L_P = L - L_S \tag{49}$$

where $L - L_S$ is the non-SOE labour endowment of the economy.

A equilibrium is again given by a value of λ and equilibrium embodies maximization of utility subject to household budget constraints with implied trade balance. The departure from Pareto optimality remains that for workers in each SOE the marginal value of additional effort in production differs the marginal value of extra leisure. The added feature of the more complex model is that marginal supply of manufacturing output to the market will come from competitive firms and so departures from Pareto optimality now occur with intra-marginal SOE production and the associated distortion of leisure consumption by workers in the SOE.

4. Numerical Analysis of SOE Responses to Trade Liberalization in China

We have used the two formulations set out above to conduct numerical analyses which explore possible economy-wide responses to trade liberalization in China in observationally equivalent models and contrast the results to those generated by comparable simple competitive structures. We calibrate both model forms to a 2003 benchmark equilibrium data set capturing the presence of Chinese SOEs, and use similar data in calibrating a competitive model for comparison purposes.

We draw on data from the Chinese National Bureau of Statistics (NBS) (2004) (from the China Statistical Yearbook) for our calibrations. In the simple versions of both models, we treat the entire managerial sector as a simple SOE. For the more complex model forms we group the manufacturing sector in China across sectors of registration as reported in the China Statistical Yearbook and allocate each to the two manufacturing sub-sectors appearing in the model of SOEs and private firms. Sectors of registration according to the statistical yearbook are as Manufacturing 1 = State-Owned Industry, Manufacturing 2 = Collective-Owned Industry, Manufacturing 3 = Co-operative Enterprises, Manufacturing 4 = Joint Ownership Enterprises, Manufacturing 5 = Limited Liability Co-operations, Manufacturing 6 = Share Holding Enterprises, Manufacturing 7 = Private Enterprises, Manufacturing 8 = Other Enterprises, Manufacturing 9 = Enterprises with Funds from Hong Kong, Macao, and Taiwan, and Manufacturing 10 = Foreign-Funded Enterprises. We treat the first five as the SOE subsector, and the latter five as the competitive subsector in manufacturing.

From the NBS data (Table 1) the 2003 gross output of the agriculture sector (farming, forestry, animal husbandry and fishery), $P_A Y_A$, is 2,969.180 billion RMB, and the value of labour input, $W_A L_A$, is 2,614.101 billion RMB. The value of net trade (imports) in agriculture, Z_A, is 3,143.310 billion RMB. The gross industrial output, $P_M Y_M$,

Table 1. Base Case 2003 Chinese Data[1] Used in Calibrating Alternative Formulations for Managerial and Worker Control SOE Models.

1.1. Simple and complex managerial control SOE models

	World prices	Import tariffs[2] Export subsides	Wage rate	Value of output (billion RMB)	Value of labour input (billion RMB)	Value of net trade (billion RMB)
Simple model						
Agriculture	$P_A = 1$	$r_A = 16.8\%$	$W_A = 1$	$Q_A = 2969.180$	$K_A = 2614.100662$	$B_A = 3143.310256$
Manufacturing	$P_M = 1$	$r_M = -15.0\%$	$W_M = 1$	$Q_M = 14227.122$	$K_M = 7297.690729$	$B_M = -5252.792719$
More complex variant						
Agriculture	$P_A = 1$	$r_A = 16.8\%$	$W_A = 1$	$Q_A = 2969.180$	$K_A = 2614.100662$	$B_A = 3143.310256$
SOEs	$P_S = 1$	$r_S = -15.0\%$	$W_S = 1$	$Q_S = 5872.134$	$K_S = 3012.065114$	$B_S = -2168.049360$
Private Firms	$P_P = 1$	$r_P = -15.0\%$	$W_P = 1$	$Q_P = 8354.988$	$K_P = 4285.625615$	$B_P = -3084.743361$

1.2. Simple and complex worker control SOE models

	World prices	Import tariffs[2] Export subsides	Wage rate	Value of output (billion RMB)	Value of labour input (billion RMB)	Value of net trade (billion RMB)	Labour shrinking parameter
Simple model							
Agriculture	$P_A = 1$	$r_A = 16.8\%$	$W_A = 1.00$	$Q_A = 2969.180$	$K_A = 2614.100662$	$B_A = 3143.310256$	$\lambda_A = 1.00$
Manufacturing	$P_M = 1$	$r_M = -15.0\%$	$W_M = 0.75$	$Q_M = 14227.122$	$K_M = 7297.690729$	$B_M = -5252.792719$	$\lambda_M = 0.75$
More complex variant							
Agriculture	$P_A = 1$	$r_A = 16.8\%$	$W_A = 1.00$	$Q_A = 2969.180$	$K_A = 2614.100662$	$B_A = 3143.310256$	$\lambda_A = 1.00$
SOEs	$P_S = 1$	$r_S = -15.0\%$	$W_S = 0.75$	$Q_S = 5872.134$	$K_S = 3012.065114$	$B_S = -2168.049360$	$\lambda_S = 0.75$
Private Firms	$P_P = 1$	$r_P = -15.0\%$	$W_P = 1.00$	$Q_P = 8354.988$	$K_P = 4285.625615$	$B_P = -3084.743361$	$\lambda_P = 1.00$

1. *Sources*: National Bureau of Statistics (NBS) of China (2004), Yu (2004) and BBCE (2004), and CHINANEWS (2003 and 2004).
2. See discussion of these values in the text.

is 14,227.122 billion RMB, and the value of labour input, $W_M L_M$, is 7,297.69072 billion RMB. The value of net trade (exports) in manufacturing, Z_M, is −5,252.79722 billion RMB.

We define physical units for agricultural and manufacturing products to be related to these value observations following the Harberger and Shoven and Whalley units convention that in the initial benchmark equilibrium data world prices, $P_A = P_M = 1$ and wage rates $W_A = W_M = 1$. There is no information that we can use from base data to yield λ through calibration, and so we assume $\lambda = 0.75$ in manufacturing in the base data and then perform sensitivity analysis around this value.

We use literature sources for both import tariffs and export subsidy rates for China's agricultural and manufacturing trade. The export subsidy for manufacturing reflects tax preferences for exports given to foreign-owned enterprises. The average tariff rate on imports (agricultural good) is $r_A = 16.8\%$ (from Yu, 2004, and BBCE, 2004), and the average export subsidy (subsidy rate on the manufacturing good) is $r_M = -15.0\%$ (from CHINANEWS, 2003 and 2004). These two compound in their effects on relative domestic prices relative to world prices.[3]

These data sources thus yield a benchmark data set that we are able to use in calibrating our two models in both their simple and more complex forms. The resulting model parameter values are set out in Tables 2 and 3. In calibration, for the managerial control model first order conditions imply no value directly for the exponent in the production function. For the worker control model, calibration is unable to use first order conditions to yield share parameters on leisure in preferences for workers in manufacturing enterprises. These we set equal to 0.25 and then also perform sensitivity analysis around this setting. For the simple model variants we group the five SOE sectors and five private firms into two composite sectors. For the more complex model variants, we use five separate sector SOEs and five private competitive sectors.

We have performed numerical simulation analyses for various forms of trade liberalization in China using both SOE model formulations set out above, and also using their simple and more complex forms. Using the model parameterizations generated by calibration we can then parametrically vary

[3]From these literatures sources, the average import tariff rate on agricultural goods is 16.8%, and the average export subsidy rate on agricultural goods is 8.5%. The average import tariff rate on manufacturing goods is 10.3%, and the average export subsidy rate on manufacturing goods is 15.0%.

Table 2. Calibrated Model Parameters for Simple and More Complex Managerial Control SOE Models.

	Scalar parameter production side	Power parameter production side	Scalar parameter utility side	Rent (billion RMB)	Total labour
Simple model					$L = 9911.791391$
Agriculture	$\phi_A = 2.491973$	$\alpha_A = 0.880412$	$\theta_A = 0.404843$		
Manufacturing	$\phi_M = 21.198691$	$\alpha_M = 0.750000$	$\theta_M = 0.595157$	$R_M = 6929.431271$	
More complex variant					$L = 9911.791391$
Agriculture	$\phi_A = 2.491973$	$\alpha_A = 0.880412$	$\theta_A = 0.404843$		
SOEs	$\phi_S = 16.991384$	$\alpha_S = 0.750000$	$\theta_S = 0.245646$	$R_S = 2860.068886$	
Private firms	$\phi_P = 134.745314$	$\alpha_P = 0.512942$	$\theta_P = 0.349511$		

Table 3. Calibrated Model Parameters for Simple and More Complex Worker Control SOE Model Variants.

	Scalar parameter production side	Power parameter production side	Share parameter utility side			Rent (billion RMB)	Total labour
Simple model ($\theta'_{MM} = 0.25$)							$L = 12344.354967$
Agriculture	$\phi_A = 2.491973$	$\alpha_A = 0.880412$	$\theta_{AA} = 0.404843$		$\theta_{AA} = 0.595157$		
Manufacturing	$\phi_M = 21.198691$	$\alpha_M = 0.750000$	$\theta_{MA} = 0.303632$		$\theta_{MM} = 0.446368$	$R_M = 6929.431271$	
More complex variant ($\theta'_{SS} = 0.20$)							$L = 10915.813096$
Agriculture	$\phi_A = 2.491973$	$\alpha_A = 0.880412$	$\theta_{AA} = 0.404843$	$\theta_{AS} = 0.245646$	$\theta_{AP} = 0.349511$		
SOEs	$\phi_S = 16.991384$	$\alpha_S = 0.750000$	$\theta_{SA} = 0.323874$	$\theta_{SS} = 0.196517$	$\theta_{SP} = 0.279608$	$R_S = 2860.068886$	
Private firms	$\phi_P = 134.745314$	$\alpha_P = 0.512942$	$\theta_{PA} = 0.404843$	$\theta_{PS} = 0.245646$	$\theta_{SP} = 0.349511$		

the import tariff and export subsidy rates and assess the economy wide behavioural response. This allows us to assess the welfare implications of alternative trade policy changes in China capturing SOE behavioural response using the two models' formulations. We can also compare the results we generate to a comparable competitive case by also calibrating a simple competitive model with decreasing returns to scale production and sector specific rents using the same data sets for each SOE model. In each experiment we perform we first calibrate the relevant model to the 2003 benchmark data set out in Table 1, and then vary both import tariff and export subsidy rates and compute the relevant new equilibria. We make welfare comparisons across equilibria using Hicksian equivalent variations expressed as a % of GDP.

Table 4 reports the welfare impacts of moving to free trade in five different model formulations all calibrated to the same base case data. These are the simple and more complex managerial control models, the simple and more complex worker control models described above, and a simple competitive model. The differences in model results are striking. Moving to free trade in a simple competitive model implies a welfare gains of 3.4% of income, but in a simple managerial control model a welfare loss of 22.7% and a sharply smaller welfare loss of 4.1% in the complex managerial control model. The simple and complex worker control model implies a welfare loss of 9% and the more complex worker control mald a welfare gain, but this is larger than in the competitive model. These results thus suggest that the analytical formulation used to represent SOE behaviour when analyzing responses to trade liberalization in China can make a large difference.

The 22.7% loss when moving to free trade in the simple managerial control model is especially striking. This is a reflection of a number of features. First, a loss occurs when moving to free trade since with average

Table 4. Impacts of Trade Liberalization in Managerial Control SOE, Worker Control SOE, and Competitive Models.

	Hicksian equivalent variations of welfare change relative to base case as % of base case income in moving to free trade
Simple Managerial Control SOE Model	−22.7266%
Complex Managerial Control SOE Model	−4.1381%
Simple Worker Control SOE Model	−9.2977%
Complex Worker Control SOE Model	12.5506%
Competitive Model	3.4560%

product pricing of labour the marginal product of labour in manufacturing is below the wage. Relative to Pareto optimality the SOE is too large, trade interventions correct for this departure from Pareto optimality and removing them thus implies a welfare loss. Secondly, in the data we use manufacturing accounts for nearly 80% of activity in the economy. We ignore services in our benchmark data, and our data are consistent with the widely used figure that 60% of China's GDP is in manufacturing. Thirdly,

Table 5. Sensitivity Analyses of Trade Liberalization Impacts in Managerial and Worker Control SOE Models.

	Hicksian eqivalent varations of welfare change relative to base case as % of base case income in moving to free trade			
	Simple managerial control SOE model	Complex managerial control SOE model	Simple worker control SOE model	Complex worker control SOE model
$\alpha = 0.70$	−22.8080%	−4.1850%	−8.8539%	12.7262%
$\alpha = 0.75$	−22.7266%	−4.1381%	−9.2977%	12.5506%
$\alpha = 0.80$	−22.6420%	−4.0918%	−9.6983%	12.3919%

Table 6. Impacts of Separate Trade Policy Instrument Removal in Managerial Control SOE, Worker Control SOE, and Competitive Models (Hicksian EVs as % of Base Case Income When Moving to Free Trade).

	Hicksian eqivalent varations of welfare change relative to base case as % of base case income in moving to free trade
6.1. Elimination of import tariff on agricultural imports	
Simple Managerial Control SOE Model	−14.0029%
Complex Managerial Control SOE Model	−6.5716%
Simple Worker Control SOE Model	−8.4655%
Complex Worker Control SOE Model	6.5037%
Competitive Model	−4.2198%
6.2. Elimination of export subsidy on manufacturing exports	
Simple Managerial Control SOE Model	−19.5777%
Complex Managerial Control SOE Model	−7.4557%
Simple Worker Control SOE Model	−0.7591%
Complex Worker Control SOE Model	5.0255%
Competitive Model	−1.9449%

the size of the loss moving to free trade depends critically on both the size of the gap between average and marginal product, and their slopes. This gap is large in the base case, and the slope of both marginal and average product functions shallow.

The 4.1% loss in the worker control case when moving to free trade reflects a smaller size for the SOE sector relative to the whole of manufacturing, and the feature that marginal source of supply now comes from competitive firms and it is the intra-marginal SOE production that is now provided by an enterprise that is too large.

Table 5 reports on sensitivity analyses in the simple and complex SOE models varying α_M (the production function exponent) around the control case value of 0.75. These variations make little difference to results.

Table 6 reports results by model type involving the separate elimination of import tariffs (on agriculture) and export subsidies (on manufacturing).

Table 7. Impacts of Trade Policy Change Beyond Free Trade in Model Types (Hicksian EVs as % of Base Case Income for Alternative % Joint Reductions) (in Both Import Tariffs on Agricultural Imports and Export Subsidies on manufacturing Exports).

% Joint reduction in both import tariffs and export subsidies	Simple managerial control SOE model	Complex managerial control SOE model	Simple worker control SOE model	Complex worker control SOE model	Competitive model
0	0.0000%	0.0000%	0.0000%	0.0000%	0.0000%
10	−5.9595%	−0.7184%	−0.5743%	1.1549%	0.7226%
20	−9.2311%	−1.2472%	−1.2698%	2.3279%	1.3549%
30	−11.7650%	−1.6720%	−2.0648%	3.5226%	1.8969%
40	−13.8877%	−2.0391%	−2.9422%	4.7413%	2.3500%
50	−15.7363%	−2.3774%	−3.8878%	5.9849%	2.7171%
60	−17.3854%	−2.7063%	−4.8902%	7.2533%	3.0025%
70	−18.8815%	−3.0390%	−5.9398%	8.5456%	3.2120%
80	−20.2562%	−3.3849%	−7.0285%	9.8604%	3.3525%
90	−21.5322%	−3.7500%	−8.1498%	11.1960%	3.4313%
100	−22.7266%	−4.1381%	−9.2977%	12.5506%	3.4560%
110	−23.8526%	−4.5505%	−10.4675%	13.9225%	3.4336%
120	−24.9207%	−4.9871%	−11.6549%	15.3106%	3.3705%
130	−25.9396%	−5.4464%	−12.8563%	16.7146%	3.2720%
140	−26.9162%	−5.9256%	−14.0686%	18.1347%	3.1422%
150	−27.8566%	−6.4218%	−15.2889%	19.5722%	2.9842%
160	−28.7659%	−6.9317%	−16.5148%	21.0288%	2.8000%
170	−29.6483%	−7.4523%	−17.7442%	22.5072%	2.5908%
180	−30.5078%	−7.9816%	−18.9751%	24.0103%	2.3572%
190	−31.3476%	−8.5178%	−20.2058%	25.5414%	2.0990%
200	−32.1707%	−9.0603%	−21.4346%	27.1043%	1.8159%

Removing each produces results that are smaller than movements to free trade, but the signs are the same as these two as elements compound with each other in their trade effects. As in Table 4, there are large differences in results across models.

Tablc 7 reports results of changes in trade policies which go beyond free trade, either by having a reduction in, rather than a removal of, import tariffs and export subsidies, or in having greater than 100% reductions. In the competitive model, a 100% reduction in tariffs and export subsidies maximizes the welfare gain, implying that in this model free trade is the best policy. In the simple and more complex managerial control models, welfare losses increase continuously and beyond a 100% reduction. This suggests that in these model variants, increases in the level of trade protection rather than moves towards free trade are welfare-preferred. In the worker control models, free trade is again best policy.

Table 8 reports optimal policy interventions in the simple and more complex managerial control SOE models for alternative value of α_M, and also for the worker control model. As noted above, for the worker control model free trade is the best policy, whereas in the managerial control models

Table 8. Optimal Trade Policies in Managerial Control and Worker Control SOE Models (Hicksian EVs as % of Base Case Income for Alternative % Joint Reductions) (% reduction in Import Tariffs and Export Subsidies).

	Optimal joint reductions in import tariffs and export subsidies	Optimal reduction in import tariffs	Optimal reduction in export subsidies
8.1. Simple managerial control SOE model			
$\alpha_M = 0.70$	−0.0795%	−0.0998%	−0.0670%
$\alpha_M = 0.75$	−0.7099%	−2.3541%	−1.0170%
$\alpha_M = 0.80$	−3.0408%	−6.6764%	−2.9350%
8.2. Complex managerial control SOE model			
$\alpha_M = 0.70$	−10.9169%	−38.1336%	−15.2859%
$\alpha_M = 0.75$	−19.6042%	−67.1161%	−27.6610%
$\alpha_M = 0.80$	−30.2607%	−102.3328%	−41.3000%
8.3. Simple worker control SOE model			
$\alpha_M = 0.70$	−18.9400%		39.4000%
$\alpha_M = 0.75$	−22.5500%		32.1300%
$\alpha_M = 0.80$	−32.2000%		24.8300%

increases in existing levels of protection as in the base case data are welfare-preferred.

5. Conclusions

In this chapter we present analytical formulations of SOE behavioural response to trade policy change which we apply to the Chinese case. Our analyses are motivated both by the significance of communally-controlled enterprise structures in economies such as China, and the seeming lack of analytical work in existing literature capturing their behavioural response. At the same time we note that OECD style competitive structures are now widely used in policy evaluation numerical simulation work on China.

We present two alternative formulations of SOE behavioural response to policy change. In the first of these, management controls enterprise behaviour with political appointees whose losses are re-capitalized through the banking system and who are assumed to maximize enterprise size so as to yield the largest potential personal networking benefits to management. In this case, labour is paid its average rather than its marginal product and free trade is not best policy. In the second, workers collectively control enterprise behaviour and meet the enterprise budget constraint given employment and wage rates, and otherwise satisfice using surplus labour for moonlighting or second jobs. Again free trade is not the best policy.

Model results using 2003 data indicate welfare losses rather than welfare gains from trade liberalization and effects that are potentially very large. We compare model results to those from comparable competitive structures calibrated to the same data set, and results show both differences of sign and large quantitative variants. We conclude that explicit analytical representations of SOE behavioural response is needed when assessing policy change such as trade liberalization in China.

References

Bai, C. and Y. Wang (1998). Bureaucratic Control and the Soft Budget Constraint, *Journal of Comparative Economics*, 26: 41–61.

Bigsten, A., X. Liu and J. Zheng (2002). Efficiency, Technical Progress, and Best Practice in Chinese State Enterprises, *China Economic Quarterly*, 1: 521–540.

BBCE (2004). Blue Book of China's Economy, Spring 2004.

Bonin, J. and Y. Huang (2002). Foreign Entry into Chinese Banking: Does WTO Membership Threaten Domestic Banks? *The World Economy*, 25: 1077–1093.

Broadman, H. G. (2001). The Business(es) of the Chinese State, *The World Economy*, 24: 849–875.

Chen, J., J. Yang, Q. Yu and W. Zhang (2002). Investment Pattern of Non-State Owned Firms in China, *China Economic Quarterly*, 1: 501–520.

CHINANEWS (2003). *WWW.CHINANEWS.COM.CN*, Available at http://www.chinanews.com.cn/n/2003-09-17/26/347701.html.

CHINANEWS (2003). *WWW.CHINANEWS.COM.CN*, Available at http://202.106.184.148//n/2003-10-14/26/356427.html.

CHINANEWS (2004). *WWW.CHINANEWS.COM.CN*, Available at http://www1.cei.gov.cn/hottopic/doc/zjzt2002011/200401122446.html.

Cull, R. and L. C. Xu (2000). Bureaucrats, State Banks, and the Efficiency of Credit Allocation: The Experience of Chinese State-Owned Enterprises, *Journal of Comparative Economics*, 28: 1–31.

Cull, R. and L. C. Xu (2003). Who Gets Credit? The Behavior Bureaucrats and State Banks in Allocating Credit to Chinese State-Owned Enterprises, *Journal of Development Economics*, 71: 533–559.

Fan, G., W. Hai, Y. Jin and W. T. Woo (1994). How Successful has Chinese Enterprise Reform Been? Pitfalls in Opposite Biases and Focus, *Journal of Comparative Economics*, 18: 410–437.

Ghosh, M. and J. Whalley (2000). *State-Owned Enterprises, Shirking and Trade Liberalization*, NBER Working Paper No. 7696, CESifo Working Paper No. 300, University of Western Ontario Working Paper, and University of Warwick Working Paper.

Gilbert, J. and T. Wahl (2002). Applied General Equilibrium Assessments of Trade Libereralization in China, *The World Economy*, 25: 697–731.

Hertel, T. W. and T. L. Walmsley (2001). China's Accession to the WTO: Timing is Everything, *The World Economy*, 24: 1019–1049.

Ianchovichina, E. and W. Martin (2004). *Economic Impacts of China's Accession to the WTO*, Bhattasali Deepak, Shantong Li and Will Martin, (eds.) China and the WTO, Chapter 13: 211–236.

Lee, Y. (1997). Bank Loans, Self-Financing, and Grants in Chinese SOEs: Optimal Policy under Incomplete Information, *Journal of Comparative Economics*, 24: 140–160.

Li, G. and L. Xu (2001). State-Owned Enterprise, Labour Redundancy, and Job Creation, *China Economic Quarterly* 1: 97–110; Forthcoming in Journal of Development Economics.

Liu, D. (2002). Managers in State-Owned Enterprises: Ability, Efforts, and Productive Efficiency — A Case Study of the Iron and Steel Industry in China, *China Economic Quarterly*, 1: 419–434.

Wang, Z. (2003). The Impact of China's WTO Accession on Patterns of World Trade, *Journal of Policy Modeling*, 25: 1–41.

Whalley, J. (1985). *Trade Liberalization among Major World Trading Areas*, MIT Press.

Whalley, J. and X. Xin (2005). *The Growth Performance of China's FDI and Non-FDI Economies*, Available at http://www.ssc.uwo.ca/economics/workshop/epri/XianDec14.pdf.

Yang, Y. (2001). China's Integration into the World Economy: Implications for Developing Countries, IMF Working Paper No. WP/03/245.
Yin, X. (2001). A Dynamic Analysis of Overstaff in China's State-Owned Enterprises, *Journal of Development Economics*, 66: 87–99.
Yu, Y. (2004). *China's Trade Policy*, Available at http://www.apec.org.au/docs/China04YuYongding.pdf.

INDEX